Law

First edition September 1993

ISBN 0 7517 2014 3

British Library Cataloguing-in-Publication Data

A catalogue record for this book
is available from the British Library

Printed in Great Britain by
Ashford Colour Press, Gosport, Hampshire

Published by

BPP Publishing Limited
Aldine House, Aldine Place
London W12 8AW

We would like to acknowledge the assistance given by Louise Dunford of the
University of Portsmouth in the preparation of this book.

CONTENTS

PREFACE

FIRST YEAR Study Guides are a new series targeted specifically at the needs of:

- first year students taking business studies degrees;
- students taking business-related modules of other degrees;
- HND students;
- others requiring business information at this level.

This *Law* Study Guide has been written with two key goals in mind.

- To present a substantial and useful body of knowledge on law at degree level. This is not just a set of revision notes - it explains the subject in detail and does not assume prior knowledge.

- To make learning and revision as easy as possible. Each chapter:

  - starts with clear objectives;
  - contains numerous exercises;
  - includes a chapter roundup summarising the points made; and
  - ends with a quick quiz.

The philosophy of the series is thus to combine techniques which actively promote learning with a no-nonsense, systematic approach to the necessary factual content of the course.

BPP Publishing have for many years been the leading providers of targeted texts for students of professional qualifications. We know that our customers need to study effectively in order to pass their exams, and that they cannot afford to waste time. They expect clear, concise and highly-focused study material. We expect first year degree and HND students to be equally demanding. And we have addressed the specific requirements of degree courses: each title has been developed in consultation with university lecturers.

We believe that the resulting material will prove to be the most helpful - and cost-effective - resource available to today's business students.

BPP Publishing
September 1993

If you would like to send in your comments on this Study Guide, please turn to the review form on page 347.

HOW TO USE THIS BOOK

This Study Guide can simply be read straight through from beginning to end, but you will get far more out of it if you keep a pen and paper to hand. The most effective form of learning is *active learning*, and we have therefore filled the text with exercises for you to try as you go along. We have also provided objectives, a chapter roundup and a quick quiz for each chapter. Here is a suggested approach to enable you to get the most out of this book.

(a) Select a chapter to study, and read the objectives in the box at the start of the chapter.

(b) Next read the chapter roundup at the end of the chapter (before the quick quiz and the solutions to exercises). Do not expect this brief summary to mean too much at this stage, but see whether you can relate some of the points made in it to some of the objectives.

(c) Next read the chapter itself. Do attempt each exercise as you come to it. You will derive the greatest benefit from the exercises if you write down your solutions before checking them against the solutions at the end of the chapter.

(d) As you read, make use of the 'notes' column to add your own comments, references to other material and so on. Do try to formulate your own views. In law, many things are matters of interpretation and there is often scope for alternative views. The more you engage in a dialogue with the book, the more you will get out of your study.

(e) When you reach the end of the chapter, read the chapter roundup again. Then go back to the objectives at the start of the chapter, and ask yourself whether you have achieved them.

(f) Finally, consolidate your knowledge by writing down your answers to the quick quiz. You can check your answers by going back to the text. The very act of going back and searching the text for relevant details will further improve your grasp of the subject.

Further reading

While we are confident that the FIRST YEAR Study Guides offer excellent range and depth of subject coverage, we are aware that you will be encouraged to follow up particular points in books other than your main textbook, in order to get alternative points of view and more detail on key topics. We recommend the following books as a starting point for your further reading on *Law*.

Smith and Bailey, *The Modern English Legal System*, 2nd edition 1991, Sweet & Maxwell

Smith and Keenan, *English Law*, 10th edition 1992, Pitman

Cheshire Fifoot and Furmston, *Law of Contract*, 12th edition 1991, Butterworths

Gower, *Principles of Modern Company Law*, 5th edition 1992, Sweet & Maxwell

1 THE NATURE AND SOURCES OF ENGLISH LAW

> **Your objectives**
>
> After completing this chapter you should:
>
> (a)   understand the nature of law;
>
> (b)   know the main sources of law;
>
> (c)   understand the relationship between common law and equity;
>
> (d)   know the main equitable maxims;
>
> (e)   know how to refer to cases, and how cases are reported;
>
> (f)   understand the concept of Parliamentary sovereignty;
>
> (g)   know the stages a bill passes through before it becomes an Act of Parliament;
>
> (h)   understand the need for delegated legislation;
>
> (i)   know the subsidiary sources of law;
>
> (j)   be able to distinguish between *ratio decidendi* and *obiter dicta*;
>
> (k)   know which courts can create binding precedents, and which courts are so bound;
>
> (l)   be able to assess the advantages and disadvantages of the system of precedent;
>
> (m)   know the canons and general principles of statutory interpretation and the statutory sources of help in interpretation.

1   The nature of law

The laws of any country are those rules which the nation through its law-enforcing machinery makes compulsory by imposing penalties for law-breaking. The body of law is not static but changes and develops. In this process it reflects the values and institutions of each era. Any study of English law as it now is (for the time being) requires a brief explanation of the process of historical development which has made it what it is.

Although English law has many features which are common to other national legal systems, it also has some distinctive features of its own. It differs from the law of many Western European countries (and also Scotland) in having absorbed only a small amount of Roman law. Secondly, English law is case law made by decisions of the courts to a much greater extent than the law of many other countries. However, English law shares with most other legal systems a fundamental distinction between civil and criminal law.

fundamental – essential, primary, original.

2   Sources of English law

The term 'sources of law' is used in several different senses.

(a)   The *historical sources* are common law and equity.

equity – fairness, the application of the principles of justice to correct or supplement the law.

BPP Publishing

(b) The *legal sources* are the means by which the law is currently brought into existence. There are four legal sources:

  (i)   case law (or judicial precedent);

  (ii) legislation (or statute law);

  (iii) European Community (EC) law;

  (iv) custom.

(c) The *subsidiary sources* are not currently responsible for the direct creation of law. They include Law Merchant, Roman Law and Canon Law.

3 Historical sources of law

English law's historical sources are those procedures, rules and ways of thinking which have given rise to today's current sources of law. A legal problem may be decided on the rules of the legal sources, but these in turn (particularly judicial precedent) have been derived from the historical sources of common law and equity.

Common law

At the time of the Norman Conquest in 1066 there was no system of law common to the whole country. Rules of local custom were applied by local manorial courts. To improve the system, the King sent royal commissioners on tour (circuit) to different parts of the realm to deal with crimes and civil disputes. These commissioners, who often heard their cases with the assistance of a local jury, at first applied the local customary law of the neighbourhood. On their return from circuit the commissioners sat in the royal courts at Westminster to try cases there. In time the commissioners developed rules of law, selected from the differing local customs which they had encountered, as a common law *(ius commune)* which they applied uniformly in all trials (before the King's courts) throughout the kingdom.

To commence an action before any of these courts, the plaintiff obtained from the main royal office, the Chancery, an order (a writ) issued under the King's authority and addressed to the Sheriff of the county in which the defendant resided, by which the Sheriff was required to ensure that the defendant appeared for the trial. The writ specified the ground of complaint and gave a brief summary of the facts on which the plaintiff required judgement. Writs could only be issued in one of the established forms, which were grounds of action. If there was no appropriate writ it was not possible to have one of a new type in order to bring a grievance before the royal courts. This principle was slightly relaxed in 1285 but the common law system, based on the availability of standard writs, was still very rigid and hence an inadequate means of providing justice.

The procedure of common law courts was also unsatisfactory. A *plaintiff* (a person bringing a legal action, as opposed to a *defendant*, the other party) might lose his case owing to a minor technicality of wording or be frustrated by specious defences, deliberate delay or corruption, or find himself unable to enforce a judgement given in his favour because there was no suitable common law remedy.

Exercise 1

In what sorts of cases (other than crimes) might the payment of damages, the standard common law remedy, be inadequate?

Equity

Citizens who could not obtain redress for grievances in the common law courts petitioned the King to obtain relief by direct royal intervention. These petitions came before the King in Council and by custom were referred to the principal civil minister, the Chancellor. In dealing with each petition his concern was to establish the truth of the matter and then to impose a just solution without undue regard for technicalities or procedural points.

Because the principles on which the Chancellor decided points were based on fair dealing between two individuals as equals, these principles became known as equity. Equity depends upon the exercise of discretion following the dictates of *informed conscience*.

The system of equity, developed and administered by the Court of Chancery, was not an alternative to the common law, but a method of adding to and improving on the common law. This interaction of common law and equity produced three major changes.

(a) *New rights.* Equity recognised and protected rights for which the common law gave no safeguards. If, for example, A transferred property to the legal ownership of B to pay the income of the property to C (in modern law B is a trustee for C), the common law simply recognised that B was the owner of the property and ignored B's obligations to C. Equity recognised that B was the owner of the property at common law but insisted, as a matter of justice and good conscience, that B must comply with the terms of the trust imposed by A (the settlor) and pay the income to C (the beneficiary).

(b) *Better procedure.* Equity could be more effective than common law in bringing a disputed matter to a decision.

(c) *Better remedies.* The standard common law remedy for the successful plaintiff was the award of monetary compensation, damages, for his loss. Equity was able to order the defendant to do what he had agreed to do *(specific performance),* to abstain from wrongdoing *(injunction),* to alter a document so that it reflected the parties' true intentions *(rectification)* or to restore the pre-contract status quo *(rescission).*

The development of equity was based on a number of 'equitable maxims', or principles. These are still applied today if an equitable remedy is sought. The following are examples.

(a) *He who comes to equity must come with clean hands.* To be fairly treated, the plaintiff must have acted fairly himself. For example in the case *D and C Builders v Rees 1966* the defendant could not plead a defence of equitable estoppel because she had tried to take advantage of the plaintiff's financial difficulties.

(b) *Equality is equity.* The law attempts to play fair and redress the balance; hence what is available to one person must be available to another. As an example, equity does not allow the remedy of specific performance to be granted against a minor, and it does not allow a minor to benefit from the remedy either.

(c) *He who seeks equity must do equity.* This is similar to (a) above. A person wanting equitable relief must be prepared to act fairly himself. For example a mortgagor wishing to redeem his security under the principle of 'equity of redemption' must give reasonable notice of this to the mortgagee.

(d) *Equity looks at the intent, not the form.* However a person may try to pretend that he is doing something in the correct form, equity will look at what he is actually trying to achieve. For example, if an agreed damages clause in a contract is not a genuine estimate of likely loss, equity will treat the clause as a penalty clause.

Common law and equity: later developments

In theory, equity accepted common law rights but insisted that they should be exercised in a just fashion. The practical effect was nonetheless that a decision of the Court of Chancery often reversed or conflicted with common law rules. At one stage, the Court of Chancery went so far as to issue orders by which litigants were forbidden to bring an action at common law to enforce strict common law rights. The rivalry between Chancery and common law courts was resolved in 1615 by a decision of the King (in the *Earl of Oxford's Case*) that where common law and equity conflict, equity must prevail.

Equity was not in its origins a consistent code of law: it was simply disconnected intervention in legal disputes. Each Chancellor (and the Chancery judges acting under his authority) applied a personal and sometimes arbitrary standard of what he considered fair. From the sixteenth century onwards, however, the Chancellor and his deputies were usually recruited from the legal profession trained in common law. Under common law influence, equity become a consistent body of doctrine and at least as technical as the common law.

Thus the common law, administered in royal courts, was supplemented and sometimes overruled by principles of equity administered in the Court of Chancery. A plaintiff who began proceedings in one set of courts might after years of expensive litigation find that for some technical reason, he could not obtain the desired result but must abandon his case and begin again in the other courts. This dual court system was ended by the Judicature Acts 1873 - 1875 which amalgamated the English courts. It is now possible to rely on any principle of common law or equity in any court of law. In case of conflict equity still prevails over common law.

Although the courts have been amalgamated, common law and equity remain distinct. Where common law applies it tends to be automatic in its effect. Equity recognises the common law, as it always did; it sometimes offers an alternative solution but the court has discretion as to whether or not it will grant an equitable remedy in lieu of a common law one.

If, for example, breach of contract is proved, the plaintiff will at least get common law damages as compensation for his loss automatically; in certain circumstances the court may, at its discretion, provide an alternative remedy of equity. It may, for instance, order the defendant to perform the contract rather than allow him to buy his way out of his contractual obligations by paying damages. The discretionary nature of equitable remedies means that a person who wins an action will not necessarily get the remedy he wants.

Case: Miller v Jackson 1977
The Court of Appeal held that a cricket club had committed both negligence and nuisance by allowing cricket balls to be struck out of the ground into M's adjoining premises. However, the court refused to grant the injunction that M had sought. They awarded damages instead on the grounds that the interest of the public in being able to play and watch cricket on a ground where it had been played for over 70 years should prevail over the hardship of a few individual householders who had only recently purchased their homes.

Exercise 2

How does the recognition of trusts illustrate the principle that equity prevails over common law?

4 Legal sources of law

The development of common law and equity has led to one of the main legal sources of law, case law, and informs much of the other main source, legislation

Case law (judicial precedent)

Both common law and equity are the product of decisions in the courts. They are judge-made law but based on a principle of consistency. Once a matter of principle has been decided (by one of the higher courts) it becomes a *precedent*. In any later case to which that principle is relevant the same principle should (subject to certain exceptions) be applied. This doctrine of consistency, following precedent, is expressed in the maxim *stare decisis,* 'to stand by a decision'.

Judicial precedent is based on three elements.

(a)   There must be adequate and reliable reports of earlier decisions.

(b)   There must be rules for extracting from an earlier decision on one set of facts the legal principle to be applied in reaching a decision on a different set of facts.

(c)   Precedents must be classified into those which are binding and those which are merely persuasive.

Point (a), the reporting of cases, is discussed immediately below. The points concerning legal reasoning and how binding precedents should be interpreted are dealt with later.

There are major series of law reports on general law published weekly and then bound as annual volumes. In addition there are other special series of reports, for example of tax cases, commercial cases and industrial relations cases. At a hearing in court, the barrister who cites a case as a precedent will read aloud from the reported judgement.

Every case has a title, usually (in a civil case) in the form *Brown v Smith*, that is Brown (plaintiff) versus Smith (defendant). In the event of an appeal the plaintiff's name is still shown first, whether he or she is the appellant or the respondent. Some cases are cited (for technical reasons of procedure) by reference to the subject matter, such as *Re Enterprises Limited* (a company case) or *Re Black's Settlement* (a trust case) ('re' means 'about'); or in shipping cases by the name of the ship, for example *The Wagon Mound*. In a full citation the title of the case is followed by abbreviated particulars of the volume of the law reports in which the case is reported, for example *Best v Samuel Fox & Co Ltd (1952)* 2 All ER 394 (The report is at p 394 of Vol. 2 of the All England Reports for 1952). The same case may be reported in more than one series of law reports and sometimes under different names.

As regards content:

(a)   each report begins with a summary (a *head note*) of the points of law established by the case and a list of the earlier cases cited as precedents at the hearing;

(b)   the verbatim text of the judgement follows as given in court but with any minor corrections which the judge decides to make at the proof stage.

It is only decisions of the higher courts, that is the High Court, the Court of Appeal and the Judicial Committee of the House of Lords, which are included in the general law reports. Only the important cases are included in the law reports, though certain libraries hold copies of judgements in unreported cases.

Exercise 3

If you saw a case cited as *The Moorcock*, what would you conclude about the case?

Legislation (statute law)

Legislation is enacted by Parliament. Until the United Kingdom entered the European Community (the EC) in 1973 the UK Parliament was completely sovereign: its law-making powers were unfettered.

unrestrained.

Parliamentary sovereignty means that:

(a) Parliament is able to make the law as it sees fit. It may repeal earlier statutes, overrule case law developed in the courts or make new law on subjects which have not been regulated by law before;

(b) no Parliament can legislate so as to prevent a future Parliament changing the law:

> *Case: Vauxhall Estates v Liverpool Corporation 1932*
> If compensation for compulsory purchase were assessed under an Act of 1919 the plaintiffs would receive £2,370, whereas if it were assessed under an Act of 1925 they would only receive £1,133. The Act of 1919 provided that any Act inconsistent with it would have no effect.
>
> *Held:* this provision did not apply to subsequent Acts because a Parliament cannot bind its successors. In addition the 1925 Act by implication repealed the 1919 Act so far as it was inconsistent with it. The plaintiffs therefore received £1,133;

(c) judges are bound to apply the relevant statute law however distasteful to them it may be. But judges have to *interpret* statute law, and they may find a meaning in a statutory rule which those members of Parliament who promoted the statute did not intend.

In practice, Parliament usually follows certain conventions which limit its freedom. It does not usually enact statutes which alter the law with retrospective effect or deprive citizens of their property without compensation. In addition to making new law and altering existing law, Parliament may make the law clearer by passing a *codifying statute* (such as the Sale of Goods Act 1979) to put case law on a statutory basis, or a *consolidating statute* to incorporate an original statute and its successive amendments into a single statute (such as the Companies Act 1985).

Parliamentary procedure

A proposal for legislation is often originally aired in public in a Government green paper. After comments are received a white paper is produced, which sets out the aim of the legislation. It is then put forward in draft form as a bill, and may be introduced into either the House of Commons or the House of Lords, the two houses of Parliament. When the bill has passed through one house it must then go through the same stages in the other house. When it has passed through both houses it is submitted for the Royal Assent which in practice is given on the Queen's behalf by a committee of the Lord Chancellor and two other peers. It then becomes an Act of Parliament (or statute). It comes into effect at the start of the day on which Royal Assent is given, or (if the Act itself so provides) at some other time or on a commencement date set by statutory instrument.

Most bills are public bills, which means that they are of general application. They may be introduced by the government or by a private member (any member of Parliament acting on his or her own initiative). A private bill has a restricted application: for example, a local authority may promote a private bill to give it special powers within its own area. Private bills undergo a different form of examination at the committee stage.

If the House of Commons and the House of Lords disagree over the same bill, the House of Lords may delay the passing of the bill for a maximum of one year (except for financial measures, such as the annual Finance Act). It may veto any bill which tries to extend the life of Parliament beyond five years, and it may veto any private bill.

6

In each House the successive stages of dealing with the bill are as follows.

(a) *First reading:* publication and introduction into the agenda: no debate.

(b) *Second reading:* debate on the general merits of the bill but no amendments at this stage.

(c) *Committee stage:* the bill is examined by a standing committee of about 20 members, representing the main parties and including some members at least who specialise in the relevant subject. The bill is examined section by section and may be amended. If the bill is very important all or part of the committee stage may be taken by the House as a whole sitting as a committee.

(d) *Report stage:* the bill as amended in committee is reported to the full House for approval. If the government has undertaken in committee to reconsider various points it often puts forward its final amendments at this stage.

(e) *Third reading:* this is the final approval stage at which only verbal amendments may be made.

Exercise 4

Many countries have bills of rights, which cannot be changed by normal legislative procedures. What aspect of Parliamentary sovereignty would make it difficult to give a bill of rights for the UK such a secure position?

Delegated legislation

To save time in Parliament it is usual to set out the main principles in the body of an Act as numbered sections and to relegate the details to schedules (at the end of the Act) which need not be debated though they are visible and take effect as part of the Act. But even with this device there is a great deal which cannot conveniently be included in Acts. It may for example be necessary, after an Act has been passed, for the government to consult interested parties and then produce regulations, having the force of the law, to implement the Act, to fix commencement dates to bring the Act into operation or to prescribe printed forms for use in connection with it. To provide for these and other matters a modern Act usually contains a section by which power is given to a minister, or a public body such as a local authority, to make subordinate or delegated legislation for specified purposes only.

This procedure is unavoidable for various reasons.

(a) Parliament has not time to examine these matters of detail.

(b) Much of the content of delegated legislation is technical and is better worked out in consultation with professional, commercial or industrial groups outside Parliament.

(c) If new or altered regulations are required later, they can be issued in a much shorter time than is needed to pass an amending Act.

The disadvantages of delegated legislation are that Parliament loses control of the law-making process and that a huge mass of detailed law appears piecemeal each year. It is difficult for persons who may be affected by it to keep abreast of the changes. Yet ignorance of the law is not accepted as an excuse for infringing it.

Delegated legislation appears in various forms. Ministerial powers are exercised by *statutory instrument* (including emergency powers of the Crown exercised by Orders in Council). Local authorities are given statutory powers to make *bye-laws*, which apply within a specific locality.

7

Parliament does exercise some control over delegated legislation by restricting and defining the power to make rules and by keeping the making of new delegated legislation under review. Some statutory instruments do not take effect until approved by affirmative resolution of Parliament. Most other statutory instruments must be laid before Parliament for 40 days before they take effect. During that period members may propose a negative resolution to veto a statutory instrument to which they object.

There are standing scrutiny committees of both houses whose duty it is to examine statutory instruments with a view to raising objections if necessary, usually on the grounds that the instrument is obscure, expensive or retrospective.

As explained above, the power to make delegated legislation is defined by the Act which confers the power. A statutory instrument may be challenged in the courts on the ground that it is *ultra vires*, that is that it exceeds the prescribed limits, or on the ground that it has been made without due compliance with the correct procedure. If the objection is valid the court declares the statutory instrument to be void.

Custom

In early mediaeval times the courts created law by enforcing selected customs. Custom is now of little importance as a source of law, but it is still classified as a legal source of law.

In disputes over claims to customary rights, such as a right to use the land of another or to remove things from it, the alleged custom may be established subject to the following conditions.

(a) It must have existed since *time immemorial*, in theory since 1189 AD. It usually suffices to show that the custom has existed without interruption as far back as records (if any) go.

(b) It must have been enjoyed *openly as of right*. If it has only been enjoyed secretly, by force or with permission of a landowner, it is not a custom for legal purposes.

(c) The custom must be reasonable, certain in its terms, consistent with other custom or law and exercised within a definite locality.

In determining the implied terms of a contract, the court may take account of local or trade customs which the parties intended should be part of their contract.

Case: Hutton v Warren 1836
The parties were landlord and tenant of a farm. The landlord gave notice to the tenant to quit. Disputes arose as to the tenant's obligation to continue to cultivate the farm until the notice expired and as to his entitlement to allowances for work done and seed supplied.

Held: these matters were to be resolved according to local custom which had been incorporated in the contract.

Exercise 5

An Act of Parliament gives the Chancellor of the Exchequer power to fix the rate of a tax on land values by statutory instrument. The Chancellor of the Exchequer issues a statutory instrument extending the tax to the values of shareholdings. On what ground could the statutory instrument be challenged?

8

5   Subsidiary sources of law

The main sources of law as set out above are judicial precedent (derived from common law and equity) and parliamentary and EC legislation. However, a number of subsidiary sources have had some influence on the law's development, and are still recognisable today.

The law merchant

In mediaeval times, traders (who were often foreigners) submitted their disputes to courts at main ports, fairs and markets which applied mercantile custom. The law of negotiable instruments was brought to England as a commercial practice recognised by bankers and traders in Northern Italy, Germany and elsewhere in late mediaeval times. The work of these courts was absorbed (with the law merchant) into common law in the seventeenth century.

Roman law

Although it is the basis of most continental systems of law, Roman law is of little importance as a source of English law. Its influence was mainly felt in the ecclesiastical courts and in the rules relating to the requirements of a valid will. A soldier's privileged will (an informal will) is an example of a current law which has Roman origins.

Ecclesiastical law

Like the courts of the law merchant, the ecclesiastical courts were independent of the common law courts. They mainly dealt with offences against morality, such as adultery and slander. They also had jurisdiction over the law of succession. They kept their jurisdiction until 1857.

Codes of practice

In recent years some statutes have provided for codes of practice to be drawn up to supplement the law. These codes are usually prepared by appropriate bodies as guides to recommended practice, for example codes on picketing at a factory gate in the course of an industrial dispute or dealings between traders and their consumer customers. Such codes are not law and it is not unlawful to disregard them. But in any legal proceedings the court may take account of compliance with or disregard of a code of practice in deciding whether, for instance, a person has behaved reasonably (if that is a legal obligation imposed on him in general terms, as it is, for instance, in the unfair dismissal rules of employment law).

6   Case law

Judges inevitably create law. Sometimes an Act of Parliament will deliberately vest a wide discretion in the judiciary. In other cases there may be no statutory provision and no existing precedent relevant to the particular dispute. Even so, the doctrine of judicial precedent is based on the view that it is not the function of a judge to make law, but to decide cases in accordance with existing rules.

The doctrine of judicial precedent is designed to provide consistency in the law. In order that this should be done in a coherent manner, three things must be considered when examining a precedent before it can be applied to a case.

(a)   The *ratio decidendi* must be identified.

(b)   The material facts must be the same.

(c)   The earlier court must have had a superior (or in some cases, equal) status to the later court.

9

Ratio decidendi and *obiter dicta*

A judgement will start with a description of the facts of the case and probably a review of earlier precedents and possible alternative theories. The judge will then make statements of law applicable to the legal problems raised by the material facts. Provided these statements are the basis for the decision, they are known as the *ratio decidendi* of the case. The *ratio decidendi* (reason for deciding) is the vital element which binds future judges. If a judge's statements of legal principle do not form the basis of the decision, or if his statements are not based on the existing material facts but on hypothetical facts, they are known as *obiter dicta* (said by the way) A later court may respect such statements, but it is not bound to follow them. They are only of *persuasive* authority.

> *Case: Rondel v Worsley 1969*
> The House of Lords stated an opinion that a barrister could be held liable for negligence when not acting as an advocate, and that a solicitor would be immune from action when acting as an advocate. Since the case actually concerned the liability of a barrister when acting as an advocate these opinions were *obiter dicta*.

It is not always easy to identify the *ratio decidendi*. The same judgement may appear to contain contradictory views of the law in different passages. In decisions of appeal courts, where there are three or even five separate judgements, the members of the court may reach the same conclusion but give different reasons. The *ratio* may also be mingled with *obiter* statements. Many judges help by indicating in their speeches which comments are *ratio* and which are *obiter*.

Exercise 6

A case hinges upon whether clementines are oranges. The judgement contains the remark 'clementines are oranges, just as peanuts are nuts'. How does this remark illustrate the distinction between *ratio decidendi* and *obiter dicta*?

The status of courts

A court's status has a significant effect on whether its decisions are binding, persuasive or disregarded.

(a) The Judicial Committee of the House of Lords stands at the apex of the judicial system. Its decisions are binding on all other English courts. The House of Lords generally regards itself as bound by its own earlier decisions but it reserves the right to depart from its own precedents in exceptional cases.

(b) The Court of Appeal's decisions are binding on all English courts except the House of Lords. It is bound by its own previous decisions and by those of the House of Lords: *Young v Bristol Aeroplane Co 1944.* However, the Criminal Division may deviate from its own previous decisions where to follow a decision would cause injustice to the appellant; the need for justice exceeds the desire for certainty where human liberty is at stake: *R v Gould 1986.*

(c) A single High Court judge is bound by decisions of higher courts but not by a decision of another High Court judge sitting alone (though he would treat it as strong persuasive authority). When two or more High Court judges sit together as a Divisional Court, their decisions are binding on any other Divisional Court (and on a single High Court judge sitting alone).

(d) Lower courts (the Crown Court, county courts and magistrates' courts) do not make precedents, and their decisions are not usually reported. They are bound by decisions of the higher courts.

Apart from binding precedents as described above, reported decisions of any court (even if lower in status) may be treated as *persuasive* precedents: they may be, but need not be followed in a later case. Reported decisions of the Judicial Committee of the Privy Council (which is a court of appeal from certain Commonwealth countries), of higher courts of Commonwealth countries which have a common law legal tradition and of courts of the United States of America may be cited as persuasive precedents. With persuasive precedents much depends on the personal reputation of the judge whose earlier decision is cited.

Distinguishing the facts

Apart from identifying the *ratio decidendi* of an earlier case, it is also necessary to consider how far the facts of a previous case and the current case are similar. Facts are never identical. If the differences appear significant the court may distinguish the earlier case on the facts and thereby avoid following it as a precedent.

Overruling

A court of higher status is not only free to disregard the decision of a court of lower status in an earlier case. It may also deprive it of authority and expressly overrule it. This does not does not affect the outcome as regards the defendant and plaintiff in the earlier decision; it only affects the precedents to be applied in later cases.

Reversing

A case in the High Court may be taken on appeal to the Court of Appeal. If the latter court reverses the former decision, that first decision cannot be a precedent, and the reversing decision becomes a precedent. However, if the original decision had been reached by following a precedent, then reversing that decision overrules the precedent which formed the *ratio*.

If, in a case before the House of Lords, there is a dispute about a point of European Community (EC) law it must be referred to the Court of Justice (of the EC) for a ruling. English courts are also required to take account of principles laid down by the Court of Justice in so far as these are relevant. The Court of Justice does not, however, create or follow precedents as such.

Avoidance of a binding precedent

Even if a precedent appears to be binding, a court may decline to follow it:

(a) by distinguishing the facts;

(b) by declaring the *ratio decidendi* obscure, particularly when a decision by three or five judges gives as many *rationes decidendi*;

(c) by declaring that the previous decision was made *per incuriam*, that is without taking account of some essential point of law, such as an important precedent;

(d) by declaring the precedent to be in conflict with a fundamental principle of law, for example where a court has failed to apply the doctrine of privity of contract: *Beswick v Beswick 1968*;

(e) by declaring the precedent to be too wide. For example, the duty of care to third parties found in *Donoghue v Stevenson 1932* has since been considerably refined;

(f) because the earlier decision has been subsequently overruled by another court or by statute.

BPP Publishing

Exercise 7

A brings an action against B, and the case is finally settled in favour of B in the Court of Appeal. 15 years later, C brings an action against D on very similar facts, and the case of A v B is the only relevant precedent. However, the case of C v D is finally decided by the Judicial Committee of the House of Lords, which overrules A v B and gives judgement in favour of C. Can A do anything to get judgement against B?

The advantages and disadvantages of precedent

Many of the strengths of judicial precedent also indicate some of its weaknesses. Generally the arguments revolve around the principles of consistency, clarity, flexibility and detail.

Consistency. The whole point of following binding precedent is that the law is decided fairly and predictably. In theory therefore it should be possible to avoid litigation because the result is a foregone conclusion. However, judges are often forced to make illogical distinctions to avoid an unfair result, which combined with the wealth of reported cases serves to complicate the law.

Clarity. Following only the reasoning in ratio statements should lead to statements of principle for general application. In practice, however, the same judgement may be found to contain propositions which appear inconsistent with each other or with the precedent which the court purports to follow.

Flexibility. The real strength of the system lies in its ability to change with changing circumstances since it arises directly out of the actions of society. The counter-argument is that the doctrine limits judges' discretion and they may be unable to avoid deciding in line with a precedent which produces an unfair result. Often the deficiency may only be remedied by passing a statute to correct the law's failings.

Detail. Precedents state how the law applies to facts, and it should be flexible enough to allow for details to be different, so that the law is all-encompassing. However, judges often distinguish cases on facts to avoid following a precedent. The wealth of detail is also a drawback in that it produces a vast body of reports which must be taken into account; again, though, statute can help by codifying rules developed in case law.

The most famous (adverse) description of case law is that made by Jeremy Bentham, when he called it 'dog's law'. Precedent follows the event, just as beating a dog follows the dog disobeying his master: before the dog transgressed, the offence did not exist. It can be answered, however, that a thing can only be prevented when it is seen to be harmful, and that this is only usually seen when harm has already been done.

7   The interpretation of statutes

Statutes, including delegated legislation, are expressed in general terms. For example, a Finance Act may impose a new tax on transactions described as a category; it does not expressly impose a tax of a specified amount on a particular transaction by a particular person. If a dispute arises as to whether or how a statute applies to particular acts or events, the courts must interpret the statute and decide whether or not it applies to a given case.

In statutory interpretation the court is concerned with what the statute itself provides. It is not required to take account of what may have been said in parliamentary discussion, and it may only consider statements by a government spokesman explaining the intended effect of the bill when the statements are clear and the legislation is ambiguous or obscure, or leads to absurdity *(Pepper v Hart 1992)*. A report of a committee or commission recommending legislation is not to be used as a guide to the interpretation of a statute.

Unless the statute contains express words to the contrary it is presumed that the following 'canons' of statutory interpretation apply, although any of them may be rebutted by contrary evidence.

(a)   A statute does not alter the existing law nor repeal other statutes.

(b)   If a statute deprives a person of his property, say by nationalisation, he is to be compensated for its value.

(c)   A statute does not have retrospective effect to a date earlier than its becoming law.

(d)   A statute does not bind the Crown.

(e)   Any point on which the statute leaves a gap or omission is outside the scope of the statute.

(f)   A statute has effect only in the UK; it does not have extraterritorial effect.

(g)   A statute cannot impose criminal liability without proof of fault (some modern statutes rebut this presumption by imposing *strict liability*, that is liability even without any intention to commit a crime).

(h)   A statute does not run counter to international law and should be interpreted so as to give effect to international obligations.

In practice a statute usually deals expressly with these matters (other than (e)) to remove any possible doubt.

Exercise 8

A statute given Royal Assent on 15 July 1993 provides that it shall come into force on 1 January 1993 and that another statute given Royal Assent on 14 April 1993 shall be repealed. Is either of these provisions invalid?

Since judges are called upon to interpret statutes, a system has been developed to guide them. This consists of statutory assistance and a set of general principles.

Statutory assistance consists of:

(a)   the Interpretation Act 1978, which defines certain terms frequently found in legislation;

(b)   interpretation sections of Acts, defining various terms;

(c)   preambles or long titles to Acts, which often direct the judge as to the Act's intentions and objects. Private Acts must have preambles but Public Acts have recently only contained long titles. Preambles may only be used to resolve an ambiguity. They may not be used when the enacted words are already clear: *Attorney-General v Ernest Augustus (Prince) of Hanover 1957*;

(d)   sidenotes, summary notes in the margin, which may be used to give a general interpretation of the sections to which they are attached.

In interpreting the words of a statute the courts use the following general principles.

(a)   *The literal rule:* words should be given their ordinary grammatical sense. Normally a word should be construed in the same literal sense wherever it appears throughout the statute. The courts will use standard dictionaries to aid them in their interpretation.

(b)   *The golden rule:* a statute should be construed to avoid a manifest absurdity or contradiction within itself.

> *Case: Re Sigsworth 1935*
> The golden rule was applied to prevent a murderer from inheriting on the intestacy of his victim although he was, as her son, her only heir on a literal interpretation of the Administration of Estates Act 1925.

(c)   *The contextual rule:* a word should be construed in its context. It is permissible to look at the statute as a whole to discover the meaning of a word in it.

(d)   *The mischief rule:* if the words used are ambiguous and the statute discloses (perhaps in its preamble) its purpose, the court will adopt the meaning which is likely to give effect to that purpose (that is, to take account of the mischief or weakness which the statute is intended to remedy).

> *Case: Gardiner v Sevenoaks RDC 1950*
> The purpose of an Act was to provide for the safe storage of flammable cinematograph film wherever it might be stored on 'premises'. A notice was served on G who stored film in a cave, requiring him to comply with the safety rules. G argued that 'premises' did not include a cave.
>
> *Held:* the purpose of the Act was to secure the safety of persons working in all places where film was stored. Insofar as film was stored in a cave, the word 'premises' included the cave.

(e)   *The eiusdem generis rule:* statutes often list a number of specific things and end the list with more general words. In that case the general words are to be limited in their meaning to other things of the same kind *(eiusdem generis)* as the specific items which precede them.

> *Case: Evans v Cross 1938*
> E was charged with driving his car in such a way as to 'ignore a traffic sign'. He had undoubtedly crossed to the wrong side of a white line painted down the middle of the road. 'Traffic sign' was defined in the Act as 'all signals, warning signposts, direction posts, signs or other devices'. Unless, therefore, a white line was an 'other device', E had not ignored a 'traffic sign' and had not committed the offence charged.
>
> *Held:* 'other devices' must be limited in its meaning to signs of the sorts mentioned in the list which preceded it. Thus restricted it did not include a painted line which was quite different.

(f)   *Expressio unius est exclusio alterius:* to express one thing is by implication to exclude anything else. For example, a statutory rule on 'sheep' does not include goats.

(g)   *In pari materia:* if the statute forms part of a series which deals with similar subject matter, the court may look to the interpretation of previous statutes on the assumption that Parliament intended the same thing.

The courts have been paying more attention to what Parliament intended in recent times. This is partly an extension of the mischief rule. In October 1988, for example, the Attorney-General issued a statement interpreting the word 'obtain' in the Company Securities (Insider Dealing) Act 1985. This was in order that the courts should apply the law for the purpose for which it was enacted by Parliament. A more purposive approach is also being taken because so many international and EC regulations have to be interpreted by the courts.

BPP Publishing

Case: Re Attorney-General's reference (No 1) 1988
The accused had received unsolicited information from a merchant banker telling him of a forthcoming merger. He knew that this was price-sensitive information and instructed is broker to buy shares in one of the companies, later netting a profit of £3,000. The Act sets out the offence of 'knowingly obtaining' such information. His defence was that he had obtained it passively, not actively.

Held: both the Court of Appeal and the House of Lords rejected this interpretation on the grounds that the effect of the legislation would be lessened if it were followed.

The House of Lords has decided that it is permissible for the courts to refer to reports, by certain bodies, which led to the statute in question: *Davis v Johnson 1978* For example reports by the Law Commission or by committees appointed by the Government may be used, as described in a judgement by Lord Diplock, 'to identify the mischief which the legislation is intended to remedy but not for the purpose of construing the enacting words.'

It is open to the UK courts to decide that a British statute should be interpreted according to British court rules. EC directives need not be taken into account: *Duke v GEC Reliance Systems Ltd 1988.*

Exercise 9

A statute applies to 'lions, tigers, leopards and other felines'. Is it likely to apply to domestic cats?

Chapter roundup

(a)   Laws are rules enforced by the State. English law is largely case law, with little Roman law.

(b)   The sources of law are the historical sources, the legal sources and the subsidiary sources.

(c)   Common law developed after the Norman Conquest, but became too rigid to give just results in many cases.

(d)   Equity gave more discretion to do justice than common law, and new rights and remedies, but fair dealing was expected from litigants expecting to be treated fairly themselves.

(e)   Common law and equity remain separate, although both are applied in all courts. Equity prevails over common law.

(f)   Case law is the application of reported cases to later cases. Several series of law reports are published.

(g)   Statute law is made by Parliament, which subject to the UK's membership of the European Community has unfettered legislative powers.

(h)   A bill goes through two readings, a committee stage, a report stage and a third reading in each house of Parliament before receiving the Royal Assent.

(i)   Much detailed legislation is delegated to Government departments exercising powers conferred by Acts of Parliament.

(j)   Customs may be a source of law, so long as the customs in question satisfy certain criteria.

(k)   The subsidiary sources of law are the law merchant, Roman law, ecclesiastical law and codes of practice.

(l)   Decided cases can fix the law for the purposes of future cases heard before certain courts, through the doctrine of precedent.

(m)   The binding element in an earlier decision is the *ratio decidendi*, not the *obiter dicta*.

(n)   The House of Lords binds all courts except itself. The Court of Appeal and a Divisional Court of the High Court bind themselves and all lower courts.

(o)   A court can avoid following a precedent on several grounds.

(p)   Statutes need to be interpreted to determine their application to different cases. There are canons of statutory interpretation, concerned with a statute's scope and its impact on the law and on persons, and there are also rules of statutory interpretation, concerned with the detailed interpretation of the words of a statute. There are also some statutory aids to interpretation.

Quick quiz

1   How was the common law first developed?

2   Give some examples of equitable maxims.

3   Can a successful plaintiff be certain of obtaining a desired equitable remedy?

4   What are the normal contents of a report of a case?

5   What is meant by Parliamentary sovereignty?

6   Why is delegated legislation essential?

7   How may a code of practice influence the outcome of a court case?

8   Can *obiter dicta* in a case have any influence on the outcome of subsequent cases?

9   When may the Court of Appeal deviate from its own previous decisions?

10   What does it mean to say that a court's decision was taken *per incuriam*?

11   List the canons of statutory interpretation.

12   What is the mischief rule?

Solutions to exercises

1   The defendant might, for example, have agreed to sell a unique work of art to the plaintiff, and might then refuse to go through with the sale.

2   Common law would only recognise trustees' rights as legal owners of the trust property. Equity makes those rights subject to beneficiaries' interests.

3   It concerns a ship.

4   No Parliament can bind its successors.

5   It would be *ultra vires*.

6   'Clementines are oranges' is the *ratio decidendi*. 'Peanuts are nuts' is an *obiter dictum*.

7   No: A v B cannot be reopened.

8   Both provisions are valid.

9   No: the *ejusdem generis* rule applies.

BPP Publishing

2 THE ENGLISH LEGAL SYSTEM

Your objectives

After completing this chapter you should:

(a)   understand the difference between civil and criminal liability;

(b)   know the system of courts, and the appeals available;

(c)   know the jurisdiction of each of the courts;

(d)   know the different divisions of the High Court;

(e)   understand the structure of the legal profession.

---

1   Civil and criminal liability

The distinction between criminal and civil liability is central to the legal system and to the way in which the court system is structured.

Crime

A crime is conduct prohibited by the law. The State (in the form of the Crown Prosecution Service) is the usual prosecutor in a criminal case because it is the community as a whole which suffers as a result of the law being broken. However, private individuals may also prosecute (although this is rare). Persons guilty of crimes are punished by fines or imprisonment.

In a criminal trial, the burden of proof to convict the *accused* rests with the *prosecution*, which must prove its case *beyond reasonable doubt*.

Civil proceedings

Civil law exists to regulate disputes over the rights and obligations of persons dealing with each other. The State has no role in a dispute over, for instance, a breach of contract. It is up to the persons involved to settle the matter in the courts if they so wish. The general purpose of such a course of action is to impose a settlement, sometimes using financial *compensation* in the form of the legal remedy of damages, sometimes using equitable remedies such as injunctions or other orders. There is no concept of punishment.

In civil proceedings, the case must be proved on the *balance of probability*. Terminology is different from that in criminal cases; the *plaintiff* sues the *defendant*, and the burden of proof may shift between the two.

The main areas of civil liability are contract and tort. Both are forms of relationship between persons.

(a)   A *contract* is a legally binding agreement, breach of which infringes one person's legal right given by the contract to have it performed.

BPP Publishing

Notes

(b) A *tort* is a wrong committed by one person against another (such as a libel), infringing general rights given by the law. Hence for there to be liability there need not have been any pre-existing personal relationship before the tort was committed.

Exercise 1

Why is the standard of proof in criminal trials not beyond *all* doubt?

2 The structure of the legal system

The courts have to be organised to accommodate the working of the law. There are four main functional aspects of the court system which underlie its structure.

(a) *Civil and criminal law* differ so much in substance and procedure that they are administered in separate courts.

(b) *Local courts* deal with must small legal proceedings. But important civil cases, in which large sums of money are at stake, begin in the High Court in London.

(c) Although the courts form a single system, there is some *specialisation* both within the High Court (split into three divisions) and in other courts with separate functions.

(d) There is a system of *review by appeals* to higher courts.

Under the Supreme Court Act 1981, the Court of Appeal, the High Court and the Crown Court comprise the Supreme Court. The diagram below gives an overall view of the whole court system.

BPP Publishing

CIVIL COURT STRUCTURE

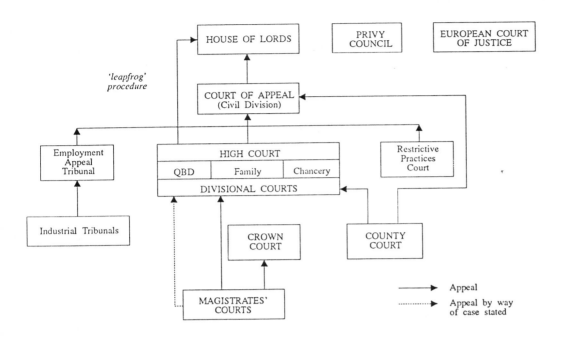

CRIMINAL COURT STRUCTURE

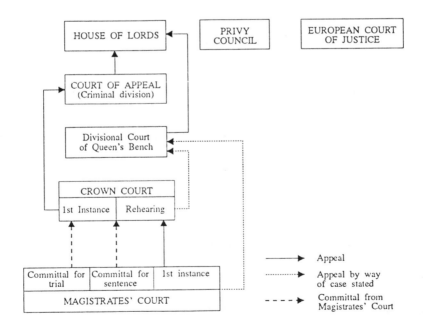

BPP Publishing

Note that in criminal cases the Crown Court is at once a court of first instance and an appellate court. A court of first instance is one where a case is originally heard in full. An appellate court is a court to which an appeal is made against the original ruling or the sentence.

If an appellate court finds in favour of the appellant the original decision is reversed. This is different from overruling which happens when a higher court finds a lower court's precedent to be wrong. Although the precedent is overruled and hence not followed again, the overruling has no effect on the actual outcome of the original case.

Exercise 2

A sues B in the High Court, and judgement is given in favour of A. B then appeals to the Court of Appeal. If A later appeals to the House of Lords, what may we conclude about the judgement given in the Court of Appeal?

---

3 The courts

As can be seen, some courts deal only with civil cases and some only with criminal cases. Most, however, can deal with both. We will now look at the structure and jurisdiction of the various elements of the court system.

Magistrates' courts

Magistrates' courts deal with *criminal* cases as follows.

(a) They try summarily (without a jury) all minor offences and may try offences triable summarily or on indictment with a jury (triable either way), if the accused consents and the magistrates' court considers that the case is suitable for trial in that court.

(b) They conduct committal proceedings, which are preliminary investigations of the prosecution case, when the offence is triable only on indictment (in the Crown Court with a jury), or where it is an offence triable either way but is to be tried on indictment. If the magistrates are satisfied that the prosecution has enough evidence to justify a full trial, they commit the defendant for trial in the Crown Court.

The maximum penalties which magistrates may impose on a defendant convicted summarily of a criminal offence are six months' imprisonment and/or a fine of up to £5,000. The magistrates also have discretion to order the defendant to compensate his victim, up to £5,000. If in a summary trial the magistrates consider that their sentencing powers are inadequate they may convict and commit the defendant to the Crown Court for sentence. They may also make community service, restitution, supervision and probation orders. Under the Criminal Justice Act 1991 they may combine community service and probation orders in respect of a single offence. They may also impose curfews and enforce these by means of electronic tagging. Other miscellaneous sentences include binding over to keep the peace (a fine being payable in the event of a breach), disqualification from driving and endorsement of a driving licence.

A convicted defendant has a general right to a rehearing by a Crown Court. Either the defendant or the prosecution may appeal on a point of law only by way of 'case stated' to a Divisional Court of the Queen's Bench Division. A 'case stated' appeal is based on the idea not that magistrates (or the Crown Court) have wrongly decided the facts but that they have wrongly interpreted the law. The magistrates produce written reasons for the way in which they decided the case. These, together with the facts, are considered by the Divisional Court to ensure that the law was correctly applied. If not then the case may be sent back to the lower court with instructions as to how it should be decided.

Magistrates' *civil* jurisdiction includes various types of licensing and the enforcement of local authority rates and the council tax. The magistrates' courts also have an important role to play in the law relating to children; they are the first tier in what is in effect a Family Court in which specially trained magistrates and judges apply uniform procedures across the magistrates', county and High Courts.

Magistrates' courts are mostly staffed by lay magistrates who are not legally qualified and sit part-time. They are appointed on the Lord Chancellor's advice and are assisted by salaried, legally qualified clerks, who must be solicitors or barristers of at least five years' standing. Stipendiary magistrates sit in large towns and are salaried. They must be solicitors or barristers of at least seven years' standing. Lay magistrates sit two or three to a court; stipendiary magistrates sit alone.

Exercise 3

C is being prosecuted for an offence which is triable either way. He elects to be tried summarily, so as to ensure that he will not be sentenced to more than six months' imprisonment. Will he succeed in his aim?

County courts

County courts have *civil* jurisdiction only but deal with almost every kind of civil case arising within the local areas for which the courts are established.

County courts are involved in:

(a)   contract and tort claims (see below);

(b)   equitable matters concerning trusts, mortgages and partnership dissolution but only up to £30,000 unless the parties waive the limit;

(c)   disputes concerning land where the capital value of the land is less than £30,000;

(d)   family cases;

(e)   probate matters where the estate of the deceased is estimated to be less than £30,000;

(f)   miscellaneous matters as set out in various statutes, for example the Consumer Credit Act 1974 (no limit on jurisdiction);

(g)   some bankruptcy, company winding up and admiralty cases; and

(h)   small claims.

The allocation of cases between the High Court and county courts used to be made purely on the basis of monetary limits. This had the disadvantage that there was not always an appropriate match between the case and the judge presiding over it. In particular some cases which did not really require the relevant resources and expertise were being heard in the High Court.

The High Court and County Court Jurisdiction Order 1991 makes new arrangements for the distribution of proceedings between the High Court and county courts. Criteria are laid down for where proceedings are to be commenced and tried and where judgements are to be enforced. In particular, actions in respect of *personal injuries* are to be commenced in a county court unless the claim is worth £50,000 or more.

BPP Publishing

Actions in contract and tort worth less than £25,000 must normally be tried in a county court and those worth £50,000 or more must normally be tried in the High Court, with those in between going either way, subject to:

(a)   the 'financial substance' of the action;

(b)   whether questions of public interest are raised;

(c)   the complexity of the facts, the legal issues, the procedures or the remedies involved; and

(d)   whether transfer is likely to result in a more speedy trial.

These criteria may also be used to transfer an action worth less than £25,000 to the High Court or an action worth over £50,000 to a county court.

County court judgements for the payment of sums of money of £5,000 or more must be enforced in the High Court. If the judgement is for a sum less than £2,000 it must be enforced in the county court, with amounts between these limits being enforceable in either court.

A circuit judge usually presides in a county court. He or she is a barrister of at least ten years' standing. A recorder, a part-time appointment in the Crown Court, is a solicitor or barrister of at least ten years' standing, and may be appointed as a circuit judge if he has three years' experience as a recorder. A district judge, who must be a solicitor or barrister of at least seven years' standing, assists the circuit judge; the district judge may also hear small claims, or any other claims with the consent of the parties. The circuit judge normally sits alone, although in a limited number of civil cases there may be a jury.

To assist litigants who decide to conduct their cases in person the court may, if the amount involved does not exceed £1,000 or if the parties agree, refer a case to an arbitrator to hear and decide informally in a small claims court. The arbitrator is usually the district judge but may be another person chosen by the parties. The arbitrator's award is recorded as a county court judgement. This is a cheaper and quicker way of settling small claims in an informal atmosphere, and is often used in consumer cases, motor accident and personal injury claims, employment, tenancy, travel and debt disputes.

From the county court there is a right of appeal direct to the Civil Division of the Court of Appeal.

The practical importance of the county courts is that they deal with the majority of the country's civil litigation. Over one and a half million actions are commenced each year (about one million are for debt), although only about 5% result in trials since most actions are discontinued or settled out of court before the trial stage is reached.

Exercise 4

P sues D for breach of contract, asking for and obtaining damages of £10,000. In which court would the case be heard, and in which court would the judgement be enforced?

The Crown Court

The Crown Court is theoretically a single court forming part of the Supreme Court, but in fact it comprises local courts in large towns and also the Central Criminal Court (the Old Bailey) in the City of London. It tries all serious (indictable) offences with a jury and hears appeals and deals with committals for sentencing from magistrates' courts. It also deals with a few types of civil cases, being appeals from the magistrates' court on matters of betting, gaming and licensing. From the Crown Court there is a right of appeal on criminal matters to the

Criminal Division of the Court of Appeal. An appeal by way of 'case stated' on a point of law may also be made to a Divisional Court of the Queen's Bench division.

A circuit judge, a recorder or a High Court judge may sit in the Crown Court. Sometimes lay magistrates also sit. Very serious offences, such as murder and treason, may only be heard by a High Court judge in the Crown Court. All prosecutions for indictable offences are heard by a judge with a jury of 12 persons.

The High Court

The High Court is organised into three divisions: Queen's Bench, Chancery and Family. Except where other special courts have exclusive jurisdiction, the High Court can deal with any civil matter.

The High Court is staffed by puisne (pronounced 'puny') judges, who must be barristers of at least ten years' standing. A judge's name is written as Smith J (plural JJ), and pronounced 'Mr Justice Smith'. The Queen's Bench division is presided over by the Lord Chief Justice. The Chancery division is presided over (nominally) by the Lord Chancellor. The Family division has its own President.

In hearing a case for the first time *(at first instance)* a High Court judge sits alone. A Divisional Court of two or more High Court judges sits to hear appeals from magistrates (and from Crown Courts in respect of civil matters tried in those courts). It also exercises the supervisory jurisdiction of the Queen's Bench division.

The Queen's Bench division

The Queen's Bench division (QBD) deals mainly with common law matters such as actions based on contract or tort. It includes a separate Admiralty Court to deal with shipping matters such as charterparties, salvage and collisions at sea. It is the largest of the three divisions.

There is also within the QBD the Commercial Court which specialises in commercial cases, such as insurance claims. The Commercial Court offers a rather simpler trial procedure to meet business needs. Judges of the Commercial Court may also sit as arbitrators.

A Divisional Court of the QBD has a supervisory role over other courts. It may issue a writ of *habeas corpus*, which is an order for the release of a person wrongfully detained, and also prerogative orders against inferior courts, tribunals and other bodies such as local authorities, insofar as they have a duty to exercise a discretion fairly. There are three types of prerogative order.

(a) *Mandamus* requires a court or other body to carry out a public duty. For example, a tribunal may be ordered to hear an appeal which it has wrongly refused to hear or a local authority may be ordered to produce its accounts for inspection by a council tax payer.

(b) *Prohibition* prevents a court or tribunal from exceeding its jurisdiction (*before* it has done so).

(c) *Certiorari* orders a court or tribunal which has taken action to submit the record of its proceedings to the High Court for review. The High Court may then quash the decision but cannot substitute its own decision (as it can under the ordinary appeal procedure). The exact scope of this power of review is not clearly defined. It is exercised when an inferior court has acted illegally, exceeded its jurisdiction or reached its decision contrary to the principles of natural justice (for example without giving the person concerned the right to know of and reply to the case against him).

Application may be made for all these three remedies, together with an injunction, under a single claim for judicial review. Leave for an application for judicial review is made to a single judge, following which application is made to the QBD. A person making such an application must have the appropriate *locus standi*, that is a sufficient interest in the matter to which the application relates.

The Chancery division

This division deals with traditional equity matters such as:

(a)   trusts and mortgages;

(b)   revenue matters;

(c)   bankruptcy (though outside London this is a county court subject);

(d)   disputed wills and the administration of estates of deceased persons;

(e)   partnership and company matters.

There is a separate Companies Court within the division which deals with liquidations and other company proceedings.

The family division

This division deals with the same matters of family law as the magistrates' and county courts, except that magistrates' courts have no jurisdiction on divorce.

Exercise 5

A local authority decides not to provide education for children of school age. What action could be taken by:

(a)   a parent of a child affected?

(b)   someone from a different part of the country who thinks that the law should always be enforced?

The Restrictive Practices Court

The Restrictive Practices Court is not part of the High Court but has the same status, and appeals from it go to the Court of Appeal. It investigates the merits of agreements registered under the Restrictive Trade Practices Act 1976 and agreements falling under the Resale Prices Act 1976. In these functions it is required to have regard to EC law. It is also concerned with proceedings to prohibit practices deemed prejudicial to consumers under the Fair Trading Act 1973. Usually a High Court judge and two lay assessors from a panel appointed on the Lord Chancellor's recommendation sit.

The Employment Appeal Tribunal (EAT)

The Employment Appeal Tribunal is a court of equal status with the High Court. It hears appeals from industrial tribunals mainly on employment matters (such as unfair dismissal, redundancy pay or sex discrimination). Again, a High Court judge and two lay assessors sit. There is a right of appeal from the EAT to the Court of Appeal.

The Court of Appeal

The Civil Division of the Court of Appeal hears appeals from county courts, the High Court, the Restrictive Practices Court, the Employment Appeal Tribunal and various other special tribunals such as the Lands Tribunal. It does not conduct a complete rehearing but reviews the record of the evidence in the lower court and the legal arguments put before it. It may uphold or reverse the earlier decision or order a new trial.

BPP Publishing

The Criminal Division of the Court of Appeal hears appeals from Crown Courts. It may also be invited to review a criminal case by the Home Secretary or to consider a point of law at the request of the Attorney General. Its powers and procedures are very similar to those of the Civil Division.

There are 28 Lords Justices of Appeal, promoted from the High Court. A Lord Justice's name is written Green LJ (plural LJJ) and pronounced 'Lord Justice Green'. Three judges normally sit together. In the Criminal Division, the Lord Chief Justice presides. Both he and judges of the High Court may be selected to sit along with the 18 Civil Division judges. In the Civil Division the Master of the Rolls presides, but he may also sit in the Criminal Division. A majority decision is sufficient and dissenting judgements are expressed.

The Judicial Committee of the House of Lords

Apart from the limited jurisdiction of the Court of Justice (of the EC), the Judicial Committee of the House of Lords is the highest court of appeal of the English, Scottish and Northern Irish legal system. It hears appeals from both the civil and the criminal divisions of the Court of Appeal (and in certain circumstances directly from the High Court).

Judges are promoted from the Appeal Court to be members of the Judicial Committee of the House of Lords. They are known as Lords of Appeal in Ordinary, or Law Lords. Five judges normally sit together, though there may be only three. Majority decisions are sufficient and dissenting judgements are expressed.

The Judicial Committee of the Privy Council (JCPC)

Some countries of the Commonwealth (though not many) still retain a right of appeal from their national courts to the Privy Council. The Judicial Committee is (with a slightly different membership) in effect the same body as the Judicial Committee of the House of Lords. It also deals with appeals from the English ecclesiastical courts.

Exercise 6

When might it be appropriate for the Court of Appeal to order a new trial, rather than simply reviewing the earlier proceedings in a lower court and upholding or reversing the earlier decision?

---

4 The legal profession

The legal profession is divided into two mutually exclusive groups, barristers and solicitors. The two groups have some shared arrangements for basic training but, before qualifying, the recruit must take his advanced training in one or the other branch exclusively. It is not possible to be a member of both, though individuals may transfer from one to the other.

Solicitors

Solicitors are the general practitioners of the legal profession and provide many services to their clients which do not involve them in court proceedings. Generally solicitors may only appear as advocates for their clients before magistrates' and county courts. In most other court proceedings the solicitor prepares the case and retains one or more counsel (barristers) to appear in court as advocates for his client, although it is sometimes possible for clients to brief barristers without the intervention of solicitors. The individual conduct and collective affairs of solicitors are subject to regulation (partly on a statutory basis) by the Law Society. It is common for solicitors to practise as partners in a firm, but they may not carry on business through companies.

Barristers

Barristers are members of one of the four Inns of Court, the Inner Temple, the Middle Temple, Gray's Inn and Lincoln's Inn, and obtain their admission to the bar (to practise in the courts) after taking examinations set by the Council of Legal Education and satisfying certain other conditions. They are required to complete a year's pupillage in professional training in the chambers of a practising barrister (in London or a provincial city). Although groups of barristers share the occupation of chambers (and the services of a clerk of chambers and his assistants), they are not allowed to enter into partnership.

Barristers are specialists in advocacy in court, but much of their working time is spent in chambers conducting conferences with instructing solicitors and their clients. There is also a great deal of paperwork, for example drafting legal documents and opinions. Barristers are consultants who usually (but not always) deal with lay clients only through solicitors. The Bar Council has approved proposals which allow direct access by certain professionals (such as accountants and engineers).

There are advantages and disadvantages to the division of the legal profession into two branches. The present system gives the public greater access to barristers than a fused system would. Under fusion barristers would probably join the larger legal firms. The present system, by keeping advocacy in the hands of specialists, also means that judges hear clear arguments in trials. Those who argue in favour of fusion would point to duplication of effort, unnecessary division of responsibility, the high cost of paying more than one expert and the overlaps which already exist, particularly in the field of advocacy.

Legal executives

Finally, mention should be made of the legal executives who are employed by firms of solicitors to do professional work. Some may be qualified as members of the Institute of Legal Executives, though this is not obligatory. A legal executive is usually a specialist in one type of work only, such as litigation, conveyancing or trust administration.

Exercise 7

If a non-lawyer requires the services of a barrister in order to argue a case in court, what useful work can a solicitor do before a barrister is instructed?

Chapter roundup

(a) Crimes offend against society as a whole, and criminals are prosecuted, usually by the State.

(b) Civil proceedings are brought by the person who has suffered loss, the aim being compensation.

(c) The courts are structured in a system which allows for appeals.

(d) Magistrates' courts deal mainly with minor crimes, although they have some civil jurisdiction.

(e) County courts only have civil jurisdiction, and do not generally deal with cases where very large amounts are at stake.

(f) The Crown Court deals with serious crimes.

(g) The High Court deals with substantial civil cases. It has three divisions, the Queen's Bench division, the Chancery division and the Family division. It also has a supervisory jurisdiction over other courts and authorities.

(h)   The Court of Appeal hears appeals from lower courts. It has both a civil division and a criminal division.

(i)   The Judicial Committee of the House of Lords is the final appellate court.

(j)   Other courts include the Restrictive Practices Court, the Employment Appeal Tribunal and the Judicial Committee of the Privy Council.

(k)   The legal profession is divided into solicitors and barristers. Solicitors deal with members of the public directly, and have only limited advocacy rights. Barristers generally deal with members of the public through solicitors, and can act as advocates in all courts.

Quick quiz

1   How does the standard of proof differ between civil and criminal proceedings?

2   Which courts comprise the Supreme Court?

3   What is the difference between summary trial and trial on indictment?

4   What civil jurisdiction do magistrates' courts have?

5   List the types of case which may be dealt with in a county court.

6   Who may hear a case in the Crown Court?

7   What are the three types of prerogative order which may be issued by the Queen's Bench division of the High Court?

8   What matters are dealt with by the Chancery division of the High Court?

9   What matters are dealt with by the Restrictive Practices Court?

10   From which courts does an appeal lie to the Court of Appeal?

11   Which body regulates the conduct of solicitors?

12   What sorts of work do barristers do apart from advocacy?

Solutions to exercises

1   Nothing can be proved beyond all doubt.

2   In the Court of Appeal, judgement was given in favour of B.

3   No: he might be convicted in a magistrates' court and then committed to the Crown Court for sentencing.

4   The case would probably be heard in a county court, but the judgement would be enforced in the High Court.

5   A parent could seek a *mandamus* order. Someone from another part of the country would have no *locus standi* and could do nothing.

6   When there was new evidence (perhaps from new witnesses) to consider.

7   A solicitor can ensure that the client has an adequate case, and can compile evidence and ensure that the facts are presented to the barrister in an orderly fashion.

BPP Publishing

3 EUROPEAN COMMUNITY LAW

Your objectives

After completing this chapter you should:

(a) understand the composition and role of the European Community (the EC);

(b) know the names and functions of the law-making EC institutions;

(c) understand the role of the Court of Justice, and how it hears cases;

(d) know what general principles of law are applied by the Court of Justice;

(e) understand the notions of direct applicability and direct effect of EC law;

(f) know how treaty provisions, regulations and directives differ;

(g) know how EC law can be enforced in national courts;

(h) appreciate the supremacy of EC law over national law.

1   The European Community

The European Community exists to promote free trade and competition, economic integration and the harmonisation of law. Political union is a possible long-term goal. It has 12 European states as members. The United Kingdom joined in 1973. The other members are Ireland, Denmark, Germany, the Netherlands, Luxembourg, Belgium, France, Spain, Portugal, Italy and Greece. There are actually three communities, the European Community (formerly the European Economic Community), the European Coal and Steel Community and the European Atomic Energy Community, but for our purposes we can regard them all as one, which we shall refer to as the European Community (the EC).

The EC was set up by the Treaty of Rome, and this treaty is the legal foundation for the powers of EC institutions. The original treaty has been amended, most notably by the Treaty on European Union (the Maastricht treaty). We will refer to the treaties entered into by the member states as 'the EC treaties'.

The EC generates much law, mainly on economic and social matters such as competition between businesses, working conditions and the free movement of people within the EC. The legislative process is independent of national legislatures, such as the United Kingdom Parliament, although it is controlled by government ministers from the member states. EC law can be enforced through the national courts in the member states and through the Court of Justice. If EC law conflicts with national law, EC law takes priority. EC law should thus be seen as a separate system of law, independent of national systems and overriding them where necessary.

In this chapter, we will have to consider the institutions of the EC, the member states, natural persons (human beings) and legal persons (for example companies, which are recognised as separate legal entities in their own right). For simplicity, we will refer to member states as 'states' and to natural and legal persons as 'persons'.

BPP Publishing

2 The law-making institutions of the EC

EC law is generated by three institutions working together. These are the Council of Ministers, the Commission and the Parliament.

The Council of Ministers

The Council of Ministers comprises one government minister from each state. The ministers who attend meetings vary with the subjects to be discussed. Thus agriculture ministers would attend a meeting to discuss farming matters, and foreign affairs ministers would attend to discuss responses to a war being waged outside the EC. The Council considers proposed legislation submitted to it by the Commission, and may decide to adopt it. It also gives the Commission the necessary powers to implement legislation. The Council is the closest of the three law-making institutions to the governments of the states, because it comprises ministers from those governments. It has more power in the EC legislative process than the other two institutions: it can block legislation which it does not approve of, and it can ensure that legislation which it wants is put forward. It normally takes decisions by 'qualified majority vote': larger states have more votes than smaller states, but the five largest states cannot win a vote against the other seven states combined.

The Commission

The Commission comprises 17 commissioners, one or two nominated by each state. Once the members of the Commission have been nominated, the Commission as a whole is subject to approval by the Parliament. The Parliament can also at any time insist that the whole Commission resign and be replaced by a new Commission (again nominated by the states). The commissioners act in the interests of the EC as a whole, and do not put forward the views of the states which nominated them. The Commission proposes new laws for consideration, and it also ensures that existing EC law is applied. It can impose fines on persons. If a state is not fulfilling its obligations under EC law, the Commission can take the case to the Court of Justice, which can require compliance with EC law, and impose a fine on the state if it still fails to comply.

The Parliament

The Parliament (often referred to as the European Parliament) is directly elected by the citizens of the states. Its role is largely advisory. It cannot make law in the way in which the UK Parliament can. The Commission must submit all its proposals for legislation to the Parliament as well as to the Council of Ministers. The Parliament can propose amendments, but if the Council of Ministers does not approve of an amendment it can override the Parliament by a unanimous vote.

Exercise 1

The Council of Ministers wishes to pass a new EC law.

(a) Could a single state prevent its being passed, assuming that no amendments had been proposed?

(b) Could a single state prevent its being passed in its unamended form if an amendment had been proposed by the Parliament?

BPP Publishing

3 The Court of Justice

The Court of Justice (CJ), often referred to as the European Court of Justice, is the court which hears legal actions connected with EC law. There is no long hierarchy of courts allowing for several appeals, as there is in the UK, but some actions may be heard by the Court of First Instance (see below), with the possibility of an appeal to the CJ.

The procedure of the CJ is in the continental tradition, so its proceedings are inquisitorial rather than adversarial: that is, the court takes an active part in trying to find out what happened and what should be done. In an English court, the court leaves it to the parties to an action to come up with evidence and legal arguments, and then decides between the parties. The CJ has 13 judges and six advocates-general, all of whom are appointed by states but are independent of the states which appointed them. There are extensive written stages, in which evidence and arguments are exchanged, before a court hearing takes place. At a hearing, the parties can put their cases but the court is also given the opinion of an advocate-general on the case. He or she is impartial, and offers reasoned submissions. A single majority judgement is given, and the views of dissenting judges are not published.

The CJ's jurisdiction is limited to that set out in the EC treaties. This is as follows.

(a) It can hear disputes between states or between the Commission and a state relating to matters covered by an EC treaty.

(b) It can consider the legality of acts or omissions of the Council of Ministers, the Commission or the Parliament, and it can declare that any of these institutions has violated the EC treaties. An action may be brought by a state, by the Council of Ministers or by the Commission. In addition, the Parliament may bring an action in order to protect its prerogatives.

(c) It can hear appeals by persons, for example against fines imposed by the Commission for breaches of EC law.

(d) It can interpret EC law when asked to do so by a court in a state. This is called giving a preliminary ruling. The final court of appeal in each state (the House of Lords in the UK) must refer such questions of interpretation to the CJ. Lower courts may do so. Such a reference to the CJ is made merely to establish the meaning of EC law. The case is still decided by the relevant national courts.

(e) It can, at the request of the Council of Ministers or of the Commission, give an advisory opinion on whether their proposals are compatible with existing EC law.

The CJ cannot interpret, apply, enforce, repeal or annul legislation or administrative acts of states, and it cannot pronounce on their validity under national law. The CJ applies the following general principles of law, which have been evolved in cases.

(a) The protection of fundamental human rights.

(b) Equality (for example in cases of discrimination on the ground of gender or religion).

(c) The protection of legitimate expectations. Thus a farmer who had temporarily given up his right to sell milk was allowed to enforce the restoration of that right to him at the end of the agreed period, because he could legitimately expect that it would be restored (*Mulder v Minister of Agriculture and Fisheries 1989*).

(d) Proportionality. Administrative measures, such as penalties, should not be excessive.

(e) Legal certainty. Earlier decisions of the CJ are normally followed, so that people can be reasonably confident of what the law is in an area which the CJ has considered in the past. However, the CJ is not legally bound by its own previous decisions.

BPP Publishing

The Court of First Instance

The Court of First Instance is attached to the CJ. It has 12 judges and no advocates-general. It can hear certain cases which would otherwise go to the CJ. There is a right of appeal from its decisions to the CJ, but only on a matter of law.

Exercise 2

A builder bought some land, and built a house for his own use on it. Under EC law, value added tax is chargeable when business assets are applied for private use. Could either or both of the following questions be referred to the Court of Justice by a national court?

(a)   Is this a case of business assets being applied for private use?

(b)   How much was the land worth? (Assume that there is no doubt as to the correct method of valuation.)

---

4   Types of EC Law

EC law may be made in several ways. Although all EC law is supreme over the law of states, the way in which it is made is important for two reasons.

(a)   It affects the way in which the EC law comes into force in states. In some cases it comes into force without any further action. Such law is said to be directly applicable.In other cases it only comes into force when national legislation is enacted in states.

(b)   It affects the types of rights and obligations which arise under the EC law. States may acquire rights, or persons may acquire rights which they may enforce against states or against each other. EC law which itself creates rights which persons may enforce is said to have direct effect. Such rights must be protected by the courts in the states; there is no need to go to the CJ to take legal action on the basis that EC legislation has direct effect. If the rights are against other persons, the law has horizontal effect. If the rights are against states, the law has vertical effect.

The two main categories of EC law are primary legislation, which is given in the EC treaties, and secondary legislation, which is given in regulations, directives and decisions. EC institutions may also issue recommendations and opinions, but these have no binding force.

The EC treaties

The EC treaties are self-executing, that is they do not require any other legal backing in order to become law in the states. They become law on their ratification by the states. Treaties are therefore directly applicable. The normal procedure is for the heads of governments to indicate their agreement to a treaty by signing it, but that agreement needs to be ratified by national governments acting with their parliaments' authorities.

Each EC treaty is divided into numbered articles. Most articles of EC treaties have direct effect. Whether this is horizontal effect or vertical effect depends on the nature of the article. Thus articles granting individuals the right to live and work in any state have vertical effect, because such a right would be enforced against a state where an individual wished to live or work. Articles intended to ensure free competition, on the other hand, would be more likely to have horizontal effect, because they would be enforced against persons engaging in anti-competitive trade practices.

31

Some treaty articles do not have direct effect. This may be because they state that further legislation is required, or because they give states discretionary power on their application. In the latter case, their effect is subject to the exercise of that discretion.

The direct effect of treaty articles has been upheld by the Court of Justice in several cases. In an early case, *Van Gend en Loos v Nederlandse Tariefcommissie 1963*, it appeared to be important that the treaty article in question should contain a clear negative prohibition (in that case a prohibition on imposing new customs duties or increasing existing duties). In some other cases in the 1960s, notably *Costa v Ente Nazionale per l'Energia Elettrica 1964*, this prohibition rule was affirmed, but in later cases it has not been applied and treaty articles have been held to have direct effect even if they do not contain negative prohibitions. Thus an article requiring states to ensure that nationals of other states should (if suitably qualified) be able to practise their professions was held to have direct effect in *Reyners v Belgium 1974*. The horizontal effect of treaty articles was illustrated in *Robert Bosch GmbH v de Geus 1962*, which concerned a sole agency agreement for the distribution of Bosch products in the Netherlands.

Regulations

EC regulations are directly applicable in all states, and they also have direct effect. This effect may be either horizontal or vertical, depending on the content of the regulation. Regulations are also generally applicable. This means that they apply to all persons meeting certain criteria, rather than to named persons. For example, a regulation might be expressed to apply to all businesses with annual turnovers exceeding 5bn ecus (European currency units). It would not be expressed to apply to X plc and Y AG, even if those companies happened to be the only businesses with annual turnovers exceeding 5bn ecus. A regulation is binding in its entirety, and takes priority over any conflicting national law.

Case: Leonisio v Italian Ministry of Agriculture and Forestry 1972
Signora Leonisio was entitled, under a regulation, to a premium from the Italian state because she had slaughtered some cattle. The Italian state claimed that it did not have to pay the premium, because it had not gone through the budgetary procedures needed under Italian law for such payments to be made.

Held: the premium must be paid. Italian national law could not be used to defeat the regulation.

Case: EC Commission v United Kingdom (Re Tachographs) 1979
A regulation concerning tachographs in vehicles required states to enact national legislation. The United Kingdom did not incorporate the whole of the regulation in the UK legislation.

Held: states must not implement regulations in an incomplete or selective way. The UK had therefore not fulfilled its EC obligations.

Directives

EC directives are not directly applicable. They are binding on the states to which they are addressed, but only as to the result to be achieved. That is, they set out specific aims (such as allowing companies to have only one shareholder), but they leave it to states to alter national law so as to achieve those aims within a specified period.

A directive may have vertical direct effect, so as to give persons a remedy if a state fails to implement a directive. Legal action may only be taken against the state or its emanations, and it is limited so as not to interfere with any discretion the state may be given under the directive in how to implement it. The state may not take action against persons on the basis of an unimplemented directive.

Case: Marshall v Southampton and South-West Hampshire Area Health Authority 1986
A female employee was required to retire at a younger age than a male employee would
have been, on the basis that the UK state pension age was 60 for women and 65 for men.

Held: this policy of different retirement ages for men and women breached a directive on
equal treatment of men and women. The employee could rely on the directive against her
employer, which was an emanation of the state.

A local authority was held to be an emanation of the state in *R v London Boroughs Transport
Committee 1990*. In *Foster and others v British Gas plc 1988*, it was held that British Gas
(pre-privatisation) was an emanation of the state, because it was under state control and had
powers greater than those which would normally apply in relations between individuals.

A directive cannot have direct horizontal effect, giving persons rights against each other, but
a similar effect has been achieved by requiring that national law be interpreted in conformity
with directives.

Case: Marleasing SA v La Commercial Internacional De Alimentacion SA 1992
A directive which had not been implemented in Spain set out all the grounds on which
the incorporation of a company could be declared void. Spanish law included another
ground. The case hinged on whether that extra ground could be used.

Held: Spanish law must be interpreted so as to make it consistent with EC law. The extra
ground could not be used, and the rights of the persons involved in the case were to be
decided accordingly.

Decisions

EC decisions are addressed to particular states or persons, and are binding on the addressees.
They are issued by the Commission to enforce the application of EC law.

Exercise 3

If a state refused to change its national law in order to implement a directive, what would
it have to do in order not to continue in breach of its treaty obligations?

---

5 The supremacy of EC law

As has been said already, EC law overrides national law when the two conflict, and national
parliaments have surrendered some of their sovereignty to EC institutions. In this final
section, we will look at the way in which this supremacy of EC law is achieved.

For the UK to reach the position in which directly applicable EC law alters UK law without
UK legislation, the UK Parliament had to surrender some of its sovereignty using its existing
procedures. This was achieved by the European Communities Act 1972, which allows EC law
to alter UK law without further UK legislation.

The supremacy of EC law over national law is to be enforced by the national courts. National
legislatures have given law-making powers to EC institutions, but they cannot be prevented
from passing laws which contradict EC law. If they do so, it is the duty of the national courts
to enforce the EC law and override the national law. This rule was stated clearly in
Simmenthal SpA v Commission 1979. The House of Lords applied this rule in the *Factortame
case*.

Case: Factortame Ltd v Secretary of State for Transport (No 2) 1991
Under a British statute, 75% of directors and shareholders in companies operating British-registered fishing vessels had to be British. A UK company controlled by Spanish nationals claimed that this law was incompatible with EC law forbidding discrimination against nationals of other EC states.

Held: the supremacy of EC law had to be ensured. The House of Lords therefore temporarily suspended the UK statute while the interpretation of the EC law was considered by the CJ. Thus the House of Lords directly overrode the will of the UK Parliament.

Chapter roundup

(a) The EC is an association of 12 states. EC law generally concerns economic and social matters.

(b) There are three law-making EC institutions. The Council of Ministers has the final say on new law. The Commission proposes new law and enforces existing EC law. The Parliament's role is largely advisory.

(c) The Court of Justice hears legal actions. It can hear disputes involving EC institutions and disputes between states. It also interprets EC law when asked to do so by national courts. It applies certain general legal principles.

(d) EC law may be directly applicable. It may also have direct effect, horizontal and/or vertical.

(e) Treaties and regulations are generally directly applicable and have direct effect. Directives are not directly applicable, but require national legislation to bring them into force. They may however have direct effect in favour of persons against the state or its emanations.

(f) EC law is supreme over national law. This supremacy is enforced by the national courts.

Quick quiz

1 List the members of the EC.

2 How is the Commission appointed?

3 Can the Parliament make law?

4 To what extent does the Court of Justice follow its earlier decisions?

5 What is the role of the Court of First Instance?

6 When does an article of an EC treaty not have direct effect?

7 To what extent are directives binding on states?

8 What was the significance of the *Factortame* case?

Solutions to exercises

1 (a) No: only a qualified majority vote would be needed.

  (b) Yes: unanimity is required to override an amendment proposed by the Parliament.

2 (a) Yes: this is a question of the interpretation of EC law.

  (b) No.

3 It would have to leave the EC.

4 THE SETTLEMENT OF DISPUTES

Your objectives

After completing this chapter you should:

(a)   understand why litigation is not always advisable;

(b)   know how judgement may be obtained without a trial;

(c)   know the stages in an action in the High Court;

(d)   know the stages in an action in a county court;

(e)   understand the need for injunctions;

(f)   understand the nature of *Mareva* injunctions and *Anton Piller* orders;

(g)   be aware of the advantages and disadvantages of arbitration;

(h)   know the main terms implied in an arbitration agreement;

(i)   be able to outline the stages in arbitration, and the powers of an arbitrator;

(j)   know the extent to which courts may become involved in cases subject to arbitration;

(k)   be aware of the extent of legal aid;

(l)   know the main tribunals available to settle disputes, and their jurisdictions.

---

1   Commercial disputes

Most of this text is concerned with the principles relating to business law. It is important to have a clear grasp of this underlying theory because it forms the basis for deciding which party to a dispute is entitled to succeed in his claim. But there are numerous *practical* points which affect the outcome of commercial disputes. Settlements are often arrived at not as a result of the relative merits of the parties' cases, but from negotiations within, or outside, the framework of litigation.

Businesspeople tend to regard commercial disputes as being just one more test of the managerial and negotiating skills which they bring to bear on other aspects of their work. Knowledge of legal principles is important because it can indicate the strength of a negotiating position. But the legal merits of a case may never be put to the test and settlements out of court are common.

Even when litigation is decided on, legal theory is only one aspect of the problem and there may be practical difficulties to overcome.

(a)   If a plaintiff is successful, he will usually want to obtain financial compensation. Before commencing litigation he should be convinced that the defendant has sufficient assets to make it worthwhile. There is no point in seeking recompense from someone with no resources.

(b)   Even if the party at fault is financially sound, he may resist the judgement of the court, perhaps by transferring his assets outside the jurisdiction of the court.

BPP Publishing

(c) An injured party may feel that he has a strong legal case and still refrain from action. This might be because he cannot afford the risk of losing and the associated costs, or because a court case might damage his reputation or otherwise harm his long-term interests.

In this chapter we will look at some of the practical and procedural aspects of business law. We will begin by describing the stages in litigation and then proceed to discuss the process of arbitration. Note that we are considering civil, not criminal, law: the object is to obtain a remedy, not to inflict a punishment.

Exercise 1

P wishes to sue D, a person with whom he has regular business dealings, for breach of contract. The damages sought would be £3,000, and the total legal costs (mostly borne by the loser) would be about £800. P could only seek damages, and not any equitable remedy, because of the maxim that he who comes to equity must come with clean hands. D's easily realisable assets are worth about £3,000. What factors should P consider before deciding whether to take legal action?

---

2   Litigation

The object of litigation is firstly to obtain judgement from the court in favour of the person seeking it, and secondly to make sure that that judgement is enforced.

The system of litigation in England is *adversarial*. This means that the parties to a dispute put forward their cases and the court adjudicates on the matters presented to it. It is not the business of the court to look beyond the evidence presented so as to find other evidence which might be relevant. One criticism which has been made of the adversarial system is that important evidence may not be taken into account. It can happen, for example, that a piece of evidence is known to only one of the parties in dispute, and is not brought forward by him because it tells against his case.

Commercial disputes involving large sums are usually heard in the High Court, either in the Queen's Bench Division or in the Chancery Division. Each of these Divisions has specialist courts within it: for example the Commercial Court is a part of the Queen's Bench Division. Actions in both Divisions are usually heard by a judge, but judges in the Chancery Division may delegate to solicitors acting as *Masters*. Actions in the Queen's Bench Division may also be heard by Masters, but the similarity of title conceals an important difference in function. Queen's Bench Masters are barristers exercising independent jurisdiction rather than acting merely as delegates of a judge.

Obtaining judgement

There are some circumstances in which judgement may be given without trial. The most important are judgement in default, summary judgement and judgement on admissions.

Judgement in default may be given if the defendant fails to meet the specified time limits either in announcing his intention to contest the case or in presenting his defence.

Summary judgement is available when it appears that the defendant has no proper defence and is going through the motions of contesting the case merely to cause delay and trouble to the plaintiff.

Judgement on admissions may occur where a defendant admits some part of the plaintiff's claim, but disputes the rest. It is then open to the plaintiff to apply for any judgement that he may be entitled to on the basis of the admission, without waiting for resolution of any other points that may still be in dispute.

A contested action in the High Court

The stages in a contested High Court action are:

(a)   the issue and service of a writ;

(b)   the return of an acknowledgement of service;

(c)   the pleadings;

(d)   the close of pleadings and discovery;

(e)   the summons for directions;

(f)   the trial.

The stages before the trial itself are referred to as the *interlocutory* stages. Each of them is considered below.

A *writ* must first be served on the defendant. As a minimum this must state the ground of action and the relief sought; the plaintiff may wish in addition to set out his statement of claim (see below).

The writ must be accompanied by a form of *acknowledgement of service*. If he wishes to contest the plaintiff's claim, the defendant must return this form to the court within fourteen days. If he fails to do so, he makes himself liable to judgement in default.

The *pleadings* define the issues which will eventually be brought before the court. Neither party will be allowed to bring before the court any grounds of claim or defence which he has not already adduced in his pleadings and for this reason the drafting of pleadings must be done with great care.

The exchange of pleadings is begun by the plaintiff who serves a *statement of claim* on the defendant. This must be done within a prescribed time and similar time limits apply to the submission of a defence by the defendant.

Once the pleadings have been completed, *discovery* takes place. Each party must disclose to the other all relevant documents which are or have been in his possession.

The final step before the trial is a *summons for directions* by which the parties may seek directions for further discovery, amendment of pleadings or any other tidying up that may be necessary.

Finally, the *trial* itself takes place. After opening speeches by counsel for both parties, the witnesses are brought forward to be examined and cross-examined. The proceedings conclude with closing speeches by counsel and the judge's delivery of his judgement. In general, costs will be awarded to the successful party, but he will rarely be fully reimbursed for all his costs.

Exercise 2

How do the interlocutory stages help to ensure that as many cases as possible are settled before trial?

BPP Publishing

A contested action in the county court

County court procedure is similar, but somewhat simpler and less expensive than a High Court action. The plaintiff applies to the county court office, setting out the nature of his claim and particulars of the defendant, who must normally reside or carry on business within the county court district. The registrar issues a summons which, among other things, specifies a *return day*. The summons and particulars of the plaintiff's claim must be served on the defendant personally or at his address, or by post, not less than 21 days before the return day. The defendant may, within 14 days of receiving the summons, pay into court the whole amount claimed, or as much as he agrees is due, plus costs, or file a defence setting out his rejection of the plaintiff's claim. Alternatively he may appear on the return day to dispute the claim or to admit the claim and ask for time to pay.

The final stage before trial of a defended case is a *pre-trial review* by the court registrar (following enactment of the Courts and Legal Services Act 1990 a district judge will preside). He may make various appropriate orders according to the circumstances. Unless the action is disposed of by his order, the registrar fixes a date for the hearing if the case is in his opinion ready for trial. The trial will be conducted in the same manner as a trial in the High Court. There is not usually a jury but there are exceptions in for example, actions for malicious prosecution or false imprisonment and some personal injury cases.

3 Interlocutory matters

In many cases, the eventual award of damages in court may be an inadequate remedy for a plaintiff. The courts have developed other procedures which may assist him, some of which are used between the commencement of proceedings and the trial. One of the most commonly applied for is an *injunction*.

Any *injunction* is an order restraining a defendant from committing some act before the trial comes to be heard. A plaintiff may apply to the court for an injunction, which is an equitable remedy preventing breach of duties or infringement of intellectual property rights. It is common for the plaintiff to apply *ex parte* in the first instance, that is without giving notice to the defendant. If the judge is convinced by the case he makes out, he will grant an *interim* injunction for a short period during which the defendant will be formally notified, and allowed to make representations. Alternatively, the court may make an *interlocutory* injunction, which applies until the full hearing of the case; it is for a determined period, whereas an interim injunction may be varied between hearings.

Because the plaintiff may not be ultimately successful in the trial, he must give an undertaking to pay damages to the defendant if he fails in his case. This is to compensate the defendant for the prejudice caused by an injunction.

Mareva injunctions

A recent development in this field is the *Mareva* injunction. A successful plaintiff may be unable to enforce judgement if the defendant's assets have been transferred outside the jurisdiction of the court or otherwise dissipated: *Barclay-Johnson v Yuill 1980*. If the plaintiff can convince the court that he has a good case and that there is a danger of the defendant's assets being exported or dissipated, he may be awarded an injunction which restricts the defendant's dealing with the assets at all, either at home or by taking them abroad.

The *Mareva* injunction is named from the case of *Mareva Compania Naviera SA v International Bulkcarriers SA 1975*, but it has now been given statutory effect by s 37 of the Supreme Court Act 1981. The terms which the court will impose in granting such an injunction may vary, but they will not be so restrictive as to prevent the defendant from the ordinary running of his business, from paying ordinary business debts or having an ordinary way of life. The injunction is designed to prevent the defendant's assets from being exported or dissipated; it does not attempt to give the plaintiff any charge over the assets or to place the plaintiff in a preferential position compared with other creditors who may have claims on the assets.

The court will not grant a *Mareva* injunction unless:

(a) there is a 'good arguable case' on the part of the plaintiff;

(b) the court has jurisdiction over the case, and the defendant has available assets within that jurisdiction;

(c) there exists a genuine risk that if the injunction is not granted then:

(i) the assets will be removed or dissipated; or

(ii) the defendant will not satisfy the plaintiff's claim; and

(d) the balance of convenience is in favour of the injunction.

Anton Piller orders

A procedural aid for plaintiffs who suspect that their products (usually tape, film, video or computer goods) are being copied is the *Anton Piller* order, named after the case of *Anton Piller KG v Manufacturing Processes Ltd 1976*. In this case a German manufacturer feared that his English agent would pass on details of a new range of computer equipment to a competitor. The German company applied for an *ex parte* injunction authorising its solicitor to enter the agent's premises in order to inspect, and if necessary remove, the relevant documents.

The great benefit of the *Anton Piller* order is that it is granted *ex parte*, that is on the application of the plaintiff alone and without reference to the defendant. Ordinary *inter partes* injunctions are often inadequate because with notice of the plaintiff's intentions the defendant has the opportunity to destroy the evidence. An *Anton Piller* order can be applied for before either issue or service of a writ.

It is normal for the plaintiff's agent (normally a solicitor) to execute the order on the defendant's premises. If necessary the agent will be accompanied by police. As well as admitting the plaintiff to premises, the order often also requires the defendant to reveal the names and addresses of anybody else engaged in the copying scheme. In addition, the plaintiff may obtain an injunction restraining him from warning those persons.

Quia timet injunction

A *quia timet* injunction may be granted to restrain the commission of a threatened infringement. For example, the defendant might be erecting a building which, if completed, would infringe the plaintiff's right to light.

Exercise 3

X is planning to emigrate and to move all of his assets abroad. Y, who is opposed to this plan for personal reasons, brings an action against X which is unlikely to succeed, and then asks for a *Mareva* injunction in order to delay X in moving his assets abroad. Is Y's plan likely to succeed?

4   Commercial arbitration

Arbitration is an alternative to litigation in commercial disputes. As a process, it has much more in common with a businessperson's other commercial activities than does litigation. It is often preferred for that reason. However, arbitration only exists within the framework of law, and the court's jurisdiction cannot be ousted.

Some of the advantages of arbitration are as follows.

(a)   The proceedings are less formal and more flexible than litigation.

(b)   In some cases, arbitration may be quicker and cheaper than litigation, although since the parties must often bear the arbitrator's costs and remuneration directly, this is not always so.

(c)   The parties can select an arbitrator in whom they have confidence.

(d)   The person chosen is likely to be familiar with the commercial activities of the parties.

(e)   The hearing is usually in private, so avoiding publicity.

(f)   The atmosphere of an arbitration is more friendly than that of a court action. This is a point of some importance if the parties intend to continue their commercial dealings with each other.

Nevertheless, arbitration suffers from some disadvantages compared with litigation.

(a)   Plaintiff and defendant are bound to observe certain time limits in litigation, and so an arbitration procedure may provide more scope for deliberate time-wasting by a defendant.

(b)   A judge has power to grant interim relief (such as an injunction) or curtail proceedings by means of a summary judgement. An arbitrator's powers are less extensive.

(c)   Judges exercise their profession after many years of training in the process of weighing evidence and interpreting law. Arbitrators may be unqualified in such matters, and hence their decisions may be subjective.

In England, arbitration is regulated by the Arbitration Acts 1950, 1975 and 1979 and the Consumer Arbitration Agreements Act 1988. The 1950 Act is the principal Act. The 1975 Act gives effect to the 1958 New York Convention on the Recognition and Enforcement of Foreign Arbitral Awards. The 1979 Act makes miscellaneous additions to the law and limits appeals to the courts.

The Consumer Arbitration Agreements Act 1988 regulates the extent to which a consumer is bound by a clause in a contract requiring disputes to be referred to arbitration. Such a clause may not be enforced against a party entering into the agreement as a consumer (if the cause of action is within the county court's jurisdiction) unless the consumer gives written consent *after* differences arise. Except where the dispute could qualify as a 'small claim' the court may order that it should go to arbitration where it is satisfied that the consumer's interest will not be damaged.

Arbitration agreements and procedure

Disputes are most likely to be referred to arbitration under the terms of an *arbitration agreement*. An arbitration agreement is defined in s 32 Arbitration Act 1950 as 'a written agreement to submit present or future differences to arbitration, whether an arbitrator is named therein or not'. Although an arbitration agreement may by made orally, the Arbitration Acts only apply to written agreements. The definition includes not only *executory* agreements (agreements that disputes will be referred to arbitration) but also agreements to submit disputes to arbitration after they have arisen.

BPP Publishing

Certain provisions are implied into an arbitration agreement unless a contrary intention is expressed.

(a)   The parties to the agreement must submit to being examined on oath by the arbitrator and must produce all relevant documents which may be called for.

(b)   The award made by the arbitrator is final and binding on the parties.

(c)   The arbitrator can normally offer specific performance of a contract.

(d)   An interim award may be made.

The procedure for an arbitration may sometimes be similar to that of a court action. The usual first step is to arrange a meeting between the arbitrator and the parties, and from there to move on to pleadings and discovery. The hearing itself may well be similar to a trial, though less formal. But there are important differences between the two processes. For example, an arbitrator is not normally bound by the rules of evidence and procedure that would apply in a court.

An arbitrator's powers in the interlocutory stages of an arbitration are less than those of a judge in an action. For example, he has no power to enter summary judgement or to penalise either party for failure to comply with his orders. However, the High Court is able to make interlocutory orders for an arbitration in much the same way as for an action. Since enactment of the Arbitration Act 1979 the arbitrator's own position has been strengthened: if either party fails to comply with his orders he may apply to the High Court for power to act, in effect, as a judge might do.

Exercise 4

Why should it be harder for a consumer to become bound by an arbitration clause in a contract than for a businessperson to become bound by one?

The involvement of the courts

The main object of the Arbitration Act 1979 was to limit the right of parties to an arbitration to apply to a court in the event of disagreement over the outcome of arbitration. The Act:

(a)   limits the right to refer a preliminary point of law to the High Court;

(b)   limits the right of appeal on a point of law;

(c)   requires the arbitrator in certain cases to state reasons for his awards; and

(d)   allows for the right of appeal to be expressly excluded by agreement between the parties.

The referral of preliminary points of law

Although a party to arbitration proceedings may apply to the court for settlement of a preliminary point of law before full arbitration proceedings are commenced, this is only allowed if the arbitrator agrees, both parties agree or the leave of the court is obtained.

The court will only grant leave to refer a preliminary point of law if the point of law to be clarified is capable, on clarification, of settling the parties' entire dispute *(Universal Petroleum Co Ltd v Handels und Transport Gesellschaft GmbH 1987)* and also significant cost savings are anticipated as a result of the referral.

BPP Publishing

The right of appeal on a point of law

Provided either both parties agree to an appeal or the court gives leave an appeal may be made to the court on a point of law. Leave is not given lightly by the court, and is limited to cases where the point is of general public importance. In addition the arbitrator's decision must not be *prima facie* wrong in law: *The Antasios 1984*.

The reasons for an arbitrator's award

With the court's leave, application may be made to the court for an order to obtain detailed reasons for the arbitrator's decision. Again the court is sparing in granting such orders.

Exclusion of the right of appeal

Although generally the law resists attempts to limit access to judicial review, parties in an arbitration may make an 'exclusion agreement' which prevents the parties from appealing on a point of law or referring preliminary points of law.

In domestic cases (where both parties reside in the UK) and in international cases relating to insurance or shipping matters, the exclusion agreement is only valid if it is entered into *after* the arbitration proceedings have begun. In other international cases it is valid even if entered into *before* such proceedings.

An exclusion agreement should not be confused with:

(a) a *Scott v Avery* clause, which makes it a condition precedent to court proceedings that arbitration proceedings should have commenced first; and

(b) an *Atlantic Shipping* clause which requires that, unless arbitration proceedings are commenced within a certain time period, the right of recourse to the courts is lost.

Both these types of clause have been upheld in the courts, since they do not totally oust the court's jurisdiction.

Exercise 5

To what extent would the advantages of arbitration be lost if it were easier to get the court to intervene?

---

5 Legal aid

Legal aid is a payment out of state funds to provide legal advice or representation, by either solicitors or barristers, for people who would otherwise be unable to afford it. The grant of legal aid in both civil and criminal matters is governed by the Legal Aid Act 1988 and the regulations passed under it and under earlier legislation. It is administered by the Legal Aid Board.

In *criminal cases*, application for aid is made to the court of trial. The applicant must submit a written statement as to his means and the court must be satisfied that it is desirable in the interests of justice for legal aid to be given, and that the applicant's means are such that he needs assistance to meet the costs of the case. When assessing the 'interests of justice' the clerk of the court will consider whether there is a serious risk that the accused will lose his liberty, job or reputation. If there is such a risk, legal aid is more likely to be granted. Nevertheless, there is concern that these criteria are not being applied consistently.

BPP Publishing

In *civil proceedings*, legal aid is only available to persons of very limited means. A person must satisfy a means test both on 'disposable income' and 'disposable capital'. He must also satisfy a 'merits test': has he a good arguable case with which, if he were paying his own costs, a solicitor would advise him to proceed? Two types of help are available.

(a) *Legal advice and assistance*. Under this scheme solicitors can undertake work falling short of court appearances. There is a relatively low limit on the value of this work, but it may be extended with the consent of the local area office of the Legal Aid Board.

(b) *Legal aid*. This is available for nearly all civil court hearings (except defamation). It is administered by local Legal Aid Board offices. Depending upon his financial position, the applicant for legal aid may receive legal services free of charge or he may be required to make some contribution to the total cost.

6 Administrative tribunals

Administrative tribunals are specialised courts established by statute to deal with disputes between government agencies and individuals or between two individuals in a simpler and less formal way than is possible in a court of law. Some of the more important ones are listed below.

(a) *Social security tribunals*. An individual who is refused a social security benefit may have his claim referred to a local tribunal consisting of a chairman (usually a lawyer) and two members from panels representative of employers and of employees. Either party may appeal from the decision of the tribunal to a National Insurance Commissioner who is a barrister or solicitor of at least ten years' standing. On a point of law there is a further right of appeal to the High Court.

(b) *The Land Tribunal*. This tribunal deals with disputes over the value of property, for example for compulsory purchase purposes. An experienced lawyer and a qualified valuation expert usually preside.

(c) *Rent tribunals*. These assess rents of certain furnished dwellings. County courts assess rents of unfurnished dwellings.

(d) *ACAS*. The Advisory, Conciliation and Arbitration Service has various functions including conciliation in disputes between employer and employee before such disputes go to an industrial tribunal.

(e) *Industrial tribunals*. These have membership similar to that of social security tribunals. They deal mainly with claims for compensation for unfair dismissal, redundancy pay, equal pay and sex discrimination. There is a right of appeal to the Employment Appeal Tribunal (EAT).

(f) *Administrative enquiries*. Some statutes, such as the town and country planning legislation, provide that objectors may put their case at a public enquiry conducted by an *inspector* (a professionally qualified expert) appointed by a minister. The inspector makes a report to the minister who takes the final decision.

Administrative tribunals offer a quicker and less expensive method of resolving a dispute than the court. But they may make mistakes of law or fail to convince interested parties that a fair and impartial hearing has been given.

The working of this system of administrative tribunals is supervised by a Council on Tribunals. In many instances, especially industrial tribunals, there is a statutory right to appeal from a tribunal to a court on points of law. The High Court may also make prerogative orders to prevent or remedy errors and injustices. At the appeal stage (but not usually in the proceedings before the lower tribunal) the applicant may be able to obtain legal aid.

BPP Publishing

Domestic tribunals

Within some professions, trade associations and trade unions, there are *domestic tribunals* which deal with charges of professional misconduct or breach of membership obligations. Some of these domestic tribunals are established by statute, for example the Solicitors' Disciplinary Tribunal and the disciplinary panel of the General Medical Council. Others are created merely by contract between the members of the relevant body who, on becoming members, agree to submit to a code of rules, including disciplinary procedures. This is the position in, for example, trades unions. If a domestic tribunal is established by law there is often a statutory right of appeal. The High Court may make prerogative orders to remedy misconduct by a domestic tribunal where there is no other relief available.

Exercise 6

A group of employees who are being made redundant and their employer are in dispute. Name two bodies other than the courts which might be involved in settling the dispute.

Chapter roundup

(a) A negotiated settlement may be preferable to litigation, in order to avoid legal costs or publicity, or to ensure that the compensation sought is actually received.

(b) Judgement may be obtained without trial, by obtaining judgement in default, summary judgement or judgement on admissions.

(c) Before a High Court action reaches trial, there are several interlocutory stages, in which each party learns about the other party's case. The parties thus have the opportunity to reach an agreement, but if the case does go to trial it is already clear what the issues are.

(d) County court procedure is simpler than High Court procedure.

(e) Injunctions may be sought to govern the actions of the parties prior to trial. A *Mareva* injunction prevents assets from being taken outside the jurisdiction of the court, and an *Anton Piller* order prevents illicit copies of goods from being destroyed.

(f) Arbitration offers an alternative to litigation in the settlement of commercial disputes. Contracts may incorporate arbitration agreements just in case disputes arise.

(g) Even if arbitration is used, the courts may still become involved in settling preliminary points of law or in hearing appeals on points of law.

(h) Legal aid is available to make legal advice and representation available to those without means, but it is very limited.

(i) Administrative tribunals deal with particular types of dispute more cheaply and quickly than the courts could.

BPP Publishing

Quick quiz

1   What does it mean to say that the system of litigation in England is adversarial?

2   What are the stages in a contested action in the High Court?

3   What are the stages in a contested action in a county court?

4   To what extent will the terms of a *Mareva* injunction be limited so as not to be too restrictive?

5   What are the main disadvantages of arbitration compared with litigation?

6   What conditions must be satisfied for a court to hear an appeal from an arbitration on a point of law?

7   List six administrative tribunals, and state the types of case which they deal with.

Solutions to exercises

1   (a)   Will P end up having to pay his own legal costs (and perhaps D's, if they reduce the £3,000 available)?

    (b)   Will D be put out of business?

    (c)   Even if D remains in business, will he refuse to have further dealings with P?

2   When the parties disclose their cases, it may become clear that one has a much stronger case than the other, so that a settlement would be sensible.

3   No: a *Mareva* injunction will only be granted if the plaintiff has a good arguable case.

4   An arbitration clause is likely to be stipulated by the seller of goods to a consumer, and the consumer must either accept it or not buy the goods. A consumer may also not understand its significance.

5   Someone doing badly in an arbitration would try to get the decision reversed by the courts, thus leading to delay and further expense.

6   ACAS and an industrial tribunal.

5 FORMATION OF CONTRACT

Your objectives

After completing this chapter you should:

(a) understand the nature of a contract;

(b) appreciate the circumstances in which legal relations are or are not intended;

(c) know what constitutes a valid offer, and how it may be terminated;

(d) know how an offer may be accepted, and how acceptance may be communicated;

(e) understand the circumstances in which contracts may arise without offer and acceptance;

(f) understand the need for consideration, and know the three types of consideration;

(g) appreciate the need for consideration to be sufficient;

(h) know the uses of promissory estoppel;

(i) understand the doctrine of privity of contract.

---

1   What is a contract?

A contract is an agreement which legally binds the parties. Sometimes contracts are referred to as enforceable agreements. This is rather misleading since one party cannot usually *force* the other to fulfil his part of the bargain. He will usually be restricted to the remedy of damages.

The underlying theory is that a contract is the outcome of 'consenting minds', each party being free to accept or reject the terms of the other. To speak of consenting minds is also misleading.

(a) Parties are judged by what they have said, written, or done, not by what is in their minds: an objective standard is applied.

(b) Mass production and nationalisation have led to the standard form contract: the individual must usually take it or leave it. For example, a customer has to accept his supply of electricity on the electricity company's terms.

(c) Public policy sometimes requires that the freedom of contract should be modified. For example, the Consumer Credit Act 1974 and the Unfair Contract Terms Act 1977 regulate the extent to which contracts can contain certain terms.

(d) The law will sometimes imply terms into contracts because the parties are expected to observe certain standards of behaviour. A person is bound by those terms even though he has never agreed to them, or never even thought of them; for example, sections 12-15 Sale of Goods Act 1979 imply terms as to title, fitness and quality of goods into all contracts for the sale of goods.

The essential elements of a contract are that:

(a) the parties *intend to create legal relations* between themselves;

46

(b)   it is an agreement made by *offer and acceptance*; and

(c)   it is a bargain by which the obligations assumed by each party are supported by *consideration* (value) given by the other. However, a gratuitous promise is binding if made by deed.

2   The intention to create legal relations

An agreement is not a binding contract unless the parties intend thereby to create legal relations. Where the parties have not expressly denied such intention, what matters is not what the parties have in their minds, but the inferences that reasonable people would draw from their words or conduct.

Case: Carlill v Carbolic Smokeball Co 1893
The manufacturers of a patent medicine published an advertisement by which they undertook to pay '£100 reward .... to any person who contracts ... influenza, colds, ... after having used the smoke ball three times daily for two weeks.' The advertisement added that £1,000 had been deposited at a bank 'showing our sincerity in this matter'. C read the advertisement, bought the smoke ball at a chemist's shop, used it as directed for eight weeks and while doing so contracted influenza; she then claimed her £100 reward. In their defence the manufacturers argued that:

(a)   the offer was so vague that it could not form the basis of a contract; it specified no period of immunity after use;

(b)   it was mere sales promotion, or 'puff', not intended to create legal relations;

(c)   it was not an offer to make a contract which could be accepted since it was offered to the whole world;

(d)   C had not supplied any consideration; and

(e)   C had not communicated to them her acceptance of their offer.

Held: it was an offer to the whole world which C could accept and had accepted. Specific communication was clearly not expected. Legal relations had been intended (as shown by the deposit of £1,000), and C had supplied consideration by buying the product. Point (a) did not succeed since the court found that the terms of the offer were sufficiently clear.

Any express statement by the parties of their intention not to make a binding contract is conclusive.

Case: Rose and Frank v J R Crompton & Bros 1923
A commercial agreement by which A (a British manufacturer) appointed B to be its distributor in USA expressly stated that it was 'not subject to legal jurisdiction' in either country. A terminated the agreement without giving notice as it required, and refused to deliver goods ordered by B although A had accepted these orders when placed.

Held: the general agreement was not legally binding but the orders for goods were separate and binding contracts.

Exercise 1

A manufacturer of vitamin pills states in an advertisement that the regular use of its product is likely to improve the user's health, but says nothing more. A user notices no improvement in his health, and wonders whether he can sue for breach of contract on the basis of *Carlill's* case. What are the significant differences from that case which would mean that there would be no basis for an action for breach of contract (although there might be other grounds of action)?

Domestic arrangements

In most agreements no intention is expressly stated. If it is a domestic agreement between husband and wife, relatives or friends it is presumed that there is no intention to create legal relations unless the circumstances point to the opposite conclusion. However, where agreements between husband and wife or other relatives relate to property matters the courts are very ready to impute an intention to create legal relations.

Case: Balfour v Balfour 1919
The husband was employed in Ceylon. He and his wife returned to the UK on leave but it was agreed that for health reasons she would not return to Ceylon with him. He promised to pay her £30 a month as maintenance. Later the marriage ended in divorce and the wife sued for the monthly allowance which the husband no longer paid.

Held: an informal agreement of indefinite duration made between husband and wife (whose marriage had not then broken up) was not intended to be legally binding. Similarly, use of uncertain words such as 'I'll pay you £15 as long as I can manage it' will lead the court to conclude that legal relations were not intended: *Gould v Gould 1969*.

Case: Merritt v Merritt 1970
The husband had left the matrimonial home, which was owned by him, to live with another woman. The spouses met and held a discussion in the husband's car in the course of which he agreed to pay her £40 a month out of which she agreed to keep up the mortgage payments on the house. The wife refused to leave the car until the husband signed a note of these agreed terms and an undertaking to transfer the house into her sole name when the mortgage had been paid off. The wife paid off the mortgage but the husband refused to transfer the house to her.

Held: in the circumstances, an intention to create legal relations was to be inferred and the wife could sue for breach of contract.

Domestic arrangements extend to those between people who are not related but who have a close relationship of some form. The nature of the agreement itself may lead to the conclusion that legal relations were intended.

Case: Simpkins v Pays 1955
A woman, her granddaughter and a paying boarder all took part together in a weekly competition organised by a Sunday newspaper. The arrangements were informal and the entries were made in the grandmother's name. One week they won £750; the paying boarder was denied a third share by the other two.

Held: there was a 'mutuality of agreement' amongst the parties, amounting to a joint enterprise. As such it was not a 'friendly adventure' as the defendant claimed, but a contract.

Commercial agreements

When businessmen enter into commercial agreements it is presumed that there is an intention to enter into legal relations unless this is expressly disclaimed or the circumstances displace that presumption.

Case: Edwards v Skyways 1964

In negotiations over the terms for making an employee redundant, the employer undertook to make an ex gratia payment to him, a payment without admission of previous liability.

Held: the denial of previous liability did not suffice to rebut the presumption that the agreed terms were intended to be legally binding in their future operation.

It was held in 1969 that procedural agreements between employers and trade unions for the settlement of disputes are not by their nature intended to give rise to legal relations in spite of their elaborate and very legal contents: *Ford Motor Co v AUEW 1969*. That view has been confirmed by statute: s 18 Trade Union and Labour Relations Act 1974.

The presumption that commercial agreements are legally binding needs to be expressly rebutted; however, for many years, holding companies have given 'comfort letters' to creditors of subsidiaries which purport to give some comfort as to the ability of the subsidiary to pay its debts. Such a letter has always been presumed in the past not to be legally binding, and the decision in the following case gives the reasons for such a presumption.

Case: Kleinwort Benson Ltd v Malaysian Mining Corporation Bhd 1989

The plaintiffs lent money to the defendant's subsidiary, having received a letter from the defendant stating:

'It is our policy to ensure that the business is at all times in a position to meet its liabilities to you.'

On the collapse of the International Tin Council the subsidiary went into liquidation, and the bank claimed from its holding company, MMC.

Held: (a)   the bank had clearly acted on the strength of the letter and so believed it to be of legal force;

(b)   the defendant had failed to ensure that its subsidiary's liabilities could be met;

(c)   the onus was on the defendant who claimed the letter was intended to have no legal effect to prove that was so.

The Appeal Court found that the statement of policy was a representation of fact and not a promise that the policy would continue in the future. This promise could not be implied where it was not expressly stated. Because both parties were well aware that in business parlance a 'comfort letter' imposed moral and not legal responsibilities, it was held not to have been given with the intention of creating legal relations. The defendant's breach of moral responsibility was of no concern to the court.

Oral agreements made during the course of negotiations are not binding.

Case: Walford v Miles 1991

The defendants were negotiating the sale of a business to the plaintiffs. The plaintiffs agreed not to withdraw from negotiations and the defendants agreed to break off negotiations with a third party. The defendants, however, continued to negotiate with the third party and sold the business to the third party.

Held: the oral agreement to withdraw from negotiations with the third party (the 'lock-out' agreement) was in effect simply an agreement to continue to negotiate and was not legally enforceable. An agreement to negotiate is not enforceable in English law. A 'lock-out' agreement may in principle be valid, providing a time limit is specified (none was specified here) and that there is consideration (as there was here).

Exercise 2

A widow tells her adult son that he can stay at her house temporarily so long as he does his share of domestic chores. Is there likely to be a contract under which accommodation is supplied in return for housework?

3   Offer

An offer is a definite promise to be bound on specific terms, and a contract will only normally exist if an offer is made and accepted. An offer must not be vague.

Case: Gunthing v Lynn 1831
The offeror offered to pay a further sum for a horse if it was 'lucky'.

Held: the offer was too vague.

However, if an apparently vague offer can be made certain by reference to the parties' previous dealing or the customs of the trade, then it will be regarded as certain.

An offer must be distinguished from the mere supply of information and from an invitation to treat (negotiate). Only an offer in the proper sense (made with the intention that it shall become binding when accepted) may be accepted so as to form a binding contract.

Case: Harvey v Facey 1893
A telegraphed to B 'Will you sell us Bumper Hall Pen? Telegraph lowest cash price.' B replied 'Lowest price for Bumper Hall Pen £900.' A telegraphed to accept what he regarded as an offer; B made no further reply.

Held: B's telegram was merely a statement of his price if a sale were to be agreed. It was not an offer which A could accept. No contract had been made.

To display goods in a shop window or on the open shelves of a self service shop (with a price tag), or to advertise goods for sale is to invite customers to make offers to purchase. The shopkeeper makes an 'invitation to treat', not an offer to sell.

Case: Fisher v Bell 1961
A shopkeeper was prosecuted for offering for sale an offensive weapon by exhibiting a flick knife in his shop window.

Held: the display of an article with a price on it in a shop window is merely an invitation to treat. It is not an offer for sale.

Case: Pharmaceutical Society of Great Britain v Boots Cash Chemists (Southern) 1952
Certain drugs may only be sold 'under the supervision of a qualified pharmacist.' It was alleged that this rule had been broken by Boots who put supplies of these drugs on open shelves in a self service shop. Boots, however, contended that there was no sale until a customer brought the goods which he had selected to the cash desk at the exit and offered to buy them. A qualified pharmacist was stationed at this point.

Held: Boots were correct in their analysis of the situation. The court commented that if it were true that a customer accepted an offer to sell by removing goods from the shelf he could not then change his mind and put them back; it would be breach of contract. Plainly neither Boots nor their customers intended such a result.

An offer may only be accepted by a person to whom the offer has been made. But it is possible to make an offer (which may be in any form) to the members of a group or even to the public at large for acceptance by those persons who wish to do so: *Carlill's case*.

Exercise 3

The following conversation takes place between A and B.

A: Would you be interested in buying my car?

B: Yes, but I would only give you £800 for it.

A: I would want £850 at least.

B: Very well, I accept your offer to sell the car to me for £850.

At this point, is A bound to sell the car to B for £850?

---

4   Termination of an offer

An offer may only be accepted (so as to form a contract) while the offer is still open. An offer is terminated (and can no longer be accepted) if:

(a)   it has expired by lapse of time;

(b)   the offeror has revoked it;

(c)   the offeree has rejected it; or

(d)   the offeree dies or (usually) if the offeror dies.

An offer may be expressed to last for a *specified time*. It then expires at the end of that time. If however, there is no express time limit it expires after a *reasonable time*. What is reasonable depends on the circumstances of the case, on what is usual and to be expected.

Case: Ramsgate Victoria Hotel Co v Montefiore 1866
M applied to the company for shares and paid a deposit to the company's bank. Five months later the company sent him an acceptance by issue of a letter of allotment. M contended that his offer had expired and could no longer be accepted.

Held: M's offer was for a reasonable time only and five months was much more than that. The offer had lapsed.

The offeror may *revoke* his offer at any time before acceptance. If he undertakes that his offer shall remain open for acceptance for a specified time he may nonetheless revoke it within that time, unless by a separate contract (an option agreement) he has bound himself to keep it open for the whole of the specified time.

Case: Routledge v Grant 1828
G offered to buy R's house, requiring acceptance within six weeks. Within the six weeks G withdrew his offer.

Held: as there was no option agreement (for which consideration must be given), G could revoke his offer at any time.

Revocation may be by express statement or by an act of the offeror indicating that he no longer regards the offer as in force. But however he revokes it, his revocation does not take effect (and the offer continues to be available for acceptance) until the revocation is

---

51

communicated to the offeree, either by the offeror or by any third party who is a sufficiently reliable informant.

Case: Byrne v Van Tienhoven 1880
The offeror was in Cardiff: the offeree in New York. The sequence of events was as follows.

1 October   Letter of offer posted in Cardiff.

8 October   Letter of revocation posted in Cardiff.

11 October   Letter of offer received in New York and telegram of acceptance sent; this was confirmed by letter posted on 15 October.

20 October   Letter of revocation received in New York. The offeree had meanwhile re-sold the contract goods.

Held: the letter of revocation could not take effect until received (20 October); it could not revoke the contract made by acceptance of the offer on 11 October. Simply posting a letter does not revoke the offer until it is received.

Case: Dickinson v Dodds 1876
A, on 10 June, wrote to B to offer property for sale at £800, adding 'This offer to be left open until Friday 12 June, 9.00 am.' On Thursday 11 June B delivered a letter of acceptance to an address at which A was no longer residing so that A did not receive it. A later sold the property to another buyer. C, who had been an intermediary between A and B, informed B that A had sold to someone else. On Friday 12 June, before 9.00 am, C delivered to A a duplicate of B's letter of acceptance.

Held: A was free to revoke his offer and had done so by sale to a third party; B could not accept the offer after he had learnt from a reliable informant (C) of A's revocation of the offer to B.

An offer may be *rejected* outright or by a counter-offer made by the offeree. Either form of rejection terminates the original offer. If a counter-offer is made the original offeror may accept it, but if he rejects it his original offer is no longer available for acceptance.

Case: Hyde v Wrench 1840
W offered to sell property to H for £1,000. H made a counter offer of £950 which W rejected three weeks later. H then informed W that he (H) accepted the original offer of £1,000.

Held: the original offer of £1,000 had been terminated by the counter offer of £950; it could not therefore be accepted.

Death of the offeree terminates the offer. Death of the offeror terminates the offer unless the offeree accepts it in ignorance of the offeror's death, and the offer is not of a personal nature.

Exercise 4

X offers to sell some rare books to Y. Before Y has decided whether to accept the offer, she hears from X's solicitor (whom Y knows acts in that capacity) that X has withdrawn the offer. Y then tries to accept the offer, on the ground that revocation was not communicated by X himself. Must X sell the books to Y?

BPP Publishing

5   Acceptance

Acceptance may be by express words or (as in *Carlill's* case) by action. It may also be implied by conduct.

> *Case: Brogden v Metropolitan Railway Co 1877*
> For many years B supplied coal to M. He suggested that they should enter into a written agreement and M's agent sent a draft to him for consideration. B made some alterations and additions and returned the amended draft to M's agent indicating that he (B) approved it. M's agent took no further action on it. B continued to supply coal to M and the parties applied to their dealings the special terms of the draft agreement. But they never signed a fair copy of it. B later denied that there was any agreement between him and M.
>
> *Held:* the draft agreement became the contract between the parties as soon as M ordered and B supplied coal after the return by B of the draft to M's agent.

There must, however, be some act on the part of the offeree to indicate his acceptance. Mere passive inaction is not acceptance.

> *Case: Felthouse v Bindley 1862*
> After previous negotiations had produced an agreed price P wrote to J offering to buy a horse for £30.75, adding 'If I hear no more about him, I consider the horse mine at that price'. J intended to accept but did not reply and owing to a misunderstanding the horse was sold at auction to someone else. P sued the auctioneer for conversion (misappropriation) of P's property.
>
> *Held:* there could be no acceptance by silence in these circumstances. The offeror cannot impose acceptance merely because the offeree does not reject the offer.

Goods which are sent or services which are rendered to a person who did not request them are not 'accepted' merely because he does not return them to the sender. His silence is not acceptance of them, even if the sender includes a statement that he is deemed to have agreed to buy and/or pay unless he rejects them: Unsolicited Goods and Services Act 1971. Indeed, provided the goods were sent with a view to his acquiring them otherwise than for a trade or business, and he has not agreed to pay for or to return them, the recipient may treat them as an unsolicited gift. However if, within six months, the sender tries to repossess them or the recipient unreasonably prevents repossession the goods are not deemed to be his.

Acceptance must be unqualified agreement to the terms of the offer. Acceptance which introduces any new terms is a rejection and counter-offer.

A counter-offer may be accepted by the original offeror; this will have the effect of creating a binding contract.

> *Case: Butler Machine Tool Co. v Ex-cell-O Corp (England) 1979*
> The plaintiff offered to sell tools to the defendant. Their quotation included details of their standard terms and conditions of sale. The defendant 'accepted' the offer, enclosing their own standard terms. The plaintiff acknowledged acceptance by returning a tear-off slip from the order form.
>
> *Held:* the defendant's order was really a counter-offer. The plaintiff had accepted this by returning the tear-off slip.

Acceptance 'subject to contract'

It is possible, however, to respond to an offer without accepting or rejecting it by a request for information or by acceptance 'subject to contract'. Acceptance 'subject to contract' is neither acceptance nor rejection by counter offer. It means that the offeree is agreeable to the terms of the offer but proposes that the parties should negotiate a formal (usually written) contract on the basis of the offer. Neither party is bound until the formal contract is signed.

Acceptance 'subject to contract' must be distinguished from outright and immediate acceptance on the understanding that the parties wish to replace the preliminary contract later with another more elaborate one. Even if the immediate contract is described as 'provisional', it takes effect at once.

> *Case: Branca v Cobarro 1947*
> A vendor agreed to sell a mushroom farm under a contract which ended 'this is a provisional agreement until a fully legalised agreement drawn up by a solicitor and embodying all the conditions herewith stated is signed.'
>
> *Held:* the parties were bound by their provisional contract until, by mutual agreement, they made another to replace it.

Exercise 5

When the two parties to a contract for a sale of goods each put forward their own standard conditions of sale or purchase, in respect of what matters would the two sets of conditions be likely to differ?

Tender

A 'tender' is a term often used in commercial dealings. A tender is an estimate submitted in response to a prior request. When a person tenders for a contract, he is making an offer to the person who has advertised a contract as being available. An invitation for tenders does not amount to an offer to contract with the person quoting the best price, except where the person inviting tenders makes it clear that he is in fact making an offer, for example by the use of words such as 'we confirm that if the offer made by you is the best offer received by us we bind ourselves to accept such offer': *Harvela Investments Ltd v Royal Trust Co of Canada Ltd 1985*.

The term tender can be used in two distinct senses.

(a)   A tender to perform one task, such as building a new hospital, is an offer which can be accepted.

(b)   A tender to supply or perform a series of things, such as the supply of vegetables daily to a restaurant is not accepted until an order is placed. It is a standing offer.

The acceptance of a tender to perform one task will create a binding contract, unless it is expressly stipulated that there will be no contract until formal documents are executed. In contrast, where a tender is made to supply goods in 'such quantities as you may order' (up to a stated amount), the person to whom the tender is submitted does not incur liability merely by accepting it and he is not bound to place any orders unless he has expressly undertaken to do so. The successful tender is regarded as a standing offer which the other party converts into a series of contracts by placing specific orders (which are acceptances). Until orders are placed there is no contract and the tenderer can terminate his offer.

The communication of acceptance

The general rule is that acceptance must be communicated to the offeror and is not effective until this has been done.

Case: Entores v Miles Far Eastern Corporation 1955
The legal issue was whether a contract had been made in London (within the jurisdiction of the English court) or abroad (outside it). The offeror sent an offer by telex to the offeree's agent in Amsterdam and the latter sent an acceptance by telex.

Held: the acceptance took effect (and the contract was made) when the telex message was printed out on the offeror's terminal in London.

But the offeror may by his offer dispense with communication of acceptance. For example, the offer to Mrs Carlill merely required that she should buy and use the smokeball. This was sufficient acceptance although not reported to the manufacturer.

The offeror may call for acceptance by specified means. Unless he stipulates that this is the only method of acceptance which suffices, the offeree may accept by some other means (if it is equally advantageous to the offeror).

Case: Yates Building Co v R J Pulleyn & Sons (York) 1975
The offer called for acceptance by registered or recorded delivery letter. The offeree sent an ordinary letter which arrived without delay.

Held: the offeror had suffered no disadvantage and had not stipulated that acceptance must be made in this way only. The acceptance was valid.

In *Tinn v Hoffman 1873* it was said that a telegram or even an oral message could be sufficient acceptance of an offer inviting acceptance 'by return of post'.

Use of the post

The offeror may expressly or by implication indicate that he expects acceptance by letter sent through the post. The acceptance is then complete and effective as soon as a letter (if it is correctly addressed and stamped and actually put in the post) is posted, even though it may be delayed or lost altogether in the post.

Case: Adams v Lindsell 1818
L made an offer by letter to A requiring an answer 'in course of post'. The letter of offer was misdirected and somewhat delayed in the post. A posted a letter of acceptance immediately. But L assumed that the absence of a reply within the expected period indicated non-acceptance and sold the goods to another buyer.

Held: the acceptance was made 'in course of post' (no time limit was imposed) and effective when posted.

The intention to use the post for communication of acceptance may be deduced from the circumstances, for example if the offer is made by post, without express statement to that effect.

Case: Household Fire and Carriage Accident Insurance Co v Grant 1879
G handed a letter of application for shares to the company's agent in Swansea with the intention that it should be posted (as it was) to the company in London. The company posted an acceptance (a letter of allotment) which was lost in the post.

Held: the parties intended to use the Post Office as their common agent and delivery of the letter of allotment to the Post Office was acceptance of G's offer.

In a case such as *Grant's*, the offeror may be unaware that a contract has been made by acceptance of his offer. If that possibility is clearly inconsistent with the nature of the transaction (and of course if the offeror so stipulates), the rule (complete acceptance by posting) is excluded and the letter of acceptance takes effect only when received.

Exercise 6

With the usual rules on acceptance by post, the offeror does not know that the offer has been accepted until a day or two after acceptance: he is therefore legally bound without knowing that he is. Although this is unsatisfactory, why would it be equally unsatisfactory to rule that acceptance takes place when the offeror receives the letter of acceptance?

---

6   Agreement without offer and acceptance

Offer and acceptance are merely a means of establishing the fact of agreement. But it is doubtful whether an agreement effected by any other means suffices to make a contract. This view is supported by the House of Lords decision in *Gibson v Manchester City Council 1979*, when the House overruled the Court of Appeal, disagreeing with Lord Denning who had said 'there is no need to look for strict offer and acceptance. You should look at the correspondence as a whole and at the conduct of the parties.' In general therefore offer and acceptance are essential to make a contract. Problems may however arise in reward cases, with cross-offers and with collateral contracts.

Reward cases

If A offers a *reward* to anyone who finds and returns his lost property and B, in ignorance of the offer, does in fact return it to him, is B entitled to the promised reward? There is agreement by conduct, but B is not accepting A's offer since he is unaware of it. There is no contract by which A is obliged to pay the reward to B: *R v Clarke 1927*.

However, acceptance may still be valid even if the offer was not the sole reason for it being made.

> *Case: Williams v Carwardine 1833*
> A reward was offered to bring criminals to book. W, an accomplice in the crime, supplied the information, with knowledge of the reward but moved primarily by remorse at her own part in the crime.
>
> *Held:* as the information was given with knowledge, the acceptance was related to the offer despite the fact that remorse was the prime motive.

Cross-offers

If, after an inconclusive discussion, X writes to offer to buy property from Y and Y at the same time writes to offer to sell the property to X on the same terms, these *cross-offers* establish agreement, but neither offer has been accepted. It has been held *(Tinn v Hoffman 1873)* that cross offers cannot constitute a contract, although this was only a majority decision and may still be challenged.

Collateral contracts

A collateral contract, although not expressly entered into by the parties to it, arises when a statement which is not part of the principal contract is nevertheless part of another contract related to the same subject matter. This means that a person not party to the principal contract can, if a collateral contract exists, sue on the collateral contract.

BPP Publishing

Case: Shanklin Pier v Detel Products 1951

D gave assurances to S, the owner of a pier, that paint manufactured by D would be satisfactory and durable if used in repainting S's pier. S, in his contract with T for the repainting of the pier, specified that T should use D's paint. The paint proved very unsatisfactory and the remedial work cost £4,127.

Held: although S could not sue D on the contract of sale of the paint, to which he was not a party, the contract between S and T requiring the use of D's paint (to be purchased and supplied by T) was the consideration for a contract between S and D, by which D guaranteed that D's paint was of the quality described.

Exercise 7

Mary contracts with Peter to do some computer programming for him. Peter asks Mary to subcontract some of the work to Jane, whom Peter believes (on the strength of Jane's assurance) to be a competent programmer. Jane proves to be unable to do the work she has agreed to do. Who may sue Jane, and on what grounds?

---

7 The nature of consideration

A promise given in a contract is only binding on the promisor if it is supported by consideration or if the promise is in the form of a deed. A contract not made by deed is a *simple contract*. In such a contract, the law looks for an element of *bargain:* a contractual promise is one which is not purely gratuitous. Consideration is what the promisee must give in exchange for the promise to him.

The accepted full length definition of consideration (given in *Currie v Misa 1875*) states that consideration is either an advantage to the promisor or a detriment incurred by the promisee. A better definition adopted by the House of Lords in *Dunlop v Selfridge 1915* is as follows.

'An act or forbearance of one party, or the promise thereof, is the price for which the promise of the other is bought, and the promise thus given for value is enforceable'.

Unilateral and bilateral contracts

A person who wishes to benefit from a contract must either promise to do something or must actually do something. We shall see below that in each case there is a different type of consideration, executory or executed respectively. Each type also creates a different type of contract.

(a) *Unilateral contract.* If one person does something at another's request, in return for a reward, he both accepts the offer of a reward and gives consideration. This is a unilateral contract, best demonstrated by *Carlill's* case. An example is a commission agreement with an estate agent. An agent instructed to find a purchaser is under no obligation to act; however when he does act and fulfil his client's request, the latter's promise to pay commission becomes enforceable.

(b) *Bilateral contract.* One person promises to do something in response to a promise by the other party. Both thereby provide consideration.

Letters of intent

The distinction between unilateral and bilateral contracts may be of importance when there are disputes concerning contracts which were intended to come into effect but which never did. In such a case, A may request B to commence work on a project on the strength of a

Law

'letter of intent' to contract. Even though the contract may never come into being, the initial request and subsequent activity together resemble a unilateral contract. As such B is entitled to reasonable remuneration for the work completed.

> *Case: British Steel Corporation v Cleveland Bridge and Engineering Co Ltd 1984*
> The defendants were engaged as subcontractors on a construction contract which required use of a particular type of steel frame. They approached the plaintiffs who had appropriate specialist experience, with a view to engaging them to work on the frame. After negotiations they sent the plaintiffs a letter of intent and set out terms. The plaintiffs began work, although they made it clear that the terms proposed were unacceptable. They delivered the goods and sued for their value.
>
> *Held:* there was no contract, since no agreement had been reached on such matters as progress payments or liability for late delivery. The plaintiff was however entitled to reasonable remuneration on a *quantum meruit* basis (how much the work done was worth).

Exercise 8

P and Q are neighbours. P undertakes not to sell part of his garden to a developer in return for a promise by Q to pay £1,000 to P. Q then claims that because P has not actually given Q anything, but has merely refrained from action, Q's promise to pay £1,000 is not supported by consideration and is not binding. Is Q correct?

8 Executory, executed and past consideration

Executed consideration is an act in return for a promise. If, for example, A offers a reward for the return of lost property, his promise becomes binding when B performs the act of returning A's property to him. A is not bound to pay anything to anyone until the prescribed act is done.

Executory consideration is a promise given for a promise. If, for example, a customer orders goods which a shopkeeper undertakes to obtain from the manufacturer, the shopkeeper promises to supply the goods and the customer promises to accept and pay for them. Neither has yet done anything but each has given a promise to obtain the promise of the other. It would be breach of contract if either withdrew without the consent of the other.

Anything which has already been done *before* a promise is given in return is *past* consideration which as a general rule is not sufficient to make the promise binding. In such a case the promisor may by his promise recognise a moral obligation, but he is not obtaining anything in exchange for his promise (as he already has it before the promise is made).

> *Case: Re McArdle 1951*
> Under a will the testator's children were entitled to a house at their mother's death. In the mother's lifetime one of the children and his wife lived in the house with the mother. The wife made improvements to the house. The children later agreed in writing to repay to the wife the sum of £488 which she spent on improvements, but at the mother's death they refused to do so.
>
> *Held:* at the time of the promise the improvements were past consideration and so the promise was not binding.

In three cases past consideration for a promise does suffice to make the promise binding.

BPP Publishing

(a) Past consideration is sufficient to create liability on a bill of exchange (such as a cheque) under s 27 Bills of Exchange Act 1882. Most cheques are issued to pay existing debts.

(b) After six (or in some cases twelve) years the right to sue for recovery of a debt becomes statute-barred by the Limitation Act 1980. If, after that period, the debtor makes written acknowledgement of the creditor's claim, it again becomes enforceable at law. The debt, although past consideration, suffices.

(c) When a request is made for a service this request may imply a promise to pay for it. If, after the service has been rendered, the person who made the request promises a specific reward, this is treated as fixing the amount to be paid under the previous implied promise rather than as a new promise.

Exercise 9

In *Roscorla v Thomas 1842*, the plaintiff contracted to buy a horse from the defendant. After the contract was made, the defendant told the plaintiff that the horse was sound. It later turned out to be vicious, so the plaintiff sued. What was the nature of the consideration for the promise that the horse was sound, and why did the plaintiff fail?

---

9 Sufficiency of consideration

Consideration must be sufficient, that is it must have some value. The value may however be nominal, for example 50p in consideration of a promise worth £1 million, or it may be very subjective. The law only requires an element of bargain, not that it shall be a good bargain. That is, consideration need not be adequate.

Case: Chappell & Co v Nestle Co 1959
As a sales promotion scheme, N offered to supply a record to anyone who sent in a postal order for 1/6d (7.5p) and three wrappers from 6d (2.5p) bars of chocolate made by N. C owned the copyright of the popular tune on the record. In a dispute over royalties the issue was whether the wrappers, which were thrown away when received, were part of the consideration for the promise to supply the record (which N obtained in bulk for 4d (1.67p) each from the recording company).

Held: N had required that wrappers be sent (for obvious commercial reasons). It was immaterial that the wrappers when received were of no economic value to N. The wrappers were sufficient consideration.

Case: Thomas v Thomas 1842
By his will a husband expressed the wish that his widow should have the use of his house during her life. The executors allowed the widow to occupy the house in return for her undertaking to pay a rent of £1 per annum. They later said that their promise to let her occupy the house was not supported by consideration.

Held: compliance with the husband's wishes was not consideration (no economic value attached to it), but the nominal rent was sufficient consideration though inadequate as a rent.

As stated earlier, forbearance or the promise of it may be sufficient consideration if it has some value or amounts to giving up something of value. A promise not to pursue a genuine but disputed claim may be consideration. Even forbearance without any promise may suffice. But a promise not to perform an act which the promisor had no intention of performing anyway does not suffice as consideration: *Arrale v Costain Engineering 1976*; nor does waiver of a claim known to be hopeless, or abstention from pressing a purely moral claim: *White v Bluett 1853*.

Insufficient consideration

If there is already a contract between A and B, and B promises additional reward to A if he (A) will perform the contract, there is no consideration to make that promise binding; A assumes no extra obligation and B obtains no extra rights or benefits.

Case: Stilk v Myrick 1809
Two members of the crew of a ship deserted in a foreign port. The master was unable to recruit substitutes and promised the rest of the crew that they should share the wages of the deserters if they would complete the voyage home. The shipowners however repudiated the promise.

Held: in performing their existing contractual duties the crew gave no consideration for the promise of extra pay and the promise was not binding. (In *Hartley v Ponsonby 1857*, where desertions had reduced the crew below the workable minimum, the crew were held to have provided consideration by doing more than their contractual duties.)

However, the courts appear to be taking a slightly different line recently on the payment of additional consideration. The line seems to be that the principles of consideration will not be applied if the dispute before the court can be dealt with on an alternative basis.

Case: Williams v Roffey Bros & Nicholls (Contractors) Ltd 1990
W agreed to refurbish a block of flats for R at a fixed price of £20,000. The work ran late and so R, concerned that the job might not be finished on time and that they would in that event have to pay money under a penalty clause in another contract, agreed to pay W an extra £10,300 to ensure the work was completed on time. R later refused to pay the extra amount.

Held: the fact that there was no apparent consideration for R's promise was not held to be important, and in the court's view both R and W derived benefit from the promise. The telling point was that R's promise had not been extracted by duress or fraud: it was therefore binding.

If A promises B a reward if B will perform his existing contract with C, there is consideration for A's promise since he obtains a benefit to which he previously had no right and B assumes new obligations.

Performance of an existing obligation imposed by statute, such as to appear as a witness when called upon in a lawsuit, is no consideration for a promise of reward. But if some extra service is given that is sufficient consideration.

Case: Glasbrook Bros v Glamorgan CC 1925
At a time of industrial unrest, colliery owners asked for and agreed to pay for a special police guard on the mine. Later they repudiated liability saying that the police had done no more than perform their public duty of maintaining order.

Held: the police had done more than perform their general duties. The *extra* services given were consideration for the promise to pay.

BPP Publishing

Exercise 10

A contracted with B to repair B's roof for £500. B then said that he would pay A an extra £200 to do the work which he was already obliged to do, even though there was no risk that A would otherwise do the work late or to an unsatisfactory standard. How could this promise of extra money be made legally binding without any other change in the terms agreed between A and B?

Waivers of existing rights

If X owes £100 to Y but Y agrees to accept a lesser sum, say £80, in full settlement of Y's claim, that is a promise by Y to waive his entitlement to the balance of £20. The promise, like any other, should be supported by consideration. In other words, payment on the day that a debt is due of less than the full amount of the debt is not consideration for a promise to release the balance.

Case: Foakes v Beer 1884
Y obtained judgement against X for the sum of £2,091 with interest. By a written agreement Y agreed to accept payment by instalments of the sum of £2,091. Later Y claimed the interest.

Held: Y was entitled to the debt with interest. No consideration had been given by X for waiver of any part of Y's rights against him.

There are, however, exceptions to the rule that the debtor (X) must give consideration if the waiver is to be binding.

(a) If X arranges with a number of creditors that they will each accept part payment in full settlement, that is a bargain between the creditors. X has given no consideration but he can hold the creditors individually to the agreed terms.

(b) If a third party (Z) offers part payment and Y agrees to release X from Y's claim to the balance, Y has received consideration from Z against whom he had no previous claim.

(c) If X offers and Y accepts anything to which Y is not already entitled (for example goods instead of cash, or payment before the due date) the extra thing will be sufficient consideration for the waiver (*Pinnel's case 1602*).

(d) The principle of *promissory estoppel* may prevent Y from retracting his promise with retrospective effect.

Promissory estoppel

If a creditor (Y) makes a promise (unsupported by consideration) to the debtor (X) that Y will not insist on the full discharge of the debt (or other obligation), and *the promise is made with the intention that X should act on it and he does so* (by more than just making part payment), Y is estopped (prohibited) from retracting his promise, unless X can be restored to his original position. This last point will prevent Y from retracting his waiver with retrospective effect, though it may allow him to insist on his full rights in the future.

Case: Central London Property Trust v High Trees House 1947
In 1939, Y let a block of flats to X at an annual rent of £2,500. It was difficult to let the individual flats in wartime. Y agreed in writing to accept a reduced annual rent of £1,250. No time limit was set on the arrangement but it was related to wartime conditions. The reduced rent was paid from 1940 to 1945 and X let flats during the period on the basis of its expected liability to pay rent under the head lease at £1,250 only. In 1945 the flats were fully let. Y made a test claim for rent at the full annual rate of £2,500 for the final two quarters of 1945.

BPP Publishing

Held: Y was entitled to the full annual rent of £2,500 for the period for which this was claimed; the agreement to reduce the rent was a temporary expedient only. Denning J was of the opinion that had Y sought arrears for the earlier period (1940-45), he would have failed.

The precise scope of promissory estoppel is still uncertain (though the principle is now well established) but two limitations are clear.

(a) *It only applies to a promise of waiver which is entirely voluntary.*

> *Case: D and C Builders v Rees 1966*
> X owed £482 to Y (a small firm of builders). Y, which was in acute financial difficulties, reluctantly agreed to accept £300 in full settlement (in order to obtain the money quickly). X had been aware of and had exploited Y's difficulties ('he was held to ransom' said Lord Denning). The builder later claimed the balance.

> *Held:* the debt must be paid in full. Promissory estoppel only applies to a promise voluntarily given. In this important case it was also held that payment by cheque (instead of in cash) is normal and gives no extra advantage which could be treated as consideration for the waiver under the rule in *Pinnel's* case.

(b) *It applies only to a waiver of existing rights.* A promise which creates new obligations is not binding unless supported by consideration in the usual way. The principle is 'a shield not a sword'.

> *Case: Combe v Combe 1951*
> A wife obtained a divorce decree *nisi* against her husband. He then promised her that he would make maintenance payments. The wife did not apply to the court for an order for maintenance but this forbearance was not at the husband's request. The decree was made absolute; the husband paid no maintenance; the wife sued him on his promise. In the High Court the wife obtained judgement on the basis of promissory estoppel.

> *Held:* (in the Court of Appeal) promissory estoppel 'does not create new causes of action where none existed before. It only prevents a party from insisting on his strict legal rights when it would be unjust to allow him to enforce them'. The wife's claim failed.

Exercise 11

C pays her daughter D a monthly allowance of £200. In January, C promises to increase this to £400 a month from April. On the strength of this promise, D incurs various financial obligations in March. C then changes her mind, and does not increase the allowance. Why would D be unable to rely on the doctrine of promissory estoppel to enforce the promised increase?

---

10 Privity of contract

The principle of privity of contract has two overlapping aspects: consideration must move from the promisee, and only the parties to a contract can enforce it.

Consideration must move from the promisee

As consideration is the price of a promise, the price must be paid by the person who seeks to enforce the promise.

If, for example, A promises B that (for a consideration provided by B) A will confer a benefit on C, then C cannot as a general rule enforce A's promise since C has given no consideration for it.

Case: Tweddle v Atkinson 1861

T married the daughter of G. On the occasion of the marriage T's father and G exchanged promises that they would each pay a sum of money to T. The agreement between the two fathers expressly provided that T should have enforceable rights against them. G died without making the promised payment and T sued G's executor (A) for the specified amount.

Held: T had provided no consideration for G's promise. In spite of the express terms of the agreement, T had no enforceable rights under it.

It is not essential that the promisor should receive any benefit from the promisee. In *Tweddle's* case each father as promisee gave consideration by his promise to the other but T was to be the beneficiary of each promise. Each father could have sued the other on his promise but his claim would have been for damages and he would have recovered nothing since he himself suffered no loss.

Only the parties to a contract may enforce it

As a general rule, only a person who is a party to a contract has enforceable rights or obligations under it.

Case: Dunlop v Selfridge 1915

D, a tyre manufacturer, supplied tyres to X, a distributor, on terms that X would not re-sell the tyres at less than the prescribed retail price. If X sold the tyres wholesale to trade customers, X must impose a similar condition on those buyers to observe minimum retail prices (such clauses were legal at the time though prohibited since 1964 by the Resale Prices Act). X resold tyres on these conditions to S, the Oxford Street store. Under the terms of the contract between X and S, S was to pay to D a sum of £5 per tyre if it sold tyres to customers below the minimum retail price. S sold tyres to two customers at less than the minimum price. D sued to recover £5 per tyre.

Held: D could not recover damages under a contract (between X and S) to which D was not a party. This is the leading case (decided in the House of Lords) on privity of contract.

A party to a contract who imposes a condition or obtains a promise of a benefit for a third party can usually enforce it. Damages cannot be recovered on the third party's behalf unless the contracting party is suing as agent or trustee, since a plaintiff can only recover damages for a loss he has suffered. Thus only nominal damages can be given if the contract was only for a third party's benefit. Other remedies may be sought however.

Case: Beswick v Beswick 1968

P transferred his business to A, his nephew, in consideration for a pension and, after his death, a weekly annuity to P's widow. Only one annuity payment was made. The widow, as her husband's administratrix, sued for an order of specific performance.

Held: as her husband's representative, the widow was successful in enforcing the contract for a third party's (her) benefit. The House of Lords held that she would not have succeeded if she had only been the intended recipient.

Where the contract is one which provides something for the enjoyment of both the contracting party and third parties, such as a family or other group holiday, the contracting party is entitled to substantial damages for his loss of benefit: *Jackson v Horizon Holidays Ltd 1975.*

Notes

If the contract is broken and the contracting party seeks damages on the other people's behalf he can also recover for the loss suffered by those other people: *Woodar Investment Development Ltd v Wimpey Construction UK Ltd 1980*.

There is some inconsistency in the case law, but the general tenor is that a seller of goods cannot impose conditions which pass with the goods to a third party even if the latter buys with knowledge of the conditions. There are, however, special rules of the law of property which enable a person to impose restrictions on land to pass with the land from one owner to the next.

There are a number of real or apparent exceptions to the general rule of privity of contract.

(a) In a contract between A and B by which B is to confer a benefit on C, A may constitute himself a trustee for C. C as beneficiary may then enforce the contract against B.

(b) The benefit of a contract may be transferred by assignment, or by negotiation of a bill of exchange.

(c) There are statutory exceptions which permit a person injured in a road accident to claim against the motorist's insurers, and which permit husband and wife to insure his or her own life for the benefit of the other under a trust which the beneficiary can enforce: Road Traffic Act 1972; Married Women's Property Act 1882.

(d) An undisclosed principal may adopt a contract made for him by an agent.

Exercise 12

Civil law, unlike criminal law, mainly deals with matters which are of no general interest to the community. How is this fact related to the doctrine of privity of contract?

Chapter roundup

(a) A contract is a legally binding agreement between the parties. A contract only arises if there is an intention to create legal relations. Such an intention is assumed to be present in business agreements and absent in domestic arrangements, but either presumption may be rebutted.

(b) Not every suggestion that a transaction be entered into is an offer. The display of goods in a shop, for example, is an invitation to treat.

(c) An offer may lapse or be revoked, or it may be rejected by the offeree. A counter-offer amounts to a rejection.

(d) Acceptance may be by express words or action, or it may be implied by conduct. Mere inaction is not sufficient for acceptance. Where there is a standing offer, each acceptance creates a separate contract.

(e) Acceptance needs to be communicated to the offeror. Acceptance by post generally takes effect when the letter of acceptance is posted, but in some cases only when the letter is received by the offeror.

(f) There are special rules for reward cases (the claimant must have been aware of the offer of a reward), for cross-offers (there is no contract) and for collateral contracts.

(g) Consideration, which may be either executory or executed but not past, is required when a contract is not made by deed.

(h) Consideration must be sufficient (have some value), but it need not be adequate (have a value similar to the value of what is given in return). A promise to perform existing obligations is not in general sufficient consideration.

(i) Waivers of existing rights mostly need to be supported by consideration, but there are some exceptions involving third parties, and promissory estoppel may apply.

BPP Publishing

(j)   Consideration must move from the promisee, and in general only a party to a contract may enforce it. These rules make up the doctrine of privity of contract.

Quick quiz

1   When may it be misleading to presume that a contract is the outcome of consenting minds?

2   Give three essential elements of a binding agreement.

3   What is the effect of a statement in a business agreement that it is not intended to create legal relations?

4   How do the courts deduce the intention of the parties (to create legal relations or not to do so) from the terms of a domestic or family agreement?

5   What sorts of domestic agreement are the courts willing to interpret as legally binding?

6   When is a commercial agreement never intended to create legal relations?

7   Do any of the following constitute an offer which becomes a contract if accepted?

    (a)   A statement of the price of goods

    (b)   An advertisement

    (c)   A display of goods

8   How is an offer terminated?

9   When is revocation of an offer effective?

10   Can an offer be accepted by doing nothing if the offer so provides?

11   What is the effect of acceptance 'subject to contract'?

12   What is the effect of accepting a tender?

13   What is the effect of posting a letter accepting an offer made by letter to the offeree?

14   May a contract be formed without offer and acceptance?

15   What is a collateral contract?

16   In what circumstances is something which is done before a promise is made sufficient consideration to make the promise binding?

17   If, in return for a promise, the promisee hands over something which no longer has any value, has he given sufficient consideration to make the promise binding?

18   Is acceptance of part payment of an existing debt binding on the person who accepts it or may he still claim the unpaid balance?

19   Explain the doctrine of promissory estoppel and indicate the limitations placed upon it.

20   Is it possible for a person to enforce a contract if he is not a party to it?

Solutions to exercises

1   The claim is vague and there is no offer of any particular reward or compensation.

2   No: legal relations are unlikely to be assumed.

3   No: 'I would want £850 at least' is an invitation to continue to treat.

4   No: X's revocation of his offer has been effectively communicated.

5   Delivery arrangements, responsibility for damage in transit, time for payment and the right to reject the goods. You may well have thought of other examples.

6   With the alternative suggested, the acceptor would not know for a day or two whether or not he had succeeded in accepting the offer.

7   Mary may sue Jane for straightforward breach of contract. Peter may sue Jane on the contract under which she assured him of her skills, his contract with Mary being consideration.

8   No: forebearance (as by P) can be consideration.

9   The plaintiff failed because the consideration for the promise (the plaintiff's purchase of the horse) was past consideration.

10   The promise would have to be by deed.

11   Promissory estoppel does not create new causes of action where none existed before. D never had any right to the increased allowance.

12   In general, only the parties to a contract are affected by it, so only they may sue on it.

BPP Publishing

6 TERMS OF CONTRACT

Your objectives

After completing this chapter you should:

(a) understand the effects of incompleteness in the terms of a contract;

(b) understand the concepts of condition, warranty and innominate term;

(c) know the limitations on the use of oral evidence for contract terms;

(d) understand the distinction between representations and contract terms;

(e) know how terms may be implied into a contract;

(f) know which contracts must be in specified forms;

(g) know the limitations on the effectiveness of exclusion clauses;

(h) appreciate how exclusion clauses may fail to be effectively incorporated into a contract;

(i) know how exclusion clauses are interpreted;

(j) know the main provisions of the Unfair Contract Terms Act 1977.

1   The terms of contract

As a general principle the parties may by their offer and acceptance include in their contract whatever terms they like, but certain legal rules apply.

(a) The terms must be sufficiently complete and precise to produce an agreement which can be binding. If they are vague there may be no contract.

(b) The terms of the contract are usually classified as *conditions* or as *warranties* according to their importance.

(c) If the parties express the terms in writing, the introduction of oral evidence of the terms of the contract is restricted.

(d) Statements made in the pre-contract negotiations may become terms of the contract or remain as representations to which different rules attach.

(e) In addition to the express terms of the agreement, additional terms may be implied by law.

(f) Terms which exclude or restrict liability for breach of contract *(exemption* or *exclusion clauses)* are restricted in their effect or overridden by common law and statutory rules.

2   Incomplete contracts

A legally binding agreement must be complete in its terms. Otherwise there is no contract, since the parties are still at the stage of negotiating the necessary terms.

BPP Publishing

Case: Scammell v Ouston 1941

An agreement for the purchase of a van provided that the unpaid balance of the price should be paid over two years 'on hire purchase terms'.

Held: there was no agreement since it was uncertain what terms of payment were intended. Hire purchase terms vary as to intervals between payments, interest charges to be added and so on.

It is always possible for the parties to leave an essential term to be settled by specified means outside the contract. For example, it may be agreed to sell at the ruling open market price (if there is a market) on the day of delivery, or to invite an arbitrator to determine a fair price. The price may even be determined by the course of dealing between the parties.

If the parties use meaningless but non-essential words, for example by use of standard printed conditions some of which are inappropriate, such phrases may be disregarded.

If however the parties expressly agree to defer some essential term for later negotiation there is no binding agreement. This is described as 'an agreement to agree' which is void, as the parties may subsequently fail to agree.

Exercise 1

A contract contains a term which states that the price shall be £50,000 unless the parties agree otherwise within seven days of the contract's being signed. Why does this not invalidate the contract?

---

3   Conditions and warranties

The terms of the contract are usually classified by their relative importance as conditions or warranties. A *condition* is a term vital to the contract. Non-observance of a condition will affect the main purpose of the agreement. Breach of a condition entitles the party not in breach to treat the contract as discharged. A *warranty* is a less important term. It does not go to the root of the contract, but is subsidiary to the main purpose of the agreement. Breach of a warranty only entitles the injured party to claim damages.

Case: Poussard v Spiers 1876

Madame Poussard agreed to sing in an opera throughout a series of performances. Owing to illness she was unable to appear on the opening night and the next few days. The producer engaged a substitute who insisted that she should be engaged for the whole run. When Mme Poussard had recovered the producer declined to accept her services for the remaining performances.

Held: failure to sing on the opening night was a breach of condition which entitled the producer to treat the contract for the remaining performances as discharged.

Case: Bettini v Gye 1876

An opera singer was engaged for a series of performances under a contract by which he had to be in London for rehearsals six days before the opening performance. Owing to illness he did not arrive until the third day before the opening.

Held: the rehearsal clause was subsidiary to the main purpose of the contract. Breach of the clause must be treated as breach of warranty, so the producer was bound to accept the

BPP Publishing

singer's services though he could claim damages (if he could prove any loss) for failure to arrive in time for six days' rehearsals.

Determining whether a contractual term is a condition or a warranty is clearly very important. Classification depends on the following issues.

(a) Statute often identifies implied terms specifically as conditions or warranties. Such identification must be followed by the courts. An example is the Sale of Goods Act 1979.

(b) Case law may also define particular clauses as conditions: *The Mihalis Angelos 1971*.

(c) Where statute or case law does not shed any light, the court will consider the intention of the parties *at the time the contract was made* as to whether a broken term was to be a condition or a warranty: *Bunge Corporation v Tradax SA 1981*. They tend to lean away from interpretation as a condition, because of the drastic consequences of breach of a condition.

Innominate terms

Where the term broken was not clearly intended to be a condition, and neither statute nor case law define it as such, it cannot necessarily be assumed that the term is a warranty. Instead, the contract must be interpreted; only if it is clear that in no circumstances did the parties intend the contract to be terminated by breach of that particular term can it be classed as a warranty. Such intention may be express or be implied from surrounding circumstances. Where it is not clear what the effect of breach of the term was intended to be, it will be classified by the court as innominate, intermediate or indeterminate (the three are synonymous).

The consequence of a term being classified as innominate is that the court must decide what is the actual effect of its breach. If the nature and effect of the breach is such as to deprive the injured party of substantially the whole benefit which it was intended he should obtain under the contract then it will be treated as a breached condition, so that the injured party may terminate the contract and claim damages.

Case: Hong Kong Fir Shipping Co Ltd v Kawasaki Kisa Kaisha Ltd 1962
The defendants chartered a ship from the plaintiffs for a period of 24 months. A term in the contract stated that the plaintiffs would provide a ship which was 'in every way fitted for ordinary cargo service'. They were in breach of this term since the ship required a competent engine room crew which they did not provide. Because of the engine's age and the crew's lack of competence the ship's first voyage was delayed for weeks and further repairs were required at the end of it. The defendants purported to terminate the contract so the plaintiffs sued for beach of contract on the grounds that the defendant had no right to terminate; the defendants claimed that the plaintiffs were in breach of a contractual condition.

Held: (a) The term was innominate and could not automatically be construed as either a condition or a warranty.

(b) The term would be construed in the light of the actual consequences of the actual breach.

(c) The consequences of the breach were not so serious that the defendants could be justified in terminating the contract as a result.

(d) The defendants were in breach of contract for terminating it when they did.

Exercise 2

A company contracts for the purchase of 200 mobile telephones 'immediately suitable for use in the UK'. Assume that this term is innominate. How would the court classify it if:

(a)   the telephones supplied required tuning to particular frequencies, a task taking two minutes for each one?

(b)   use of the telephones supplied was illegal in the UK, and they could not be modified to make their use legal?

4   Oral evidence relating to contracts in writing

The general rule is that if a contract is or includes a written document, oral evidence may not be given to 'add to, vary or contradict' the document. There are the following exceptions to the rule.

(a)   Oral evidence may be given of trade practice or custom.

(b)   Evidence may be given to show that the parties agreed orally that their written consent should not take effect until a *condition precedent* had been satisfied.

(c)   Oral evidence may be given as an addition to a written contract if it can be shown that the document, such as printed conditions of sale, was not intended to comprise all the agreed terms. But the presumption is that a contract document is the entire contract until the contrary is proved.

> *Case: SS Ardennes 1951*
>
> A printed bill of lading (for shipment of a cargo of oranges) provided that the ship might go 'by any route ... directly or indirectly' to London. The shipowners' agent had given an oral undertaking that the vessel would sail directly from Spain to London.
>
> *Held:* evidence might be given of the oral undertaking as a term overriding the bill of lading.

(d)   Oral evidence may be adduced to correct a written agreement which contains a mistake.

5   Representations and contract terms

If something said in pre-contract negotiations proves to be untrue, the party misled can only claim for breach of contract if the statement became a term of the contract. Otherwise his remedy is for misrepresentation only (explained in the next chapter). Even if the statement is not repeated or referred to in making the contract it may be treated as a contract term. But such factors as a significant interval of time between statement and contract or the use of a written contract making no reference to the statement suggest that it is not a term of the contract. If, however, the party who makes the statement speaks with special knowledge of the subject it is more likely to be treated as a contract term.

> *Case: Bannerman v White 1861*
>
> In negotiations for the sale of hops the buyer emphasised that it was essential to him that the hops should not have been treated with sulphur. The seller replied explicitly that no sulphur had been used. It was later discovered that a small proportion of the hops (bought in by the seller from another grower) had been treated with sulphur.
>
> *Held:* the absence of sulphur was intended to be a term of the contract.

> *Case: Oscar Chess v Williams 1959*
>
> A private motorist negotiated the sale of an old car to motor dealers in part exchange for a new car. The seller stated (as the registration book showed) that his car was a 1948

model. In fact it was a 1939 model (and the registration book had been altered by a previous owner).

Held: the statement was a mere representation. The seller was not an expert and the buyer had better means of discovering the truth.

6   Implied terms

Additional terms of a contract may be implied by law.

(a)   The parties may be considered to enter into a contract subject to a custom or practice of their trade. For example, when a farm is let to a tenant it may be an implied term that local farming custom on husbandry and tenant rights shall apply: *Hutton v Warren 1836.* But any express term overrides a term which might be implied by custom.

> *Case: Les Affreteurs v Walford 1919*
> A charter of a ship provided expressly for a payment to be made on signing the charter. There was a trade custom that it should only be paid at a later stage.
>
> *Held*: an express term prevails over a term otherwise implied by custom.

(b)   Terms may be implied by statute. In some cases the statute permits the parties to contract out of the statutory terms (thus the terms of partnership implied by the Partnership Act 1890 may be excluded). In other cases the statutory terms are obligatory. The protection given by the Sale of Goods Act 1979 to a consumer who buys goods from a trader cannot be taken away from him.

(c)   Terms may be implied if the court concludes that the parties intended these terms to apply and did not mention them because they were taken for granted.

The parties may take something obvious for granted. For example, if a person undertakes to do work, such as the conveyance of a property, in which he claims to be proficient, it is an implied term that he will show reasonable skill in doing the work. In such cases the 'officious bystander' test is applied; if an officious bystander had intervened to remind the parties that in formulating their contract they had failed to mention a particular point they would have replied 'of course ... we did not trouble to say that; it is too clear'.

> *Case: The Moorcock 1889*
> The owners of a wharf agreed that a ship should be moored alongside to unload its cargo. It was well known to both wharfingers and shipowners that at low tide the ship would ground on the mud at the bottom. At low tide the ship rested on a ridge concealed beneath the mud and suffered damage.
>
> *Held:* it was an implied term, though not expressed, that the ground alongside the wharf (which did not belong to the wharfingers) was safe at low tide since both parties knew that the ship must rest on it.

The terms to be implied in this way are those necessary to complete the contract and give it 'business efficacy.' Terms will not be implied to contradict the express terms of the contract (see *Walford's* case above) nor to provide for events which the parties did not contemplate in their negotiations.

Exercise 3

A qualified accountant undertakes to prepare a client's tax return. The accountant then finds that the tax return form has been redesigned, and that his computer system cannot cope with the new design. Could he claim that there was no term in the contract stating that he should be able to prepare a return in the new form, and that he is therefore not obliged to prepare the return?

7 The required form of contracts

As a general rule a contract may be made in any form - in writing, by word of mouth or even by implication from conduct. For example, a customer in a self-service shop takes his selected goods to the cash desk, pays for them and walks out. There is a contract of sale although not a word has been spoken; the till receipt is merely evidence of payment and is not essential to the contract.

To the general rule there are some exceptions.

(a) *Contract by deed*. Some rights and obligations, such as a transfer of title to land, or a lease of land for a period of three years or more, or a promise not supported by consideration (such as a covenant to make annual payments to a charity) must be in the form of a deed.

(b) *Contracts in writing*. Some types of contract (mainly commercial) are required to be in the form of a written document, usually signed by at least one of the parties. This category includes bills of exchange, hire purchase agreements and agreements relating to land.

(c) *Contracts which must be evidenced in writing*. Certain types of contract may be made orally but are not enforceable in a court of law unless there is written evidence of their terms. The important contract falling under this head is that of guarantee.

A deed used to be referred to as a contract under seal, but under s 1 of the Law of Property (Miscellaneous Provisions) Act 1989 an individual need not seal a deed. It is a written document (on paper, parchment or other substance) which has been signed by the person executing it (and sealed if created by a corporate body with a common seal) and is expressed on its face to be a deed. Signature must be witnessed. To be validly executed by an individual, the document must be delivered to the other party by the individual or his agent. A contract by deed is binding even though no consideration is given or received.

A contract for the sale or other disposition of land or of any interest in land (such as the grant of a lease) must be in writing, incorporating all the expressly agreed terms and signed by or on behalf of each party to the contract: s 2 Law of Property (Miscellaneous Provisions) Act 1989. Note that s 2 does not apply to the grant of a short lease or a contract made at public auction. These may be enforced if they are only evidenced in writing.

A contract for the sale of land must be distinguished from the actual document which transfers the title to that land, that is the conveyance (unregistered land) or transfer (registered land). The contract promises to transfer title at a future date (usually four weeks hence) and must be in writing. The conveyance or transfer must be by deed and will therefore also be in writing. A contract promising to grant a lease must be in writing but the lease itself, if it is for three years or more, must be by deed.

Exercise 4

A agrees to transfer his house to B in 28 days time at a price of £100,000. Both parties sign the contract, but neither signature is witnessed. Is the contract binding?

8   Exclusion clauses

If the parties negotiate their contract from positions of more or less equal bargaining strength and expertise, neither the courts nor Parliament have usually interfered. But there has been strong criticism of the use of exclusion (or exemption) clauses in contracts made between manufacturers or sellers of goods or services and private citizens as consumers. In such cases there may be great inequality. The seller puts forward standard conditions of sale which the buyer may not understand and must accept if he wishes to buy.

In those conditions the seller may try to exclude or limit his liability for failure to perform as promised, for breach of contract or negligence, or he may try to offer a 'guarantee' which in fact reduces the buyer's rights.

When considering the validity of exclusion clauses the courts have had to strike a balance between:

(a)   the principle that parties should have complete freedom to contract on whatever terms they wish; and

(b)   the need to protect the public from unfair exemption clauses in standard form contracts used by large companies.

The main limitations on exclusion clauses are now contained in the Unfair Contract Terms Act 1977 which applies to clauses excluding or restricting liability in contract or tort.

An exclusion clause which is not void by statute may still be ineffectual. The courts have generally sought to protect the consumer from the harsher effects of exclusion clauses in two ways.

(a)   An exclusion clause must be properly *incorporated* into a contract before it has any legal effect.

(b)   Exclusion clauses are *interpreted* strictly; this may prevent the application of the clause.

The incorporation of exclusion clauses

If a person signs a document containing a clause restricting his rights he is held to have agreed to the restriction even if he had not read the document. But this is not so if the party who puts forward the document for signature gives a misleading explanation of its legal effect.

> *Case: L'Estrange v Graucob 1934*
> A sold to B, a shopkeeper, a slot machine under conditions which excluded B's normal rights under the Sale of Goods Act 1893. B signed the document without reading the relevant condition.
>
> *Held:* the conditions were binding on B since she had signed them. It was not material that A had given her no information of their terms nor called her attention to them.

> *Case: Curtis v Chemical Cleaning Co 1951*
> X took her wedding dress to be cleaned. She was asked to sign a receipt on which there were conditions by which the cleaners disclaimed liability for damage however it might arise. Before signing X enquired what was the effect of the document and was told that it restricted the cleaner's liability in certain ways and in particular placed on X the risk of damage to beads and sequins on the dress. The dress was badly stained in the course of cleaning.
>
> *Held:* the cleaners could not rely on their disclaimer since they had misled X as to the effect of the document which she signed.

Exercise 5

A contract between P and Q includes a clause excluding P's liability in certain circumstances. When Q enquires as to the meaning of this clause, P replies that he does not wish to provide an oral interpretation, but that Q must read the clause for herself. Q reads the clause and signs the contract. P later seeks to rely on the exclusion clause, and Q claims that P should have interpreted the clause for her. The clause itself is not misleadingly phrased. Is Q likely to prevent P from relying on the clause?

Prior information on clause in unsigned documents

Many contracts are entered into without the parties signing a document. In such cases, exclusion clauses may be stated on notices or tickets. However, since the terms of the contract are fixed at the moment of acceptance of the offer, an exclusion clause cannot be introduced thereafter (except by mutual consent). Each party must be aware of an exclusion clause *at the time of entering into the agreement* if it is to be binding.

Case: Olley v Marlborough Court 1949
A husband and wife arrived at a hotel and paid for a room in advance. On reaching their bedroom they saw a notice on the wall by which the hotel disclaimed liability for loss of valuables unless handed to the management for safe-keeping. The wife locked the room and handed the key in at the reception desk. A thief obtained the key and stole the wife's furs from the bedroom.

Held: the hotel could not rely on the notice disclaiming liability since the contract had been made previously (when the room was booked and paid for) and the disclaimer was too late.

Complications can arise when it is difficult to determine at exactly what point in time the contract is formed so as to determine whether or not a term is validly included.

Case: Thornton v Shoe Lane Parking Ltd 1972
X saw a sign saying 'Parking' outside the defendant's carpark. He drove up to the unattended machine and was automatically given a ticket. He had seen a sign disclaiming liability for damage to cars before obtaining the ticket and when he received the ticket he saw that it contained words which he did not read. In fact these made the contract subject to conditions which, if he had looked hard enough in the carpark, also excluded liability for injury. When he returned to collect his car (which had been stacked in a special machine) there was an accident in which he was badly injured.

Held: the contract was formed before he got the ticket (the offer was the 'parking' sign; acceptance was parking his car so as to receive a ticket) so reference on the ticket to conditions was too late for the conditions to be included as contractual terms. Note that since UCTA 1977 the personal injury clause would be void anyway.

An exception to the rule that there be prior notice of the clause is where the parties have had consistent dealings with each other in the past, and the documents used then contained similar clauses.

Sufficient information on clauses

The courts will not treat an exclusion clause as a term of the contract unless the party affected by it was sufficiently informed of it when he accepted it.

(a)   The exclusion clause must be put forward in a document which gives reasonable notice that liability conditions are proposed by it: *Interfoto Picture Library Ltd v Stiletto Visual*

Programmes Ltd 1988. It must be shown that this document is an integral part of the contract and is one which could be expected to contain terms.

Case: Chapelton v Barry UDC 1940

There was a pile of deck chairs and a notice stating 'Hire of chairs 2d (0.83p) per session of 3 hours'. The plaintiff took two chairs, paid for them and received two tickets which he put in his pocket. One of the chairs collapsed and he was injured. The defendant council relied on a notice on the back of the tickets by which it disclaimed liability for injury.

Held: the notice advertising chairs for hire gave no warning of limiting conditions and it was not reasonable to communicate them on a receipt. The disclaimer of liability was not binding on the plaintiff.

Case: Thompson v LMS Railway 1930

An elderly lady who could not read asked her niece to buy her a railway excursion ticket on which was printed 'Excursion: for conditions see back'. On the back it was stated that the ticket was issued subject to conditions contained in the company's timetables. These conditions excluded liability for injury.

Held: the conditions had been adequately communicated and therefore had been accepted.

(b) If the parties have had previous dealings (not on a consistent basis) then the person to be bound by the exclusion clause may be sufficiently aware of it (as a proposed condition) at the time of making the latest contract.

(i) For this purpose it is necessary to show in a consumer contract that he actually knew of the condition; it is not sufficient that he might have become aware of it.

Case: Hollier v Rambler Motors 1972

On three or four occasions over a period of five years H had had repairs done at a garage. On each occasion he had signed a form by which the garage disclaimed liability for damage caused by fire to customers' cars. On the latest occasion, however, he did not sign the form. The car was damaged by fire caused by negligence of garage employees. The garage contended that the disclaimer had by course of dealing become an established term of any contract made between them and H.

Held: the garage was liable. There was no evidence to show that H knew of and agreed to the condition as a continuing term of his contracts with the garage.

(ii) But in a commercial contract it is sufficient to show that, by a previous course of dealings, the other party has constructive if not actual notice of the term: *British Crane Hire Corporation Ltd v Ipswich Plant Hire 1974*.

Exercise 6

Customers of a self service shop take goods from the shelves and then walk down a corridor to a till. A conspicuous notice is hung across this corridor incorporating an exclusion clause into contracts for the purchase of goods from the shop. Could a customer claim that the exclusion clause was invalid because he had selected goods before seeing the notice?

BPP Publishing

The battle of the forms

In contracts between traders each may put forward his own standard conditions stipulating that all other conditions are thereby excluded. In any such 'battle of forms' it has to be decided by reference to the particular facts which set of conditions is the basis of the contract.

Case: Butler Machine Tool Co v Ex-cell-O Corp (England) 1979
Buyer and seller each put forward conditions expressed to prevail over any others. The order placed by the buyer had a 'tear-off' acknowledgement slip by which the supplier accepted the order on the terms and conditions set out in the order. The seller signed and returned the acknowledgement slip with a letter referring to its previous quotation (which included the seller's conditions of sale).

Held: the buyer's conditions had been accepted by the seller. The reference to the previous quotation must be taken as an indication merely of the technical specification of the goods.

The interpretation of exclusion clauses

In deciding what an exclusion clause means, the courts interpret any ambiguity against the person at fault who relies on the exclusion. This is known as the *contra proferentem* rule (against the person relying on it). Liability can only be excluded or restricted by clear words. In particular, if the clause gives exclusion in unspecific terms it is unlikely to be interpreted as covering negligence on his part unless that is the only reasonable interpretation.

Case: Hollier v Rambler Motors 1972
The facts are given above.

Held: as a matter of interpretation the disclaimer of liability could be interpreted to apply (a) only to accidental fire damage or (b) to fire damage caused in any way including negligence. It should therefore be interpreted against the garage in the narrower sense of (a) so that it did not give exemption from fire damage due to negligence.

Case: Alderslade v Hendon Laundry 1945
The conditions of contracts made by a laundry with its customers excluded liability for loss of or damage to customers' clothing in the possession of the laundry. By its negligence the laundry lost A's handkerchief.

Held: the exclusion clause would have no meaning unless it covered loss etc due to negligence. It did therefore cover loss by negligence.

When construing an exclusion clause the court will also consider the *main purpose rule*. By this, the court presumes that the clause was not intended to defeat the main purpose of the contract, although of course the presumption may be rebutted. In order to rebut the presumption the party relying on the clause must show that its wording is sufficiently precise and relevant. In the context of a clause in a supplier's standard term contract which allows the supplier to render performance in a substantially different manner, the main purpose rule is supplemented by s 3 UCTA 1977 which provides that such a term must be reasonable.

Fundamental breach

There used to be some doubt on how far an exclusion clause can exclude liability in a case where the breach of contract was a failure to perform the contract altogether (a fundamental breach). In the case given below the House of Lords overruled some earlier decisions of the Court of Appeal and so the legal position is now reasonably clear.

BPP Publishing

Case: Photo Productions v Securicor Transport 1980

Securicor agreed to guard the plaintiffs' factory under a contract by which Securicor were excluded from liability for damage caused by any of their employees. One of the Securicor guards deliberately started a fire which caused much damage. It was contended (on the authority of earlier decisions of the Court of Appeal) that Securicor had entirely failed to perform their contract since they had not guarded the factory and so they could not rely on any exclusion clause in the contract.

Held: (a)   there is no principle that total failure to perform a contract deprives the party at fault of any exclusion from liability provided by the contract;

       (b)   it is a question of interpretation of the exclusion clause whether it is widely enough expressed to cover total failure to perform;

       (c)   the exclusion clause was wide enough to cover the damage which had happened;

       (d)   as the fire occurred before the Unfair Contracts Terms Act 1977 was in force the Act could not apply here. But if it had done it would have been necessary to consider whether the exclusion clause was reasonable.

The question of fundamental breach is only likely to be relevant when the requirement of reasonableness imposed by the Unfair Contract Terms Act 1977 does not apply.

Exercise 7

A road haulage company's standard conditions exclude liability for delays caused by factors beyond the company's control. Would this exclusion be interpreted to cover a delay due to a driver choosing to use minor roads because he found motorway driving boring, given that it is the company's policy never to interfere with drivers' choices of routes?

---

9   The Unfair Contract Terms Act 1977

Before we consider the specific term of UCTA, it is necessary to describe how its scope is restricted.

(a)   In general the Act only applies to clauses inserted into agreements by commercial concerns or businesses. In principle private persons may restrict liability as much as they wish.

(b)   The Act does not apply to contracts:

      (i)   for the creation or transfer of patents;

      (ii)   of insurance;

      (iii)   for the creation or transfer of interests in land;

      (iv)   for company formation or securities transactions.

The Act uses two techniques for controlling exclusion clauses: some types of clauses are void, whereas others are subject to a test of reasonableness. The main provisions of the Act are as follows.

Exclusion of negligence liability (s 2)

'Negligence' covers breach of contractual obligations of skill and care, the common law duty of skill and care and the common duty of occupiers of premises under the Occupiers' Liability Acts 1957 and 1984.

(a) A person cannot, by reference to any contract term, restrict his liability for death or personal injury resulting from negligence. Note also that manufacturers who do not have a contract with the consumer now have liability for death or injury caused by defective products, whether they were negligent or not (Consumer Protection Act 1987).

(b) In the case of other loss or damage, a person cannot restrict his liability for negligence unless the term is reasonable.

Standard term contracts and consumer contracts (s 3)

The person who imposes the standard term, or who deals with the consumer, cannot *unless the term is reasonable:*

(a) restrict liability for his own breach or fundamental breach; or

(b) claim to be entitled to render substantially different performance or no performance at all.

Unreasonable indemnity clauses (s 4)

A clause whereby one party undertakes to indemnify the other for liability incurred in the other's performance of the contract is void if the party giving the indemnity is a consumer, unless it is reasonable.

Guarantees of consumer goods (s 5)

The terms of a guarantee of goods cannot exclude or restrict liability for loss or damage caused by defects of the goods in consumer use.

Sale and supply of goods (ss 6-7)

Any contract for the sale or hire purchase of goods cannot exclude the implied condition that the seller has a right to sell or transfer ownership of the goods.

A *consumer* contract for the sale of goods, hire purchase, supply of work or materials or exchange of goods cannot exclude or restrict liability for breach of the conditions relating to description, quality, fitness for the purpose for which sold and sample implied by the Sale of Goods Act 1979 and the Supply of Goods and Services Act 1982. In a non-consumer contract these implied conditions may be excluded if the exclusion clause is reasonable. Note that a business may be dealing as a consumer if it makes an unusual transaction such as buying a car for one of its directors: *R&B Customs Brokers Ltd v UDT Ltd 1987.*

Misrepresentation (s 8)

Any attempt to exclude liability for misrepresentation must satisfy a test of reasonableness. This section applies to private individuals as well as businesses.

Exercise 8

A contract for the sale of a washing machine to a consumer contains the following clause: 'The seller undertakes to repair any defects arising within the first 12 months free of charge, and the buyer shall accordingly not be permitted to return the machine if it does not work at the time of sale'. A consumer would normally have a statutory right to return the machine if it did not work at the time of sale. Has this right been effectively excluded by the clause?

BPP Publishing

The statutory text of reasonableness (s 11)

The term must be fair and reasonable having regard to all the circumstances which were, or which ought to have been, known to the parties when the contract was made. The burden of proving reasonableness lies on the person seeking to rely on the clause. Statutory guidelines have been included in the Act to assist in the determination of reasonableness although the court has discretion to take account of all factors. For the purposes of ss 6 and 7, the court will consider:

(a)   the relative strength of the parties' bargaining positions and in particular whether the customer could have satisfied his requirements from another source;

(b)   whether any inducement (such as a reduced price) was offered to the customer to persuade him to accept a limitation of his rights and whether any other person would have made a similar contract with him without that limitation;

(c)   whether the customer knew or ought to have known of the existence and extent of the exclusion clause (having regard, where appropriate, to trade custom or previous dealings between the parties);

(d)   if failure to comply with a condition (for example failure to give notice of a defect within a short period) excludes or restricts the customer's rights, whether it was reasonable to expect when the contract was made that compliance with the condition would be practicable;

(e)   whether the goods were made, processed or adapted to the special order of the customer.

With regard to all of the above sections of UCTA 1977, the test of reasonableness for an exclusion clause looks at:

(a)   the resources which the party who seeks to restrict liability has available for the purpose of meeting the liability if it arises; and

(b)   how far that person could cover himself by insurance.

The person who is aiming to rely on the clause's reasonableness must prove that it is reasonable.

The definition of consumer (s 12)

A person deals as a consumer if:

(a)   he neither makes the contract in the course of a business, nor holds himself out as doing so;

(b)   the other party does make the contract in the course of a business; and

(c)   the goods are of a type ordinarily supplied for private use or consumption.

Exercise 9

A contract under which a consumer buys a 20 volume encyclopaedia contains a clause excluding liability for defects not notified within a week of delivery. Two weeks after delivery, the buyer finds that several pages which should have been printed are blank. Will the seller be able to rely on the exclusion clause?

Chapter roundup

(a)   If a purported contract omits an essential term, and gives no means for settling that term, there is no contract.

(b)   A condition is a term which is vital to a contract, and its breach allows the party not in breach to treat the contract as discharged. Breach of a warranty, on the other hand, only entitles the injured party to damages.

(c)   Innominate terms can only be classified as conditions or warranties once the effects of their breach can be assessed.

(d)   Oral evidence may only be adduced to assist in the interpretation of a written contract in certain limited circumstances.

(e)   Statements made in the course of negotiations may not become terms of a contract at all. They may only amount to representations.

(f)   Some terms may be implied by law, whereas others are so obvious that they are implied under the officious bystander test.

(g)   Transfers of land and gratuitous promises must be by deed. Bills of exchange, hire purchase agreements and contracts for the sale of land must be in writing. Contracts of guarantee must be evidenced in writing.

(h)   Exclusion clauses are not automatically illegal, but some such clauses are ruled out to prevent abuses of economic power by one party.

(i)   Exclusion clauses must be properly incorporated into a contract at or before the time of acceptance, and must not be presented in a misleading manner.

(j)   Exclusion clauses are interpreted strictly, against the person seeking to rely on them.

(k)   The Unfair Contract Terms Act 1977 makes certain exclusion clauses void, and others void unless they are reasonable.

Quick quiz

1   What is the difference between a condition and a warranty?

2   Explain the significance of an innominate term.

3   When may oral evidence add to a written contract?

4   What is the difference between a representation and a contract term?

5   In what circumstances may additional terms, not expressed in the contract, nonetheless be implied as part of it?

6   What contracts relating to an interest in land may still be enforceable even if they are only evidenced in writing?

7   When will a court treat an exclusion clause as void because the affected party was not properly informed?

8   What effect does the fact that parties have had previous dealings have on an exclusion clause?

9   If there is ambiguity in an exclusion clause, how does the court interpret the clause?

10   What is the main purpose rule?

11   When may liability for negligence never be excluded?

12   What tests are applied to determine the reasonableness of an exclusion clause?

13   How does UCTA 1977 define a consumer?

Solutions to exercises

1   If there is no agreement, a definite price (£50,000) is automatically fixed.

2   (a)   A warranty

    (b)   A condition

80

3   No: it is an implied term that a qualified accountant can prepare a tax return in any form required by the Inland Revenue.

4   Yes: the contract (as opposed to the transfer) need not be in the form of a deed, so a witness is not required.

5   No: Q has not been misled.

6   No: the exclusion clause was notified before the contract was made at the till.

7   No: the company could choose to control drivers' choices of routes.

8   No: a consumer contract cannot exclude the term that goods are fit for their purpose.

9   No: it is not reasonable to expect a consumer to find all printing defects in a 20 volume work within the first two weeks of use.

BPP Publishing

7 VITIATING FACTORS

1 Contractual capacity

It is a prerequisite for forming a binding agreement that both parties should have the capacity to enter into it. In certain circumstances certain types of person do not have that capacity, namely minors, persons suffering from mental incapacity and companies.

Minors

The legal capacity of minors (persons under the age of 18) is determined by the Minors' Contracts Act 1987. A contract between a minor and another party may be:

(a) *valid*, binding in the usual way;

(b) *voidable*, binding unless and until the minor rescinds the contract; or

(c) *unenforceable* against the minor unless he ratifies (adopts) it; but the other party is bound.

Valid contracts of a minor

Two sorts of contract are valid and binding on a minor:

(a) contracts for the supply of goods or services which are necessaries; and

(b) a service contract for the minor's benefit.

If goods or services which are necessaries are delivered to a minor under a contract made by him, he is bound to pay a reasonable price (not the contract price if that is excessive) for them: s 3 Sale of Goods Act 1979. Necessaries are goods suitable to the condition in life of the minor and to his actual requirements at the time of sale and delivery. Services may also be necessaries.

BPP Publishing

Suitability is measured by the living standards of the minor. Things which are in ordinary use may be necessaries even though they are luxurious in quality, if that is what the minor ordinarily uses. Food, clothing, professional advice and even a gold watch have been held to be necessaries. However, in some cases it is clear that a broad definition of necessaries has been adopted, not for the benefit of the minor, but to protect traders who gave credit to young people from wealthy families. It has been said that an item of 'mere luxury' cannot be a necessary, for example a racehorse, but that a luxurious item of utility such as an expensive car may be a necessary. Expensive items bought as gifts are not usually necessaries, but an engagement ring to a fiancee can be.

The second test is whether the minor requires the goods for the personal *needs* of himself (or his wife or child if any). Goods required for use in a trade are not necessaries, nor are goods of any kind if the minor is already well supplied with them and so does not need any more.

Case: Nash v Inman 1908
N was a tailor who had solicited orders from I, a minor of extravagant tastes. N sued I on bills totalling £145 for clothes, including eleven fancy waistcoats, supplied over a period of nine months. It was conceded that the clothes were suitable for I but it was shown that he was already amply supplied with clothing.

Held: the clothes were not necessaries since, although quite suitable for his use, the minor had no need of them. It was immaterial that N was unaware that I was already well supplied.

Case: Mercantile Union Guarantee Corporation v Ball 1937
A minor obtained a lorry on hire purchase terms for use in his road haulage business.

Held: this was not a contract for necessaries since the lorry was required for business, not personal use. Under the hire purchase contract the owner could recover the lorry as still his property, but could not enforce payment of the hire purchase instalments.

If a minor uses borrowed money to pay for necessaries the lender can stand in the shoes of the supplier who has been paid with the lender's money, and the lender may recover so much of his loan as corresponds to a reasonable price for the necessaries.

A service contract for the minor's benefit is also binding on a minor.

Case: Doyle v White City Stadium 1935
D, who was a minor, obtained a licence to compete as a professional boxer. Under his licence (which was treated as a contract of apprenticeship or vocation) he agreed to be bound by rules under which the British Boxing Board of Control could withhold his prize money if he was disqualified for a foul blow (as in fact happened). He asserted that the licence was a void contract since it was not for his benefit.

Held: the licence enabled him to pursue a lucrative occupation. Despite the penal clause, it was beneficial as a whole.

Apart from the test of benefit, the contract must relate to education or training, or to some occupation or vocation.

Voidable contracts of a minor

A minor may enter into a contract by which he acquires an interest of a continuing nature. Such contracts are voidable by the minor during his minority and within a reasonable time after attaining his majority. Until he rescinds (avoids) the contract it is binding. If he rescinds it before his majority, he may withdraw his rescission within a reasonable time afterwards. If he rescinds it, he is relieved of any future obligations. There are four categories of these voidable contracts:

(a) contracts concerning land, for example leases;

(b) purchases of shares in a company;

(c) partnership agreements;

(d) marriage settlements.

Unenforceable contracts of a minor

All other contracts entered into by a minor are described as unenforceable: the minor is not bound (though he may ratify the contract after his majority) but the other party is bound. If he is to be bound the minor must ratify the contract within a reasonable time after his majority. Once ratified the contract is valid and is enforceable both by and against the ex-minor.

Where a contract is voidable and is rescinded by the minor, or where it is unenforceable and is not ratified by the minor, any guarantee of the contract given by a person capable of giving a guarantee is still valid. In addition, a minor may be required to return property which he acquired under a rescinded or unenforceable contract.

Exercise 1

A minor makes a contract for the purchase of food for his own consumption. He eats all the food without over-eating. The food includes luxurious items such as quails' eggs. The actual price for the items supplied is £130, but a reasonable price would be £90 and the minor could have obtained a comparable amount of nutrition by spending £50 on more ordinary types of food. The minor borrows £130 to pay for the goods, but then refuses to repay the lender. How much may the lender recover?

Mental incapacity

If a person who is temporarily insane, under the influence of drugs or drunk enters into a contract it is binding on him unless he is at the time incapable of understanding the nature of the contract and the other party knows or ought to know of his disability.

When necessaries are supplied (not as a gift but with the intention of obtaining payment) to a person under such disability, he must pay a reasonable price for them in any event (s 3 Sale of Goods Act 1979). The rules are similar to those applicable to minors.

Companies

Companies and other artificial legal persons, such as local authorities, do not have unlimited contractual capacity. Often they are limited in what they can do by their constitutions, which only give them certain powers. Actions done outside those powers are said to be *ultra vires*. *Ultra vires* contracts are void, so neither party can enforce their terms.

The *ultra vires* rule as it applies to companies is now of very limited effect following the Companies Act 1989.

2   Mistake

The general rule is that a party to a contract is not discharged from his obligations because he is mistaken as to the terms of the contract or the relevant circumstances. The terms of the contract are established by offer and acceptance; what the parties may think or intend should

Notes

not override those terms or render the contract void. There are, however, limited categories of *operative mistake* which render the contract void.

Operative mistake may be classified as follows.

(a) *Common mistake:* there is complete agreement between the parties but both are equally mistaken as to some fundamental point.

(b) *Mutual mistake:* the parties are at cross-purposes but each believes that the other agrees with him and does not realise that there is a misunderstanding.

(c) *Unilateral mistake:* one party is mistaken and the other is aware of this fact.

Only a mistake of fact can render a contract void: a mistake of law cannot have this effect.

Common mistake

If the parties make a contract relating to subject matter which unknown to both of them does not exist, there is no contract between them.

Case: Couturier v Hastie 1852
A contract was made in London for the sale of a cargo of corn shipped from Salonika. Unknown to the parties the cargo had meanwhile been sold by the master of the ship at Tunis since it had begun to rot. The London purchaser repudiated the contract and the agent who had sold the corn to him was sued (as a *del credere* agent he had indemnified his principal against any losses arising from such a repudiation).

Held: the claim against the agent failed. The corn was not really in existence when the contract was made; the contract was void.

Case: Galloway v Galloway 1914
A man and a woman entered into a separation agreement relating to their apparent status as husband and wife. Neither then knew that their marriage was null and void.

Held: the contract related to non-existent subject matter (the marriage) and was void.

The rule on non-existent subject matter *(res extincta)* has been extended to the infrequent cases where a person buys what already belongs to him *(res sua)*. In such cases the contract cannot be performed because there is nothing to buy.

Case: Cochrane v Willis 1865
Under a family settlement A would inherit property on the death of his brother B. B had become bankrupt in Calcutta and, to save the property from sale to a third party, A agreed with B's trustee in bankruptcy in England to purchase the property from B's bankrupt estate. Unknown to A and B's trustee, B had already died in Calcutta and so the property had passed to A by inheritance before he bought it.

Held: the contract was void and A was not liable to pay the agreed contract price.

Exercise 2

A rogue claims that a new island has just been formed in the Atlantic Ocean by a volcanic eruption, and that he owns the sea bed and therefore the island. He sells the alleged island to a dupe, although no such island exists. Why, although the subject matter does not exist, is this not a case of common mistake?

BPP Publishing

The leading case on both parties being equally mistaken on some fundamental point (a decision of the House of Lords) left open the question as to whether common mistake could be extended any further.

Case: Bell v Lever Bros 1932

L, the controlling shareholder of a Nigerian Company, appointed B to be the managing director of the latter company for five years. Before five years had elapsed, B became redundant owing to a merger and L negotiated with B for the cancellation of his service agreement on payment to B of £30,000. Later L discovered that while serving as managing director, B had used inside information to trade in cocoa on his own account. This was serious misconduct for which B might have been summarily dismissed. B was said to have forgotten the significance of his past conduct in negotiating the cancellation of his service agreement and it was treated as a case of common mistake, not unilateral mistake. L's claim to recover £30,000 from B was that there had been a common mistake as to an essential quality of the subject matter, since the service agreement for which L had paid £30,000 was in fact valueless to B since he could have been dismissed without compensation.

Held: L's claim must fail. It was not a case of non-existent subject matter. If L's claim was correct in its theoretical basis there was not here a sufficiently fundamental mistake as to the 'quality' of the subject matter. Modern opinion is inclined to interpret the decision to mean that no mistake as to mere 'quality' of the subject matter can ever make the contract void for mistake (but equitable relief is sometimes given).

But common mistake resulting in a contract void *ab initio* was upheld in the following case (decided in the High Court), in which the principles were clearly analysed.

Case: Associated Japanese Bank (International) v Credit du Nord SA 1988

A rogue, B, entered into a sale and leaseback agreement with the plaintiff to fund the purchase of four machines, identified by serial numbers. The defendant guaranteed the transaction as a leasing agreement. The plaintiff advanced £1m to B, who made one quarterly repayment before being arrested for fraud, and adjudged bankrupt. The machines did not exist, and so the plaintiff sued to enforce the guarantee. The defendant claimed the contract was void for common or mutual mistake since the non-existence of the machines made the subject of the contract essentially different.

Held:

(a)   the law exists to uphold rather than destroy agreements;

(b)   the law on a mistake as to quality exists to cope with unexpected and exceptional circumstances;

(c)   in order to be 'operative' a mistake must be shared by the parties and relate to facts as they existed at the time of the agreement;

(d)   the subject-matter of the contract must be rendered essentially and radically different to that which the parties believed to exist; and

(e)   a party must have reasonable grounds for believing a common mistake for it to be operative.

The non-existence of the machines in the principal contract (the lease) on which the secondary contract (the guarantee) relied was so fundamental as to render the subject matter 'essentially different'. Hence there was common mistake: the guarantee was void and could not be enforced.

Mutual mistake

If the parties are at cross purposes without either realising it, the terms of the contract usually resolve the misunderstanding in favour of one or the other.

Case: Tamplin v James 1880

J went to an auction to bid for a public house. J believed that the property for sale included a field which had been occupied by the publican. But the sale particulars, which J did not inspect, made it clear that the field was not included. J was the successful bidder but when he realised his mistake refused to proceed with the purchase. The auctioneer had been unaware of J's mistake.

Held: J was bound to pay the price which he had bid for the property described in the particulars of sale. The contract was quite clear and his mistake did not invalidate it.

The parties may, however, have failed to reach any agreement at all if the terms of the contract fail to identify the subject matter. Such a mistake renders the contract void.

Case: Raffles v Wichelhaus 1864

A and B agreed in London on the sale from A to B of a cargo of cotton to arrive 'Ex Peerless from Bombay'. There were in fact two ships named Peerless with a cargo of cotton from Bombay; one sailed in October and the other in December. B intended the contract to refer to the October sailing and A to the December one.

Held: as a preliminary point B could show that there was an ambiguity and that he intended to refer to the October shipment. If the case had gone further (there is no record that it did) the contract would have been void.

If the subject matter is adequately identified, a misunderstanding concerning its *qualities* does not make the contract void. If each party is unaware that the other intends subject matter of a different quality (and has not contributed to the misunderstanding by lack of precision on his side), he may perform his side of the contract according to his intention although the other party was expecting something different.

Case: Smith v Hughes 1871

Oats were bought by sample. The buyer believed that they were old oats. The seller (who was unaware of the buyer's impression) was selling new oats which are less valuable. On discovering that they were new oats the buyer refused to complete the sale.

Held: the contract was for the sale of 'oats' and the buyer's mistake as to a quality (old or new oats) did not render the contract void. The seller was entitled to deliver and to receive payment for his oats.

Exercise 3

X owned two racehorses, Mercury and Hermes. Y offered to buy one of the horses, but after a contract was made it transpired that Y thought he was to buy Mercury, and X thought he was to sell Hermes. Would this be a case of mutual mistake if the contract referred to:

(a)   Hermes, but Y had not read the contract carefully?

(b)   X's racehorse, with no name being given?

Unilateral mistake

A unilateral mistake is usually (but not invariably) the result of misrepresentation by one party. The party misled is entitled to rescind the contract for misrepresentation but it may then be too late to recover the goods. Title to the goods passes to the dishonest party under a contract which is voidable and he may re-sell them to an innocent third party who is entitled to retain them (since the rogue still had title at the time of the re-sale to him). If, on the other hand, the contract is void for mistake at the outset, no title passes to the dishonest party and it may be possible for the party misled to recover his goods. The difference between a voidable and a void contract determines which of two innocent persons is to bear the loss caused by fraud.

Most of the case law on this type of mistake is concerned with mistake of identity. A contract is only void for mistake by the seller about the buyer's identity if the seller intended to sell to someone different from the actual buyer. If that is the position the seller never intends to sell to the actual buyer and the contract with him is void. In any other case the contract is valid when made, though it may later be rescinded since it may be voidable for misrepresentation.

The parties may negotiate the contract by correspondence without meeting face to face. If the buyer fraudulently adopts the identity of another person known to the seller with whom the seller intends to make the contract, the sale to the actual buyer is void.

> *Case: Cundy v Lindsay 1878*
> Blenkarn, a dishonest person, wrote to C from '37 Wood St, Cheapside' to order goods and signed the letter so that his name appeared to be 'Blenkiron & Co', a respectable firm known to C, with their offices at 123 Wood St. The goods were consigned to Blenkiron & Co at 37 Wood St and Blenkarn re-sold the goods to L. C sued L for conversion to recover the value of the goods (for which L had already paid Blenkarn in good faith).
>
> *Held:* C intended to sell only to B & Co and no title passed to Blenkarn. The mistake over the Wood St address was reasonable. L was liable to C for the value of the goods.

But if the buyer fraudulently adopts the alias of a non-existent person who could not have been known to the seller, the contract is only voidable for misrepresentation.

> *Case: King's Norton Metal Co v Edridge Merrett & Co 1897*
> K received an order for goods from 'Hallam & Co', an alias assumed by a rogue called Wallis. The letterhead indicated that H & Co had substantial premises and overseas branches. K had not previously dealt with or heard of H & Co. On receiving the goods (consigned to H & Co) W re-sold them to EM and K sued EM for the value of the goods.
>
> *Held:* K intended to sell to the writer of the letter, who was W trading as H & Co. The misdescription of H & Co as a substantial firm induced a mistake as to the quality of creditworthiness, not as to identity. W acquired title to the goods and EM in turn acquired title before the contract between K and W was rescinded by K. EM was not accountable for the value of the goods.

Face to face transactions

When the parties meet face to face it is generally inferred that the seller intends to sell to the person whom he meets. The latter may mislead the seller as to the buyer's creditworthiness by assuming a false identity. But even if he takes the identity of a real person about whom the seller makes enquiries, there is no mistake of identity which renders the contract void. It is merely voidable for misrepresentation and the loss falls on the seller.

BPP Publishing

Case: Phillips v Brooks 1919

A rogue entered a jeweller's shop, selected various items which he wished to buy and proposed to pay by cheque. The jeweller replied that delivery must be delayed until the cheque had been cleared. The rogue then said that he was Sir George Bullough, a well known person, and the jeweller checked that the real Sir George Bullough lived at the address given by the rogue. The rogue then asked to take a ring away with him and the jeweller accepted his cheque and allowed him to have it. The rogue pledged the ring to the defendant, a pawnbroker, who was sued by the jeweller to recover the ring.

Held: the action must fail. There was no mistake of identity which made the contract void but only a mistake as to the creditworthiness of the buyer. Good title had passed to the rogue until the contract was avoided.

The Court of Appeal reached a similar decision on substantially similar facts in *Lewis v Avery 1971*. The Court of Appeal did not follow its own earlier decision in *Ingram v Little 1960* (contract void for mistake in similar circumstances). Ingram's case is inconsistent with the others and it is unlikely to be followed now. Both *Lewis's* and *Ingram's* cases were sales of a car to a stranger who appeared in response to an advertisement with an elaborate and plausible story of being a well-known person whom the seller had never met.

Exercise 4

A rogue telephones a supplier to place an order for goods. He claims to represent a respectable firm with which the supplier has had previous dealings, and he arranges to collect the goods in person later the same day. The cost is to be charged to the firm's account with the supplier. The rogue meets the supplier when he comes to collect the goods. Why might the contract still be void, despite this face to face contact?

Mistakes over documents - *non est factum*

The law recognises the problems of a blind or illiterate person who signs a document which he cannot read. If it is not what he supposes he may be able to repudiate it as not his deed *(non est factum)*. The relief is not now restricted to the blind or illiterate but will not ordinarily be given to a person who merely failed to read what it was within his capacity to read and understand.

In the *Saunders* case described below the House of Lords reviewed earlier case law and laid down conditions which must be satisfied in repudiating a signed document as *non est factum*: there must be a fundamental difference between the legal effect of the document signed and that which the person who signed it believed it to have, and the mistake must have been made without carelessness on the part of the person who signs.

Case: Saunders v Anglia Building Society 1971 (also known as *Gallie v Lee 1971*)
Mrs Gallie, a widow of 78, agreed to help her nephew, Parkin, to raise money on the security of her house provided that she might continue to live in it until her death. Parkin did not wish to appear in the transaction himself since he feared that his wife, from whom he was separated, would then enforce against him her claim for maintenance. Parkin therefore arranged that Lee, a solicitor's clerk, should prepare the mortgage. As a first step Lee produced a document which was in fact a transfer of the house on sale to Lee. However, Lee told Mrs Gallie that the document was a deed of gift to Parkin and she signed it at a time when her spectacles were broken and she could not read. Lee then mortgaged the house as his property to a building society. Lee paid nothing to Mrs Gallie or to Parkin. Mrs Gallie sought to repudiate the document as *non est factum*.

Held: Mrs Gallie knew that she was transferring her house and her act in signing the document during a temporary inability to read amounted to carelessness. The claim to repudiate the transfer failed.

Case: Lloyds Bank plc v Waterhouse 1990

The bank obtained a guarantee from a father as security for a loan to his son to buy a farm. It also took a charge over the farm. The father did not read the guarantee because he was illiterate (which he did not tell the bank) but he did enquire of the bank about the guarantee's terms. As a result he believed that he was guaranteeing only the loan for the farm. In fact he signed a guarantee securing all the son's indebtedness to the bank. The son defaulted and the bank called on the father's guarantee for that amount of the son's debts which was not repaid following the farm's sale.

Held: the father had made adequate attempts to discover his liability by questioning the bank's employees (he was not careless). They had caused him to believe he was signing something other than he believed. This was a case of both *non est factum* and negligent misrepresentation.

In a case where the signature to a document is obtained by fraud the person who signs can rescind the contract between himself and the fraudster (as in the *Waterhouse* case above). The defence of *non est factum* need only be raised when an honest third party has acquired rights on the document and therefore rescission is not available..

Equitable reliefs for mistake

Rescission is an equitable remedy which is available when the contract is voidable. A different type of relief, *rectification*, may be claimed when the document does not correctly express the common intention of the parties. A party who applies for rectification must show that:

(a)   the parties had a 'common intention', though it need not have become a binding agreement, and they retained that common intention at the time of signing the document; and

(b)   the document does not correctly express their common intention.

It is also possible occasionally to obtain other equitable relief for mistake if it does not render the contract void. No general principle can be deduced from the cases except that such relief is only likely to be given to relieve unfairness. Unless it is unfair, a party who has made a non-operative mistake must abide by his contract. Two examples will illustrate the practice.

Equity will sometimes impose a compromise on the parties.

Case: Solle v Butcher 1950

Extensive improvements were made to what had been a flat at a controlled rent. Both landlord and tenant believed (common mistake) that the flat had therefore ceased to be subject to rent control. It was let at a rent of £250 a year. The original controlled rent was £140 a year but if the landlord had served a notice on the tenant in time he could have had the controlled rent increased to almost £250 a year on account of the improvements. After the period for claiming increased rent had expired it was discovered that the flat was still subject to rent control. The tenant sought to recover the excess rent and the landlord to rescind the lease.

Held: the tenant should have the choice between a surrender of the lease and accepting a new lease at a controlled rent increased to make allowance for the landlord's improvements.

BPP Publishing

If A was aware of B's mistake but did not bring it about by misrepresentation (so that B is not entitled to rescind), the court may refuse an order for specific performance since A is seeking to take unfair advantage of a mistake of the other party.

Exercise 5

In what ways does the remedy of rectification differ from the defence of *non est factum*?

---

3 Misrepresentation

A statement made in the course of negotiations may become a term of the contract. If it is a term of the contract and proves to be untrue, the party who has been misinformed may claim damages for breach of contract. If, however, the statement does not become a term of the contract and it is untrue, the party misled may be able to treat it as a misrepresentation and rescind (cancel) the contract, or in some cases, recover damages. *The contract is voidable for misrepresentation.*

A misrepresentation is:

(a) a statement of *fact* which is untrue;

(b) made by one party to the other *before* the contract is made in order to induce the latter to enter into the contract; and

(c) an *inducement* to the party misled actually to enter into the contract: it must relate to a matter of some importance and have been relied on by the party misled.

> *Case: Horsfall v Thomas 1862*
> H made a gun to be sold to T and, in making it, concealed a defect in the breech by inserting a metal plug. T bought the gun without inspecting it. The gun exploded and T claimed that he had been misled into purchasing it by a misrepresentation (the metal plug) that it was sound.
>
> *Held:* T had not inspected the gun at the time of purchase and the metal plug could not have been a misleading inducement because he was unaware of it, and therefore did not rely on it when he entered into the contract.

Since to be actionable a representation must have induced the person to enter into the contract, it follows that he must have known of its existence, allowed it to affect his judgement and been unaware of its untruth. However, the misrepresentation may still be actionable even though it was not the *only* reason the person entered into the contract: *Edgington v Fitzmaurice 1885* (plaintiff subscribed for debentures partly on the strength of a prospectus containing a misrepresentation and partly because he mistakenly believed that he would obtain a charge over property).

Representation

In order to analyse whether a statement may be a misrepresentation, it is first of all necessary to decide whether it could have been a representation at all.

(a) A statement of fact is a representation.

(b) A statement of law, intention, opinion or mere sales talk is not a representation.

(c) Silence is not usually a representation.

BPP Publishing

A statement of opinion or intention is a statement that the opinion or intention exists, but not that it is a correct opinion or an intention which will be realised. In deciding whether a statement is a statement of fact or of opinion, the extent of the speaker's knowledge as much as the words he uses determines the category to which the statement belongs.

> *Case: Smith v Land and House Property Corporation 1884*
> A vendor of property described it as 'let to F (a most desirable tenant) at a rent of £400 per annum for 27½ years thus offering a first class investment'. In fact F had only paid part of the rent due in the previous six months by instalments after the due date and he had failed altogether to pay the most recent quarter's rent.
>
> *Held:* the description of F as a 'desirable tenant' was not a mere opinion but an implied assertion that nothing had occurred which could make F an undesirable tenant. As a statement of fact this was untrue.

A statement of the law is not a representation and hence no remedy is available if it is untrue. However, most representations on law are statements of the speaker's opinion of what the law is; if he does not in fact hold this opinion then there is a misrepresentation of his state of mind and hence a remedy may be available. In addition, a statement of foreign law is a representation.

Exercise 6

P sells a car to Q. Which of the following statements by P to Q could be misrepresentations?

(a)   'The car can do 120 mph.'

(b)   'I have enjoyed driving the car.'

(c)   'You should get the brakes checked before you agree to buy the car.'

As a general rule neither party is under any duty to disclose what he knows. If he keeps silent that is not a representation. But there is a duty to disclose information in the following cases.

(a)   What is said must be complete enough to avoid giving a misleading impression. A half truth can be false.

> *Case: R v Kylsant 1931*
> When inviting the public to subscribe for its shares, a company stated that it had paid a regular dividend throughout the years of the depression. This clearly implied that the company had made a profit during those years. This was not the case since the dividends had been paid out of the accumulated profits of the pre-depression years.
>
> *Held:* the silence as to the source of the dividends was a misrepresentation since it distorted the true statement that dividends had been paid.

(b)   There is a duty to correct an earlier statement which was true when made but which may become untrue before the contract is completed.

(c)   In contracts of 'utmost good faith' *(uberrimae fidei)* there is a duty to disclose the material facts which one knows. Contracts of insurance fall into this category.

BPP Publishing

Made by one party to another

The person to whom a representation is made is entitled to rely on it without investigation, even if he is invited to make enquiries.

Case: Redgrave v Hurd 1881
R told H that the income of his business was £300 per annum and produced to H papers which disclosed an income of £200 per annum. H queried the figure of £300 and R produced additional papers which R stated showed how the additional £100 per annum was obtained. H did not examine these papers which in fact showed only a very small amount of additional income. H entered into the contract but later discovered the true facts and he refused to complete the contract.

Held: H relied on R's statement and not on his own investigation. H had no duty to investigate the accuracy of R's statement and might rescind the contract.

Although in general a misrepresentation must have been made by the misrepresentor to the misrepresentee, there are two exceptions to the rule.

(a) A misrepresentation can be made to the public in general, as where an advertisement contains a misleading representation.

(b) The misrepresentation need not be made directly on a one-to-one basis. It is sufficient that the misrepresentor knows that the misrepresentation would be passed on to the relevant person.

Case: Pilmore v Hood 1873
H fraudulently misrepresented the turnover of his pub so as to sell it to X. X had insufficient funds and so repeated the representations, with H's knowledge, to P. On the basis of this P purchased the pub.

Held: H was liable for fraudulent misrepresentation even though he had not himself misrepresented the facts to P.

Exercise 7

R sells some farmland to S. Before the contract is made, R states that the land is good for grazing. In fact it is good for grazing sheep, but not cattle. R also suggests that S might like to get an independent opinion on the quality of the land. Has R made a misrepresentation to S?

Types of misrepresentation

Misrepresentation is classified (for the purpose of determining what remedies are available) as:

(a) *fraudulent misrepresentation:* a statement made with knowledge that it is untrue, or without believing it to be true, or recklessly careless whether it be true or false;

(b) *negligent misrepresentation:* a statement made in the belief that it is true but without reasonable grounds for that belief;

(c) *innocent misrepresentation:* a statement made in the belief that it is true and with reasonable grounds for that belief.

BPP Publishing

Case: Derry v Peek 1889

D and other directors of a company published a prospectus inviting the public to apply for shares. The prospectus stated that the company (formed under a special Act of Parliament) had statutory powers to operate trams in Plymouth, drawn by horses or driven by steam power. The Act required that the company should obtain a licence from the Board of Trade for the operation of steam trams. The directors assumed that the licence would be granted whenever they might apply for it, but it was later refused.

Held: the directors honestly believed that the statement made was true and so this was not a fraudulent misrepresentation.

Under the Misrepresentation Act 1967, which was not then in force, this would probably have been negligent misrepresentation since there were no *reasonable* grounds for the statement. Negligent misrepresentation may be at common law (involving breach of a duty of care owed) or under the statutory protection of the Misrepresentation Act 1967 (when the defendant must disprove his negligence). Under the Act no duty of care need be shown.

Remedies for misrepresentation

In a case of *fraudulent* misrepresentation the party misled may, under common law, rescind the contract (since it is voidable), refuse to perform his part of it and/or recover damages for any loss by a common law action for deceit (which is a tort).

In a case of *negligent* misrepresentation the party misled may, under equitable principles, rescind the contract and refuse to perform his part under it. In order to gain a remedy, the plaintiff must show that the misrepresentation was in breach of a duty of care which arose out of a special relationship.

Case: Esso Petroleum Co Ltd v Mardon 1976

E negligently told M that a filling station, the tenancy for which they were negotiating, had an annual turnover of 200,000 gallons. This induced M to take the tenancy, but in fact the turnover never rose to more than 86,000 gallons.

Held: E owed a special duty of care and was in breach. Damages were awarded to M.

In a case of *innocent* misrepresentation the party misled may also, in equity, rescind the contract and refuse to perform his part of it. He is not ordinarily entitled to claim damages for any additional loss.

The Misrepresentation Act 1967

Under the Misrepresentation Act 1967 a victim of negligent misrepresentation claim damages for any actual loss caused by the misrepresentation. It is then up to the party who made the statement to prove, if he can, that he had reasonable grounds for making it and that it was not in fact negligent. If the maker of the statement proves that he had reasonable grounds for believing, and in fact did believe up to the time the contract was made, that the facts represented were true then he has a defence that he was not negligent. This placing of the burden of proof on the maker of the statement makes an action under the Act easier for the victim to win than an action at common law.

Under the Misrepresentation Act 1967 s 2(2) the court may in the case of non-fraudulent (negligent or innocent) misrepresentation award damages *instead* of rescission. This may be a fairer solution in some cases. But damages may only be awarded instead of rescission if the right to rescind has not been lost.

Damages in cases of misrepresentation are intended to put the injured party in the position he would have been in if he had never made the contract. Whatever the type of

BPP Publishing

misrepresentation, unforeseeable as well as foreseeable losses are recoverable, provided the losses are not too remote.

Case: Royscot Trust Ltd v Rogerson & Others 1991
In a hire purchase agreement for a car the dealer agreed a price of £7,600 with the hirer and took a £1,200 deposit. The plaintiff finance company agreed to finance the transaction but, because it stipulated a 20% deposit, the dealer (innocently) misrepresented the price and deposit at £8,000 and £1,600 respectively. The agreement was executed between the plaintiff and the hirer but the latter, after paying £2,774.76, dishonestly sold the car to an innocent third party who acquired good title. The plaintiff claimed damages from the dealer of £3,624.24, being the difference between the price for which it bought the car from the dealer and the amount paid to it by the hirer.

Held: as in a case of fraudulent misrepresentation, the plaintiff was entitled to recover for any loss which flowed from the dealer's misrepresentation, even if this could not have been foreseen. Because hire purchase cars are often dishonestly sold by hirers, the loss was also not too remote.

Exercise 8

X negotiates to sell some paper to Y. X tells Y that the paper is suitable for colour printing, whereas in fact it is only suitable for black and white printing. In making the statement to Y, X relies on statements made to him by the (reputable) paper merchant who supplied the paper to him, and on the independent opinion of a printer who had inspected the paper. However, two days before the contract is made (but after X makes his statement to Y), that printer tells X that he made a mistake and that the paper is not suitable for colour printing. Could X's misrepresentation to Y be treated as negligent?

Loss of the right to rescind

The principle of rescission is that the parties should be restored to their position as it was before the contract was made. The right to rescind is lost in any of the following circumstances.

(a)   If the party misled *affirms the contract* after discovering the true facts he may not afterwards rescind. For this purpose it is not necessary that he should expressly affirm the contract. Intention to affirm may be implied from conduct indicating that the party is treating the contract as still in operation. In a number of cases concerned with untrue prospectuses, subscribers have lost the right to rescind by continuing to exercise their rights as shareholders even though they did not realise that this would be the effect. Mere inaction over a period of time may also be treated as affirmation.

(b)   If the parties can no longer be restored to substantially the pre-contract position, the right to rescind is lost.

Case: Clarke v Dickson 1858
The contract related to a business which at the time of the misrepresentation was carried on by a partnership. It was later reorganised as a company and the plaintiff's interest was with his consent converted into shares. He later sought to rescind.

Held: the conversion of the plaintiff's interest in the partnership into shares in the company was an irreversible change which precluded restoration to the original position. The right to rescind had been lost.

(c) If the rights of third parties, such as creditors of an insolvent company, would be prejudiced by rescission, it is too late to rescind.

(d) Lapse of time may bar rescission where the misrepresentation is innocent. Where misrepresentation is fraudulent, lapse of time does not, by itself, bar rescission because time only begins to run from the discovery of the truth.

No other barrier exists to the right to rescission thanks to s 1 Misrepresentation Act 1967; in particular, the fact that the contract has been performed (a conveyance of land has been completed) does not mean that it cannot be rescinded for misrepresentation. But thanks to s 2(2) the court may avoid unnecessary punishment by ordering damages instead of rescission.

Rescission is often an illusory remedy because it may be too late to rescind when the truth is discovered. It may be more advantageous to the party misled to sue for damages for negligent misstatement under the law of tort. Generally, though, s 2(1) Misrepresentation Act 1967 is more popular because the onus of disproving negligence shifts to the defendant, and no special relationship need be proved. For the role of a special relationship in the tort of negligent misstatement, see Chapter 15, Section 6.

Any clause of a contract which excludes liability for misrepresentation in making the contract is void unless it satisfies the test of reasonableness imposed by the Unfair Contract Terms Act 1977.

Contracts *uberrimae fidei*

As indicated earlier, the general rule is that a party to a contract has no duty to disclose what he knows which may affect the willingness of the other party to enter into the contract, either spontaneously or in answer to questions.

When a public company offers its shares or debentures by means of listing particulars or a prospectus, it must include in the printed document all the information prescribed by the Financial Services Act 1986. This is not strictly an obligation of utmost good faith but its effect is very similar.

Three types of contract carry a duty of utmost good faith *(uberrimae fidei)*, which means that failure to disclose material facts gives rise to a right for relief:

(a) contracts of insurance;

(b) contracts preliminary to family arrangements, such as land settlements; and

(c) contracts where there is a fiduciary relationship, such as exists between solicitor and client, or partner and partner.

Exercise 9

Is it reasonable that when a contract of insurance is proposed to an insurer, the onus is on the proposer to disclose all relevant facts?

---

4   Duress

A person who has been induced to enter into a contract by duress or undue influence is entitled to avoid it at common law: the contract is *voidable* at his option, because he has not given his genuine consent to its terms.

BPP Publishing

Duress is fundamentally a threat. This may be of physical violence, imprisonment, damage to goods or business or even breach of a contract.

In older cases it has been held that threatened seizure of goods or property is not duress as it should be limited to threats of physical harm or imprisonment. But in some recent decisions the courts have set aside contracts made under 'economic duress'.

Case: The Atlantic Baron 1979
The parties had reached agreement on the purchase price of a ship. There was then a currency devaluation and the vendor claimed a 10% increase in price. The purchaser refused to pay. The vendor then stated that if the extra was not paid he would terminate the contract and amicable business relations would not continue. The purchaser then agreed to pay the increased price.

Held: the threat to terminate the contract and discontinue amicable business relations amounted to economic duress. The contract was therefore voidable.

Case: Atlas Express Ltd v Kafco (Exporters and Distributors) Ltd 1989
K had a big order to fulfil with W for a supply of baskets. K negotiated with A that deliveries should be made at £7.50 each. This was confirmed by telex. Later A decided that £7.50 was not enough and drew up an updated 'agreement'. A's driver arrived at K's depot with the update and said that he would not collect goods unless K signed the update. K protested but was unable to speak to someone in charge at A. Being bound to supply to W, K signed under protest and continued to pay only the original agreed amount.

Held: A could not enforce the higher payment since consent had been obtained by economic duress: K would have suffered dire consequences if it had been unable to supply W.

Exercise 10

A indicates to B that she would probably supply microcomputers of a specified type to B at £1,200 each. When A and B meet to agree a contract, A says that the price per computer will be £1,300, and says that unless B accepts this price he will have to go elsewhere. Both A and B know that the lowest price available elsewhere is £1,400. Why is this not a case of economic duress?

---

5 Undue influence

A contract (or a gift) is *voidable* if the party who made the contract or gift did so under the undue influence of another person (usually the other party to the transaction). This is an equitable relief.

To succeed in a claim for undue influence, it must be shown that:

(a) a relationship of trust and confidence existed (in some cases this is assumed);

(b) the weaker party did not exercise free judgement in making the contract;

(c) the resulting contract is to the manifest disadvantage of the weaker party and the obvious benefit of the stronger; and

(d) the weaker party has sought to avoid the contract as soon as the undue influence ceased to affect him or her.

BPP Publishing

Relationship of trust and confidence

When the parties stand in certain relationships the law assumes that one has undue influence over the other. These relationships include the following in which the stronger party is mentioned first (this is not an exhaustive list).

(a) Parent and minor child (*sometimes* even if the child is an adult)

(b) Guardian and ward

(c) Trustee and beneficiary under the trust

(d) Religious adviser and disciple

(e) Doctor and patient

The following relationships are not assumed to be ones in which undue influence is exerted, although this assumption may of course be rebutted.

(a) Bank and customer

(b) Husband and wife

(c) Employer and employee

It is possible to argue that any other relationship in which one person places trust and confidence in another has given the latter the opportunity for undue influence. The courts will look at all the facts in ascertaining whether in a particular case undue influence has in fact been exercised.

> *Case: Williams v Bayley 1866*
> A bank official told an elderly man that the bank might prosecute his son for forgery and to avoid such action the father mortgaged property to the bank.
>
> *Held:* there is no presumption of undue influence in the relation of the bank and customer but it could be proved to exist (as was in this case) by the relevant facts.

It is perfectly possible for a relationship to exist where one person places trust and confidence in another without a resulting contract being voidable for undue influence. It is only where the stronger person steps outside a fair and businesslike relationship and obtains a benefit from the abuse of trust that undue influence arises: *National Westminster Bank v Morgan 1985*.

Free judgement

If it appears that there is undue influence, the party who is deemed to have the influence may resist the attempt to set aside the contract by showing that the weaker party did in fact exercise free judgement in making the contract. A person who has undue influence is presumed to have used it but this presumption is rebuttable. In rebuttal it is usually necessary to show that the person, otherwise subject to undue influence, was advised by an independent adviser to whom the material facts were fully disclosed and that adequate consideration was given: *Inche Noriah v Shaik Allie bin Omar 1929*.

> *Case: Lloyds Bank v Bundy 1975*
> On facts very like those of *Williams v Bayley* above (except that the son was in financial difficulty and the bank required additional security for its loan to him) a customer gave the bank a charge over his house.
>
> *Held:* the bank could not itself give independent financial advice to a customer on a matter in which the bank was interested as a creditor. Since the bank had not arranged for the customer to have independent advice the charge in favour of the bank would be set aside.

BPP Publishing

However, there may be undue influence even where the defendant tries to rebut the presumption by showing that the plaintiff has refused independent advice.

Case: Goldsworthy v Brickell 1987
G, an 85 year old man entered into an agreement to give tenancy of a farm to B, who had been helping him run it. The terms were highly favourable to B, but G had rejected opportunities to consult a solicitor. G sought for the agreement to be rescinded.

Held: although there had been no domination (see Morgan's case below), the fact that the agreement's terms were clearly unfair and that G placed trust in B meant that the presumption could not be rebutted by showing that free exercise of judgement was allowed. G could rescind.

Exercise 11

A religious adviser suggests to a disciple that he should give half of his property to a religious order. The adviser points out that the disciple should seek independent advice, and recommends that he consult another adviser who is a member of the same order. The disciple does so consult, but goes ahead with the gift by deed. Could the presumption of undue influence be rebutted?

Manifest disadvantage

A transaction will not be set aside on the ground of undue influence unless it can be shown that the transaction is to the manifest disadvantage of the person subjected to undue influence. The case below also demonstrates that a presumption of undue influence will not arise merely because a confidential relationship exists, provided that the person in whom confidence is placed keeps within the boundaries of a normal business relationship.

Case: National Westminster Bank v Morgan 1985
A wife (W) signed a re-mortgage of the family home (owned jointly with her husband H) in favour of the bank, to prevent the original mortgagee from continuing with proceedings to repossess the home. The bank manager told her in good faith, but incorrectly, that the mortgage only secured liabilities in respect of the home. In fact, it covered all H's debts to the bank. W signed the mortgage at home, in the presence of the manager, and without taking independent advice. H and W fell into arrears with the payments and soon afterwards H died. At the time of his death, nothing was owed to the bank in respect of H's business liabilities. The bank sought possession, but W contended that she had only signed the mortgage because of undue influence from the bank and, therefore, it should be set aside.

Held: the manager had not crossed the line between explaining an ordinary business transaction and entering into a relationship in which he had a dominant influence. Furthermore, the transaction was not unfair to W. Therefore, the bank was not under a duty to ensure that W took independent advice. The order for possession was granted.

Despite the words 'dominant influence' in Lord Scarman's judgement in the Morgan case, the Court of Appeal stated subsequently in *Goldsworthy v Brickell 1987* (see above), in an apparent move away from the House of Lords position, that an influence stopping short of a dominant one may be sufficient to allow the court to set the contract aside on the basis of undue influence. Once trust has been shown to have existed, it is then necessary to demonstrate manifest disadvantage rather than that the position of trust has been abused and exercised as a dominating influence: *Woodstead Finance Ltd v Petrou 1986.*

The case below identifies what is and is not 'manifest disadvantage'.

Case: Bank of Credit and Commerce International v Aboody 1988
Mrs A purchased the family home in 1949 and it was registered in her sole name. Mr A ran a business in which his wife took no interest but in 1959 she became a director of his company on the understanding that she would have to do nothing. Between 1976 and 1980 she signed three guarantees and three mortgages over her house. Mr A deliberately concealed matters from his wife. The company collapsed due to Mr A's fraud and the bank sought to enforce the guarantees against Mr and Mrs A.

Held: there had been actual undue influence over his wife by Mr A but Mrs A had suffered no manifest disadvantage since, at the time she signed the documents, her husband's business was comfortably supporting her and there was no indication that it would not continue to do so. She had benefited from the business which she secured.

Loss of the right to rescind

The right to rescind for undue influence is lost if there is delay in taking action after the influence has ceased to have effect.

Case: Allcard v Skinner 1887
Under the influence of a clergyman, A entered a Protestant convent and in compliance with a vow of poverty transferred property worth about £7,000 to the order. After ten years A left the order and became a Roman Catholic. Six years later she demanded the return of the unexpended balance of her gift.

Held: it was a clear case of undue influence since, among other things, the rules of the order forbade its members to seek advice from any outsider. But A's delay of six years after leaving the order in making her claim, debarred her from setting aside the gift and recovering her property. (This is an example of the equitable doctrine of 'laches' or delay.)

The right to rescission is also lost if the party affirms the contract by performing obligations without protest, or if an innocent third party has acquired rights.

Exercise 12

A has undue influence over B. A would very much like to live in B's house, so A persuades B to sell the house to him for £80,000 when its open market value is £10,000 less. B then regrets selling the house, which she was very fond of. Could B have the transaction set aside on the ground of undue influence?

---

6 Void and illegal contracts

Some types of contract cannot be enforced in a court of law because they are unlawful in themselves or disapproved as contrary to public policy. The following categories may be distinguished.

(a) *Void by statute*

  (i) Certain wagering contracts

  (ii) Restrictive trading agreements

  (iii) Resale price maintenance agreements

(b)   *Void at common law on the grounds of public policy*

    (i)   Restraint of trade contracts

    (ii)   Contracts prejudicial to marriage or parental obligations

    (iii)   Contracts to oust the jurisdiction of the courts in relation to private matters, such as agreements not to prove in bankruptcy

(c)   *Illegal, void and prohibited by statute*

    (i)   Cartel agreements

    (ii)   Contracts made in breach of licence requirements

(d)   *Illegal and void at common law as contrary to public morals or the interests of the state*

    (i)   Agreements to commit a crime or tort, such as assault or defrauding the Revenue

    (ii)   Contracts to promote sexual immorality

    (iii)   Contracts to promote corruption in public life

    (iv)   Contracts to oust the court's jurisdiction in relation to a matter of concern to the public, such as contracts not to prosecute for crimes

All such contracts are *void* and neither party can enforce them. In general, money paid or property transferred under a contract which is merely void may be recovered. If the void part can be separated from the other terms without rendering the agreement meaningless, then the remainder may be valid. But if the contract is also illegal the courts will not (subject to some exceptions) assist a party to recover his money or property.

Effects of an illegal contract

If the contract is obviously illegal in its inception or if the contract appears to be legal but both parties intend to accomplish an illegal purpose by it, neither has an enforceable right at law against the other.

> *Case: Pearce v Brooks 1866*
> The plaintiffs, who were coachbuilders, let a carriage described as 'of a somewhat intriguing nature' to a prostitute. They knew that she was a prostitute and the jury found (although they denied it) that they also knew that she intended to parade along the streets in the carriage as a means of soliciting clients and would pay for the carriage out of her immoral earnings. She failed to pay the agreed amount and they sued to recover it.
>
> *Held:* although the letting of a carriage is not obviously unlawful, to do so to facilitate known immoral purposes is an illegal contract which will not be enforced.

If one party in performing a contract does an act prohibited by statute, the act only may be illegal or the whole contract may be illegal. It depends on whether or not the statute was intended to prohibit the whole contract from being formed.

> *Case: Archbolds v Spanglett 1961*
> S contracted to carry whisky belonging to A in a van which was not licensed to carry goods which did not belong to him. In carrying the whisky S therefore committed a crime. The whisky was stolen on the journey and A sued for damages. S pleaded the illegality as his defence.
>
> *Held:* the defence failed because:
>
> (a)   the statute in question did not prohibit the contract expressly or by implication; and
>
> (b)   A did not know that S did not have the correct licence.

Although money paid or property transferred under a contract which was illegal from its inception cannot generally be recovered, there are two exceptions.

(a)   If one party is less at fault than the other then the less blameworthy (for example, a party who was less aware of the rules or under pressure from the other) may be permitted to recover.

> *Case: Hughes v Liverpool Victoria Legal Friendly Society 1916*
> A grocer insured the lives of customers who owed him money. This was legal since he had an insurable interest. The policies lapsed and an insurance agent persuaded the grocer's wife to take them up, assuring her that this was lawful. It was illegal since she was not their creditor and had no insurable interest. On discovering that the policies were void she sued to recover premiums paid.
>
> *Held:* she might recover her money since she had been persuaded by fraud to enter into an illegal contract.

(b)   A party to an illegal contract who repents of it and withdraws without performing the illegal acts under it may be permitted to recover money or property.

Exercise 13

J runs an illegal radio station. K, who runs a local business and who is aware of the illegality of the radio station, arranges to have some advertisements broadcast. K pays J in advance, but the advertisements are broadcast at the wrong time of day and have little effect. K wishes to sue J. Why is K in a worse position than was Archbolds in *Archbolds v Spanglett 1961*?

A related transaction, even if legal in itself, is usually void and illegal because of its connection with an illegal contract. However, if the contract is illegal under statute in its formation, any legal 'severable' (separately identifiable) parts may be enforced if:

(a)   the illegal promise is not the main or only consideration given;

(b)   the illegal promise is independent of the others; and

(c)   it is not illegal on grounds of public policy to enforce the rest.

If the contract is legal at its inception and one party later performs his side of it for illegal purposes, the other innocent party may recover money paid or property transferred or payment for services rendered (while in ignorance of the illegality).

A contract of insurance is distinguished from a wagering contract by the existence of an insurable interest. If there is no insurable interest the contract is illegal and void. In outline the rules on insurable interest are as follows.

(a)   *Property:* the person who insures must have legal ownership of the property insured or a legal interest in it. One can only insure someone else's property if one has an interest in it. A bailee who has possession of another person's property with liability for its safekeeping has an insurable interest.

(b)   *Events:* one may insure against an event, for example rain which would spoil a garden fete, if one has a financial interest in its success. For the same reason one may insure against the death of one's debtor.

(c)   *Lives:* one may only insure the life of oneself, one's spouse and other persons whose deaths would cause loss to the insured.

BPP Publishing

Contracts void at common law

Contracts in restraint of trade are by far the most important examples of this type of void agreement. However, the other two categories should not be forgotten.

Contracts prejudicial to the state of marriage include any agreement which restricts a person's freedom to marry. Hence an agreement not to marry someone, or to marry only one person or one from a set of persons, is void. Similarly, a contract, whereby a person agrees for a money payment to procure a marriage is void.

Contracts to oust the court's jurisdiction are those whereby the parties agree not to apply to the courts no matter what may happen. For example, a separated husband and wife may draw up a contract whereby one agrees to pay maintenance to the other. Any clause in it that the recipient should not seek to enforce the contract in court is void as it seeks to oust the court's role.

Note that it is perfectly allowable for parties to agree in a contract that disputes should be referred to arbitration rather than to the courts, because arbitration is an effective and independent alternative to the court. What is avoided by the common law is an attempt to agree that a path of recourse to the law which is there as of right should be closed off.

Exercise 14

Jane of her own volition takes out an insurance policy on the life of a famous actress with whom she has no other connection. The actress does not die within the term of the policy. Why can Jane not rely on *Hughes v Liverpool Victoria Legal Friendly Society 1916* to recover the premiums she has paid?

Contracts in restraint of trade

Any restriction on a person's normal freedom to carry on a trade, business or profession in such a way and with such persons as he chooses is a restraint of trade. A restraint of trade is treated as contrary to public policy and therefore void unless it can be justified under the principles explained below. If a restraint is void the remainder of the contract by which the restraint is imposed is usually valid and binding: it is merely the restraint which is struck out as invalid.

The objection to a restraint of trade is that it denies to a community useful services which would otherwise be available. On the other hand, it is recognised that a restraint may be needed to protect legitimate interests. A restraint of trade may therefore be justified and be enforceable if:

(a)   the person who imposes it has a legitimate interest to protect;

(b)   the restraint is reasonable between the parties as a protection of that interest; and

(c)   it is also reasonable from the standpoint of the community.

In principle any restraint of trade may be subject to scrutiny by reference to the tests set out in the previous paragraph. But where the parties have agreed upon it in the normal course of business and on the basis of equal bargaining strength, it is accepted that the restraint is justifiable and valid without detailed examination. In practice the doctrine of restraint of trade is applicable only to:

(a)   restrictions on employees;

(b)   restrictions on vendors of businesses;

(c)   petrol solus agreements;

(d)   one-sided agreements.

Restrictions on employees

An employer may (in consideration of the payment of wages) insist that the employee's services shall be given only to him while the employment continues. But any restraint imposed on the employee's freedom to take up other employment (or to carry on business on his own account) *after* leaving the employer's service is void unless it can be justified. Such a restraint, if reasonable in its extent, may be valid if it is imposed to prevent the employee from making use of the trade secrets or trade connections (business goodwill) of the employer, since these are interests which the employer is entitled to protect.

An employee who has access to *trade secrets* such as manufacturing processes or even financial and commercial information which is confidential, may be restricted to prevent his using such information after leaving his present job.

In contrast to trade secrets the employer has no right to restrain an employee from exercising a *personal skill* acquired in the employer's service.

If the employer imposes the restraint to protect his connection with his customers or clients, he must show that the employee had something more than a routine contact with them. The restraint is only valid if the nature of the employee's duties gives him an intimate knowledge of the affairs or requirements of customers such that, if he leaves to take up other work, they might follow him because of his knowledge (as distinct from his personal skill).

> *Case: Fitch v Dewes 1921*
> D was successively an articled clerk and a managing clerk in the employment of F, a solicitor practising at Tamworth. D undertook never to practise as a solicitor (after leaving F) within seven miles of Tamworth.
>
> *Held:* the restraint was valid since D's knowledge of the affairs of F's clients should not be used to the detriment of F. (In modern practice a restriction unlimited in time would probably be treated as excessive.)
>
> *Case: S W Strange v Mann 1965*
> A bookmaker employed M to conduct business, mainly by telephone, with his clients. M's contract of service restricted his freedom to take similar employment.
>
> *Held:* the contact between M and his employer's clients was too remote to give him the required influence over them. The restraint was void.

Exercise 15

A computer programmer is employed by a computer manufacturer. In the course of her work she acquires a detailed knowledge of the workings of the computers produced by her employer, including some features not known to other manufacturers. In learning these features, she learns new programming skills which could be applied to a wide range of computers. She has said that she would accept the incorporation into her contract of a restriction on her future employment, in consideration of an increase in her holiday entitlement. Try to draft a restriction which would distinguish between her personal skill and her knowledge of trade secrets, and which would only restrict her use of the latter.

BPP Publishing

If the employer can show that the restraint is imposed to protect his legitimate interest he must next show that it is reasonable between the parties, that is no more than is necessary to protect his interest. Many restraints have been held void because they prohibited the employee from working in a wider area than the catchment area of the employer's business, or restricted him for an excessively long time.

The modern practice is generally to restrain an employee only for a short time (a year or two) within an area related to the employer's business or to prohibit him only from soliciting or doing business with customers known to him.

If the restraint is too wide the entire restriction is usually void and not merely the excess which is unreasonable. The court will not rewrite an excessive restraint by limiting it to that part which might be reasonable.

Case: Office Angels Ltd v Rainer-Thomas and O'Connor 1991
The defendants' contracts of employment included clauses stating that, for a period of six months after leaving the plaintiff's employ, they would neither solicit clients of the business nor engage in similar business within a radius of 3 kilometres of the branch in the City of London. The defendants left and set up their own business in a nearby location. An injunction was obtained preventing this in the High Court. The defendants appealed.

Held: the restraint on the poaching of clients was reasonable, but the area of restraint was not. The *whole* restraint clause was void.

The blue pencil rule

In some cases however, the court has concluded that the parties did not intend by the words used to adopt as wide a restraint as the words might impose and have struck out the words which are too wide. This is the 'blue pencil' rule of simple deletion.

Case: Home Counties Dairies v Skilton 1970
A milk roundsman's contract of employment prohibited him, for one year after leaving his employment, from selling *milk or dairy produce* to customers of the employer to whom the roundsman had supplied his employer's goods during the final six months of his employment.

Held: the words 'or dairy produce' were excessive since they would prevent the employee from engaging in a different trade, such as a grocery shop. As the object of the restraint was to protect the employer's connection with customers who purchased their milk, the restraint would be upheld in respect of milk supplied only.

Case: Littlewoods Organisation v Harris 1977
H was employed by L to prepare their half-yearly mail order catalogues, and had access to much confidential information about the mail order business. His contract prohibited him for one year after leaving L from working for any company of the GUS group, L's principal UK competitor in the mail order business. But GUS carried on many other business activities in the UK and abroad. H left L and joined GUS in their mail order business. L sued to enforce the restraint on H.

Held: as the purpose of the restraint was to protect L's trade secrets in its mail order business, the restraint would be enforced as a prohibition against working for GUS in its UK mail order business only. This was, however, a majority decision of the Court of Appeal. In his dissenting judgement, Browne LJ restated the previously accepted view that the blue pencil rule (as the phrase implies) can only be used to delete words which are excessive and not to rewrite the restraint by adding limitations to it or altering its sense. It may well be that the courts, although more sympathetic to the employer than they used to be, will continue on the lines indicated by Browne LJ.

A restraint (in a contract of service) which is reasonable between the parties is not, by definition, prejudicial to the public interest.

Attempts by employers to enforce restraints by indirect means, such as the conditions of eligibility for pension benefits or mutual agreements between employers not to engage former employees of each other, have been dealt with under the same principles as restraints directly imposed by the contract of employment. Thus judgement may be given against an association of employers, even though they have no contract with the person concerned.

Case: Greig v Insole 1978
The Test and County Cricket Board sought to ban commercial World Series cricketers from test and county cricket by means of a change of their rules.

Held: the change of rules was *ultra vires* since it was an unreasonable restraint of trade.

Exercise 16

An employer imposes a restraint on employees' future employment which is stated to apply 'throughout the UK for 20 years after the termination of employment, but if this is held to be excessive the restraint shall apply over whatever area and period the court shall deem to be reasonable'. Why is this tactic unlikely to succeed?

Restraints on vendors of businesses

A purchaser of the goodwill of a business obviously has a right to protect what he has bought by imposing restrictions to prevent the vendor doing business with his old customers or clients. But the restraint must protect the business sold and it must not be excessive.

Case: Nordenfelt v Maxim Nordenfelt Guns and Ammunition Co Ltd 1894
N had developed a new firing mechanism for guns and carried on, among other things, a business manufacturing these guns and their ammunition. When he sold the assets and goodwill of the business he entered into an agreement, later duplicated when the business merged with another, that he would not engage directly or indirectly in a wide number of gun-related activities or any other competing business for 25 years except on its behalf.

Held: the covenant as it related to guns was valid but the term as to competition was void since it went much further than could reasonably be required to protect the business.

Case: British Reinforced Concrete Engineering Co v Schelff 1921
S carried on a small local business of making one type of road reinforcement. He sold his business to BC which carried on business throughout the UK in making a range of road reinforcements. S undertook not to compete with BC in the sale or manufacture of road reinforcements.

Held: the restraint was void since it was widely drawn to protect BC from any competition by S. In buying the business of S, BC was only entitled to protect what they bought: a local business making one type of product and not the entire range produced by BC in the UK.

BPP Publishing

Case: Allied Dunbar (Frank Weisinger) Ltd v Frank Weisinger 1987
The defendant had sold his business to A, for a sum which included £386,000 as consideration for F, a financial consultant who had built up his successful business from scratch, not to be employed in a similar capacity for 2 years.

Held: the restraint was valid, since it was agreed after equal negotiation, paid for and reasonable in itself.

For goodwill to be protected it must actually exist. The courts will not allow 'protection of goodwill' to be a smokescreen for barefaced restraint of competition.

Case: Vancouver Malt & Sake Brewing Co Ltd v Vancouver Breweries Ltd 1934
The defendant was licensed to brew beer but in fact only produced sake. It sold its business and agreed to a term restraining it from brewing beer for 15 years. It later began to produce beer and the purchaser sought to enforce the restraint.

Held: since the seller did not, at the time of sale, produce beer the purchaser only paid for tangible assets because there was no beer-brewing goodwill to sell. The purchaser had not provided consideration for the promise not to produce beer and so he could not enforce it.

Petrol solus agreements

In most cases exclusive distributor or supply agreements are valid since the manufacturer and distributor bargain in a position of equal strength and do not create an oligopoly to the detriment of the public. But in the petrol trade the major suppliers are very large international oil companies and the distributors are small scale petrol filling stations. Agreements by which the proprietors of petrol filling stations agree (in consideration of a lump sum payment or other commercial advantage such as long-term finance) to purchase all their petrol from one supplier are valid only if the duration of the agreement is not excessive. It is accepted that the supplier is entitled to acquire and enforce monopoly rights of supply. Such arrangements are reasonable between the parties. But the public interest requires that any such restriction should be accepted only for a reasonable period.

Case: Esso Petroleum Co v Harper's Garage 1969
H had two petrol filling stations and had agreed to purchase all its petrol supplies for both stations from E. In consideration of this undertaking, E agreed to grant a rebate of 1d (0.42p) per gallon on the normal price and to make a loan of £7,000 to H, secured by a mortgage over one of the filling stations. For one filling station the monopoly rights of E were to last for 4½ years and for the other (by the terms of the mortgage) for 21 years. The mortgage could not be paid off in less than 21 years. H broke its undertaking and E sued to enforce it.

Held: in both cases a personal restraint of trade had been imposed on H. It was not merely a restriction on the use of land even though the longer restriction was imposed by a mortgage. Both must be examined under the principles of restraint of trade since arrangements of this kind, unlike some exclusive distributor agreements, were not to be regarded as reasonable by their nature alone. Solus agreements of this type were, however, reasonable if limited to a short period. The 4½ year restriction was valid but the 21 year restriction on the second filling station was void.

One-sided agreements

Other business agreements of a type which do not usually require justification may nonetheless do so if they are one-sided.

BPP Publishing

Case: Schroder Music Publishing Co v Macaulay 1974

An unknown songwriter made a five year agreement with music publishers on their standard terms. The composer had to assign to the publishers (for a royalty) the copyright to any music which he had written before the contract started or which he might write during the five years, but they had no obligation to publish any of his compositions. The agreement was automatically extended from five to ten years if it yielded at least £5,000 in royalties. The publishers could terminate the agreement at any time by giving one month's notice; M had no such right.

Held: this was restraint of trade which was void unless it could be justified. It was so one-sided - the publishers obtained a monopoly of the composer's output without any commitment to publish his work - that it was unreasonable and void.

Exercise 17

F bought G's supermarket, with G accepting a restraint on carrying on 'any comparable retail business' in the locality within the following year. Would this be likely to prevent G from opening a bookshop nearby within six months?

Chapter roundup

(a) Contracts made by a minor are binding on the minor if they are for the supply of necessaries, or if they are service contracts which are for the minor's benefit. Other contracts made by a minor are either voidable or unenforceable. The contractual capacity of the mentally incapacitated and of companies is also limited.

(b) Not all mistakes render a contract void. The three classes of operative mistake are common mistake (both parties have the same, wrong, understanding), mutual mistake and unilateral mistake.

(c) Common mistake may arise when the subject matter of the contract does not exist. Mutual mistake sufficient to render a contract void may arise when the subject matter is not identified, but a mistake as to quality is not normally sufficient to render a contract void. Unilateral mistake may arise when one party is mistaken as to the identity of the other party.

(d) The defence of *non est factum* may be raised when someone has signed a document which he could not read, but not when he has merely not troubled to read it.

(e) The main remedies for mistake are rescission and rectification, but other equitable remedies may also be available.

(f) A misrepresentation is a false statement of fact which induced the party to whom it was made to enter into the contract. Silence is only a misrepresentation in special cases.

(g) Misrepresentation may be fraudulent, negligent or innocent. In all cases rescission may be available, but this is only available in equity unless the misrepresentation is fraudulent. Damages may also be claimed except in the case of innocent misrepresentation. However, where the misrepresentation was not fraudulent, the court may award damages instead of rescission. In any case, the right to rescission is easily lost.

(h) A contract entered into under duress, whether physical threats or economic duress, is voidable.

(i) Contracts entered into under undue influence are voidable in equity. Several family and professional relationships give rise to a presumption of undue influence, but a contract will only be set aside if it is to the manifest disadvantage of the person influenced. The right to rescind can be lost.

(j) Certain contracts are void, and of these some are illegal. Neither party to an illegal contract acquires rights against the other party, except that the party less at fault may be allowed to recover property.

BPP Publishing

(k) If a contract includes a term which is in restraint of trade, that term is liable to be struck out unless the party imposing it has a legitimate interest to protect and the term is reasonable.

(l) Restraints on employees may limit their use of trade secrets, but not their use of personal skills. Restraints must be appropriately limited in geographical scope and in duration. Restraints on the vendors of businesses must protect the business sold and must not be excessive.

(m) Petrol solus agreements must be limited in duration. One-sided agreements in restraint of trade may be held to be void.

Quick quiz

1 How may a minor's different general contractual liabilities be classified?

2 In what circumstances may a minor be bound to pay for goods?

3 In what circumstances may a minor be bound by a contract of apprenticeship or vocation?

4 When is a person who is insane or drunk not bound by a contract which he enters into?

5 Explain the difference between common, mutual and unilateral mistake.

6 Give examples of contracts rendered void by common mistake.

7 In what circumstances does a contract become void for mistake by one party over the identity of the other?

8 What is a misrepresentation and how does it differ from a statement of opinion?

9 When may silence be construed as misrepresentation?

10 What are the three different kinds of misrepresentation?

11 What are the remedies available to a party who has been misled by negligent misrepresentation by the other party to the contract?

12 In what circumstances may a party misled by misrepresentation be unable to rescind the contract?

13 What types of contract are *uberrimae fidei*?

14 Distinguish between duress and undue influence.

15 How is undue influence established?

16 What is manifest disadvantage and when need it be shown?

17 How may the right (based on undue influence) to rescind a contract be lost?

18 Which contracts are (a) void and (b) illegal?

19 What is a restraint of trade?

20 What must be shown in order to validate a restraint of trade?

21 Illustrate the types of circumstance in which an employee may be subject to a valid restraint on his freedom to take other employment.

Solutions to exercises

1 £90

2 The rogue knew that the subject matter did not exist.

3 (a) No: the subject matter was adequately identified.

   (b) Yes.

4 The contract was made on the telephone, before the rogue met the supplier.

5   *Non est factum* applies when the person pleading it never intended to enter into the contract, and may only be raised when an honest third party has acquired rights. Rectification applies when the parties did intend to contract, but a document fails to express their common intention.

6   (a) and (b). Both are statements of fact.

7   Yes.

8   Yes: when the contract was made, X had lost his reasonable grounds for believing that his representation was true.

9   It may be argued to be reasonable because the insurer has no way of knowing the full range of potentially relevant facts.

10 There was no pre-existing contract in which B was trapped, and B was still being offered a bargain.

11 No: the advice was clearly not independent.

12 No: B has not suffered manifest disadvantage.

13 The whole contract was illegal, and K knew of the illegality.

14 Jane took out the policy voluntarily.

15 One possible answer would be as follows.

    'The employee shall not disclose confidential information about the workings of the employer's computers, and shall not use programming techniques relating only to computers of similar design, but she shall not be prevented from using programming techniques of more general application.'

16 The court will not rewrite an excessive restraint.

17 No: a bookshop is not likely to compete with a supermarket to any significant degree, even though some supermarkets sell a few books.

BPP Publishing

8 DISCHARGE OF CONTRACT

Your objectives

After completing this chapter you should:

(a) know what is necessary for a contract to be discharged by performance;

(b) understand how a contract may be discharged by an agreement which is binding on the parties;

(c) know the types of repudiatory breach of contract, and how anticipatory breach may arise;

(d) understand the circumstances in which frustration arises and when it cannot be pleaded;

(e) know the position of the parties following frustration;

(f) know which losses may give rise to damages, and how damages are computed;

(g) be able to distinguish between liquidated damages and penalty clauses;

(h) understand the limitations on action for the price;

(i) understand the effects of termination and affirmation;

(j) know the uses of *quantum meruit*, specific performance, injunction and rescission;

(k) know how actions for breach of contract may be limited by the passage of time;

(l) understand how liability in quasi-contract may arise.

1   How a contract comes to an end

A party who is subject to the obligations of a contract may be discharged from those obligations in one of four ways. The agreement is then at an end. The four ways are performance, agreement, breach and frustration.

2   Performance

This is the normal method of discharge. Each party fulfils or performs his contractual obligations and the agreement is then ended. As a general rule contractual obligations are discharged only by complete and exact performance. *Partial* performance does not usually suffice, nor does incorrect performance.

Case: Moore v Landauer 1921
The contract was for the supply of tinned fruit from Australia packed in cases of 30 tins each. The ship was seriously delayed and presumably the buyers no longer wished to accept delivery. They argued that the sellers had failed to perform the contract since about half the shipment was packed in cases of 24 tins each. There was no evidence that this departure from the terms of the contract affected the market value of the goods.

Held: the buyers might reject the goods since they were not of the contract description and so the contract had not been discharged by performance.

BPP Publishing

Time of performance

If one party fails to perform at the *agreed time* he may perform the contract later: the contract continues in force, unless prompt performance is an essential condition. In that case the injured party may refuse late performance and treat the contract as discharged by breach (see below and also the case of *Poussard v Spiers* in the chapter on the terms of contract). Where time is not of the essence the injured party may claim damages for any loss or expense caused by the delay but must accept late performance.

If the parties expressly agree that 'time shall be of the essence' so that prompt performance is a condition, that is conclusive and late performance does not discharge obligations. If they make no such express stipulation the following rules apply.

(a)   In a commercial contract, time of performance (other than the time of payment) is usually treated as an essential condition.

(b)   In a contract for the sale of land (unless it fluctuates in value or is required for business use) equity may permit the plaintiff to have an order for specific performance even if he is late.

(c)   If time was not originally of the essence, either party may make it so by serving on the other (after the time for performance has arrived) a notice to complete within a reasonable time.

> *Case: Charles Rickards v Oppenheim 1950*
> The contract was to build a Rolls-Royce chassis within seven months. When this period expired without delivery the purchaser agreed to wait another three months. As the chassis had still not been built by then, he served a notice requiring completion within four weeks; if this were not done he would cancel the order. He did cancel it but the makers tendered delivery three months after he had done so.
>
> *Held:* although the purchaser had at first waived his rights (by the three month extension) he could, by serving reasonable notice to complete, make time of the essence and treat the contract as discharged if there was no performance within the period of the notice.

Exercise 1

In a contract for B to build an extension to A's house, time is not originally of the essence but it becomes clear that B is running seriously behind schedule. When B has only done half of the work, A serves a notice to complete the work within three days. B fails to do so. Why is this unlikely to entitle A to terminate the contract?

Complete performance

As a general rule the contract price is not payable unless there is complete performance. However, the other party may prevent performance. In that case the offer ('tender') of performance is sufficient discharge. For example, if the buyer will not accept delivery of goods and the seller sues for breach of contract, the seller need only show that he tendered performance by offering to deliver. This will discharge him by performance if he can show that the other party had a reasonable chance to examine whether performance really was tendered, such as whether goods tendered were those ordered. This is because performance only serves as discharge if it is precise. Where the obligation is to pay money, tender of payment must be followed by payment into court to show a continuing willingness to perform.

There is no general right to demand proportionate payment for partially completed work.

Case: Cutter v Powell 1795

P employed C as second mate of a ship sailing from Jamaica to Liverpool at a wage for the complete voyage of 30 guineas. C died at sea when he had completed about three quarters of the voyage. C's widow sued for a proportionate part of the agreed sum.

Held: C was entitled to nothing unless he completed the voyage.

There are a number of exceptions, cases where part payment of the contract price may be recovered in exchange for incomplete performance.

(a)   The contract may provide for performance by instalments with separate payment for each of them (a *divisible or severable contract*).

 Case: Taylor v Laird 1856

 The plaintiff agreed to captain a ship up the River Niger at a rate of £50 per month. He abandoned the job before it was completed. He claimed his pay for the months completed.

 Held: he was entitled to £50 for each complete month. Effectively this was a contract that provided for performance and payment in monthly instalments.

(b)   The other party may prevent complete performance. The party so prevented from completing is entitled to be paid for what he has done under the doctrine of *quantum meruit*.

(c)   The other party may accept partial performance and must then pay for it. For example, A orders a dozen bottles of beer from B; B delivers ten which is all he has in stock. A may reject the ten bottles but if he accepts them he must pay for ten bottles at the appropriate rate.

(d)   The doctrine of *substantial performance* may be applied, especially in contracts for building work. If the building contractor has completed the essential work and in doing so has completed a very large part of it, he may claim the contract price less a deduction for the minor work outstanding. This may also be regarded as a deduction of damages for breach of warranty when the contract price is paid.

 Case: Sumpter v Hedges 1898

 S undertook to erect buildings on the land of H for a price of £565. S abandoned the work when it was only 60 per cent completed. H completed the work using materials left on his land by S. S sued for (i) the value of his materials and (ii) the value of his work (so far as it had not already been paid for).

 Held: H must pay for the materials since he had elected to use them but he had no obligation to pay the unpaid balance of the charges for work done by S before abandoning it. It was not a case of substantial performance of the contract.

 Case: Hoenig v Isaacs 1952

 I employed H to decorate I's flat at a total price of £750, to be paid as the work progressed. After paying £400, I objected to the quality of the work and refused to pay the balance for the completed work. The cost of putting right incomplete or defective work was assessed at the trial at £56.

 Held: I must pay the balance owing of the total price of £750 less an allowance of £56.

Since most contracts discharged by performance involve the payment of money, it is necessary to analyse how money should be applied to a series of debts.

(a) The debtor paying the money may identify *at the time of payment* to which debt it should be applied. If he pays one of two debts and denies the other's existence, then it should be inferred that he is not paying the latter.

(b) The creditor receiving the money may identify it *at any time* as he chooses. This right may be excluded by statute, for example by the Consumer Credit Act 1974.

(c) The rule in *Clayton's* case states that, where there is a running or current account (such as one with a bank or with a major supplier), each payment is appropriated to the earliest debt. This is subject to contrary agreement or express intention.

A third party may validly discharge a contract by performance. The validity depends on whether the creditor agrees.

(a) *Creditor consents:* discharge will be effective only if the third party is an agent of the debtor or if the act is subsequently ratified. Different performance to that required by the contract may then suffice.

(b) *Creditor does not consent:* discharge is effected provided the contract terms are exactly performed, and so long as the creditor is proved to be indifferent to that mode of performance: that is, he had not stipulated personal performance. It is the debtor and not the third party who is liable however.

Exercise 2

P regularly makes sales on credit to Q, and maintains an account for Q. On 31 January, Q sends P a cheque for £450. At that date, the amounts outstanding are a debt of £200 incurred on 4 January, one of £170 incurred on 12 January and one of £300 incurred on 20 January. Q is not satisfied with the quality of the goods supplied on 12 January, and does not wish to pay for them. Need he take any action to ensure that he does not pay for those goods?

---

3   Agreement

A contract may include provision for its own discharge by imposing a *condition precedent*, which prevents the contract from coming into operation unless the condition is satisfied. Alternatively, it may impose a *condition subsequent* by which the contract is discharged on the later happening of an event; a simple example of the latter is provision for termination by notice given by one party to the other.

In any other case the parties may agree to cancel the contract before it has been completely performed on both sides. But the agreement to cancel is itself a new contract for which consideration must be given (unless it is a contract for release by deed).

If there are unperformed obligations of the original contract on both sides (it is an executory contract), each party provides consideration for his own release by agreeing to release the other (*bilateral* discharge).

But if one party has completely performed his obligations, his agreement to release the other from his obligations *(unilateral discharge)* requires consideration, such as payment of a cancellation fee (called *accord and satisfaction*).

If the parties enter into a new contract to replace the unperformed contract, the new contract provides any necessary consideration. This is called *novation* of the old contract.

BPP Publishing

4   Breach of contract

A party is said to be in breach of contract where, *without lawful excuse*, he does not perform his contractual obligations precisely. This may be because he refuses to perform them, he fails to perform them, he incapacitates himself from performing them or he performs them defectively.

A person has a lawful excuse not to perform primary contractual obligations (that is, what he promised to do under his side of the bargain) where:

(a)   performance is impossible;

(b)   he has tendered performance but this has been rejected;

(c)   the other party has made it impossible for him to perform; or

(d)   the contract has been discharged through frustration.

Breach of contract gives rise to a secondary obligation to pay the other party damages but, unless breach is treated as repudiation, the primary obligation to perform the contract's terms remains.

Repudiatory breach

A repudiatory breach is a serious actual breach of contract. It does not automatically discharge the contract. The injured party has a choice. He can elect to treat the contract as repudiated by the other, recover damages and treat himself as being discharged from his primary obligations under the contract. This is termination of the contract for repudiatory breach. Alternatively, he can elect to affirm the contract.

Types of repudiatory breach

Repudiatory breach giving rise to a right either to terminate or to affirm arises in the following circumstances.

(a)   *Refusal to perform (renunciation)*
One party renounces his contractual obligations by showing that he has no intention to perform them nor to be otherwise bound by the contract. Such refusal may be express or implied.

(b)   *Failure to perform an entire obligation*
An entire obligation is one where complete and precise performance of it is a precondition (a condition precedent) of the other party's performance. Usually partial performance alone is not sufficient. Thus a contractual condition is often an entire obligation, so failure to perform the acts required by a condition can amount to a repudiatory breach.

(c)   *Incapacitation*
Where a party, by his own act or default, prevents himself from performing his contractual obligations he is treated as if he refused to perform them. For instance, where A sells a thing to C even though he promised to sell it to B he is in repudiatory breach of his contract with B.

Exercise 3

J contracts to sell a painting to K, and K contracts to sell it to L. However, when the time comes for the contract between J and K to be completed, K refuses to pay for the painting so J will not let him have it. Which two types of repudiatory breach arise in relation to the two contracts?

115

Anticipatory breach

A party may break a condition of the contract merely by declaring in advance that he will not perform it when the time for performance arrives, or by some other action which makes future performance impossible. The other party may treat this as *anticipatory breach* and can choose between treating the contract as discharged forthwith and allowing the contract to continue until there is an actual breach.

The risk is that, in the latter case, the party guilty of anticipatory breach may subsequently change his mind and perform the contract after all. If the contract is allowed to continue in this way the parties may be discharged from their obligations without liability by some other cause which occurs later.

> *Case: Hochster v De La Tour 1853*
> T engaged H as a courier to accompany him on a European tour commencing on 1 June. On 11 May T wrote to H to say that he no longer required his services. On 22 May H commenced legal proceedings for anticipatory breach of contract. T objected that there was no actionable breach until 1 June.
>
> *Held:* H was entitled to sue as soon as the anticipatory breach occurred on 11 May.

> *Case: Avery v Bowden 1855*
> There was a contract to charter a ship to load grain at Odessa within a period of 45 days. The ship arrived at Odessa and the charterer told the master that he did not propose to load a cargo. The master remained at Odessa hoping the charterer would change his mind - that is, he did not there and then treat the contract as discharged by the charterer's anticipatory breach. Before the 45 days for loading cargo had expired the outbreak of the Crimean war discharged the contract by frustration.
>
> *Held:* the shipowner, through the master, had waived his right to sue for anticipatory breach (with a claim for damages). The contract continued and had been discharged later by frustration without liability for either party.

If the innocent party elects to treat the contract as still in force despite the other party's anticipatory breach, the former may continue with his preparations for performance and recover the agreed price for his services. But any claim for damages will be assessed on the basis of what the plaintiff has really lost.

> *Case: The Mihalis Angelos 1971*
> There was a charter of a ship to be 'ready to load at Haiphong' (in Vietnam) on 1 July 1965. The charterers had the option to cancel if the ship was not ready to load by 20 July. On 17 July the charterers repudiated the contract believing (wrongly) that they were entitled to do so. The shipowners accepted the repudiation and claimed damages. On 17 July the ship was still in Hong Kong and could not have reached Haiphong by 20 July.
>
> *Held:* the shipowners were entitled only to nominal damages since they would have been unable to perform the contract and the charterers could have cancelled it without liability on 20 July.

Exercise 4

X contracts to sell a computer to Y. Ten days before the date for delivery and payment, Y tells X that he does not intend to go ahead with the purchase. Does X need to deliver the computer immediately in order to secure his legal position against Y?

116

5 Frustration

If it is impossible to perform the contract when it is made, there is usually no contract at all: it is void and each party is released from performing any obligation after the frustrating event. In addition, the parties are free to negotiate 'escape clauses' or *force majeure* clauses covering impossibility which arises after the contract has been made. If they fail to do so, they are, as a general rule, in breach of contract if they find themselves unable to do what they have agreed to do: *Paradine v Jane 1647*.

The rigour of this principle is modified by the doctrine that in certain circumstances a contract may be discharged by frustration (subsequent impossibility). If it appears that the parties assumed that certain underlying conditions would continue, the contract may be frustrated if their assumption proves to be false. An alternative theory of the doctrine of frustration is that the parties should be discharged from their contract if altered circumstances render the contract fundamentally different in its nature from the original contract made by the parties. This alternative avoids imputing to the parties assumptions which in fact never occurred to them. They simply did not foresee what would happen. Frustration does not render a contract void *ab initio*, rather it discharges it automatically as to the future. Contracts have been discharged by frustration in the following circumstances.

(a) *Destruction of the subject matter*

Case: Taylor v Caldwell 1863
A hall was let for a series of concerts on specified dates. Before the date of the first concert the hall was destroyed by fire. The concert organiser sued the owner of the hall for damages for failure to let him have the use of the hall as agreed.

Held: destruction of the subject matter rendered the contract impossible to perform and discharged the contract. This case was the origin of the doctrine of frustration.

(b) *Personal incapacity to perform a contract of personal service*

Case: Condor v Barron Knights 1966
C, aged 16, contracted to perform as drummer in a pop group. His duties, when the group had work, were to play on every night of the week. He fell ill and his doctor advised that he should restrict his performances to four nights per week. The group terminated his contract.

Held: a contract of personal service is based on the assumption that the employee's health will permit him to perform his duties. If that is not so the contract is discharged by frustration.

Case: F C Shepherd & Co Ltd v Jerrom 1986
J entered into a contract of apprenticeship with S & Co. Subsequently he was sentenced to a period of borstal training following a conviction for conspiring to assault and to cause affray. He served 39 weeks. The employers told J's father that they were not prepared to take J back.

Held: the contract has been discharged by frustration.

Other instances of frustration in this category are where the person dies, is called up for military service or is interned in wartime.

(c) *Government intervention or supervening illegality*

Case: Re Shipton, Anderson & Co etc 1915
The contract was for the sale of wheat stored in a Liverpool warehouse. It was requisitioned by the government under emergency wartime powers.

Held: it was no longer lawful for the seller to deliver the wheat. The contract had been discharged by frustration. Supervening illegality, for example owing to outbreak of war (as in *Avery v Bowden*), or government intervention to restrain or suspend performance of the contract is a common cause of frustration.

(d)   *Non-occurrence of an event if it is the sole purpose of the contract*

Case: Krell v Henry 1903
A room overlooking the route of the coronation procession of Edward VII was let for the day of the coronation for the purpose of viewing the procession. The coronation was postponed owing to the illness of the King. The owner of the room sued for the agreed fee.

Held: the contract was made for the sole purpose of viewing the procession. As that event did not occur the contract was frustrated.

Case: Herne Bay Steamship Co v Hutton 1903
A steamboat was hired for two days to carry passengers round the naval review at Spithead which had been arranged as part of the coronation celebrations. The review was cancelled owing to the King's illness but the steamboat could have taken passengers for a trip round the assembled fleet.

Held: the royal review of the fleet was not the sole occasion of the contract. The owner of the steamboat was entitled to the agreed hire charge less what he had earned from the normal use of the vessel over the two day period.

(e)   *Interruption which prevents performance of the contract in the form intended by the parties*

Case: Jackson v Union Marine Insurance Co 1874
There was a contract for a charter of a ship to proceed immediately to load cargo for San Francisco. Off the coast of Wales the ship went ashore and could not be refloated for a month. Thereafter she would need repairs to make her fit for the voyage. Meanwhile the charterers hired another vessel.

Held: the interruption had put an end to the contract in the commercial sense: it was no longer possible to perform the contract intended. The contract was discharged by frustration. There are numerous other interruption cases. In deciding whether it is a case of frustration the test applied is whether the interruption takes away from the agreed duration of the contract so much of it as to alter the fundamental nature of the contract insofar as it can be performed at all; contrast the *Tsakiroglou* case in the next paragraph.

Exercise 5

A small company of coal merchants has contracts to supply householders. The main lorry driver of the company dies suddenly, and the remaining staff cannot manage to deal with all the orders placed. A householder whose order is not fulfilled sues for breach of contract. Why can the company not plead discharge by frustration on the basis of personal incapacity?

118

A contract is *not* discharged by frustration in the following circumstances.

(a) *If an alternative mode of performance is still possible*

Case: Tsakiroglou & Co v Noblee and Thorl GmbH 1962
There was a contract for the sale of 300 tons of Sudan groundnuts to be delivered to Hamburg. The normal and intended method of shipment from Port Sudan (on the Red Sea coast) was by a ship routed through the Suez Canal to Hamburg. Before shipment the Suez Canal was closed; the sellers refused to ship the cargo arguing that it was an implied term that shipment should be via Suez or alternatively that shipment via the Cape of Good Hope would make the contract 'commercially and fundamentally' different, so that it was discharged by frustration.

Held: both arguments failed. There was no evidence to support the implied term argument nor was the use of a different (and more expensive) route an alteration of the fundamental nature of the contract sufficient to discharge it by frustration.

(b) *If performance suddenly becomes more expensive*

Case: Davis Contractors v Fareham UDC 1956
DC agreed to build 78 houses at a price of £94,000 in eight months. Labour shortages caused the work to take 22 months and cost £115,000. DC wished to claim frustration so that they could then claim for their work on a *quantum meruit* basis.

Held: hardship, material loss or inconvenience did not amount to frustration; the obligation must change such that the thing undertaken would, if performed, be a different thing from that contracted for.

(c) *If one party has accepted the risk that he will be unable to perform*

Case: Budgett & Co v Binnington & Co 1891
A bill of lading provided that if the consignee could not unload his cargo within ten days, demurrage (compensation) would be payable. A strike prevented the unloading during the ten days.

Held: the consignee had accepted the risk and must pay the demurrage as agreed.

(d) *If one party has induced frustration by his own choice between alternatives*

Case: Maritime National Fish v Ocean Trawlers 1935
There was a contract for the hire of a trawler for use in otter trawling. The hirers had four other trawlers of their own. They applied to the Canadian government for the necessary licences for five trawlers but were granted only three licences. They nominated three of their own trawlers for the licences and argued that the contract for the hire of a fifth trawler had been frustrated since it could not lawfully be used.

Held: the impossibility of performing the hire contract was the result of a choice made by the hirers: the trawler on hire could have been nominated for one of the three licences. This was not a case for discharge by frustration.

In most cases the rights and liabilities of parties to a contract discharged by frustration are regulated by the Law Reform (Frustrated Contracts) Act 1943 as follows.

(a) Any money paid under the contract by one party to the other is (subject to rule (b) below) to be repaid. Any sums due for payment under the contract then or later cease to be payable.

(b) A party who is liable under rule (a) to repay money received (or whose entitlement to payments already accrued due for payment at the time of frustration is cancelled), may at the discretion of the court be allowed to set off (or to recover) out of those sums the

119

whole or part of his expenses incurred in performing the contract up to the time when it is discharged by frustration. But he cannot recover from the other party his expenses insofar as they exceed sums paid or due to be paid to him at the time of discharge.

(c)   If either party has obtained a valuable benefit (other than payment of money) under the contract before it is discharged, the court may in its discretion order him to pay to the other party all or part of that value. If, for example, one party has delivered to the other some of the goods to be supplied under the contract, the latter may be ordered to pay the amount of their value to him.

Various special types of contract are excluded from the provisions of this Act. Contracts for the carriage of goods by sea, contracts of insurance and contracts for the supply of specific goods if frustrated by the perishing of the goods are not regulated by the Act but by other rules.

Where these rules do not apply, the common law provides that the loss shall lie where it falls; money paid before frustration cannot be recovered and money payable at the time of frustration remains payable, unless there is a complete failure of consideration.

Exercise 6

A contract between F and G is frustrated, and the Law Reform (Frustrated Contracts) Act 1943 applies. At the time of frustration, G has paid F £600 and F has incurred expenses of £270. G has not so far received any valuable benefit. Had the contract not been frustrated, F would have incurred further expenses of £430 and G would have paid F a further £500, giving F a profit of £400. If the court exercises its discretion in favour of F, what final settlement between F and G will be made?

---

6   Remedies available for breach of contract

A party has a number of remedies when the other party is in breach of contract.

(a)   Damages, as compensation for loss caused by the breach.

(b)   Action for the price: here the breach is failure to pay.

(c)   Termination. He may accept the other party's repudiatory breach as discharging him from having to perform his own obligations. Alternatively he may affirm the contract.

(d)   *Quantum meruit*, payment for the value of what he has done.

(e)   Specific performance, a court order to the defendant to perform the contract.

(f)   Injunction, a court order for the other party to observe negative restrictions.

(g)   Rescission, cancellation of the contract.

Damages and action for the price ((a) and (b)) are common law remedies and are most frequently sought when a remedy is needed for breach of contract, since they arise as of right. The other types are equitable remedies which are only appropriate in special circumstances.

7   Damages

Damages are a common law remedy and are primarily intended to restore the party who has suffered loss to the same position he would have been in if the contract had been performed. They are *not* meant to be a punishment, which is a criminal, not a civil, measure. In addition,

BPP Publishing

they should not allow the party to whom they are awarded to profit, nor to achieve a better result: the law will not make up for a bad bargain.

In a claim for damages the first issue is *remoteness of damage:* how far down the sequence of cause and effect should the consequences of breach be traced before they become so indirect that they should be ignored? Secondly, the court must decide how much money (the *measure of damages*) to award in respect of the breach and its relevant consequences.

Remoteness of damage

Under the rule in *Hadley v Baxendale* (below) damages may only be awarded in respect of loss as follows.

(a)　(i)　The loss must arise naturally, according to the usual course of things, from the breach; or

　　(ii)　the loss must arise in a manner which the parties may reasonably be supposed to have contemplated, in making the contract, as the probable result of the breach of it.

(b)　A loss outside the natural course of events will only be compensated if the exceptional circumstances which cause the loss are within the defendant's knowledge, actual or constructive, when he made the contract.

Case: Hadley v Baxendale 1854
H owned a mill at Gloucester which came to a standstill because the main driving shaft had broken. H made a contract with B, a carrier, for the transport of the broken shaft to the makers at Greenwich to serve as a pattern for making a new shaft. Delivery was to be made at Greenwich the following day. Owing to neglect by B delivery was delayed and the mill was out of action for a longer period than would have resulted if there had been no delay. B did not know that the mill would be idle during this interval. He was merely aware that he had to transport a broken millshaft from H's mill. H claimed for loss of profits of the mill during the period of delay.

Held: the claim must fail since B did not know that the mill would be idle until the new shaft was delivered (part (b) of the rule did not apply) and it was not a natural consequence of delay in transport of a broken shaft that the mill would be out of action meanwhile (part (a) of the rule did not apply). The importance of the shaft was not obvious; the miller might have had a spare.

Case: Victoria Laundry (Windsor) v Newman Industries 1949
N contracted to sell a large boiler to V 'for immediate use' in V's business of launderers and dyers. Owing to an accident in dismantling the boiler at its previous site delivery was delayed by a period of four months. V claimed damages for (i) normal loss of profits (£16 per week) for the period of delay and (ii) loss of abnormal profits (£262 per week) from losing 'highly lucrative' dyeing contracts to be undertaken if the boiler had been delivered on time.

Held: damages for loss of normal profits were recoverable since in the circumstances failure to deliver major industrial equipment ordered for immediate use would be expected to prevent operation of the plant: it was a natural consequence covered by the first head of the rule. The claim for loss of special profits fell under the second head of the rule; it failed because N had no knowledge of the dyeing contracts and the abnormal profits which they would yield.

The *Victoria Laundry* judgement was confirmed (but slightly reformulated) by the House of Lords in the *Heron* case (below). It has also been established in the *Parsons* case (below) that if the type of loss caused is not too remote the defendant may be liable for consequences which are much more serious in extent than could reasonably be contemplated.

121

Case: The Heron II 1969
There was a contract for the shipment of a bulk cargo of sugar from the Black Sea to Basra in Iraq. K, the shipowner, was aware that C were sugar merchants but he did not know that C intended to sell the cargo as soon as it reached Basra. The ship arrived nine days late and in that time the price of sugar on the market in Basra had fallen. C claimed damages for the loss due to the fall in market value of the cargo over the period of delay.

Held: the claim succeeded. It is common knowledge that market values of commodities fluctuate so that delay might cause loss. It was sufficiently obvious that a bulk cargo of sugar owned by merchants was destined for sale to which the market value would be relevant.

Case: H Parsons (Livestock) v Uttley Ingham 1978
There was a contract for the supply and installation at a pig farm of a large storage hopper to hold pig foods. Owing to negligence of the supplier the ventilation cowl, sealed during transit to the farm, was left closed. The pig food went mouldy. Young pigs contracted a rare disease from which they died. The pig farmer claimed damages for (i) the value of the dead pigs and (ii) loss of profits from selling the pigs when mature.

Held: illness of the pigs was to be expected as a natural consequence (the first half of the rule applied). Since illness was to be expected, death from illness (although not a normal consequence) was not too remote.

Exercise 7

Draft a clause which could have been included in the contract in *Hadley v Baxendale 1854* in order to enable Hadley to recover damages for loss of profits during any delay.

The measure of damages

As a general rule the amount awarded as damages is what is needed to put the plaintiff in the position he would have achieved if the contract had been performed. If, for example, there is failure to deliver goods at a contract price of £100 per ton and at the due time for delivery similar goods are obtainable at £110 per ton, damages are calculated at the rate of £10 per ton (Sale of Goods Act 1979 s 51 (3)). This is sometimes referred to as protecting the *expectation* interest of the plaintiff. A plaintiff may alternatively seek to have his *reliance* interest protected; this refers to the position he would have been in had he *not* relied on the contract. Because they compensate for wasted expenditure, damages for reliance loss cannot be awarded if they would put the plaintiff in a better position than he would have attained under protection of his expectation interest. A defendant may defeat a claim for wasted expenditure by showing that the plaintiff had made a bad bargain: *CCC Films (London) Ltd v Impact Quadrant Films Ltd 1985*.

More complicated questions of assessing damages can arise. The general principle is to compensate for actual financial loss.

Case: Lazenby Garages v Wright 1976
W agreed to buy a car from L at a price of £1,670 (L had previously bought the car for £1,325). W refused to accept and pay for the car. Shortly afterwards L sold the car to another buyer for £1,770. L claimed £345 (£1,670 - £1,325) from W as the profit which they would have made on a sale to W.

Held: L's claim must fail since L had suffered no loss. The argument that L might have sold a different car to the other buyer and so made profits on two sales was rejected.

BPP Publishing

Non-financial loss

At one time damages could not be recovered for any *non-financial loss* arising from breach of contract. In some recent cases, however, damages have been recovered for mental distress where that is the main result of the breach. It is uncertain how far the courts will develop this concept.

Mitigation of loss

In assessing the amount of damages it is assumed that the plaintiff will take any reasonable steps to reduce or *mitigate* his loss.

> *Case: Payzu v Saunders 1919*
> There was a contract for the supply of goods to be delivered and paid for by instalments. The purchaser failed to pay for the first instalment when due, one month after delivery. The seller declined to make further deliveries unless the buyer paid cash in advance. The buyer refused to accept delivery on those terms.
>
> *Held:* the seller was in breach of contract, as he had no right to repudiate the original contract. But the buyer should have mitigated his loss by accepting the seller's offer of delivery against cash payment. Damages were limited to the amount of the buyer's assumed loss if he had paid in advance, which was interest over the period of pre-payment.

The injured party is not, however, required to take discreditable or risky measures to reduce his loss since these are not 'reasonable'. Moreover in a case of anticipatory breach if the injured party elects to treat the contract as still in being he may continue with his own performance of it, even though in doing so he increases the loss for which, when actual breach occurs, he will recover damages.

Liquidated damages and penalty clauses

To avoid complicated calculations of loss or disputes over the amount the parties may include in their contract a formula *(liquidated damages)* for determining the damages payable for breach. In construction contracts, for example, it is usual to provide that if the building contractor is in breach of contract by late completion a deduction is to be made from the contract price (1 per cent per week subject to a maximum of 10 per cent in all is a typical example). The formula will be enforced by the courts if it is 'a genuine pre-estimate of loss' (without enquiring whether the actual loss is greater or smaller).

> *Case: Dunlop v New Garage & Motor Co 1915*
> The contract (for sale of tyres to a garage) imposed a minimum retail price (resale price maintenance was then legal). The contract provided that £5 per tyre should be paid by the buyer if he re-sold at less than the prescribed retail price or in four other possible cases of breach of contract. He did sell at a lower price and argued that £5 per tyre was a penalty and not a genuine pre-estimate of loss.
>
> *Held:* as a general rule when a fixed amount is to be paid as damages for breaches of different kinds, some more serious in their consequences than others, that is not a genuine pre-estimate of loss and so it is void as a penalty. But the general rule is merely a presumption which does not always determine the result. In this case the formula was an honest attempt to agree on liquidated damages and would be upheld, even though the consequences of the breach were such as to make precise pre-estimation almost impossible.

A contractual term designed as a penalty clause to discourage breach is void and not enforceable. The court will disregard it and require the injured party to prove the amount of his loss.

BPP Publishing

Exercise 8

Under a contract between C and D, D must pay C damages of £100 if a particular type of breach occurs. This amount is a reasonable estimate of the loss which C would suffer. The breach occurs, and C's actual loss is £200. How much must D pay C?

---

8   Action for the price

If the breach of contract arises out of one party's failure to pay the contractually agreed price due under the contract, the creditor should bring an action to recover that sum.

This is a fairly straightforward procedure but is subject to two specific limitations. The first is that an action for the price under a contract for the sale of goods may only be brought if property has passed to the buyer, unless the price has been agreed to be payable on a specific date (s 49 Sale of Goods Act 1979). Secondly, whilst the injured party may recover an agreed sum due *at the time* of an anticipatory breach whether or not he continues the contract then, sums which become due *after* the anticipatory breach may not be recovered unless he affirms the contract: that is, he carries on with his side of the bargain. Even where he does affirm the contract, he will be unable to recover the price if:

(a)   the other party withholds its cooperation so that he cannot continue with his side in order to make the price due; or

(b)   the injured party had no other reason or 'legitimate interest' in continuing his obligations than to claim damages. Such a legitimate interest may be obligations which have arisen to third parties.

These points were decided in *White & Carter (Councils) v McGregor 1961*, where the party who affirmed the contract succeeded in an action for the price.

9   Equitable remedies

Termination or affirmation

The innocent party in a case of repudiatory breach may elect to accept the contract as terminated or discharged by breach, thereby discharging himself from any further obligation to perform. Alternatively, he may affirm the contract.

Termination for repudiatory breach

To terminate for repudiatory breach the innocent party must notify the other of his decision. This may be by way of refusal to accept defects in performance, to accept further performance or to perform his own obligations.

The effects of such termination are as follows for the innocent party.

(a)   He is not bound by his future or continuing contractual obligations, and cannot be sued on them.

(b)   He need not accept nor pay for further performance.

(c)   He can refuse to pay for partial or defective performance already received.

(d)   He can reclaim money paid to a defaulter if he rejects defective performance.

(e)   He is *not* discharged from the contractual obligations which were due at the time of termination.

BPP Publishing

The innocent party can also claim damages from the defaulter for:

(a) losses sustained by him in respect of unperformed contractual obligations due at the time of default (the defaulter is in theory still bound); and

(b) losses sustained by him in relation to contractual obligations which were due in the future.

Finally an innocent party who began to perform his contractual obligations but who was prevented from completing them by the defaulter can claim reasonable remuneration on a *quantum meruit* basis.

Affirmation after repudiatory breach

If a person is aware of the other party's repudiatory breach and of his right to terminate the contract as a result but still decides to treat the contract as being in existence he is said to have affirmed the contract. Such a decision should be a conscious or active one; it is not deemed to have been made purely by virtue of the fact that a person retains defective goods while he or she decides what to do.

The effect of affirmation is that the contract remains fully in force, so each party is bound to perform existing and future obligations and may sue to enforce them. If the election is unconditional - 'I shall keep the goods despite their defects' - it may not be revoked. If it is conditional - 'I will keep the defective goods provided they are mended free of charge' - and the condition is not satisfied, the contract may then be terminated.

Exercise 9

G and H make a contract under which H is to redecorate G's lounge. After stripping the old wallpaper, H declares (without any reason) that he will not do any more work. G then notifies H that he is terminating the contract for repudiatory breach. G has already paid H £50, but refuses to pay any more. H claims a further £200 for the work done. What is likely to be the final outcome?

Quantum meruit

In particular situations, a claim may be made on a *quantum meruit* basis as an alternative to an action for damages for breach of contract.

The phrase *quantum meruit* literally means 'how much it is worth'. It is a measure of the value of contractual work which has been performed. The aim of such an award is to restore the plaintiff to the position he would have been in *if the contract had never been made*. It is a restitutory award. By contrast, an award of damages aims to put the plaintiff in the position he would have been in *if the contract had been performed*. It is a compensatory award.

Quantum meruit is likely to be sought where one party has already performed part of his obligations and the other party then repudiates the contract (repudiatory breach). Provided the injured party elects to treat the contract as terminated, he may claim a reasonable amount for the work done.

In most cases, a *quantum meruit* claim is needed because the other party has unjustifiably prevented performance.

> *Case: Planché v Colburn 1831*
> P agreed to write a book for C, who published a series for young people. P completed half of the book but then C abandoned the series, preventing P's completion.

Held: P could recover £50 as reasonable remuneration for the work done on a *quantum meruit* basis.

Because it is restitutory, a *quantum meruit* award is usually for a smaller amount than an award of damages. However where only nominal damages would be awarded (say because the plaintiff would not have been able to perform the contract anyway as in *The Mihalis Angelos 1971*) a *quantum meruit* claim would still be available and would yield a higher amount.

Specific performance

The court may in its discretion order the defendant to perform his part of the contract instead of letting him buy himself out of it by paying damages for breach.

Specific performance (which is an equitable remedy) will only be ordered in a case where the common law remedy of damages is inadequate. An order will be made for specific performance of a contract for the sale of land since the plaintiff may need the land for a particular purpose and would not be adequately compensated by damages for the loss of his bargain. He could not obtain another piece of land which is identical. For this reason specific performance of a contract for sale of goods is unlikely to be ordered unless the goods are unique and therefore no substitute could be obtained.

The order will not be made if it would require performance over a period of time and the court could not ensure that the defendant did comply fully with the order. Therefore specific performance is not ordered for contracts of employment or personal service nor usually for building contracts. By contrast, a contract for the sale of land requires only that the vendor should execute and deliver a transfer and other documents, so the order is readily enforceable.

Only contracts where consideration has passed may be remedied by an order for specific performance, since it is an equitable remedy and equity will not assist a volunteer; that is, it will not provide a remedy for someone who has given nothing.

Specific performance will be refused unless the plaintiff on his side has behaved fairly and the *principle of mutuality* is satisfied. This principle has two aspects, positive and negative.

(a)   As the purchaser of land may obtain an order for specific performance the same remedy is available to the vendor, although for him damages might be an adequate remedy.

(b)   If the plaintiff could not be ordered to perform the contract, for example, if he is a minor, the defendant will not be ordered to do so.

Exercise 10

Would specific performance of a contract for the sale of the Mona Lisa be likely to be ordered against the buyer?

Injunction

An injunction is (in this context) also a discretionary court order, requiring the defendant to observe a negative restriction of a contract. An injunction may be made even to enforce a contract of personal service for which specific performance would be refused.

Case: Warner Bros v Nelson 1937

N (the film star Bette Davis) agreed to work for a year for WB (film producers) and not during the year to work for any other film or stage producer nor 'to engage in any other occupation' without the consent of WB. N came to England during the year to work for a British film producer. WB sued for an injunction to restrain N from this work and N resisted arguing that if the restriction were enforced she must either work for WB (indirectly it would be an order for specific performance of a contract for personal service which should not be made) or abandon her livelihood.

Held: the court would not make an injunction if it would have the result suggested by N. But WB merely asked for an injunction to restrain N from working for a British film producer. This was one part of the restriction accepted by N under her contract and it was fair to hold her to it to that extent. But the court would not have enforced the 'any other occupation' restraint. Moreover, an English court would only have made an injunction restraining N from breaking her contract by taking other work in England.

An injunction is an equitable remedy limited to enforcement of contract terms which are in substance negative restraints. It is immaterial that the restraint, if negative in substance, is not so expressed.

Case: Metropolitan Electric Supply Co v Ginder 1901

G contracted to take all the electricity which he required from MES. MES sued for an injunction to restrain G from obtaining electricity from another supplier.

Held: the contract term (electricity only from MES) implied a negative restriction (no supplies from any other source) and to that extent it could be enforced by injunction.

But there must be a clear negative implication. An injunction would not be made merely to restrain the defendant from acts inconsistent with his positive obligations.

Case: Whitwood Chemical Co v Hardman 1891

H agreed to give the whole of his time to his employers, WC. In fact H occasionally worked for others. WC sued for an injunction to restrain him.

Held: by his contract H merely stated what he would do. This did not imply an undertaking to abstain from doing other things. (In *Nelson's* case above there was an express negative covenant; in *Ginder's* case it was an implied negative term of a commercial agreement. But the courts are wary of *implying* a negative restraint in a service agreement.)

Because the plaintiff may not be ultimately successful in the case, he must give an undertaking to pay damages to the defendant if he fails. This is to compensate the defendant for the prejudice caused by an interlocutory injunction.

Rescission

Strictly speaking the equitable right to rescind an agreement is not a remedy for breach of contract: it is a right which exists in certain circumstances, such as where a contract is voidable for misrepresentation, duress or undue influence.

Rescinding a contract means that it is cancelled or rejected and the parties are restored to their pre-contract condition, as if it had never been entered into.

BPP Publishing

Exercise 11

J will need 3,000 litres of liquid fertiliser over the next 12 months. He therefore contracts with K to purchase at least 2,500 litres over that period, at an agreed price which is less than the normal price because of the quantity involved. J then negotiates to buy 1,000 litres from L, so that he would only require 2,000 litres from K. K finds out about this before J makes a contract with L. Why would K not be able to obtain an injunction to ensure that J buys at least 2,500 litres from him?

10 Limitation to actions for breach

The right to sue for breach of contract becomes statute-barred after six years from the date on which the cause of action accrued, which is usually the date of the breach, not the date on which damage is suffered: s 5 Limitation Act 1980. The period is twelve years if the contract is by deed: s 8 Limitation Act 1980.

In two situations the six year period begins not at the date of the breach but later.

(a) If the plaintiff is a minor or under some other contractual disability (for example unsound mind) at the time of the breach of contract, the six year period begins to run only when his disability ceases or he dies, whichever is the earlier. If it has once begun to run it is not suspended by a subsequent disability: s 28.

(b) If the defendant or his agent conceals the right of action by fraud (which here denotes any conduct judged to be unfair by equitable standards) or if the action is for relief from the results of a mistake, the six year period begins to run only when the plaintiff discovered or could by reasonable diligence have discovered the fraud, concealment or mistake: s 32.

Where the claim can only be for the equitable reliefs of specific performance or injunction, the Limitation Act 1980 does not apply. Instead, the claim may be limited by the equitable doctrine of delay or 'laches'.

The limitation period may be extended if a debt, or any other certain monetary amount, is either acknowledged at any time or is paid in part before the original six (or twelve) years has expired: s 29. Hence if a debt accrues on 1 January 1985, the original limitation period expires on 31 December 1990. But if part payment is received on 1 January 1989, the debt is reinstated and does not then become 'statute barred' until 31 December 1994. The following conditions apply.

(a) *Acknowledgement*. The claim must be acknowledged as existing, not just as possible, but it need not be quantified. The acknowledgement must be in writing, signed by the debtor and addressed to the creditor: s 30.

(b) *Part payment*. To be effective, the part payment must be identifiable with the particular debt, not just a payment on a running account.

Exercise 12

R owes S £100. The debt is incurred on 1 July 1986, but S does not press R for payment and R forgets about the debt. On 1 July 1993, S reviews his records and discovers that the debt has never been paid. He writes to R asking for payment of 'the £500 you owe me'. R then remembers that in fact only £100 is owed, and he drafts a letter pointing out S's error. Should he send the letter?

11 Quasi-contract

In some circumstances where there is no contract the law seeks to achieve a just result by treating the persons concerned as if (*quasi* means 'as if') they had entered into a contract on the appropriate terms.

Quasi-contract relates only to the payment of money on the ground that retention of certain funds would be unjustified enrichment. No other sorts of obligation may be enforced by the law under this doctrine. Payments under quasi-contract may be:

(a)   the plaintiff paying the defendant for the defendant's use;

(b)   the plaintiff paying the defendant erroneously;

(c)   a third party paying the defendant erroneously on the plaintiff's behalf;

(d)   money paid in pursuance of an ineffective contract;

(e)   *quantum meruit*.

Examples of each of these are set out in turn below.

When the plaintiff pays money to the defendant for the latter's use and at his request, the plaintiff is entitled to its return. Alternatively, the plaintiff may recover money where:

(a)   he has paid money for which he was liable to a third party, but the real liability was on the defendant: for example, where an employee pays an on-the-spot fine for a company vehicle which is not taxed, he should be reimbursed by the employer; or

(b)   he pays money, under compulsion, to a third party and the money was owed by the defendant.

If X pays money to Y under a mistake of fact, Y is treated as if he had agreed to repay it.

Case: Norwich Union Fire Insurance Society v Price 1934
Insurers paid a claim in respect of damage to a cargo of fruit under the mistaken belief that the damage had been caused by sea water. In fact the cargo had begun to ripen so rapidly that it had been sold before it became rotten.

Held: the insurers could recover the sum which they had erroneously paid.

There is no obligation to repay money which has been paid under a mistake of law. It is often difficult, however, to distinguish mistakes of fact and of law. Money paid under a contract which is void can usually be recovered (unless the contract is also illegal).

An example of the third category would be where a third party pays money to the defendant, instructing that it be paid to the plaintiff, and the defendant promises to do so.

Where money has been paid over in pursuance of a contract which proves to be ineffective for some reason, it may have to be repaid. This could happen where:

(a)   the contract is void or illegal;

(b)   there has been total failure of consideration (for example, where a deposit is paid for a car that never materialises: the deposit can be recovered and damages may also be sought for breach);

(c)   the party in breach paid over some part of the contract price in part payment (*not* if he paid a deposit and then failed to perform).

We saw earlier how *quantum meruit* may be claimed as an alternative to damages for breach of contract. It may also be claimed in quasi-contract on the grounds that:

(a) the plaintiff has performed obligations under a contract which is void (for instance, a managing director claiming remuneration for services performed under his service contract which was void since the directors who approved it were not qualified to do so: *Craven-Ellis v Canons Ltd 1936*);

(b) at the defendant's request the plaintiff has performed tasks under a 'contract' which has not yet been finally agreed and which in the end falls through ('letter of intent' cases);

(c) necessaries have been supplied to minors, drunks or mentally disordered persons.

Exercise 13

An individual buys a radio receiver from a shop. He pays the shopkeeper an extra pound, under the impression that this is the price of a radio licence. In fact, radio licences were abolished several years ago and even when they existed, the fee was not paid to the seller of the radio. Has the buyer of the radio made a mistake of fact, a mistake of law or both?

Chapter roundup

(a) Complete and exact performance or tender thereof is generally required to discharge a contract by performance. If time is not of the essence, it may be made so by giving reasonable notice. In some cases, part payment may be recovered for incomplete performance.

(b) Contracts may be discharged by agreement, and each party normally gives consideration for being released from his obligations by releasing the other party.

(c) Repudiatory breach may be by refusal to perform, by failure to perform an entire obligation or by incapacitation. The party not in breach may treat the contract as repudiated, or may affirm the contract.

(d) In cases of anticipatory breach, the party not in breach may sue immediately or may wait to see whether the other party performs his obligations after all.

(e) A contract may be discharged by frustration when certain underlying conditions are no longer satisfied. However, changes not rendering performance impossible, or arising from one party's choices, do not discharge a contract by frustration.

(f) Losses will only be compensated by damages if they arise in the usual course of things or are within the reasonable contemplation of the parties. Damages are calculated so as to put the plaintiff in the position he would have been in if the contract had been performed. Liquidated damages will be enforced, but not penalty clauses.

(g) An action for the price is used when one party does not pay money due under the contract. Such an action is limited in its effects in cases of anticipatory breach.

(h) In cases of repudiatory breach, the party not in breach can choose between termination and affirmation of the contract.

(i) In cases of partial performance, damages may be claimed on a *quantum meruit* basis. The aim of an award is to put the plaintiff in the position he would have been in if the contract had never been made, so the profit he would have made is lost.

(j) Specific performance forces one party to perform his obligations under the contract. It will only be awarded when its enforcement is practicable. Like injunction, it is an equitable remedy. An injunction will only be granted to enforce an essentially negative restriction in a contract.

(k) Actions for breach of contract must normally be brought within six years of the breach occurring, although there are exceptions.

(l) Liability in quasi-contract arises in some cases where it is fair to impose liabilities on persons despite the absence of an actual contract.

BPP Publishing

Quick quiz

1   In what ways may a party to a contract be discharged from his obligations under it?

2   Is it a condition of a contract that it shall be performed at the appointed time?

3   In what circumstances may a party who has not completed the performance of his part of a contract be entitled to payment for what he has done?

4   How should money paid be applied to debts?

5   When must the principle of 'accord and satisfaction' be applied?

6   What types of repudiatory breach are there?

7   What are the alternatives open to an innocent party if the other party declares in advance that he will not perform his obligations?

8   Give three examples of circumstances by which a contract may be frustrated and one example of subsequent impossibility which does not frustrate and so discharge a contract.

9   What are the rules on payments to be made when a contract is discharged by frustration?

10 State the two heads of the rule in *Hadley v Baxendale*

11 What is the principle by which the court generally determines the amount payable as damages for breach of contract?

12 What is the duty to mitigate loss and on whom does it fall?

13 What is the difference between liquidated damages and a penalty for non-performance?

14 What are the effects of an innocent party's termination of a contract for repudiatory breach? What happens if the innocent party decides to affirm such a contract?

15 When may an injured party fail in an action for the price?

16 What is the purpose of a *quantum meruit* claim?

17 In what circumstances may the plaintiff obtain an order from the court requiring the defendant to perform his part of the contract?

18 On what principles will the court sometimes order the defendant not to commit a breach of contract?

19 What is meant by limitation? What are the limitation periods?

20 How may a limitation period be extended?

21 When would you expect payments to be made under quasi-contract?

Solutions to exercises

1   A has not given B a reasonable time to finish the work.

2   Q should state that the cheque is in settlement of the debt incurred on 4 January and £250 of the debt incurred on 20 January, otherwise the cheque will be applied to the debts incurred on 4 and 12 January and £80 of the debt incurred on 20 January.

3   K refuses to perform his contract with J, and K incapacitates himself in relation to his contract with L.

4   No: X may allow the contract to continue and see whether there is actual breach on the completion date.

5   Another lorry driver could have been hired: a lorry driver is not an artist hired for his unique talents, like a singer.

BPP Publishing

6   F will repay £(600 - 270) = £330 to G.

7   'If the broken shaft is not delivered to Greenwich on the next day after collection from Hadley, then Baxendale shall pay Hadley the sum of £10 for each day's delay, being the lost profits from the mill's being out of action.'

8   £100

9   G can reclaim £50 from H.

10   Yes, because it would be enforced against the seller.

11   An injunction will only be granted to enforce a negative restraint.

12   No: if he does so, he will have acknowledged the debt in writing and it will cease to be statute barred.

13   Both. It is a mistake of law to think that a radio licence is required, and a mistake of fact to think that the seller of a radio collects the fee.

BPP Publishing

9 AGENCY

Your objectives

After completing this chapter you should:

(a) understand how a relationship of agency may be created, both explicitly and by implication;

(b) understand when agency of necessity and statutory agency may arise;

(c) know the duties and rights of an agent;

(d) be aware of the different types of authority an agent may have;

(e) know the liabilities of principals and agents to third parties;

(f) understand the position of an agent acting for an undisclosed principal;

(g) know how an agency relationship may be terminated;

(h) understand the positions of certain special types of agent.

1   The creation of agency

The relationship of principal and agent is usually created by mutual consent. The consent need not generally be formal nor expressed in a written document. It is usually an express agreement even if informal. For example, P may ask A to take P's shoes to be repaired. P and A thereby expressly agree that A is to be P's agent in making a contract between P and the shoe repairer.

If the agent is to make a contract for his principal in the form of a deed, the agent must be formally appointed by a document called a power of attorney.

Agency may be created by consent which may be express, implied or retrospective (by ratification), by operation of law or by estoppel.

Implied agency

Two persons may by their relationship or their conduct to each other *imply* an agreement between them that one is the agent of the other. If, for example, an employee's duties include making contracts for his employer, say by ordering goods on his account, the employee is, by implied agreement, the agent of the employer for this purpose.

When a husband and wife live together it has in the past been usual for the wife to be responsible for obtaining household necessities such as food and clothing for herself and any children. In such matters it is implied that the husband has agreed that his wife is his agent with authority to order goods on credit, and he is liable to pay for them.

Agency by ratification

If A makes a contract on behalf of P at a time when A has no authority from P, the contract may later be ratified by P and then has retrospective effect to the time when A made the

BPP Publishing

contract. The principle of retrospective effect imposes the following conditions on agency by ratification.

(a) P must exist and have capacity to enter into the contract when it is made. For this reason a company cannot ratify a contract made on its behalf before the company is formed.

> *Case: Kelner v Baxter 1866*
> The promoters of a company to be formed to carry on an hotel business obtained stock in trade for the company from the plaintiff. The company which was formed three weeks later took over and sold the stock but failed to pay for it. The plaintiff sued the promoters who argued that they were merely agents of the company which had ratified the contract.
>
> *Held:* the company could not by ratification bind itself retrospectively to a contract made before it existed. The promoters were liable for breach of warranty of authority and must pay.

(b) In making the contract, the agent must act as agent for a principal who is named or otherwise identified as a party to the contract.

> *Case: Keighley Maxsted & Co v Durant 1900*
> An agent was authorised to buy wheat at 45/3 (£2.2625) per quarter from D. D would not sell for less than 45/6 (£2.275)and the agent bought at that price without disclosing that he was buying for a principal, KM. KM later purported to ratify the contract but failed to pay the agreed price. D sued KM on the contract.
>
> *Held:* where there is no immediate contract because the agent lacks authority, an undisclosed principal cannot adopt and ratify the contract. The principal must be capable of being ascertained at the time when the act was done *(Watson v Swann 1862)* if he is to be allowed to ratify the act afterwards.

(c) If the other party makes an offer which the agent accepts on behalf of his principal (without reservation on either side to the effect that this is subject to ratification by the principal) the principal need not ratify the contract but if he does it has retrospective effect. Hence the other party may withdraw his offer in the interval between its acceptance by the agent and the ratification by the principal.

The principal may only ratify if:

(a) he does so within a reasonable time after the agent has made the contract for him;

(b) he ratifies the whole contract and not merely parts of it;

(c) he communicates a sufficiently clear intention to ratify, either by express words or by conduct such as refusing to return goods purchased for him by an agent who lacked authority (mere passive inactivity does not amount to ratification);

(d) he is either fully informed of the terms of the contract or is prepared to ratify whatever the agent may have agreed to on his behalf.

Ratification relieves the agent of any liability for breach of warranty of authority and entitles him to claim from the principal any agreed remuneration for making the contract.

Exercise 1

David buys some coal, stating that he is acting as agent for Mary although she has not appointed him as her agent. The coal merchant lets him have two sacks of grade A coal at slightly below the market price because as part of the same contract he takes three sacks of grade B coal at slightly above the market price. When Mary learns of what has

BPP Publishing

happened, she tells the coal merchant that she will accept and pay for the grade A coal but not the grade B coal. Can the coal merchant prevent her from doing this?

Agency of necessity

By operation of law a principal may be bound by a contract made on his behalf but without his consent. This rule is of very restricted application and is generally confined to carriers, by sea or land, of goods. The principle applies when:

(a)   P entrusts goods to A for some purpose such as transporting them to a distant destination;

(b)   while the goods are in A's possession some emergency arises in which action must be taken to protect the goods;

(c)   it is not possible for A to communicate with P to obtain his instructions within the time available; and

(d)   A takes action which is reasonable to protect P's interests and not merely for the convenience of A.

When these conditions are satisfied, P is bound by any liability which A undertakes on his behalf, since an *agency of necessity* has arisen. Note that there must be an existing contractual relationship: a person cannot become the agent of necessity of another by taking charge of his property uninvited: *Jebara v Ottoman Bank 1927*.

Case: Great Northern Railway v Swaffield 1874
S delivered a horse to a railway company for transport to another station but failed to collect it on arrival as agreed. The railway company claimed from S the cost of feeding and stabling the horse arguing that if it had delivered the horse to a stable that would have been a contract made under agency of necessity and S would be bound to pay.

Held: the railway company's claim would be upheld for the reasons given.

Case: Sachs v Miklos 1948
M agreed to store furniture which belonged to S. After a considerable time had elapsed M needed the storage space for his own use. He tried to contact S to get the furniture removed but was unable to trace S. M then sold the furniture. S sued M for conversion and M pleaded agency of necessity in making the sale.

Held: there was no agency of necessity since no emergency had arisen and M had sold the furniture for his own convenience. If M's house had been destroyed by fire and the furniture left in the open M would then have been justified in selling it.

In certain circumstances agency of necessity can create agency where none existed previously, for example between the master of a ship and the owner of cargo being transported on that ship: *The Winson 1982*.

Statutory agency

It is convenient to mention here statutory rules which treat A as the agent of P without the latter's consent, but these are not cases of agency of necessity.

(a)   A repairer of goods which the owner fails to collect after due notice has been given may sell them: Disposal of Uncollected Goods Act 1952.

(b)   If A agrees to supply goods to X and A first transfers the goods to P, so that P may let them to X under a hire purchase agreement, then A is the agent of P if the hire purchase agreement falls under the Consumer Credit Act 1974.

135

Agency by estoppel

If P leads X to believe that A is P's agent, and X deals with A on that basis, P is bound by the contract with X which A has made on his behalf. This situation may arise:

(a) when A, who dealt with X as P's authorised agent, continues to do so after his authority as agent of P has been terminated but X is unaware of the termination;

(b) when A, to P's knowledge, enters into transactions with X as if A were P's agent and P fails to inform X that A is not P's agent.

Agency by estoppel can only arise where the conduct of the apparent *principal* creates it. Agency does not arise by estoppel if it is the putative agent who holds himself out as agent, not the putative principal: *Armagas v Mundogas, The Ocean Frost 1986*.

Exercise 2

Why is agency of necessity now unlikely to arise when goods are transported within Western Europe on behalf of a major company based in London?

---

2 The duties of an agent

When an agent agrees to perform services for his principal for reward there is a contract between them. But even if the agent undertakes his duties without reward he has obligations to his principal. The agent's duties are listed below.

(a) *Performance*. The agent who agrees to act as agent for reward has a contractual obligation to perform his agreed task.

> *Case: Turpin v Bilton 1843*
> A broker agreed to arrange insurance of his principal's ships but failed to do so. A ship was lost at sea.
>
> *Held:* the broker was liable to make good the loss.

An unpaid agent is not bound to carry out his agreed duties, because there is no consideration. Any agent may refuse to perform an illegal act.

(b) *Skill*. A paid agent undertakes to maintain the standard of skill and care to be expected of a person in his profession. For example, an accountant has a duty to his client to show the skill and care of a competent accountant. An unpaid agent if he acts as agent (which he need not do) must show the skill and care which people ordinarily use in managing their own affairs.

(c) *Personal performance*. The agent is presumably selected because of his personal qualities and owes a duty to perform his task himself and not to delegate it to another. But he may delegate in a few special circumstances, if delegation is necessary. Thus a solicitor acting for a client would be obliged to instruct a stockbroker to buy or sell securities on the Stock Exchange.

(d) *Accountability*. An agent must both provide full information to his principal of his agency transactions and account to him for all moneys arising from them.

(e) *No conflict of interest*. The agent owes to his principal a duty not to put himself in a situation where his own interests conflict with those of the principal; for example, he must not sell his own property to the principal, even if the sale is at a fair price.

Case: Armstrong v Jackson 1917
A client instructed his stockbroker to buy for him 600 shares of X Ltd. The broker sold to his client 600 shares which he himself owned.

Held: the sale was made in breach of the broker's duty and would be set aside.

(f)   *Confidence.* The agent must keep in confidence what he knows of his principal's affairs even after the agency relationship has ceased.

(g)   *Any benefit* must be handed over to the principal unless he agrees that the agent may retain it. Although an agent is entitled to his agreed remuneration, he must account to the principal for any other benefits. If he accepts from the other party any commission or reward as an inducement to make the contract with him, that is a bribe and the contract is fraudulent. The agent may be dismissed.

Case: Boston Deep Sea Fishing & Ice Co v Ansell 1888
A, who was managing director of the plaintiff company, accepted commissions from suppliers on orders which he placed with them for goods supplied to the company. He was dismissed and the company sued to recover the commissions from him.

Held: the company was justified in dismissing A and he must account to it for the commissions.

Even if the agent has acted honestly throughout and substantial benefits have accrued to the principal, the agent may not keep any benefit: *Boardman v Phipps 1967.*

The principal who discovers that his agent has accepted a bribe may:

(a)   dismiss the agent;

(b)   recover the amount of the bribe from him (as in *Ansell's* case);

(c)   refuse to pay him his agreed remuneration, and recover amounts already paid;

(d)   repudiate the contract with the third party;

(e)   sue both the agent and the third party who paid the bribe to recover damages for any loss. He may not recover any more than this so he may not, for instance, recover both the bribe from the agent and compensation from the third party so as to make a profit: *Mahesan v Malaysian Government Officers' Cooperative Housing Society Ltd 1978*;

(f)   seek prosecution of the agent under the Prevention of Corruption Act 1916.

Exercise 3

P appoints A as his agent, and pays A £100 for his services. P requires A to buy some explosives and to deliver them to a certain address, allegedly so that they can be used in mining. A discovers that they are actually to be used in a bank robbery. Must A carry out P's instructions, given that P has provided consideration?

---

3   The rights of an agent

The agent is entitled to be repaid his expenses and to be indemnified by his principal against losses and liabilities *(Hichens, Harrison, Woolston & Co v Jackson & Sons 1943)*. These rights are limited to acts of the agent done properly within the limits of his authority. If he acts in an unauthorised manner or negligently he loses his entitlement. He may recover expenses properly paid even if he was not legally bound to pay: for example, a solicitor who pays counsel's fees (which the counsel cannot recover at law) may reclaim this expense from his client.

The agent is also entitled to be paid any agreed remuneration for his services by his principal. The amount may have been expressly agreed or it may be implied, for example by trade or professional practice. If it is agreed that the agent is to be remunerated but the amount has not been fixed, the agent is entitled to a reasonable amount. However, a right to remuneration is not implied in every agreement.

> *Case: Way v Latilla 1937*
> An agent undertook to provide information on gold mines in West Africa. No remuneration had been agreed.
>
> *Held:* in the circumstances an agreement that there should be remuneration was implied and £5,000 was a reasonable sum to award.

Estate agents

There is a considerable body of case law on the claims of estate agents for their agreed remuneration although the property has not been sold or has been sold to a purchaser not introduced by the agent. Unless the contract states very clearly a contrary intention, the courts are inclined to hold that the parties intended commission to be paid only out of the proceeds of an actual sale to a purchaser introduced by the agent. The following matters in particular have been considered.

(a)   The principal is entitled to withdraw from the transaction: there is no implied term that he will not prevent the agent from earning his commission.

(b)   The principal may agree to pay a fee to the agent if he is able 'to find a purchaser' or 'find a person willing and able to purchase'. If a purchaser introduced by the agent then enters into a binding contract to purchase, the agent has earned his fee. If however, the purchaser whom he introduces merely makes a conditional offer to purchase, for example 'subject to contract' or 'subject to survey', the agent has not found a purchaser in the strict sense. It is doubtful whether even an unconditional offer makes the offeror a purchaser or a person willing and able to purchase. But if he does not withdraw his offer it may suffice.

> *Case: Christie, Owen and Davies v Rapacioli 1974*
> The purchaser made an offer and later paid a deposit and signed his copy of the contract. The vendors then withdrew. The agent claimed his fee for having introduced 'a person ready able and willing to purchase'.
>
> *Held:* on these facts the agent had earned his fee.

Exercise 4

A stockbroker buys shares on behalf of a client with whom he has no other connection, but owing to an oversight no prior agreement was made about the stockbroker's fees. Is it likely that the stockbroker would be able to claim a fee, and if so how might it be computed?

4 The authority of an agent

A contract made by an agent is binding on the principal and the other party only if the agent was acting within the limits of his authority. We must distinguish actual from apparent authority.

Actual authority

The *actual authority* of an agent is the authority which the principal agrees he shall have. The actual authority may be either *express* or implied from the nature of the agent's activities, from what is usual in the circumstances and so on.

The basis of *implied incidental authority* is that the principal, by appointing an agent to act in a particular capacity, gives him authority to make those contracts which are a necessary or normal incident of the agent's activities. It may cover such things as the authority to advertise when given express authority to sell goods.

Implied usual (or customary) authority is that which an agent operating in a particular market or business usually has.

Between principal and agent the latter's express authority is paramount; the agent cannot contravene the principal's express instructions by claiming that he had implied authority to act in the way he did. But as far as third parties are concerned, they are entitled to assume that the agent has implied usual authority unless they know to the contrary.

> *Case: Watteau v Fenwick 1893*
> The owner of a hotel (F) employed the previous owner H to manage it. F forbade H to buy cigars on credit but H did buy cigars from W. W sued F who argued that he was not bound by the contract, since H had no actual authority to make it, and that W believed that H still owned the hotel.
>
> *Held:* it was within the usual authority of a manager of a hotel to buy cigars on credit and F was bound by the contract (although W did not even know that H was the agent of F) since his restriction of usual authority had not been communicated.

Apparent authority

The apparent (or ostensible) authority of an agent is that which his principal represents to other persons (with whom the agent deals) that he has given to the agent. As a result an agent with limited express or usual actual authority can be held in practice to have a more extensive authority.

Apparent authority is not restricted to what is usual and incidental. The principal may expressly or by his conduct confer on the agent any amount of exceptional apparent authority. For example a partner has considerable but limited implied authority merely by virtue of being a partner. If, however, the other partners allow him to exercise a greater authority than is implied, they represent that he has it and they are bound by the contracts which he makes within the limits of this apparent authority.

For apparent authority to be created so as to bind the principal where the third party acted on it the following conditions must be met.

(a) There must be representations or holding out by the principal or by an agent acting on his behalf (*not* by the agent claiming apparent authority: *Armagas v Mundogas, The Ocean Frost 1986*).

(b) The representation must be one of fact.

(c) The third party must rely on that representation.

BPP Publishing

Exercise 5

P authorises A to buy 400 personal computers on his behalf, but instructs A confidentially not to pay more than £2,000 for any one computer. A becomes well known among computer dealers in the area as a buyer of computers for P. A buys one computer for £3,000. Must P pay for the computer?

---

5 Liability of the parties

A principal is generally liable to the third party for contracts formed by his agent within the latter's actual or apparent authority. He must therefore perform his side of the bargain.

Liability of principal for agent's fraud, torts or misrepresentations

Although apparent authority does not in itself create an agency relationship (though agency by estoppel is similar) it does mean that the alleged principal is bound even if the acts are entered into for the agent's own purposes or are fraudulent. This also applies to fraudulent acts carried out by the agent within his *actual* authority.

The principle of vicarious liability for torts is well established in employment law. It states that an employer is liable for the torts of his employee where the torts are committed in the course of his employment. Vicarious liability also applies to principals where there is no employment relationship but where the agent is acting within the limits of his or her apparent authority. Hence a principal is liable for misrepresentation and the torts of deceit, negligence and so on which are committed by an agent acting within his apparent authority. In such a case the principal can claim an indemnity from his agent if he has had to compensate a third party: *Lister v Romford Ice and Cold Storage Co Ltd 1957*.

Liability of the agent

An agent contracting for his principal within his actual and/or apparent authority generally has no liability on the contract and is not entitled to enforce it. However, the agent will be personally liable and can enforce it:

(a) when he intended to undertake personal liability, as where he signs a contract as party to it without signifying that he is an agent. In particular, he will be liable on a cheque which he signs without indicating his agency status: s 26 Bills of Exchange Act 1882. Thus a director should sign cheques 'K Black, for and on behalf of XYZ Ltd';

(b) where the principal was undisclosed (see below);

(c) where it is usual business practice or trade custom for an agent to be liable and entitled; for example, an advertising agent is liable to the media for contracts made on its client's behalf;

(d) where the agent is acting on his own behalf even though he purports to act for a principal (as in *Kelner v Baxter 1866*, where the agents thought they were acting on behalf of a company principal which was not yet in existence). This applies to any cases of agents acting for fictitious or non-existent principals;

(e) where the agent contracts by deed without having a power of attorney from the principal.

Where an agent enters into a collateral contract with the third party with whom he has contracted on the principal's behalf, there is separate liability and entitlement to enforcement on that collateral contract.

It can happen that there is joint liability of agent and principal. This is usually the case where an agent did not disclose that he acted for a principal, and is discussed below.

Breach of warranty of authority

An agent who exceeds his apparent authority will generally have no liability to his principal, since the latter will not be bound by the unauthorised contract made for him. But the agent will be liable in such a case to the third party for breach of warranty of authority.

If A purports to enter into a contract with X on behalf of P, A warrants to X that P exists and has capacity to enter into the contract, and that A has authority from P to make the contract for him. If any of these implied statements proves to be untrue, then (unless P ratifies the contract) X may claim damages from A for his loss, provided that X was unaware that A had no authority to make the contract. A is liable even though he was himself unaware that he lacked authority, for example because P had died.

Exercise 6

Joan purports to act as an agent for Daphne, even though Daphne has not asked her to do so and does not wish her to do so. Geoff is aware of these facts, although Daphne has not told him of the position. Joan buys some goods from Geoff 'as agent for Daphne', but fails to pay for them. Daphne also fails to pay for the goods. Why can Geoff not sue Joan for breach of warranty of authority?

---

6 Agents acting for undisclosed principals

If a person enters into a contract apparently on his own account as principal but in fact as agent on behalf of a principal, the doctrine of the undisclosed principal determines the position of the parties.

If the contract is not performed as agreed the third party may, on discovering the true facts:

(a) hold the agent personally bound by the contract (as the agent appeared to be contracting on his own account); *or*

(b) elect to treat the principal as the other party to the contract.

But he must elect for one or the other within a reasonable time of discovering the facts, and cannot sue both principal and agent: *Chestertons v Barone 1987*. It appears that the third party who commences legal proceedings against either agent or principal may withdraw (before judgement is given) in order to sue the other: *Clarkson Booker Ltd v Andjel 1964*. If, however, he obtains judgement against one of the principal and the agent he cannot sue the other even if the judgement is unsatisfied.

The undisclosed principal will usually intervene and enforce the contract on his own behalf against the other party since it is really his contract, not the agent's. Until such time as the principal takes this action, the agent himself may sue the third party (since he is treated as the other party to the contract).

The undisclosed principal's right to intervene in a contract made by his agent is limited to those contracts which the agent was authorised to make as agent. The principal cannot ratify an unauthorised act or seek to take over the agent's contract without the third party's consent: *Keighley, Maxsted & Co v Durant 1900*.

The undisclosed principal is also prevented from taking over a contract:

(a) where the agent, when making the contract, expressly denied that a principal was involved (this is misrepresentation);

(b)   where the contract terms are such that agency is implicitly denied:

> *Case: Humble v Hunter 1848*
> The principal (P) authorised his agent (A) to charter out his ship. A contracted with a third party for the charter of the vessel, describing himself as 'owner' of it.
>
> *Held:* the principal could not enforce the contract against the third party because the agent had implied that he was the owner and hence the principal. P's ownership contradicted the contract's terms;

(c)   where the identity of the parties is material to the third party, that is, where the third party wanted to contract with the agent and would not have contracted at all if he had known of the identity of the principal.

> *Case: Said v Butt 1920*
> A theatre critic, X, had a disagreement with the manager of a particular theatre and had been banned from attending there. He wanted to see the first night of a new play at the theatre and so asked Y, whom the manager did not know to be connected with X, to obtain a ticket for him. X was refused admission on the ticket.
>
> *Held:* X's identity was of great importance to the theatre and it would not have contracted with Y if it had known that X was his undisclosed principal. X could not enforce the contract.

Exercise 7

X plc requires some tax advice. The managing director asks Natalie, a highly respected specialist, to prepare a report for the company. She agrees to do so, but does not mention that she is in fact acting as agent for Paul, securing tax advice work for him. The managing director of X plc, on discovering this, refuses to accept Paul's services. Could Paul enforce the contract against the company?

---

7   Termination of agency

Agency is terminated by *act of the parties* in the following ways.

(a)   If an agent is employed for a particular transaction, such as sale of a house, he ceases to be an agent when the transaction is completed. In the same way, agency for a fixed period ends with the expiry of the period.

(b)   Either party may give notice to the other or they may mutually agree to terminate the agency. But certain types of agency are irrevocable.

(i)   Where the agent has 'authority coupled with an interest' and the agency has been created to protect his interests, for instance, where a debtor appoints his creditor as agent to sell the debtor's property and recover the debt from the proceeds, the principal cannot terminate the agency.

(ii)   Where the agent has begun to perform his duties and has incurred liability the principal cannot terminate the agency.

(iii)   Statute declares some agencies to be irrevocable, such as powers of attorney for a limited period expressed to be irrevocable, and powers of attorney under the Enduring Powers of Attorney Act 1985.

Agency is terminated by operation of law (with some exceptions for irrevocable agencies) by:

(a)   the death of principal or agent;

(b)   the insanity of principal or agent;

(c)   the bankruptcy of the principal, and also the bankruptcy of the agent if, as is likely, it renders him incapable of performing his duties;

(d)   frustration, for example by the agency becoming unlawful because the principal has become an enemy alien.

The termination of agency only affects the principal and agent at first, as it brings the actual authority of the agent to an end. Third parties who knew of the agency are entitled to enforce (against the principal) any later contracts made by the former agent until they are actually or constructively informed that the agency has been terminated.

For example, when a partner retires from a firm he remains an apparent member and liable on contracts of the firm made after his retirement with persons who knew him to be a partner, when he was one, until notice of his retirement has been given to those persons. Therefore, a retiring partner should advertise his retirement generally and ensure that existing suppliers and customers are actually informed of his retirement. General advertisement ensures that persons who first dealt with the firm *after* the partner's retirement cannot claim that the partner was still *apparently* a member.

Termination of agency by insanity of the principal has produced two conflicting decisions and the law is obscure.

Case: Drew v Nunn 1879
A husband when sane represented that his wife had authority to buy goods on credit as his agent. He became insane but the wife continued to buy goods from the same supplier. On recovering his sanity the husband refused to pay for the goods on the grounds that his insanity (although unknown to the supplier) had terminated the wife's authority as agent.

Held: insanity had terminated the agency as between husband and wife, but the husband was estopped from denying that his representation (that the wife was his agent) was true and must pay for the goods.

Case: Yonge v Toynbee 1910
Solicitors were instructed to defend an action on behalf of a client who later, unknown to the solicitors, became insane.

Held: the solicitors were liable to the plaintiff for breach of warranty of authority.

The Enduring Powers of Attorney Act 1985 provides that a power of attorney in the prescribed form may continue in force even though the principal becomes insane. But this procedure does not alter the law on other agency arrangements as described above.

Exercise 8

A buyer of land gives his solicitor power of attorney to sign both the contract to buy the land and a mortgage deed needed to obtain funds for the purchase. Why would the solicitor be likely to insist on an irrevocable power of attorney?

---

8 Special types of agent

Del credere agents

A *del credere* agent undertakes (in return for extra commission) responsibility for due payment of the contract price by persons whom he introduces to his principal. He undertakes that a buyer will pay for goods delivered to him but not that he will accept the goods. It is a form of financial support which is convenient where the other party's creditworthiness is unknown to the principal. A factor who sells goods on credit terms, or an advertising agent who obtains orders (for advertisements to be published in the media) may assume this liability.

A *del credere* agent undertakes to indemnify his principal against loss. The undertaking is not a guarantee and so it may be enforced without need of written evidence.

Factors or mercantile agents

A *factor* (also called a 'mercantile agent') is a person whose ordinary business is to sell goods, or consign them for sale, or to buy goods, or to raise money on the security of goods: Factors Act 1889. His principal gives him implied authority to enter into such transactions and usually gives him possession of the goods. A simple example is a motor dealer to whom the owner of a vehicle delivers the vehicle (and registration book) with authority to sell it.

A factor when in possession of goods has wider authority than an ordinary agent. When an ordinary agent has possession of goods for sale, his apparent authority is no greater than the actual authority given to him by the principal. But a factor in possession of goods, or documents of title to goods, with the consent of the owner, may sell, pledge or otherwise dispose of them so as to bind the owner (in excess of the actual authority given by him) provided that:

(a)   the factor acts in the ordinary course of his business; and

(b)   the other party acts in good faith and is unaware that the agent is exceeding his authority: Factors Act 1889 s 2.

> *Case: Folkes v King 1923*
> F delivered his car to H, a motor dealer, with instructions to sell it at a price not less than £575. The dealer sold to K (in circumstances as described above) for £340.
>
> *Held:* although the dealer had no actual authority to sell below £575 F was bound by the contract.

The purpose of the rule is to protect persons who deal with factors in ignorance of their lack of actual authority. However, the rule only applies when the goods (or documents of title) are voluntarily delivered to the factor for some purpose incidental to his business (of sale, purchase or pledging). The principal is bound even though the factor then sells or pledges without authority.

> *Case: Lloyds Bank Ltd v Bank of America National Trust 1938*
> A mercantile agent deposited commercial documents with a bank as a pledge. Later the bank allowed him to recover the documents under a 'trust receipt': he was authorised to deal with the documents but undertook to hold the proceeds in trust for the bank. He then fraudulently pledged them to another bank. The two banks both claimed the documents.
>
> *Held:* for the purpose of applying the rule, the first bank must be regarded as the 'owner'. It had given the factor possession with a view to a sale, a disposition in the course of his

144

business. The second bank (which had been unaware of the fraud) therefore had good title.

Exercise 9

F, a factor, and G his accomplice agree to act as follows. F will obtain possession of goods belonging to H, with H's consent. F will then sell the goods to G at below their market value. When H finds out what has happened, F will disappear with the proceeds and G will be left with good title to goods which he has obtained cheaply. Why will this scheme not succeed?

Brokers

There are many kinds of broker in different trades. Any broker is essentially a middleman or intermediary who arranges contracts in return for commission or brokerage. He does not usually have possession of the goods and (unlike a factor) does not deal in his own name. When a contract has been arranged he sends a 'bought note' to the buyer and a 'sold note' to the seller which evidences the existence and terms of the contract.

If a broker, even innocently, makes a contract for the sale of goods by a person who has no right to sell, the broker is liable for the tort of conversion.

Case: Hollins v Fowler 1875
The subject matter was cotton purchased through a broker from a seller who had no title. The broker merely received a commission.

Held: the true owner could recover, as damages from the broker, the full value of the cotton.

A broker may be subject to rules or trade custom. By employing such a broker the principal gives implied consent to these rules even if unaware of them.

A *confirming house* is an intermediary between a foreign buyer and a UK exporter. The exporter may know nothing of the buyer or his credit rating. The buyer employs the confirming house as guarantor and it assumes responsibility for payment of the price when the goods are shipped. It may also attend to the export formalities (customs declarations and so on) and arrange for the goods to be shipped.

An *estate agent* is an intermediary who seeks to find a buyer of a house or other property belonging to his principal. This profession is regulated by the Estate Agents Act 1979 which among other things requires an estate agent to give notice of his charges to his principal and to insure against liability for loss of any deposit paid by a buyer to the agent pending completion of the sale.

Unless the contract between principal and agent explicitly provides otherwise, the estate agent is only entitled to his commission out of the proceeds of a sale to a buyer introduced by him. He cannot have reward or compensation if the seller finds a buyer by other means or withdraws the property after a buyer has been found but before a contract of sale is agreed.

An *insurance broker* is an agent of an insurer who arranges contracts of insurance with the other party who wishes to be insured. However, in some contexts (for example, when the broker assists a car owner to complete a proposal form) he is also treated as the agent of the insured. Insurance, especially marine insurance, has complicated rules applicable to the relationships between the insurer, the broker and the insured.

Auctioneers

An auctioneer is an agent who is authorised to sell property at auction, usually in a room or place to which the public has access. He is the agent of the vendor. An auctioneer should sell only for cash (though he may accept payment by cheque). He may receive a deposit in part payment but may only pay it over to the vendor if the purchaser consents or if he defaults on the contract.

An auctioneer warrants that he has authority to sell to the highest bidder unless he announces that the seller has set a 'reserve price' (will withdraw the property if that price is not reached). He does not of course disclose what that price is. If the seller has set a reserve price and the auctioneer fails to say so, then the property must be sold to the highest bidder (and the vendor as principal will recover the deficiency from the auctioneer).

An auctioneer, like a broker, is liable in conversion to the true owner if he sells property on behalf of a principal who has no right to sell.

Bankers

The duties owed by a bank to its customer are similar to those owed by an agent, but the banker-customer contract is not one of agency in the normal run of things, such as in the operation of a current account.

Banks often do act as agents for their customers: examples are where they undertake to arrange dealings in shares or where they offer advice on investments such as life assurance and pensions.

Two difficult points arise in connection with banks' agency role.

(a) The giving of investment advice is now regulated by the Financial Services Act 1986, which (among other things) extends the financial agent's duty not to obtain reward without disclosure to the principal. Commission rates and the benefits accruing to group companies must therefore be disclosed.

(b) Many banks are financial conglomerates offering, for example, corporate finance as well as normal banking services. This situation can lead to a conflict of interest for the bank as agent, as when it is operating a company's current account while advising a predator on its takeover. This conflict must be resolved by agreement or withdrawal.

Exercise 10

The tort of conversion is any action in connection with goods which denies or is inconsistent with the true owner's title to the goods. Explain how the actions of brokers and auctioneers noted above as amounting to conversion fit this definition.

Chapter roundup

(a) An agency relationship may be created expressly, or it may be implied.

(b) A principal may, subject to certain conditions, ratify a contract made by an agent acting without authority.

(c) Agency of necessity may arise in an emergency. Agency may also arise by statute, and a principal may be estopped from denying that someone is his agent.

(d) An agent must in general perform his duties personally, and with an appropriate degree of skill. He is entitled to his agreed remuneration, but not to any other benefits.

BPP Publishing

(e) An agent also has a right to be paid his expenses and to be indemnified for losses and liabilities. There is case law on the right of estate agents to their fees.

(f) An agent's actual authority may be express or implied, and implied authority may be incidental or usual (customary). Apparent authority is the authority which third parties are led to believe the agent has.

(g) A principal is liable on contracts made by his agent within the agent's actual or apparent authority, and for the agent's misrepresentations and torts within his apparent authority. The agent is only personally liable on contracts in certain special circumstances, but he may be liable to third parties for breach of warranty of authority.

(h) Where an agency relationship is not disclosed, a third party may hold either the agent or the principal liable on a contract. An undisclosed principal's right to take over a contract may be limited.

(i) An agency may be terminated by the conclusion of the relevant transaction, by notice (although some types of agency are irrevocable) or by operation of law. Third parties need to be informed to ensure that the termination is effective.

(j) Special rules apply to *del credere* agents, to factors (mercantile agents), to brokers, to auctioneers and to bankers.

Quick quiz

1   How may an agency relationship be created?

2   Under what conditions may a person ratify a contract made without his authority but on his behalf?

3   In what circumstances may one person be an agent of necessity for another?

4   When may agency by estoppel arise?

5   What duties does an agent owe to his principal? What are the agent's rights?

6   Distinguish actual and apparent authority of an agent.

7   What is breach of warranty of authority?

8   When may an agent be liable under a contract made for a disclosed principal?

9   When is an undisclosed principal prevented from taking over a contract?

10   How may agency be terminated?

11   When has a factor wider powers than an ordinary agent?

12   Why would a buyer employ a confirming house?

13   How may an auctioneer's authority be limited?

14   What problems are encountered by a bank acting as agent of its customer?

Solutions to exercises

1   Yes: Mary must ratify the whole contract, not just part of it.

2   The carrier of the goods will usually be able to communicate with the owner.

3   No: any agent may refuse to perform an illegal act (such as facilitating a bank robbery).

4   Yes: the stockbroker's usual scale of fees could be applied.

5   Yes: A has apparent authority to buy computers, and the limitation to £2,000 per computer has not been publicised.

6   Geoff was aware of Joan's lack of authority.

7   No: the identity of the adviser is material to X plc.

8   The solicitor must ensure that funds will be available to complete the contract, and would not want to exchange contracts and then have his power to sign the mortgage deed revoked.

9   G will not get good title because he will not have bought the goods from F in good faith.

10   If a broker or auctioneer sells goods on behalf of a principal with no right to sell, he is purporting to pass title to the buyer, which denies the true owner's title.

BPP Publishing

10 SALE OF GOODS

Your objectives

After completing this chapter you should:

(a)   know what constitutes a sale of goods;

(b)   be able to define existing, future, specific and ascertained goods;

(c)   know how the price for goods may be fixed;

(d)   know what terms are implied by the Sale of Goods Act 1979;

(e)   know when time is of the essence;

(f)   appreciate the significance of the seller's title and the consequences of defective title;

(g)   know what is meant by the description of goods, and the implied conditions in a sale by sample;

(h)   know what is meant by merchantable quality and by fitness for purpose;

(i)   know when property and risk pass to the buyer;

(j)   understand the rule *nemo dat quod non habet* and the exceptions to it;

(k)   be aware of the rules on delivery;

(l)   be aware of the limits on the buyer's right to reject the goods;

(m)   know what remedies the parties may have against each other;

(n)   appreciate the effect of the Supply of Goods and Services Act 1982.

Statutory references in this chapter are to the Sale of Goods Act 1979 unless otherwise noted.

---

1   Definition of a contract for the 'sale of goods'

The main statute on the sale of goods is the Sale of Goods Act 1979. The Unfair Contract Terms Act 1977 restricts the use of contract terms which exclude the 1979 Act conditions. The Supply of Goods and Services Act 1982 for the most part extends the terms of the 1979 Act to contracts for the supply of services.

A contract for the sale of goods is defined in s 2(1) of the 1979 Act as:

'a contract by which the seller transfers, or agrees to transfer, the property in goods to a buyer for a money consideration, called the price'

Sale includes both an immediate sale, such as purchase of goods in a shop, and an agreement by which the seller is to transfer ownership (in this context called 'property') in goods to the buyer at a future date.

BPP Publishing

2 Types of goods

The rules on sale of goods make the following distinctions.

(a) *Existing goods* are those which exist and are owned by the seller at the time when the contract is made. *Future goods* are those which do not exist or which the seller does not yet own when he contracts to sell them.

(b) *Specific goods* are those which are identified as the goods to be sold at the time when the contract is made, such as 'my Ford Escort, registration no H123 ABC'. Goods which are not specific are unascertained and become *ascertained goods* when they are subsequently identified as the goods to be sold under the contract.

The main point of these distinctions is that property, that is ownership, cannot usually pass from seller to buyer unless, or until, the goods exist as specific or ascertained goods.

Goods which have perished

In a contract for sale of specific goods there are rules laid down regarding the contract's status if the goods are perishable.

(a) If, unknown to the seller, the goods have perished at the time when the contract is made, the contract is void: s 6.

(b) If the goods perish after the contract is made, without fault of either party and before the risk passes to the buyer, the contract is avoided: s 7.

In addition to simple destruction, goods may 'perish' when they deteriorate to such an extent as to lose their commercial identity. The case law is concerned mainly with rotting of produce; it is a question of degree as to when they perish.

Case: H R & S Sainsbury v Street 1972
S agreed to sell a 275 ton crop of barley to be grown on his farm to H. Due to general adverse conditions, his crop failed and only 140 tons were yielded. These he sold at a higher price to a third party.

Held: although 135 tons of produce had perished so that the contract in that respect was frustrated, S should have offered the remainder to the plaintiff. Hence the contract as a whole had not been avoided.

Exercise 1

A agrees to sell a car to B on hire purchase. B must pay regular hire charges for two years, and at the end of that period B will have an option to buy the car on payment of a further sum. Why is this not a contract for the sale of goods within the meaning of the Sale of Goods Act 1979?

---

3 The price

The definition states that there should be 'a money consideration, called the price'. This means that an exchange (barter) for other goods does not give rise to a sale of goods. However, provided some money changes hands, as with a trade-in arrangement for a car, there is a contract for the sale of goods even though goods are also given. But there can be complications regarding 'money consideration'.

Case: Esso v Commissioners of Customs & Excise 1976
With every four gallons of petrol purchased from it Esso promised to give away a free World Cup coin. Customs & Excise argued that this constituted a sale of goods and that therefore Esso had to pay purchase tax (now abolished) on all the World Cup coins it bought and gave away.

Held: there was a valid contract in respect of the World Cup coins, in that Esso had offered to give them away and any customer who purchased four gallons of petrol thereby accepted that offer and could enforce the contract. However, it was accepted that it was not a contract of sale, since the customer gave not a money consideration in return but a separate contract (for the purchase of petrol). There were two contracts, the one for the coins being a collateral contract to the one for the sale of petrol. The collateral contract was not one for the sale of goods.

The price may be fixed by the contract or in a manner set out in the contract, such as the ruling market price on the day of delivery, or by the course of dealing between the parties. If there is no agreed price, a reasonable price must be paid: s 8.

Case: Foley v Classique Coaches 1934
A bus company agreed to purchase its petrol from F 'at a price to be agreed in writing from time to time'; any dispute between the parties was to be submitted to arbitration. For three years the bus company purchased its petrol from F at the current price but there was no formal agreement on price. The bus company then repudiated the agreement arguing that it was incomplete since it was an agreement to agree on the price.

Held: in view of the course of dealing between the parties and the arbitration clause there was an agreement that a reasonable price (at any given time) should be paid. The agreement was therefore enforceable.

A reasonable price must be paid for goods delivered and accepted if a third party to whom the fixing of the price is delegated fails to do so.

4   Terms implied by the Sale of Goods Act 1979

One of the main functions of the Sale of Goods Act 1979 is to codify the terms implied into contracts of sale. As noted above, these have largely evolved from case-law. Much depends on whether an implied term is a condition or a warranty, and on whether one party to the contract is dealing as a consumer. The rules are set out below.

A sale of goods may be subject to statutory rules on:

(a)   the effect of delay in performance (s 10);

(b)   title, or the seller's right to sell the goods (s 12);

(c)   the description of the goods (s 13);

(d)   sale by sample (s 15).

(e)   the quality of the goods (s 14);

(f)   the fitness of the goods for the purpose for which they are supplied (s 14).

In addition, the Unfair Contract Terms Act 1977 prohibits or restricts the possibility of modifying these statutory rules (other than those on time) by the use of exclusion clauses as follows.

(a)   It is not possible to exclude or restrict:

(i)   the statutory terms on the seller's title in any circumstances;

151

    (ii)   the statutory terms relating to contract description or sample, quality or fitness for a purpose when the *buyer is dealing as a consumer*; that is when he is not buying in the course of a business and the seller is selling in the course of a business: UCTA 1977 s 6 and 12.

(b)   In a contract under which the buyer is not dealing as a consumer, that is when seller and buyer are both engaging in the transaction in the course of business, the terms referred to in (a) (ii) above may be excluded or restricted, but only if the exclusion or restriction satisfies a *requirement of reasonableness*. It is possible for a business to be operating as a consumer, for instance where a company purchases a car for one member of staff: *R & B Customs Brokers Ltd v UDT Ltd 1987*.

Exercise 2

If, in the case of *Esso v Commissioners of Customs & Excise 1976*, Esso had not offered a free coin with every four gallons of petrol but had instead offered 'four gallons of petrol and one World Cup coin for £2', would there have been a collateral contract for the coins?

---

5   Time of performance (s 10)

Whether time of performance is of the essence depends on the terms of the contract. If it is, then breach of it is breach of a condition, which entitles the injured party to treat the contract as discharged.

In commercial contracts for the supply of goods for business or industrial use, it will readily be assumed that time is of the essence even where there is no express term to that effect. Often one party is given a period of time within which to perform his obligation, say for delivery of goods. That party is not in breach until the whole period has elapsed without performance.

The contract may stipulate that the party should use his 'best endeavours' to perform his side by a certain time. If he fails to make that date, he must perform his obligations within a reasonable time. Under s 29, similar reasonableness is required if no date is set by the contract. In any case, time of performance stipulates a 'reasonable hour' for obligations to be performed: this is a question of fact. Hence it is not reasonable to offer delivery of perishable goods to a factory on the Friday evening before a two week shutdown of which the seller is aware.

Time for *payment* is not of the essence unless a different intention appears from the contract. For example A, a manufacturer, orders components from B and B fails to deliver by the agreed date. A can treat the contract as discharged and refuse to accept late delivery by B. But if B delivers a first instalment on time and A pays the price a week after the agreed date, B could not (under a continuing contract) refuse to make further deliveries, and treat the contract as discharged. If, however, A failed to pay altogether, that is not delay in payment but breach of an essential condition, that the price is payable in exchange for the goods (unless otherwise agreed).

6   Seller's title (s 12)

It is an implied *condition* that the seller has, or will have at the time when property in the goods is to be transferred, a right to sell the goods.

In the ordinary way the seller satisfies this condition if he has title to the goods at the moment when property is to pass to the buyer. (In this statutory code 'title' and 'property' are both used in different contexts to mean the same thing, ownership.) But the condition is broken if the seller, although he owns the goods, can be stopped by a third party from selling them: the right to transfer is essential.

Case: Niblett v Confectioners Materials 1921
A seller sold condensed milk in tins labelled with the name 'Nissly'. The well known company Nestle took legal action when the goods arrived in the UK to have them detained as infringing the Nestle trademark. The buyers were obliged to remove the labels from the tins in order to have them released from the customs warehouse in which they were held at the instance of Nestle.

Held: the seller was in breach of the implied condition that he had a 'right to sell'.

If the seller delivers goods to the buyer without having the right to sell, there is a total failure of consideration, and the buyer does not obtain the ownership of the goods which is the essential basis of the contract. If the buyer has then to give up the goods to the real owner he may recover the entire price from the seller, without any allowance for the use of the goods meanwhile.

The seller also gives implied *warranties* that the buyer shall have quiet possession of the goods and that the goods are free of any encumbrance or challenge by a third party (unless disclosed to the buyer when the contract is made): s 12(2).

Although the seller cannot contract out of these terms by stipulating that they shall not apply, he can achieve a rather similar result by undertaking to transfer only such title as he (or some third party from whom he acquired the goods) may have (or have had). This stipulation puts the buyer on notice that the seller is uncertain of title. Furthermore, the seller must disclose to the buyer any charges or encumbrances of which the seller knows. But if the buyer is prepared to buy the goods on that basis he gets what he bargained for, and there is no breach of contract if the seller's title is imperfect.

Exercise 3

A and B are in dispute over which of them owns some corn which is in A's possession. A sells the corn to C (who is unaware of the dispute) for £1,000. The dispute is then resolved in favour of B, who obtains possession of the corn from C. By that time its value has fallen to £800. How much can C recover from A?

---

7 Description of the goods (s 13)

In a contract for sale of goods by description, a *condition* is implied that the goods will correspond to the description. If a description is applied to the goods by the contract, it is a sale by description even though the buyer may have inspected the goods. If he himself asked for the goods by stating his requirements and the seller then supplies them to those requirements that is also a sale by description.

However if the buyer makes it clear that he is buying goods because of their unique qualities, and that no other item will meet his requirements, a sale is not a sale by description: *Harlingdon & Leinster Ltd v Christopher Hill Fine Art Ltd 1989.*

Where the sale is by sample as well as by description, the bulk must correspond to the sample *and* the description.

If a contract contains the phrase 'bought as seen' (as many auction sales do) then the sale is expressly not one by description: *Cavendish-Woodhouse Ltd v Manley 1984*.

'Description' is widely interpreted to include ingredients, age, date of shipment, packing, quantity and so on.

In *Moore v Landauer 1921* it was held that the mode of packing of the goods can also form part of the description where this is a substantial means of identification of the goods. In this case it did not matter that there was no effect on the value of the goods. The decision has been criticised as being unduly technical, for example by Lord Diplock in the *Ashington Piggeries* case: 'The "description" by which unascertained goods are sold is, in my view, confined to those words in the contract which were intended by the parties to identify the kind of goods which were to be supplied. It is open to the parties to use a description as broad or as narrow as they choose. But ultimately the test is whether the buyer could fairly and reasonably refuse to accept the physical goods offered to him on the grounds that their failure to correspond with what was said about them makes them goods of a different kind from those he had agreed to buy.'

If the seller uses a false description he may also commit an offence punishable under the Trade Descriptions Act 1968.

8 Sale by sample (s 15)

In a sale by sample there are implied *conditions* that:

(a) the bulk corresponds in quality with the sample;

(b) the buyer shall have a reasonable opportunity of comparing the bulk with the sample; and

(c) the goods are free of any defect rendering them unmerchantable which would not be apparent on a reasonable examination of the sample.

Exercise 4

There is a contract for the sale of '200 cases of 1958 Bordeaux wine'. If the seller were to supply wine made in 1959, is it likely that he could rely on Lord Diplock's remarks in the *Ashington Piggeries* case to force the buyer to proceed with the purchase?

---

9 Merchantable quality (s 14 (2))

There is an implied condition that goods supplied under a contract are of merchantable quality. This *condition* applies only to goods sold 'in the course of a business'; the seller must be carrying on a business or profession and make the sale in connection with that activity. Goods sold privately by a seller who is not selling in the course of a business therefore fall outside the scope of this section.

The condition applies to all 'goods supplied under the contract': not only to the goods themselves therefore but also to the packaging in which they are sold and also to any instructions provided for the use of the goods.

BPP Publishing

The condition that the goods supplied under the contract are of merchantable quality is excluded if the buyer's attention is drawn to defects before the contract is made or the buyer examines the goods before the contract is made, and that examination ought to reveal the defects.

Goods are of merchantable quality if they are as fit for the purpose for which goods of that description are commonly bought as it is reasonable to expect, having regard to any description applied to them such as 'secondhand'. The price is relevant: cheaper goods are not to be measured by the quality standard set for more expensive goods of the same type.

Case: Cehave v Bremer, The Hansa Nord 1975
There was a contract for the supply of 'citrus pulp pellets' (a raw material used in making animal feeding stuffs). On arrival at the port of destination, part of the cargo had deteriorated and the buyers rejected the entire cargo. The cargo was offered for sale and was purchased (at a much lower price) by the same buyers who used it for its intended original purpose. The sellers denied that the buyers had been entitled to reject the cargo as not being of merchantable quality.

Held: the fact that the cargo could only be sold on the market at a lower price than the contract provided was not conclusive that it was not of merchantable quality. It could be, and was, used for its purpose, making cattle food, and so by that test it was of merchantable quality.

In *Rogers v Parish (Scarborough) Ltd 1987* the Court of Appeal criticised the practice of looking to case law to provide a suitable definition of merchantable quality and insisted that the s 14(6) definition should be applied consistently and in isolation from decided cases: 'Goods of any kind are of merchantable quality if they are as fit for the purpose or purposes for which goods of that kind are commonly bought as it is reasonable to expect having regard to any description applied to them, the price (if relevant) and all the other relevant circumstances'.

If the goods can be used for only one purpose, such as a hotwater bottle (see *Priest v Last 1903* below) or a pair of underpants *(Grant v Australian Knitting Mills 1936)*, and the goods are unsuitable for that purpose, they are of unmerchantable quality. On the other hand where goods are multi-purpose, the Court of Appeal held in *Aswan Engineering Establishment Co v Lupdine Ltd 1987* that the Act does not mean that the goods must be suitable for all of the purposes for which goods of that kind are commonly bought. They will still be merchantable if they are suitable for at least one of the purposes for which they might reasonably be expected to be used.

If it is contemplated that the goods will be processed in some way before use, such as cooking or washing foodstuffs, and this treatment will remove a defect, the goods are merchantable in spite of the defect: *Heil v Hedges 1951* (the plaintiff failed to cook pork chops properly).

Once goods are found not to be of merchantable quality the seller has no defence. There is strict liability, so showing that all reasonable care was taken will not succeed.

The goods must remain of merchantable quality for a reasonable time. One of the major areas of uncertainty in consumer protection law is how long the goods must remain in satisfactory condition after transfer to the buyer. But if a fault appears soon after the transfer it will readily be concluded that the goods were not of merchantable quality when sold, for example where omnibuses broke down soon after delivery: *Bristol Tramways v Fiat Motors 1910*

If the buyer examines the goods before agreeing to buy them he is treated as discovering any defects apparent on examination, whether or not he actually discovers them, but not defects which no examination could reveal.

BPP Publishing

Merchantable quality has recently been extended to include not only the physical condition of the goods but also other qualities.

Case: Shine v General Guarantee Corporation 1988

S obtained an enthusiast's car under hire purchase. He had inspected it and assumed it had a rust warranty. He later discovered that the car had been totally submerged in water for 2 days, and so had been an insurance write-off. He stopped paying the instalments and sought to rescind the contract.

Held: although the car had no physical defects, S was entitled to rescind for breach of s 14, since merchantable quality included such fundamentals as having been previously written off.

Exercise 5

P sells an expensive new pen to Q. Q finds that it can only be made to write with difficulty. P claims that the pen is of merchantable quality, because it can write and because its casing is perfect so that it can be used as a status symbol (as expensive pens sometimes are used). Is P's claim likely to be accepted by the courts?

---

10 Fitness for purpose (s 14(3))

This *condition* applies only to goods sold 'in the course of business'.

Where the buyer expressly or by implication makes known to the seller any particular purpose for which the goods are bought, it is an implied condition that the goods supplied under the contract are reasonably fit for that purpose (whether or not that is the common purpose of such goods), unless the circumstances show that:

(a)   the buyer does not rely; or

(b)   it is unreasonable for him to rely

on the skill or judgement of the seller.

Case: Ashington Piggeries v Christopher Hill 1972

B gave S a recipe for mink food and requested that S should mix the food in accordance with the recipe and supply it to B. S told B that they had never supplied mink food before although they were manufacturers of animal foodstuffs. One of the ingredients was herring meal which had been stored in a chemical which created a poisonous substance damaging to all animals but particularly damaging to mink. As a result many of the mink died.

Held: because the poison affected all animals the food was unfit for its disclosed purpose since B relied on S's skill and judgement to the extent that S was an animal food manufacturer and should not have supplied a generally harmful food. If the poison had only affected mink then B's skill and judgement demonstrated by its supply of a recipe would have made it unreasonable to rely on S's skill or judgement.

If the goods have only one obvious purpose, the buyer by implication makes known his purpose merely by asking for the goods.

BPP Publishing

Case: Priest v Last 1903
A customer at a chemist's shop asked for a hot water bottle and was told, in answer to a question, that it should not be filled with boiling water. It burst after only five days in use.

Held: if there is only one purpose that particular purpose is disclosed by buying the goods. Because it was not an effective hot water bottle, it was in breach of s 14(3). This was followed by *Frost v Aylesbury Dairy Co 1905*: in the purchase of milk supplied to a domestic address the buyer discloses his purpose, which is human consumption.

If, however, the goods can be used for more than one purpose or there are special circumstances which affect their suitability, there is no breach of this condition unless the buyer has made an express disclosure.

Even partial reliance of the buyer on the seller's skill or judgement makes the latter subject to the condition.

Case: Cammell Laird v Manganese Bronze & Brass Co 1934
Shipbuilders ordered a ship's propeller to be manufactured by a specialist contractor. The buyers specified the materials and certain dimensions but left other details to the seller's judgement.

Held: partial reliance on the seller's skill and judgement is sufficient to bring the condition into operation as regards matters left to the seller to determine.

There is a considerable overlap between the merchantable quality and fitness for purpose conditions and the buyer can often claim that both have been broken. But if the goods are multipurpose and the buyer has disclosed that he has one purpose only, it is no defence to the seller that his goods are suitable for other purposes. They may in such a case be of merchantable quality but they are not fit for the disclosed specific purpose. The one condition is a test of general suitability and the other (where it applies) of specific suitability.

Exercise 6

R buys a filing cabinet from S, who runs an office furniture shop. R tells S that he will use the cabinet to store land certificates issued by the Land Registry, and asks S whether the cabinet is of the right size for such certificates. S replies that he does not know how large land certificates are, but R goes ahead and buys the cabinet. If the cabinet proved to be too small, why could R not claim that S had breached the condition of reasonable fitness?

11 Passing of property and risk

In a contract for the sale of goods, determining at what stage property passes is important for two reasons.

(a) The risk of accidental loss or damage is, as a general rule, borne by the owner, so the risk passes with the property in a sale of goods: s 20.

(b) The rights of parties against each other, and the rights of either party's creditors if he becomes insolvent, are also affected.

BPP Publishing

No inference is drawn merely because the seller is still in possession of the goods: they may now be owned by the buyer. Similarly, even though the buyer is in possession the seller may still be the owner.

In determining when property in goods passes the following general principles apply.

(a) No property can pass in goods which are unascertained and not yet identified as the goods to be sold under the contract: s 16.

(b) The property in specific or ascertained goods is transferred to the buyer at the time when the parties *intend* it to be transferred. Their intention may be deduced from the terms of the contract, the conduct of the parties and the circumstances of the case: s 17.

(c) Unless a different intention appears (and the parties can agree upon whatever terms they like) the rules of s 18 are applied to ascertain what their intention is on the passing of property to the buyer.

Many contracts for the supply of goods contain a clause stating that title to the goods remains with the seller until the contract price is paid. Such 'retention of title' or *'Romalpa'* clauses are a common example of the s 17 rule that title to specific goods passes when the parties so intend.

Passing of property: the s 18 rules

Rule 1. If the contract is unconditional and the goods are specific or identified, property passes when the contract is made. It is immaterial that the seller has not yet delivered the goods or that the buyer has not yet paid the price. However, the seller may, and often does, stipulate that property shall not pass until the price is paid. If the seller insists on retaining the goods or documents relating to them, such as the registration book of a car which has been sold, until the price is paid then it will readily be inferred that he intended (and the buyer agreed) that property would not pass on making the contract, but only on payment of the price.

Rule 2. If, under a contract for sale of specific goods, the seller is bound to do something to put the goods into a deliverable state, property does not pass until the seller has done what is required of him and the buyer has notice of this.

Rule 3. Where there is a contract for the sale of specific goods in a deliverable state but the seller is bound to weigh, measure or test them to fix the price, property passes when he has done so and the buyer has notice of this. The rule does not apply when it is the buyer who must take this action.

Rule 4. When goods are delivered to the buyer on approval, that is on sale or return terms, the property passes to the buyer when:

(a) he signifies to the seller that he approves, or indicates approval by dealing with them; or

(b) he retains the goods beyond the time fixed for their return without giving notice of rejection or, if no time has been fixed, if he retains them beyond a reasonable time.

Rule 5. When there is a contract for the sale of unascertained or future goods by description, and goods of that description and in a deliverable state are unconditionally appropriated to the contract by the seller with the assent of the buyer, or by the buyer with the assent of the seller, the property then passes to the buyer.

Such assent may be express or implied and given before or after the appropriation is made. For example, if the buyer orders goods to be supplied from the seller's stock he gives implied assent to the seller to make an appropriation from his stock.

To bring rule 5 into operation, something more definite is required than merely selecting or setting aside goods for delivery to the buyer. The act must be irrevocable, for example where the seller sets aside goods and also informs the buyer that they are ready for collection.

Delivery of goods to the buyer, or to a carrier for transmission to the buyer, without reserving to the seller a right of disposal, is an unconditional appropriation which brings rule 5 into operation. However, delivery to a carrier does not pass the property if identical goods destined to be sent to different buyers are mixed and need to be counted or sorted by the carrier: *Healey v Howlett and Sons 1917*. Rule 5 only applies to appropriations of goods in a deliverable state.

Exercise 7

On Monday, a contract is made for the sale of goods which are unascertained at that time. On Tuesday, the seller takes goods from stock and decides that these are the goods to be supplied to the buyer. However, the goods must first be packed. This is done on Wednesday and the buyer is notified on Thursday that this has been done and that the goods are ready for collection. On what day does property in the goods pass to the buyer?

---

12 *Nemo dat quod non habet*

The general rule is that only the owner, or an agent acting with his authority, can transfer the title in goods to a buyer. This is expressed in the Latin maxim *nemo dat quod non habet:* no one can give what he does not have.

To the general rule there are a number of *exceptions* to protect an honest buyer against loss. The exceptions fall under rules relating to:

(a) agency;

(b) estoppel;

(c) market overt;

(d) voidable title;

(e) seller in possession;

(f) buyer in possession;

(g) motor vehicles held under hire purchase;

(h) special powers of sale.

These are now discussed in turn.

Agency (s 21). If an ordinary agent sells goods without actual or apparent authority, there is usually no transfer of title to the buyer. But a mercantile agent, that is an agent whose business is selling goods for others, may have possession of goods (or documents of title to them) with the owner's consent. He can then sell them, in the ordinary course of his business, to a buyer who buys in good faith and without notice that the agent had no authority to sell (or was exceeding his authority). The buyer acquires title to the goods: s 21.

Estoppel. If, by his conduct, the true owner leads the buyer to believe that the person who makes the sale owns the goods, the true owner is prevented (estopped) from denying the seller's authority to sell. Merely to put goods in the possession of another is not to represent that he is the owner.

BPP Publishing

Market overt (s 22). If goods are sold in market overt according to the usage of the market, the buyer acquires good title if he buys in good faith and without notice of the seller's lack of title.

Market overt (open market) means a recognised public market, such as are held daily or weekly in many town squares, and any shop in the City of London. The goods must be of a type usually sold there and the sale must take place in the public part of the shop and must be a sale *by* the shopkeeper (not *to* him). Sale in any market overt must (to afford this protection) take place between sunrise and sunset.

Sale under voidable title (s 23). A person may acquire goods under a contract which is voidable, say for misrepresentation. He then has title to the goods until the contract is avoided. If he re-sells before the sale to him is avoided, to a person who buys in good faith and without notice of his defective title, that buyer obtains a good title to the goods. Normally the first contract of sale is not avoided until the person entitled to avoid it communicates his decision to the other party but if that party has disappeared other evidence of intention to avoid the first sale, such as reporting the matter to the police, will suffice: *Car & Universal Finance Co v Caldwell 1965*.

Exercise 8

A video recorder is stolen from A, and is then sold by the thief to an honest shopkeeper in the City of London. This transaction takes place at the shop counter. The shopkeeper does not have any spare display space for the video recorder, so he puts it in a storage room and displays a notice stating that he has a video recorder for sale. B enquires about the video recorder, and he is taken to the storage room to inspect it. There he agrees to buy it. A traces it to B, and B puts forward two alternative reasons why he has acquired good title to it.

(a)   He bought it in market overt.

(b)   The shopkeeper had bought it in market overt, and had therefore acquired good title which could be passed on to a buyer.

Why would neither of these reasons be sufficient to give good title to B?

Re-sale by seller in possession (s 24). If a seller, or a mercantile agent acting for him, continues in possession of the goods (or documents of title to them), and he makes a delivery of them to a person who receives them in good faith and without notice of the previous sale, the transaction takes effect as if the seller were authorised for that purpose.

Suppose that A sells specific goods to B and B, to whom the ownership of the goods passes, immediately leaves them in A's possession until B can collect them. A by mistake then re-sells the goods and delivers them to C, who is unaware of the previous sale to B. C gets good title to the goods; B's only remedy is to sue A. But if A does not actually deliver the goods to C, B has the better right.

Re-sale by a buyer in possession (s 25). The seller may permit the buyer to take possession of the goods before ownership has passed to the buyer, as when the seller makes delivery but retains title until the price is paid. If the buyer then makes a re-sale or other disposition in the normal course of business as mercantile agent, with actual delivery or transfer of the goods (or documents of title), to a person who takes them in good faith and without notice of the original seller's rights, title passes to that person as if the buyer had acted as a mercantile agent. This applies even if the buyer has a voidable title which is actually avoided (say by notifying police of the buyer's lack of title).

160

Case: Newtons of Wembley v Williams 1965
X purchased a car and paid the price by cheque. The seller stipulated that title to the car should not pass until the cheque was cleared but allowed X to take possession of the car. The cheque was dishonoured and the sellers informed the police and thereby avoided the sale to X in the only way available to them. But X sold the car for cash in an established secondhand car market to Y who took delivery forthwith.

Held: Y acquired good title since X was a buyer in possession with the seller's consent and the re-sale in the market was a disposition in the ordinary course of business of a mercantile agent. The loss must fall on the original seller if he could not recover from X.

The buyer must be a person who has 'bought or agreed to buy', which includes a person such as X in the case above. But the following are not persons who have 'bought or agreed to buy' and so are not buyers in possession:

(a)   a person with an option to buy;

(b)   a person taking goods on sale or return terms: *Edwards v Vaughan 1910*;

(c)   a hirer of goods under a hire purchase agreement (but see below);

(d)   a buyer under a regulated conditional sale agreement: s 25(2).

To be a buyer in possession, the person must have obtained possession of the goods or documents of title to goods *with the seller's consent*. It is immaterial that the seller withdraws consent after the buyer has obtained possession, and that the latter obtains possession after contracting to sell to the innocent purchaser. He is a buyer in possession provided he obtains possession before delivering possession to the innocent purchaser: *Cahn v Pockett's Bristol Channel Steam Packet Co 1899*.

However, s 25 does *not* allow good title to be given to an innocent purchaser from a buyer in possession if the latter had obtained possession from a 'seller' not entitled to sell, that is, a thief.

Case: National Mutual General Insurance Association Ltd v Jones 1988
B stole a car from A and sold it to C, who sold it to D (a car dealer) who sold it to E (another car dealer) who sold it to J (an innocent customer). J claimed that, under s 25, he obtained title from a buyer in possession acting as a mercantile agent so the loss should fall on A.

Held: s 25 only served to defeat the claim of an owner who gave possession to a buyer; it could not defeat the title of an owner whose car was stolen.

The sale of a motor vehicle acquired under hire purchase. By the Hire Purchase Act 1964 a private (but not a trade) purchaser of a motor vehicle sold by a hirer under a hire purchase agreement or a buyer under a conditional sale agreement obtains good title (although the seller had none) if the purchaser takes the vehicle in good faith and without notice that it was only let on hire purchase. The innocent buyer's purchase may be an ordinary sale or a hire purchase or conditional sale agreement. If there are intermediaries who are not private purchasers, the protection is available only to the first private purchaser. For example, A, who has a car under a hire purchase agreement, purports to sell it to B, a car dealer, who sells it to C, a private purchaser. B does not obtain title but C does. This is so even if B is a car dealer buying a vehicle for private, not business, purposes: *Stevenson v Beverley-Bentinck 1976*.

Special powers of sale. The court may order goods to be sold. Various persons, such as pawnbrokers, unpaid sellers and hotel keepers and bailees (such as dry cleaners) in possession of abandoned goods for which charges are owing, have specific powers of sale.

Exercise 9

Peter sells a car bearing the distinctive registration number DAWN 10 to Dawn Smith, who tells her friend Dawn Jones that she has just bought this car. The car is still with Peter when Dawn Jones calls on him, and attempts to buy the same car. Peter confuses the two Dawns, accepts Dawn Jones's cash and allows her to take the car away. When Dawn Smith claims the car from her, she relies on s 24 Sale of Goods Act 1979 to retain the car. Why is Dawn Jones unlikely to succeed in her claim?

---

13 Delivery

Unless otherwise agreed, the seller is entitled to receive the price before delivering the goods to the buyer, but he must deliver them as soon as the price is paid: s 28. The parties may agree on whatever delivery arrangements may suit them. But unless otherwise agreed the following rules apply.

(a) *Method:* delivery is the voluntary transfer of possession from one person to another (s 61). It may be by physical transfer of possession, or of the means of control (such as the key of a warehouse) or by arranging that a third party who has the goods acknowledges ('attorns') to the buyer that he holds them on his behalf, or by delivery of a document of title to the goods.

(b) *Place:* delivery is to be made at the seller's place of business, or if he has none at his residence, unless the goods are specific and, to the knowledge of both parties when the contract is made, the goods are at some other place. Delivery is, in those circumstances, to be at that other place.

(c) *Time:* if no time is agreed, delivery is to be made within a reasonable time and at a reasonable hour: s 29(5).

(d) *Expense:* the seller bears the expense of putting the goods into a deliverable state (for example by packing or bagging them).

Unless otherwise agreed the buyer is not obliged to accept delivery by instalments: s 30(1). He may reject a delivery of part only of the goods.

If the contract does provide for delivery by instalments with separate payment for each instalment, the contract is severable or divisible. If one or more instalments under a severable contract are defective, this may amount to repudiation of the entire contract or it may merely give a right to claim compensation for the defective deliveries only. It depends on the ratio of defective to sound deliveries and the likelihood or otherwise that future instalments will also be defective.

If the seller delivers the wrong quantity the buyer may reject the whole quantity, but if he accepts what is delivered he must pay at the contract rate for the quantity accepted. When the seller delivers too much the buyer may also accept the correct quantity and reject the rest: s 30.

If the seller delivers the contract goods mixed with other goods the buyer may reject the whole or accept the contract goods and reject others: s 30.

Where the contract requires that the goods be moved in the course of delivery:

(a) delivery to a carrier for transmission to the buyer is deemed to be delivery to the buyer unless the contrary intention appears, as when the seller consigns the goods to himself or his agent at their destination: s 32;

(b)   the seller must make a reasonable arrangement with the carrier and (if the goods are sent by sea) give the buyer notice in time to permit the buyer to arrange insurance: s 32;

(c)   the buyer must bear the risk of any deterioration necessarily incidental to the course of transit: s 33.

14   Acceptance and rejection

As already stated, acceptance of goods or part of them (unless the contract is severable), deprives the buyer of his right to treat the contract as discharged by breach of condition (for example as to the quality of the goods) on the part of the seller. But he may claim damages.

The buyer must have a reasonable opportunity to examine the goods before accepting them: s 34. On delivery the seller must give the buyer that opportunity. If the buyer either states expressly that he accepts the goods or retains the goods beyond a reasonable time for examination, he has had his opportunity and he has accepted the goods. But re-sale (possibly with delivery directly from the seller to the sub-purchaser) may give the buyer no opportunity; for example the buyer may be unaware that the goods are defective until the sub-purchaser makes complaint to him. In these circumstances the buyer is permitted to reject the goods in spite of the re-sale.

Where the seller has breached a condition the buyer may treat the contract as repudiated and hence reject the goods. The buyer does not have to return the goods to the seller - he merely has to inform the seller of his rejection: s 36.

The buyer loses his right to reject goods if:

(a)   he waives the breached condition;

(b)   he elects to treat the breach of condition as a breach of warranty;

(c)   he has accepted the goods (in a contract which is not severable); or

(d)   he is unable to return the goods because, for example, he has sold them on to a buyer who keeps them.

Exercise 10

The parties to a contract for the sale of non-perishable goods agree that the goods shall be delivered to the buyer's premises 'during normal business hours'. The seller then states that the only time of day that the goods can be delivered is 10 pm and that the goods must be accepted or rejected immediately on delivery. At that time a caretaker will be present to receive the goods, but he is not competent to inspect them. In what ways has the seller failed to meet his legal obligations?

---

15   The parties' remedies

As with any other contract, one for sale of goods may be breached. Aside from the usual common law remedies (damages, action for the price and so on) the parties have rights peculiar to this type of contract. They are categorised as:

(a)   the seller's remedies against the goods;

(b)   the seller's remedies against the buyer;

(c)   the buyer's remedies against the seller.

BPP Publishing

The remedies which are against goods are described as 'real remedies'; all others are called 'personal remedies'.

The seller's remedies against the goods

Ownership of goods often passes to the buyer before they are delivered to the buyer in exchange for the price. If the buyer then defaults, for example by failing to pay the price when due, the seller is given rights against the goods in his possession or under his control although those goods are now owned by the buyer. It is usually more satisfactory to him to retain the goods than merely to sue a buyer, who may well be insolvent, for breach of contract.

These rights are given only to an 'unpaid seller' (s 38). He is unpaid if either:

(a) the whole of the price has not been paid or tendered to him; or

(b) he has received a bill of exchange and the bill has been dishonoured.

An unpaid seller of goods which are now the property of the buyer has the following statutory rights in respect of the goods (s 39):

(a) a *lien* on the goods so long as they are in his possession;

(b) a right of *stoppage in transitu* if the buyer is insolvent and the goods are in the hands of a carrier;

(c) a right of *resale* in certain circumstances.

Lien

The unpaid seller's lien, his right to retain the goods in his possession until the price is paid or tendered, exists (s 41):

(a) where the goods are sold without any stipulation as to credit;

(b) where they have been sold on credit terms but the credit period has expired; or

(c) where the buyer becomes insolvent.

Even if part of the goods have been delivered to the buyer, the unpaid seller has a lien on the rest unless part delivery indicates his agreement to give up his lien altogether: s 42.

The unpaid seller loses his lien when he delivers the goods to a carrier or warehouseman for transmission to the buyer (unless the seller reserves a right of disposal), or when the buyer or his agent lawfully obtains possession of the goods, or when the seller waives his lien: s 43.

Lien merely gives a right to retain possession until the price is paid. It does not rescind the contract, deprive the buyer of his ownership nor entitle the seller to re-sell the goods. If ownership of the goods in the seller's possession has not yet passed to the buyer, the seller does not have lien (which is a right to retain the property of another person) but he does have a similar right to withhold delivery to the buyer (called a right of *retention*) in those circumstances where he would have lien or a right of stoppage *in transitu* if they were the buyer's goods.

Stoppage in transitu

The right of stoppage *in transitu* (s 44-45) exists when the buyer becomes insolvent. He is insolvent if he has ceased to pay his debts in the ordinary course of business or cannot pay his debts as they fall due: it is not necessary to wait until he becomes bankrupt.

While goods are in transit, neither seller nor buyer has possession of the goods since they are in the possession of a carrier. The unpaid seller may stop the goods in transit by issuing an order to the carrier. The goods cease to be in transit and the seller's right of stoppage ends:

(a) on delivery to the buyer or his agent (whether at the appointed destination or before);

(b) if the carrier acknowledges to the buyer or his agent that the goods (arrived at their original destination) are now held on behalf of the buyer; it is immaterial that the buyer may have indicated to the carrier that the goods are to be taken on to a further destination; or

(c) if the carrier wrongfully refuses to make delivery to the buyer or his agent.

But if the buyer refuses to accept the goods which remain in the possession of the carrier, they are still in transit.

When the unpaid seller exercises his right of stoppage *in transitu* he may either resume possession or give notice to the carrier of his claim pending re-delivery. But he must allow time for the carrier to transmit instructions within his organisation to give effect to the seller's notice to him: s 46.

Exercise 11

A seller of goods consigns them to a carrier for transmission to the buyer, thereby ending his lien. Why is the seller's lien not automatically replaced by a right of stoppage *in transitu* at that point?

Right of resale

As between the unpaid seller and the buyer of the goods, the seller has a *right of resale*:

(a) if the goods are of a perishable nature;

(b) if the seller gives notice to the buyer of his intention to re-sell and the buyer fails within a reasonable time to pay or tender the price; or

(c) If the seller reserves a right of resale under the contract.

If the seller does not, by resale, recover the full amount of his loss he may sue the buyer for damages for breach of contract: s 48. On a sale in these circumstances the second buyer gets good title to the goods.

If the unpaid seller, having exercised his right of lien, retention or stoppage *in transitu* re-sells the goods, the second buyer from him acquires good title even if the seller is not entitled to resell. The original buyer may in that case sue the seller for damages but he cannot recover the goods: s 48.

Retention of title clauses

Many commercial contracts now contain a retention of title clause, often known as a *Romalpa* clause after the case discussed below. Under such a clause, possession may pass to the buyer but ownership does not pass until the price is paid.

Case: Aluminium Industrie Vaassen BV v Romalpa Ltd 1976
Romalpa purchased aluminium foil on terms that the stock of foil (and any proceeds of sale) should be the property of the supplier until the company had paid to the supplier all that it owed. The receiver found that the company still held aluminium foil and proceeds of selling other stocks of foil and had not paid its debt to the supplier. The receiver applied to the court to determine whether or not the foil and the cash were assets of the company under his control as receiver.

BPP Publishing

Held: the conditions of sale were valid. The relevant assets, although in the possession of the company, did not belong to it. The receiver could not deal with these assets since his authority under the floating charge was restricted to assets of the company.

The extent to which a *Romalpa* clause protects an unpaid seller depends to a great extent on the wording of the actual clause. A retention of title clause may be effective even though goods are resold or incorporated into the buyer's products so as to lose their identity, *if* it expressly states that they can be used in these ways before title has passed: *Clough Mill Ltd v Martin 1985.*

Unless the clause expressly retains title even after resale or incorporation, the supplier is not entitled to a proportionate part of the sale proceeds or the manufactured product: *Borden (UK) Ltd v Scottish Timber Products Ltd 1979.* Where there is no express provision, resale or incorporation is conversion of the supplier's property but a third party will still get good title. The proceeds of sale are the first buyer's property and not the supplier's: *Pfeiffer Weinkellerei-Weineinkauf GmbH v Arbuthnot Factors Ltd 1988.*

If the buyer resells the goods when there is an express provision allowing resale before title passes, the proceeds of sale are held by the buyer as trustee for the supplier.

Retention clauses usually afford a remedy to the seller only in relation to sums of money owed in respect of the goods which are actually the subject of the retention clause. However, retention clauses can also cover debts due to the seller under other contracts.

Case: Armour and Carron v Thyssen Edelstahlwerke AG 1990
T transferred possession in steel strip to C under a contract of sale. C agreed that it would only acquire ownership once all debts due to T and its group companies had been paid. A were appointed receivers to C before the steel strip had been paid for; they sought to show that they could deal with the steel strip as goods of the company.

Held: since under s 17 Sale of Goods Act property is transferred when the parties to the contract intend that it be transferred and under s 19 property does not pass 'until the conditions imposed by the seller are fulfilled', T had reserved the right of disposal of the goods until the condition had been fulfilled.

Registrable charges

The buyer may seek to demonstrate that a retention clause creates a *charge* which should be registered under s 396 Companies Act 1985. This would render the clause inoperative if no such registration had taken place, as failure to register such a charge causes it to be void. However, in cases such as *Romalpa* and *Armour* this claim cannot succeed, as s 396 can only apply to charges over the property of the buyer, and the goods do not belong to the buyer.

The seller's remedies against the buyer

The seller has two possible remedies against the buyer personally.

(a)　He may bring an *action for the price* if:

    (i)　the ownership of the goods has passed to the buyer and he wrongfully neglects or refuses to pay the price according to the terms of the contract; or

    (ii)　the price is payable on a certain day (regardless of delivery) and the buyer wrongfully neglects or refuses to pay it.

In this latter case it is immaterial that property in the goods has not yet passed to the buyer or that goods have not been appropriated to the contract.

(b)　The seller may *sue for damages for non-acceptance* if the buyer wrongfully refuses or neglects to accept and pay for the goods. In this case the claim may include any expense incurred by the seller, for example in storing the goods, caused by the buyer's failure to take delivery after being requested to do so.

When the seller claims damages, the first head of the rule in *Hadley v Baxendale* applies. If there is an available market for this type of goods, the measure of damages is usually the difference between the contract price and the market price on the day when the goods should have been accepted. For example, if the market price per unit of the goods is £10 less than the contract price at the contractual delivery date that margin (plus any expenses) is the amount recoverable.

The seller's claim is sometimes for loss of profit. If in fact he has been able to re-sell the goods to another buyer at a price equal to or above the contract price, he will usually be awarded only nominal damages.

Exercise 12

Some nuts and bolts are sold to Z Ltd subject to a retention of title clause, the full text of which is as follows.

'Property in the goods shall not pass to the buyer until the buyer has paid for the goods in full'.

Before paying for the nuts and bolts, Z Ltd incorporates them into electric motors which are sold. If Z Ltd fails to pay for the nuts and bolts, what remedy might the supplier seek?

The buyer's remedies against the seller

If the seller is in *breach of a condition* of the contract, the buyer may reject the goods unless he has lost his right to do so by accepting the goods or part of them. In addition he may claim damages.

If the buyer has paid the price and the consideration has failed entirely, for example if the seller has no title or delivers goods which the buyer is entitled to reject, the buyer may sue to recover the price: s 54.

If there is a *breach of a warranty* by the seller, or if the buyer is obliged (or prefers) to deal with a breach of a condition by a claim for damages, the buyer may either reduce the amount paid to the seller by an allowance for the breach or sue for damages. The amount of damages is determined on principles similar to those of the seller's claim against the buyer.

(a)   The first head of the rule in *Hadley v Baxendale* is applied: damages arising directly and naturally from the breach in the ordinary course of events are compensated for.

(b)   The difference between the value of the goods as delivered and the value which they would have had if they had complied with the warranty or condition is the normal measure of the loss: s 53.

It is open to the buyer to base his claim on any circumstances within the general scope of these rules.

Case: Mason v Burningham 1949
The plaintiff had been sold a typewriter which turned out to be stolen property. She had to return it to the owner. In addition to the price paid she claimed damages for breach of implied warranty of quiet enjoyment including her expenditure in having the typewriter overhauled.

BPP Publishing

Held: damages should be awarded as claimed.

A buyer may also claim damages for non-delivery, calculated on the same principles as described earlier when a seller claims damages. This claim may be made if the seller either fails to deliver altogether or delivers goods which the buyer is entitled to, and does, reject.

The buyer's claim for damages for loss of profit or liability for damages arising on that contract is not affected by a resale by him, unless it can be shown that the parties to the original sale contemplated that there would be a resale.

> *Case: Williams v Agius 1914*
> There was a contract for the sale of coal at 16s.3d (81.25p) per ton. The buyers resold at 19s.6d (97.5p) per ton. The market price at the date for delivery was 23s.6d (£1.175). per ton. The sellers failed to deliver. The sellers contended that the buyer's actual loss was the difference between the contract price (16s.3d) and the resale price (19s.6d) per ton only.
>
> *Held:* the buyers should be awarded damages of 7s.3d per ton, the full difference between the market price and the contract price; the resale contract should be ignored.

In an action for breach of contract to deliver specific or ascertained goods, the court may order specific performance or delivery of the goods. But it will only do so if damages would be an inadequate remedy: s 52.

Exercise 13

Why, in a case such as *Williams v Agius 1914*, might the buyer/reseller's loss (for which he would need to be compensated) be the difference between the full market price (23s.6d per ton in that case) and the originally agreed price (16s.3d per ton in that case)?

---

16 The Supply of Goods and Services Act 1982

The Supply of Goods and Services Act 1982 (SGSA 1982) applies to certain contracts which do not fall within the definition of a sale of goods even though they do involve a transfer of ownership. The types of transaction which are covered by the Act include:

(a) *contracts of exchange or barter:* these are not contracts of sale of goods because there is no money consideration involved;

(b) *contracts of repair:* although some goods are supplied (eg spare parts) the substance of the contract is the provision of services (see below);

(c) *contracts of hire:* these are not contracts for the sale of goods because they contain no provision for ownership to pass to the hirer;

(d) *collateral contracts to the sale of goods:* for example, where a person buys a car and receives a free set of seat covers as part of a special deal, the purchase of the car is governed by the Sale of Goods Act 1979 but the seat covers, for which consideration was given by buying the car, are part of a collateral contract governed by the Supply of Goods and Services Act 1982.

The Act specifically does not cover contracts of apprenticeship or employment (s 12).

If the main purpose of a contract is, for example, the provision of skilled labour, whilst an ancillary object is the transfer of ownership of goods, the contract is one governed by the 1982 Act. Thus an accountant's contract to prepare a report is covered by the 1982 Act.

The general effect of the Act is to provide safeguards similar to those provided by the Sale of Goods Act in respect of contracts for sale of goods. Where the supply of goods is a part of the transaction, ss 2-5 of the 1982 Act implies certain terms relating to the goods. The terms implied relate to the goods supplied and are similar to those of the Sale of Goods Act 1979, dealing with strict liability regarding:

(a)   title, freedom from encumbrances and quiet possession (s 2);

(b)   description (s 3);

(c)   merchantable quality and fitness for purpose (s 4);

(d)   sample (s 5).

Under the Unfair Contract Terms Act 1977, clauses purporting to exclude or restrict liability under these headings are subject to the same rules as similar exclusion clauses in sale of goods contracts.

Where the contract is wholly or substantially for the provision of services, the 1982 Act implies a number of further terms.

(a)   Where the supplier of the service is acting in the course of a business, there are implied terms that he will carry out the service with reasonable care and skill (s 13) and within a reasonable time (s 14).

(b)   Where the consideration is not determined by the contract, there is an implied term that the party contracting with the supplier will pay a reasonable charge (s 15).

These terms are implied whether there is a supply of goods or not. But they are *not* conditions of strict liability, and may be excluded so long as such exclusion complies with the reasonableness requirement of the Unfair Contract Terms Act 1977: s 16 SGSA 1982. Because there is a difference in liability between sales of goods and supplies of services, the substance of the contract must be established and the question of strict liability for faulty goods or excludable liability for skill and care decided accordingly.

Exercise 14

Robinson v Graves 1935 concerned a contract to paint a portrait. *Marcel (Furriers) Ltd v Tapper 1953* concerned a contract for the supply of a mink jacket of a special style made to the customer's requirements. In both cases materials were worked on by skilled persons, but in one case it was held that there was a sale of goods and in the other case it was held that there was a supply of services. In which case do you think it was held that there was a sale of goods?

Chapter roundup

(a)   Contracts for the sale of goods are subject to the Sale of Goods Act 1979. In considering such contracts, we must distinguish between existing and future goods, and between specific and unascertained goods.

(b)   If the price for goods is not determined by the contract then a reasonable price must be paid.

BPP Publishing

(c)   The Sale of Goods Act 1979 implies several terms into contracts for the sale of goods, and the Unfair Contract Terms Act 1977 limits the extent to which these implied terms may be overridden.

(d)   If time is not of the essence, it may be made so. Performance must be tendered at a reasonable time.

(e)   There is an implied condition that the seller of goods has a right to sell, but the seller may put the buyer on notice that his title may be defective.

(f)   In a sale by description, the goods must match the description given. In a sale by sample, the bulk must correspond to the sample.

(g)   Goods are of merchantable quality if they are as fit for the purpose for which such goods are commonly bought as is reasonable to expect.

(h)   If the seller of goods knows the purpose for which the goods are being bought, it is normally an implied condition that the goods are reasonably fit for that purpose.

(i)   The property in goods passes when the parties intend that it shall pass. Where such intention is not otherwise made clear, the rules of s 18 Sale of Goods Act 1979 apply to fix the time. Goods are generally at the buyer's risk from the time that property passes.

(j)   A person not owning goods cannot in general transfer title to a buyer. However, there are several exceptions to protect an innocent buyer.

(k)   Goods must be delivered as agreed, but there are rules which apply in the absence of agreement.

(l)   A buyer must be given an opportunity to inspect and if necessary reject goods, but once he has accepted the goods, either explicitly or by conduct, he cannot later reject them.

(m)   An unpaid seller of goods may be able to retrieve the goods even if title has passed to the buyer. He may also attempt to protect his position by retaining title until he has been paid. Failing such remedies, the seller may sue the buyer. If the seller breaches a condition of the contract, the buyer may reject the goods. The buyer may also sue the seller for breaches of conditions or warranties.

(n)   The Sale of Goods Act 1979 applies only to sales of goods. The Supply of Goods and Services Act 1982 makes similar provisions for contracts outside the scope of the 1979 Act.

BPP Publishing

Quick quiz

1   What topics are covered by statutory conditions implied (as part of the contract) by the Sale of Goods Act 1979?

2   What is the implied condition as to the seller's right to sell the goods?

3   What is a sale of goods by description and what is implied in such a sale?

4   When are defects of quality not a breach of the condition of merchantable quality?

5   What is merchantable quality?

6   In what circumstances is it an implied condition that the goods shall be fit for the purpose for which they are bought?

7   State (in outline) the statutory rules which determine when property in goods passes. Do these rules apply to every sale of goods?

8   Give three exceptions to the rule *nemo dat quod non habet*.

9   What is a severable contract?

10   When is a buyer deemed to have accepted goods?

11   What are the seller's remedies if he is not paid?

12   What is a retention of title clause?

13   What are the buyer's remedies for breach of contract?

14   What terms are implied into a contract which is wholly or substantially for the provision of services?

Solutions to exercises

1   Until B exercises the option, there is no agreement to transfer ownership of the car.

2   No: there would have been a single contract to sell petrol and coins for cash.

3   £1,000.

4   No: although 1959 is very close to 1958, the exact year is crucial for wine.

5   No: an expensive pen should be easy to write with.

6   S made it clear that he did not have the skill or judgement which R sought to rely on.

7   Thursday: rule 2 applies.

8   (a)   B did not buy the video recorder in the public part of the shop.

   (b)   The doctrine of market overt does not apply to sales *to* the shopkeeper.

9   Dawn Jones was aware of the sale to Dawn Smith.

10   10 pm is not during normal business hours, and the seller has not given the buyer a reasonable opportunity to inspect the goods.

11   The buyer may not become insolvent, or the carrier may be the buyer's agent.

12   The seller may bring an action for the price. The retention of title clause does not mention incorporation into Z Ltd's products, so it cannot be relied upon in this case.

13   The buyer/reseller might have to buy coal from other suppliers at the market price (23s.6d per ton) in order to fulfil the contract for resale. The loss on that transaction of 23s.6d - 19s.6d = 4s. per ton would have to be added to the lost profit of 3s.3d per ton.

14   *Marcel (Furriers) Ltd v Tapper 1953*

BPP Publishing

11 CONSUMER CREDIT

Your objectives

After completing this chapter you should:

(a) understand the features of the different forms of consumer credit agreement;

(b) know which agreements are regulated by the Consumer Credit Act 1974;

(c) know how regulated agreements are classified;

(d) know how debtors under regulated agreements are protected;

(e) understand the extent to which a connected lender may be liable along with a supplier of goods;

(f) know the ways in which an agreement may be terminated;

(g) know the extent to which the courts may intervene in extortionate credit bargains;

(h) know how advertising and canvassing for consumer credit are restricted;

(i) understand the legal status of credit card transactions.

Statutory references in this chapter are to the Consumer Credit Act 1974 unless otherwise noted.

1   Forms of consumer credit

Consumer credit takes a variety of forms. The following may be identified:

(a) hire purchase agreements;

(b) conditional sale agreements;

(c) credit sale agreements;

(d) consumer hire agreements.

The simplest form is a loan to a customer which he may use to purchase whatever goods or services he requires. But the creditor often prefers to supply goods himself to the consumer on hire purchase terms so that the goods remain the creditor's property and can be recovered if the debtor defaults until the consumer has paid the price including credit charges. It is a common business practice for a trader to sell his goods to a finance company so that the latter, in providing credit to a customer of the trader, can do so under a hire purchase or related transaction. There are also other special forms of credit transaction such as those involving bank credit cards, shop budget accounts, loans by pawnbrokers on the security of chattels deposited with them and so on.

Hire purchase

There are two elements in a hire purchase transaction.

172

(a)   Goods are bailed or delivered to the possession of the hirer, for his use, by the creditor who has purchased the goods from the dealer.

(b)   The hirer has an option to purchase the goods when he has completed payment of a number of instalments which represent the cash price plus a charge for credit.

The legal effect of a hire purchase agreement is that the hirer is *not* a buyer in possession of goods, the property in which has not yet passed to him. He has an option to buy the goods but he is not bound to exercise that option. He does not yet own the goods nor can he pass ownership to another person by an unauthorised sale. This protects the owner of the goods from losing title to them: the hirer is not legally competent to deprive him of it (with an exception under the Hire Purchase Act 1964 limited to motor vehicles).

The same conditions and warranties (in substance) are implied by law in a hire purchase agreement as in a sale of goods: Supply of Goods (Implied Terms) Act 1973. There are the same restrictions on contracting out of these terms by the use of exclusion clauses as apply to agreements for the sale of goods: Unfair Contract Terms Act 1977 s 6.

Conditional sale

The conditional sale agreement was developed as a means of avoiding the controls applied to hire purchase agreements. But it no longer has this effect since the same rules apply to either type of agreement. The essential features of a conditional sale agreement are as follows.

(a)   The buyer agrees to buy goods from the creditor, who purchased them from the dealer, and to pay the price by instalments.

(b)   The buyer obtains immediate possession but the transfer of ownership is postponed until he has paid all the instalments.

(c)   He is not a buyer or person who has agreed to buy goods for the purposes of Sale of Goods Act 1979 and so he cannot transfer ownership (which he has not yet obtained) to another person.

The Sale of Goods Act 1979 applies to such agreements.

Credit sale

A credit sale agreement is an agreement under which ownership as well as possession is transferred to the buyer by the creditor without delay, but the price is payable by instalments. The buyer is free to sell before the price has been paid. Such a sale is subject to regulation (to protect the buyer) under the Consumer Credit Act 1974.

Consumer hire

A consumer hire agreement is one for the bailment or hiring of goods which fulfils the following four conditions under s 15.

(a)   It is not a hire purchase agreement.

(b)   It is capable of lasting more than three months.

(c)   It does not require the hirer to pay more than £15,000.

(d)   The hirer is not a corporate body.

Because there is no element of credit a consumer hire agreement is *not* a consumer credit agreement.

Exercise 1

In which one of a hire purchase agreement, a conditional sale agreement and a credit sale agreement can the consumer pay all the instalments required yet still not acquire ownership of the goods?

---

2   What is a regulated agreement?

The Consumer Credit Act 1974 (CCA) regulates the provision of credit. 'Credit' includes a cash loan and any other form of financial benefit including hire purchase, conditional sale and credit sale agreements. Consumer hire agreements are *not* covered.

Except in respect of extortionate credit bargains (which are discussed later in this chapter) the CCA only applies to *regulated agreements*. These are agreements meeting the following conditions set out in ss 8-9.

(a)   *Individuals* (not companies) obtain credit. The use of the phrase *consumer credit* here is rather misleading since a sole trader or partnership obtaining credit for commercial purposes is protected by the 1974 Act.

(b)   *Credit not exceeding £15,000* is provided. The amount of credit given is not the total price paid by the debtor, but that total less any initial payment paid when the agreement is made and any charges for credit. If, for example, the debtor is to pay £16,500 in total of which £500 is paid on signing the agreement, and £1,000 in interest charges, the credit given is £15,000 (£16,500 less £500 less £1,000) and so the agreement is regulated by the 1974 Act.

(c)   The agreement is not *exempt*. The CCA therefore does not apply (s 16) to:

   (i)   building society *mortgages* for the purchase of land;

   (ii)   *fixed sum* debtor-creditor-supplier agreements with four or fewer instalments;

   (iii)   running account credit which is *settled in full* (as with American Express cards);

   (iv)   agreements where the *annual percentage rate* (APR) does not exceed 13% or 1% over Base Rate;

   (v)   credit sale agreements for *less than £50* (s 17); or

   (vi)   agreements where the creditor does not act in the course of a *business*.

3   The classification of regulated agreements

The 1974 Act uses an elaborate classification of consumer credit agreements to apply rules selectively to some types but not others. Small and non-commercial agreements, for example, are not subject to all the rules. What follows applies generally both to agreements for lending money and to agreements for the supply of goods under hire purchase and related types of agreement. References to 'debtor' and 'creditor' are to the hirer and the owner of goods let under a hire purchase agreement respectively. A regulated agreement is one covered by the Act.

To understand the Act we need to look at how regulated agreements are classified. This means analysing:

(a)   the type of credit;

(b)   the nature of the credit; and

(c)   the relationship of the parties to the agreement.

The type of credit

There are two types of credit, identified by s 10 of the Act.

(a)   In *running account credit,* also known as a revolving credit, the debtor does not have to apply for further amounts of credit after making the original credit agreement but automatically has the right to further credit, although there is usually a credit limit. Common examples are bank overdrafts and shop or credit card agreements.

(b)   *Fixed sum credit* is a once-only credit, such as a single loan. If the creditor later agrees to make a further loan there are deemed to be two fixed-sum credits, since the debtor had no automatic right to receive further credit.

The nature of the credit

A distinction is made as to the nature of credit in s 11 between an agreement whereby the creditor exercises some control over the use of his finance and one where he has no such control.

(a)   *Restricted use credit* (RUC) is seen in agreements whereby

   (i)   the creditor pays the funds direct to a supplier;

   (ii)   the debtor receives a credit token (such as a credit card) which may only be used in transactions with those suppliers who have agreed to take it; or

   (iii) the creditor also acts as supplier.

(b)   *Unrestricted use credit* (UUC) is the residual category where the creditor merely supplies funds and the debtor can use them in any way he sees fit.

The relationship of the parties to the agreement

Many of the more important provisions of the Act depend on the relationship between the parties to the agreement: that is, between the debtor, the creditor (the provider of finance and owner of goods) and the supplier (the provider of or dealer in the goods).

(a)   In a *debtor-creditor (D-C) agreement* the persons who supply the finance and the goods respectively are entirely separate. Thus the use of an overdrawn current account at a bank to purchase a hi-fi from a shop is a debtor-creditor agreement.

(b)   In a *debtor-creditor-supplier (D-C-S) agreement,* there are arrangements whereby the creditor and supplier of goods are linked: s 12. An arrangement whereby a car sales agency provides credit via its linked finance house is such an agreement; so too is a credit card transaction where, although creditor and supplier are different persons, a business arrangement exists between them that the supplier will accept the creditor's card produced by the buyer.

It is important to distinguish the two types of agreement above in order to see how rights are protected under the Act. In particular a creditor is jointly and severally liable with the supplier for misrepresentations made by the supplier or for breach of contract by the supplier in a D-C-S agreement: ss 56 and 75 (connected lender liability).

A *linked transaction* is one which is subsidiary to but in some way connected with the main credit transaction: s 19. It is thus automatically terminated if the main transaction is cancelled. The following are examples of linked transactions.

(a)   An agreement to sell an item which is financed by a (main) D-C-S credit agreement

(b)   An agreement entered into in order to comply with a term in the main credit agreement (such as the term often seen in the hire purchase of a car that the purchaser will insure it for the creditor's benefit)

(c) A preliminary agreement entered into by the debtor so that the creditor will then enter into the main agreement

---

Exercise 2

George borrows £5,000 from his bank as a loan of a fixed amount at 2% over base rate for an unspecified purpose. He uses the money to buy double glazing for his house.

(a)   Is there a regulated credit agreement?

(b)   Has RUC or UUC been provided?

(c)   Is the bank liable for misrepresentations by the double glazing company?

---

4   The protection of debtors

We have seen that the main object of the 1974 Act is the protection of individual debtors. The way in which it does this can be analysed into protection given *before* the agreement is made, *at the time* the agreement is made and *after* the agreement has been made.

Protection of the debtor before the agreement is made

It often happens that a 'negotiator' is involved in the 'antecedent negotiations' of a consumer credit agreement. This can happen in two ways.

(a)   A person buying, say, a motor car and wishing to finance it by a hire purchase agreement will obtain the car from a dealer. The dealer will arrange the finance on behalf of the purchaser through a credit institution. In effect, the car dealer, acting as negotiator, is a credit broker.

(b)   A person buys goods from a shop and pays by credit card.

In these cases it is provided by s 56 of the Act that the 'negotiator' (the car dealer or the shop) is the agent of the creditor. This has two effects.

(a)   The creditor is liable for any misrepresentations made by the negotiator as though he had made them himself.

(b)   Any money paid by the debtor to the negotiator will be regarded as having been received by the creditor.

Two further rules protect the debtor who has not yet entered into a binding regulated agreement.

(a)   A debtor is not bound by any prior agreement to enter into a regulated agreement, such as an option (s 59). Without this protection, the detailed rules covering regulated agreements could be circumvented by a prior promise to enter into obligations.

(b)   The debtor may withdraw from the agreement at any time before all the formalities are completed by giving notice to the creditor, the negotiator or the creditor's agent (s 57). Thus he may withdraw up to the time when the agreement is fully executed.

Protection of the debtor at the time the agreement is made

To protect the debtor at the time the agreement is being made the Act lays down detailed requirements as to the formalities of execution and the provision of copies.

BPP Publishing

Formalities of execution

The agreement must be in writing and its form (printed) and content are prescribed by regulations to ensure that the debtor is made aware of his rights and obligations, particularly his rights of cancellation and termination. The terms of the agreement must be complete and legible and all necessary insertion of particulars in blank spaces must be made before the debtor signs the agreement. Signature must be made in the 'signature box'.

The debtor must be supplied with all 'relevant information' relating to the agreement, including the cash price, the deposit paid, the timing and number of instalments, the total charge for credit (TCC) and the annual percentage rate (APR).

Failure to comply with the required formalities in making a consumer credit agreement makes it an improperly executed agreement. It can still be enforced by the debtor but the creditor will find it either difficult or impossible to enforce. It is:

(a) *unenforceable* by the creditor (s 127) if:

(i) it did not contain the basic terms when the debtor signed it;

(ii) the requirement for copies (and notices for a cancellable agreement) were not met (see below);

(b) *difficult to enforce* in other circumstances: for example court orders will be required and security and repossession will be more difficult to enforce (ss 65 and 113). In addition s 127 gives power to the court in such a case to vary terms and impose additional conditions.

The provision of copies

When the agreement is sent or presented to the debtor for his signature, he must be provided with a copy (which he may keep) of the agreement and of any document (such as conditions of sale of goods) referred to in the agreement. If, unusually, the creditor signs at the same time, this will be the only copy the debtor receives. If, as is common practice, the agreement has to be signed by the creditor or some other person, such as a guarantor, after the debtor has signed, the debtor is entitled within seven days of the agreement becoming completely executed (being signed by all parties) to receive a *second copy* of the executed agreement and all documents referred to in it.

Exercise 3

What types of insertions in blank spaces might an unscrupulous creditor try to make after a debtor has signed an agreement, were it not for the law against doing so?

Protection of the debtor after the agreement has been made: cancellable agreements

Even after the agreement has been made and the provisions as to formalities and copies have been met the debtor is protected to a limited extent by virtue of the fact that certain agreements are cancellable.

A cancellable agreement is one (other than most agreements for loans made in land transactions to which alternative safeguards apply) made in the following circumstances.

(a) There have been *oral representations*, for example statements concerning the terms of the loan or the quality of the goods, made in the presence of the debtor by or on behalf of the person with whom the debtor negotiates before the agreement is made.

Notes

(b)   The agreement is signed by the debtor *elsewhere than at the place of business of the creditor, supplier of the goods or other negotiator: s 67.*

This rather involved definition is designed to protect the debtor who may have been persuaded to enter into the agreement by a sales representative or other agent, usually in the course of a visit to the debtor's house. In such cases the debtor has a limited opportunity to cancel the agreement even after he has signed it.

But if the debtor goes to the creditor's office to sign the agreement that is treated as a deliberate act, no longer influenced by salesmanship, and the debtor has *no right of cancellation.*

Notice and cooling off

The debtor must be given written notice of his right to cancel a cancellable agreement. If he is entitled, as he usually is, to receive a second copy of the agreement when executed, it suffices to send him by post that copy which must include a statement of his rights. If, however, he is not entitled to a second copy of the agreement (because debtor and creditor sign together), he must be sent by post a separate notice of his right of cancellation within the same period of seven days after the agreement is made.

On receiving notice of his right of cancellation the debtor has a five day 'cooling off' period in which he may exercise it. If he decides to cancel he must give notice in writing to the appropriate person (designated in the notice of his cancellation rights). It takes effect as soon as it is posted.

If the procedures for notification of rights of cancellation are not observed, the creditor may not enforce the agreement against the debtor without obtaining the leave of the court.

The effect of cancellation

The effect of cancelling an agreement depends in part on the particular circumstances. In a D-C-S agreement for restricted use credit (such as a hire purchase agreement):

(a)   the debtor is no longer bound to make payments under the agreement and may recover any payments made (or goods which he has supplied in part exchange: in some circumstances he may have their value instead);

(b)   any goods supplied to the debtor may be collected from him (at his address) by the creditor; while waiting for recovery the debtor must for 21 days take reasonable care of the goods and he has a lien on them for any money or goods (see (a) above) to be returned to him.

Where there is simply a D-C agreement for unrestricted use credit (such as a cash loan), cancellation means that the debtor must repay that amount of the loan already received with interest. The agreement continues in force in relation to repayment of the debt and interest (including terms relating to timing and method), although if he repays the loan either within one month of cancellation or before the date of the first instalment due the debtor will not have to repay interest. Cancellation of an unrestricted use credit agreement has no effect on a linked transaction unless it is also a D-C-S agreement.

Exercise 4

Susan signs a credit agreement on 4 May. The notice of her right of cancellation is posted to her on 7 May and she receives it on 9 May. She posts a notice of cancellation on 13 May and it is received on 16 May. Is her notice of cancellation effective?

BPP Publishing

5 Lenders' liability

We have seen above that a creditor may be jointly liable with a supplier where there have been misrepresentations and/or a breach of contract. We shall now look at this in a little more detail.

Misrepresentation in antecedent negotiations: s 56

The negotiator in a regulated agreement who takes part in antecedent negotiations with the debtor is a deemed agent of the creditor or owner of the goods. A negotiator is defined by s 56 as:

(a) the creditor or owner (no agency arises);

(b) the dealer in case of an HP, conditional sale or credit sale agreement; or

(c) the supplier in the case of any other D-C-S agreement, such as a credit card transactions.

The term 'antecedent negotiations' means negotiations, such as advertisements, direct communication and other dealings, which take place either before the agreement is made (say in a hire purchase agreement) or before an individual transaction under an agreement takes place (say a particular purchase under an ongoing credit card agreement).

Two examples may clarify the protection offered by these provisions.

(a) A enters into a hire purchase agreement with B (the supplier) and C (the creditor) following antecedent negotiations by B. It later transpires that B made misrepresentations. A is entitled:

    (i) to rescind the entire agreement for credit against C; and

    (ii) to rescind the agreement for the hire of goods against B.

(b) A buys a hi-fi from B using the credit card provided by C. Again it transpires that B made misrepresentations. A is entitled:

    (i) to rescind against C only that aspect of the credit agreement relating to that one transaction: the rest of the agreement for the credit card stands; and

    (ii) to rescind the agreement for the purchase of goods against B.

It is only rarely that a debtor will have to rely on the supplier's agency under s 56 in order to make a claim against the creditor as principal. Usually he will simply sue the supplier, but alternatively he can make use of the connected lender's liability under s 75.

Connected lender liability: s 75

In a D-C-S agreement there are two primary contracts: one between the debtor and the supplier (for the goods) and another between the debtor and the creditor (for the credit). Under normal principles of contract law only the parties to a contract can enforce it or be liable under it. However in D-C-S agreements the debtor is entitled to claim for breach of contract and/or misrepresentation against the creditor *provided* he also has such a claim against the supplier: s 75. Hence if A pays B for a holiday using the credit card supplied by C, and B fails to supply the holiday (he is in breach), A may claim for breach of contract against C. This right is of most help to consumers when the supplier becomes insolvent and cannot provide compensation.

Note that an important limitation on s 75 is that it applies only to transactions valued between £100 and £30,000. Transactions of less than £100 are protected only by s 56. By far the most important application of s 75 is to credit card (*not* debit card) agreements.

Where the creditor himself contracts with the debtor to supply goods or services, and where there is a conditional sale, credit sale or hire purchase agreement, with the creditor first purchasing the goods from the supplier, there is no need for ss 56 or 75. The creditor is himself liable for breach of implied terms as to title, description, quality and so on, and for misrepresentation.

Exercise 5

A buys goods costing £90 from B using a credit card provided by C. B made no representations about the goods, but they proved to be unsatisfactory and A wishes to sue for breach of contract. Does A have any claim against C?

---

6   Termination of credit agreements

Once it has come into operation, an agreement may be terminated before it is fully performed because:

(a)   the debtor elects to pay off the credit early;

(b)   the debtor elects to terminate it; or

(c)   the creditor terminates it for breach of its terms and/or default by the debtor.

Debtor's election to pay off credit

No provision in a consumer credit agreement may prevent the debtor from paying off the entire amount of credit early. He will obtain a rebate of the interest which he is required to pay under the agreement but which is not yet due. He may either give notice of his intention to repay or merely pay the balance less the rebate. In the latter case the notice immediately takes effect (although some future date may be specified on which it is to take effect).

Debtor's election to terminate

The debtor has a statutory right (which cannot be excluded by the agreement) to terminate a hire purchase or conditional sale agreement at any time, if he pays an amount which raises his aggregate payments to half of the total price plus the whole of any installation charge: s 100.

Suppose, for example, that the total price is £100 and the installation charge £10. The debtor has paid instalments of £30 in all, plus the installation charge and owes an instalment of £10. The debtor may terminate the agreement and must raise the aggregate of his payment to £60 (half of £100 plus £10). As he has paid £40 already his liability on giving notice of termination is to pay a further £20. If he had paid instalments of £50 in aggregate plus the installation charge and owed £10 as an overdue instalment he would be liable to pay that £10 since (although he has already paid half the total price) it is a payment due at the time of termination.

If the debtor considers that the above formula produces an excessive amount, he may apply to the court to order a reduction.

The debtor must of course permit the creditor to retake possession of the goods. If the debtor has not taken reasonable care of the goods while in his possession, the creditor is entitled (in addition to the sums payable as described above) to recover compensation for the damage to his goods caused by the debtor's failure to take care of them.

Creditor's right to terminate

By s 98 the creditor is allowed to terminate the agreement if the debtor is in breach of one of the contract's terms other than that relating to repayment. For example, he may terminate

---

BPP Publishing

where the debtor made misrepresentations, where the debtor has become insolvent or where the goods are destroyed. The creditor usually then has the right to repossess the goods and the debtor must pay up to half of the price. Seven days notice must be given.

If the creditor is entitled to terminate the agreement by reason of the debtor's failure to maintain the agreed payments, the creditor must first serve on the debtor a *'default notice'* which:

(a)   specifies the default alleged;

(b)   requires it to be remedied if remediable or demands compensation (if any is required) if irremediable; and

(c)   specifies a period of not less than seven days in which action is to be taken as required under (b). This gives the debtor time to apply to the court if he decides to do so: s 87.

Repossession of goods

If the debtor is in breach of a hire purchase or conditional sale agreement and he has paid at least one third of the total price for the goods (plus the whole of any installation charges) the goods are then *'protected goods'* which the creditor may only repossess from the debtor after obtaining an order of the court: s 90.

If the creditor recovers possession of protected goods without a court order, the regulated agreement is terminated and the debtor is released from all liability under the agreement: he may even recover all sums he has paid under it: s 91.

Whether or not the goods are protected the creditor may not enter premises to take possession of them except under an order of the court: s 92.

Exercise 6

David obtained credit of £3,000 under a hire purchase agreement, falsely representing that he was a homeowner. When the creditor discovers the facts, he decides to repossess the goods and terminate the agreement. At that time David has paid £1,300 and is not in arrears. How should the creditor proceed, and what is the most he can hope to obtain?

---

7   Extortionate credit bargains

Unlike the rest of the 1974 Act there is no £15,000 limit on the application of the Act to an extortionate credit bargain: s 137.

This part of the CCA gives the court the power to re-open and make appropriate orders in relation to a credit agreement made on terms which the court finds 'grossly exorbitant' or 'contrary to ordinary principles of fair dealing'. It is intended to apply, for example, to moneylending at very high rates of interest. However, the rate of interest is not the only factor considered by the court. The courts also look at 'other relevant circumstances': s 138. These circumstances include the debtor's age and business experience, the degree of sales pressure and the extent of explanations. If it does decide to reopen an agreement the court has wide powers to relieve the debtor of having to make payments beyond what is 'fairly due and reasonable': s 139.

The extortionate credit bargains provision can be used in one of two ways: as a separate action in itself or as a defence to an action brought by the creditor to enforce the agreement.

BPP Publishing

Other forms of judicial control

The county court has wide powers of regulation of consumer credit transactions falling under the 1974 Act. In particular it may grant a 'time order' allowing a debtor in default more time in which to remedy his default.

The court also has express power to order that some goods hired to the debtor shall be transferred to his immediate ownership and others returned forthwith to the creditor: s 133. This procedure can be used to clear up an unsatisfactory situation on a basis fair to both parties.

8   Consumer credit licensing, advertising and canvassing

Part III of the CCA relates to persons conducting a business dealing with regulated agreements. The aim of these provisions is to establish a system of licensing for:

(a)   consumer credit businesses and consumer hire businesses; and

(b)   ancillary businesses.

Category (a) above includes not only finance companies, but also any retailer who sells his goods on credit sale, conditional sale or hire purchase. Category (b) includes such businesses as credit brokerage, debt collecting and operating a credit reference agency. It follows that the retailer who arranges finance for his customer through a finance house is included, because he is in effect acting as a credit broker. All these businesses must be licensed under a system operated by the Director General of Fair Trading (DGFT). Anyone carrying on such a business without a licence commits an offence.

The DGFT has powers to vary, suspend, renew and withdraw licences. A regulated agreement made by an unlicensed business or through the agency of an unlicensed credit broker will generally be unenforceable against the customer. Similarly, any agreement for the services of an unlicensed ancillary business will be unenforceable against the client.

Licences granted before 1 June 1991 run for a period of 15 years. Licences granted on or after that date run for a period of 5 years.

Advertising consumer credit

Regulations made under the Act control advertisements aimed at providing credit or goods on hire to non-business customers. The objective of these regulations is to ensure that consumers have a fair impression of the product offered and a means of comparison between different products.

Advertisement must be phrased so as to fall into one of the following three categories - simple, intermediate or full.

(a)   A *simple* advertisement neither specifies a price nor contains an indication that credit or hire products are available.

(b)   An *intermediate* advertisement must, at the very least, contain an indication as to where full written credit details can be obtained.

(c)   A *full* advertisement must contain a great deal of information, the most important of which is the APR.

Warnings as to the consequences of giving security for regulated agreements are also required. It is compulsory when advertising home mortgages to include the warning 'Your home may be at risk if you do not keep up repayments on a mortgage or other loan secured on it.'

BPP Publishing

Canvassing consumer credit

'Canvassing' is 'orally soliciting an individual to enter into a credit agreement'. This is permitted if it occurs on the trade premises of either the debtor or the creditor (s 48) but it is greatly restricted off trade premises.

Canvassing off trade premises by making representations to induce a customer to make a regulated agreement arises when the canvasser:

(a)   makes oral representations during a visit by the canvasser for that purpose;

(b)   makes that visit to somewhere other than the business premises of the canvasser, creditor, supplier or consumer; and

(c)   does not make that visit in response to a request made on a previous occasion.

The controls on canvassing off trade premises are as follows.

(a)   Canvassing D-C agreements off trade premises is an offence: s 49. It is an offence even if made in response to a request unless that request is in writing and signed.

(b)   Canvassing other regulated agreements off trade premises can only be done under a licence expressly authorising such activity: s 23.

One important exception relates to overdrafts on current accounts where the canvasser is the creditor or an employee of the creditor. Such an activity is not banned nor does it require a special licence.

Exercise 7

A supplier of credit in D-C agreements sends Liz a leaflet about credit and a card for her to reply on. The card already has her name and address printed on it. It says 'Please tick the box below and post the card back to us, and a representative will call at your home to discuss credit facilities'. Liz returns the card and a representative calls. Liz decides not to take any credit. Has an offence been committed?

---

9   Credit cards

The use of a credit card involves three parties and three transactions between them.

(a)   On producing his card to a supplier for goods and/or services, the cardholder can obtain what he requires without paying for it immediately.

(b)   The supplier recovers from the credit card company the price of the goods or services less a discount which is the credit card company's profit margin.

(c)   At monthly intervals the credit card company sends to the cardholder a monthly statement. The cardholder may either settle interest free within 25 days or he may pay interest on the balance owing after 25 days. He is required to pay a minimum of 5% or £5 whichever is the lesser.

Payment by credit card is *not* a conditional payment, unlike payment by cheque where the drawer of the cheque is not discharged from his debt until the cheque has been honoured. As soon as a buyer completes and signs a valid credit card voucher which is accepted by the supplier, the buyer's obligations to the supplier are complete.

A credit limit is set for each card holder, the limit usually being well below £15,000. Hence the card issued to an individual is subject to regulation by the Consumer Credit Act 1974. In the terminology used in the Act a credit card is a 'credit token' used in a debtor - creditor - supplier agreement.

The debtor is liable for up to £50 for misuse of his credit card *before* he reports it stolen or lost. He is not liable at all after he has reported it lost or stolen or if he has reported that someone else knows the PIN. He will be had liable for all losses if he has acted fraudulently.

Exercise 8

When a credit card is used in a shop, there are three parties: the cardholder, the shop and the credit card company. There are three contracts, one between each pair of these parties. Briefly describe each of these three contracts.

Chapter roundup

(a) Consumer credit arises in simple loans and overdrafts, in credit card transactions, in revolving credit arrangements and in hire purchase, conditional sale and credit sale agreements.

(b) Agreements regulated under the Consumer Credit Act 1974 are non-exempt agreements to provide credit of up to £15,000 to individuals.

(c) Credit may be running account or fixed sum, and it may be restricted use or unrestricted use.

(d) Agreements may be debtor-creditor agreements or debtor-creditor-supplier agreements, and there may be linked transactions.

(e) A debtor is protected before an agreement is made in that a negotiator may be treated as the creditor's agent, agreements to enter into regulated agreements are not binding and the debtor may withdraw at any time before completion of the formalities.

(f) The formalities of execution protect the debtor at the time of making an agreement.

(g) Some agreements are cancellable by the debtor even after they have been made. The debtor may recover payments made, but must give up goods supplied.

(h) A creditor may be liable for misrepresentations in antecedent negotiations. Where connected lender liability arises and the debtor could sue the supplier for misrepresentation or breach of contract, he may also sue the lender.

(i) An agreement may be terminated by the debtor's election to pay off credit, by the debtor's election to terminate or (in certain circumstances) by the creditor.

(j) The courts can make orders in respect of extortionate credit bargains.

(k) Consumer credit businesses and ancillary businesses must be licensed by the Director General of Fair Trading. Advertisements for consumer credit are regulated, and canvassing consumer credit is subject to strict controls.

(l) In a credit card transaction, the buyer obtains goods or services from the supplier in return for a signed credit card slip. The only subsequent transactions are between the supplier and the credit card company (which pays the supplier), and between the credit card company and the buyer (who pays the company).

BPP Publishing

Quick quiz

1   What is (a) a hire purchase agreement and (b) a conditional sale?

2   To what transactions does the Consumer Credit Act 1974 apply?

3   What is the difference between a debtor-creditor and a debtor-creditor-supplier consumer credit agreement?

4   Give three examples of linked transactions.

5   What form must a regulated agreement take?

6   When must a debtor be given a copy of the agreement?

7   What is a cancellable regulated agreement?

8   How long after signing the agreement may a debtor in a cancellable agreement cancel?

9   What is connected lender liability?

10   What limit is placed on the amount to be paid by a hirer who terminates a hire purchase agreement before completing payment of the agreed instalments?

11   What is a default notice and what must it contain?

12   What are protected goods?

13   How may the court regulate (a) extortionate credit bargains and (b) consumer credit transactions?

14   What restrictions are contained in CCA relating to advertising and canvassing of consumer credit?

Solutions to exercises

1   A hire purchase agreement.

2   (a)   Yes

     (b)   UUC

     (c)   No

3   The rate of interest and the levels of penalties for defaults are two obvious examples.

4   Yes: 13 May is within five days of 9 May.

5   No: s 75 does not apply to transactions of less than £100, and s 56 only applies if misrepresentations are made.

6   He should seek a court order. He may obtain the goods plus a further £200 (£3,000/2 - £1,300).

7   Yes: Liz did not sign the request for a visit.

8   The shop contracts with the cardholder to supply goods in exchange for an authorisation to the credit card company to debit the cardholder's account.

     The credit card company contracts with the shop to pay the amounts due on sales less a fee charged by the credit card company.

     The cardholder contracts with the credit card company to pay amounts debited to his account.

12 CONSUMER PROTECTION

Your objectives

After completing this chapter you should:

(a) understand the role of the Director General of Fair Trading;

(b) be aware of the different types of code of practice which exist;

(c) know what constitutes a trade description and how an offence may be committed by giving one;

(d) know how statements about services, accommodation and facilities may constitute offences;

(e) know how statements about prices may constitute offences;

(f) appreciate the extent to which a consumer may sue and recover damages for negligence;

(g) understand the scope of actions for product liability.

1 Consumer protection

Under the Fair Trading Act 1973 (FTA), the post of Director General of Fair Trading (DGFT) was created. The DGFT heads the Office of Fair Trading (OFT) and has overall supervision of consumer protection. The OFT is divided into two sections dealing respectively with consumer affairs and competition. Competition is the subject of the next chapter; in this chapter we will describe various aspects of consumer affairs.

The FTA gave the DGFT a number of different functions, as follows:

(a) to identify and eliminate harmful practices;

(b) to take direct action against individual traders;

(c) to promote codes of practice.

Harmful practices

The DGFT has a general duty to keep under review commercial activities carried on in the UK, in order to establish whether the interests of consumers are suffering in any way. The OFT collates information (mainly provided by local trading standards departments) and investigates and reports on matters of public concern.

The FTA established the Consumer Protection Advisory Committee (CPAC). This is a body consisting of up to 15 members with experience in consumer affairs. The DGFT may refer to the CPAC any consumer trade practice, and will do so where the practice appears to have the effect of misleading or otherwise harming consumers. If the CPAC reports adversely on the practice, the DGFT can recommend to the Secretary of State that an order under s 22 for the control or prevention of practices which adversely affect the consumer's interest be made: s 17.

186

The Secretary of State may make orders under s 22 FTA to prevent or control consumer trade practices, infringement of which is an offence. Such orders expressly do not affect civil rights: s 26. Defences are available similar to those under the Trade Descriptions Act 1968 (see below).

Persistent offenders

The DGFT also has wide powers in respect of individual traders. Where it appears that a trader is persistently in breach of the law in such a way as to harm the interests of consumers, the DGFT will try to obtain an undertaking from the trader as to his conduct in the future: s 34(1). If that fails, he can institute proceedings in the Restrictive Practices Court: s 35. Breach of an order issued by the Restrictive Practices Court constitutes contempt and may lead to fines or imprisonment.

Persistent offenders are identified by local authority trading standards officers, who may then report them to the DGFT. Cases usually concern traders who have continued to defy the law despite warnings from the local authority in question.

Codes of practice

Codes of practice for particular trades can be classified into four groups:

(a) codes carrying the DGFT's endorsement;

(b) enforceable codes;

(c) statutory codes; and

(d) other codes of practice with limited status.

Codes of practice carrying the DGFT's endorsement

The DGFT is responsible under FTA for promoting codes of practice amongst traders. After negotiations between him and the relevant trade association a list of rules of conduct is drawn up, the objects being:

(a) to promote a high standard of trade practice; and

(b) to protect the consumer's interests.

These codes are purely voluntary in that they are not enforced by the courts, but the OFT monitors their operation and the trade associations themselves try to ensure that the standards are adhered to by their members. Common features in these codes would be an agreement not to limit legal liability except in special, stated circumstances (and obviously within the limits of the Unfair Contract Terms Act 1977), a set standard of care, a disciplinary procedure for members and agreed procedures for the settlement of disputes, such as arbitration.

Enforceable codes of practice

A code of practice which is enforceable by means of sanctions falling short of legal proceedings is known as an enforceable code. It will set down codes of conduct which can be enforced against people engaged in a certain trade or business, even though they are not members of the relevant trade body. The British Code of Advertising Practice is an example.

Statutory codes of practice

Codes which are drawn up with the involvement of government departments and the approval of the relevant minister may be given legal status.

Other codes of practice

Because of the aura of respectability imparted to a trade which has an association and a code of practice, many commercial areas have acquired codes of practice which have no status at all and afford neither legal nor practical assistance.

Exercise 1

Give some examples of trade practices (not involving collusion with other traders) which might be harmful.

---

2   Trade descriptions

The law relating to trade descriptions is contained in the Trade Descriptions Act 1968 (TDA) which replaced and considerably extended the provisions of earlier Merchandise Marks Acts, and in the Consumer Protection Act 1987 (CPA).

A consumer seeking a *civil* remedy for a false trade description will need to rely on the Misrepresentation Act 1967 or the Sale of Goods Act 1979. This is because the TDA defines *criminal* offences, and 'a contract for the supply of goods shall not be void or unenforceable by reason only of a contravention of this Act': s 35. However, the criminal court has power to order an offender to pay compensation to his victim.

There are three principal offences created by the legislation:

(a)   applying a false trade description to *goods* and supplying or offering to supply any such goods: s 1 TDA (a *strict liability* offence);

(b)   making false statements relating to *services, accommodation or facilities:* s 14 TDA; and

(c)   making misleading statements as to the price of goods: s 20 CPA.

Private individuals are not within the scope of the Act; these activities only constitute an offence if they occur *in the course of a trade or business.*

Case: Davies v Sumner 1984
The defendant was a self-employed courier who used his car almost exclusively in connection with his business as a courier. He sold the car in part exchange for a replacement vehicle.

Held: the sale transaction was incidental to the business and it was not made in the course of the business.

This case can be contrasted with another.

Case: Havering London Borough v Stevenson 1970
The defendant ran a car hire business. In accordance with his usual practice, he sold a hire car when it was of no further use to the business. A false description was given as to the mileage of the vehicle.

Held: the false description was made in the course of a trade or business.

False trade descriptions

A *trade description* (s 2 TDA) is any indication, direct or indirect, of:

BPP Publishing

(a)   quantity, size or gauge;

(b)   method of manufacture, production, processing or reconditioning;

(c)   composition: for example, this would cover a statement that an item of jewellery was made of solid silver when in fact it was only silver plated;

(d)   fitness for purpose, strength, performance, behaviour or accuracy;

(e)   any physical characteristics not included in the preceding paragraphs;

(f)   testing by any person and the results of testing: for example, this would cover a statement that the item had qualified for the kitemark of the British Standards Institution;

(g)   approval by any person or conformity with a type approved by any person: for example, this would cover a statement that a product had been recommended in the magazine *Which*;

(h)   place or date of manufacture, production, processing or reconditioning;

(i)   person by whom manufactured, produced, processed or reconditioned; or

(j)   other history, including previous ownership or use. For example, this would cover the kind of claim often made by car dealers, 'only one previous owner'.

A trade description is regarded as false in this context if it is false to a material degree (s 3(1)) and relates in some way to the sale and supply of goods.

Case: R v Ford Motor Co Ltd 1974
The defendants supplied a dealer with a new car which had been damaged at the factory in a collision, and then repaired.

Held: it was not false to describe the car as 'new' since to a material extent this was true: the car had been perfectly repaired.

False trade descriptions need not necessarily be made by the seller: a buyer can commit the offence. The statement might be made deliberately, recklessly or entirely innocently: the offence is the same.

Case: Fletcher v Budgen 1974
A car dealer negotiating to buy a car informed the owner that it could not be repaired and was only fit for scrap. The seller sold it to the dealer for £2. The dealer repaired it and advertised it for sale for £136.

Held: the buyer was guilty of an offence.

A statement which is misleading, although not false to a material degree, is still caught by the TDA.

Case: Dixons Ltd v Barnett 1988
D correctly described a telescope for sale as having a magnification of 455 times; it did not add that at that level the result was simply a blur.

Held: an offence had been committed under s 1 TDA.

Disclaimers

The motor trade industry has featured in a number of cases under the TDA, particularly in respect of the mileage and condition of used cars. It was held in *Norman v Bennett 1974* that a disclaimer as to the accuracy of the odometer given equal prominence as the figure on the odometer is a valid defence. But the disclaimer must be reasonable under the Unfair Contract

Terms Act 1977 and its terms must be as 'bold, precise and compelling' as the claim itself. A supplier who has deliberately made a false statement cannot issue a disclaimer in relation to it: *R v Southwood 1987*.

Exercise 2

Which one or more of the following might be a false trade description?

(a)   As used by the United States Army

(b)   Worthy of your serious consideration

(c)   Has won a Design Council award

(d)   Functions at room temperature

Services, accommodation and facilities

With regard to services, accommodation and facilities, s 14 TDA makes it an offence to make false statements deliberately or recklessly. The statement in question must be false 'to a material degree'. Under s 14, an element of knowledge or recklessness (*mens rea* - literally 'guilty mind') is required. Recklessness will be established even though the falsity was due to lack of thought rather than actual dishonesty. The situation here differs from the situation with regard to *goods*: false statements with regard to goods are normally an offence whether or not they were made deliberately and/or recklessly.

Statements include such things as information in a travel brochure: *R v Thomson Holidays 1974*. If the defendant knows the statement to be false, it is irrelevant that he did not know it had been made on his behalf. This may occur, for instance, where a false statement in a brochure continues to be published: *Wings Ltd v Ellis 1985*. Falsity is judged as at the time the statement was made, as where a holiday brochure indicates that a hotel is fully built when in fact the picture of it is just an artist's impression: *Yugotours Ltd v Wadsley 1988*. But if the statement was true when made, subsequent events do not then render it false: *Sunair Holidays v Dodd 1970*.

The subject matter to which s 14 TDA applies is the provision of services, accommodation and facilities as well as their nature and the time at which, manner in which or persons by whom they are to be provided. The location and amenities of any accommodation provided are covered, as are any claims as to the services, accommodation or facilities having been approved or examined by any person.

Services include professional services such as those of an architect: *R v Breeze 1973*. However, a description as to the nature of a sale (for instance, advertising a seasonal sale as a 'closing down sale') is not applied to 'facilities' and hence is not covered by s 14: *Westminster City Council v Ray Allen (Manshops) Ltd 1982*.

Misleading prices

It is an offence to make misleading statements as to price: ss 20, 21 CPA. Such misleading statement might be:

(a)   that the price is less than it really is;

(b)   that the price applied depends on facts which are not in fact the case;

(c)   that the price covers matters for which an additional charge will actually be made; or

(d)   that the price is expected to rise, fall or stay the same, when in fact the trader has no such expectation.

There are other ways in which a price description may be misleading. For example, it may be an offence to indicate a price which fails to state that VAT will be added: *Richards v Westminster Motors Ltd 1975*.

A defence exists to a prosecution under s 20 that the defendant acted with due diligence to avoid committing an offence: s 39.

The protection afforded by s 20 only operates in favour of consumers and only when the price indication is made in the course of a business. Although the protection applies to accommodation, it only affects the sale or leasing of property if it is a new house.

The prices code

A code of practice has been issued under s 25 CPA giving practical advice to retailers as to what exactly constitutes a misleading price indication. It mainly deals with some difficult issues such as price comparisons and seasonal sales. It is not automatically an offence to contravene the Code.

Defences under trade descriptions legislation

Under s 24 TDA it is a general defence for a person to prove *both* of the following.

(a)   The commission of the offence was due to:

   (i)   a mistake;

   (ii)   reliance on information supplied to the defendant;

   (iii)   the act or default of another person; or

   (iv)   an accident or some other cause beyond his control.

(b)   He took all reasonable precautions and exercised all due diligence to avoid the commission of such an offence by himself or any person under his control.

The reasonableness of precautions is often closely scrutinised; they must be more than a token gesture.

A specific defence is available to a supplier of goods. He has a defence under s 24(3) if he can show that he did not know and could not reasonably have found out:

(a)   that the goods did not conform to the description; or

(b)   that the description had been applied to the goods.

Enforcement of trade descriptions legislation

It is the duty of local weights and measures authorities to enforce the law on trade descriptions; most authorities have appointed trading standards officers to do so.

Breach of the legislation has no civil consequences, so a consumer who complains to the trading standards officer and sees a successful prosecution still has no redress. However, it is possible to obtain compensation for loss caused by a criminal act under different legislation.

Exercise 3

A boiler is advertised at a price of '£1,200 including installation'. In fact, only delivery and fixing the boiler to the wall are included, and an extra charge is made for connecting gas and water pipes. Has an offence been committed?

3 Consumer safety

A person who suffers injury or loss in connection with defective or dangerous goods may have remedies as follows.

(a) If he is the purchaser he can probably recover damages from the vendor for breach of the statutory implied conditions of quality imposed by the Sale of Goods Act 1979. If he deals as consumer he cannot be deprived of these safeguards; in any other case an attempt to exclude or restrict them is void unless it satisfies a test of reasonableness: Unfair Contract Terms Act 1977.

(b) If he suffers personal injury or damage to property by a defective product he may be able to recover damages for negligence from the manufacturer under the law of tort. Any attempt to exclude liability for personal injury or death due to negligence is void and exemption from other liability is usually subject to a test of reasonableness: Unfair Contract Terms Act 1977.

Although a supplier has no general duty at common law to take care in examining and if necessary remedying defective products supplied to him by a manufacturer, a dealer in goods which are secondhand or otherwise likely to be defective by their nature has such a duty. Thus a car dealer who sells a secondhand car should examine it to ensure that it is roadworthy: *Andrews v Hopkinson 1957*.

Negligence

To succeed in an action for negligence, the plaintiff must show:

(a) the existence of a duty of care by the defendant;

(b) a breach of that duty by the defendant; and

(c) injury or damage (or in some cases financial loss) suffered by the plaintiff as a foreseeable consequence of the breach.

Duty of care

A manufacturer's liability for physical damage or injury to users of his products has been well established since the case of *Donoghue v Stevenson 1932*, in which the House of Lords ruled that a person might owe a duty of care to another with whom he had no contractual relationship at all.

> *Case: Donoghue v Stevenson 1932*
> A purchased from a retailer a bottle of ginger beer for consumption by A's companion B. The bottle was opaque, so that its contents were not visible. As B poured the ginger beer, the remains of a decomposed snail fell into her glass from the bottle. B became seriously ill. She sued C, the manufacturer, who argued that, as there was no contract between B and him, he owed her no duty of care and so was not liable.
>
> *Held:* C was liable to B. Every person owes a duty of care to his 'neighbour', to 'persons so closely and directly affected by any act that I ought reasonably to have them in contemplation as being so affected'.

The law of negligence applies in product liability cases such as *Donoghue v Stevenson* itself where physical injury or damage results from a failure to take proper precautions, unless the consumer has a reasonable opportunity of avoiding the injury by intermediate inspection or by routine precautions.

BPP Publishing

Case: Grant v Australian Knitting Mills 1936

A purchased from a retailer a pair of underpants made by AKM. Because of AKM's negligence the garment still contained a bleaching chemical. G contracted dermatitis. AKM argued that G could have washed the garment before use, thereby removing the bleaching agent.

Held: the duty of care does not extend to preventing injury avoidable by reasonable and expected precautions at a later stage. But washing a new garment before use is not such a normal precaution. AKM was liable.

Breach of duty of care

The standard of care when a duty of care exists is that which is reasonable. This requires that the person concerned should do what a reasonable man 'guided upon those considerations which ordinarily regulate the conduct of human affairs' would do, and abstain from doing what a reasonable man would not do.

Consequential harm

For a claim to succeed, this third element must be proved. In deciding whether a claim should be allowed, the court will consider whether the breach of duty of care gave rise to the harm, and whether the harm was too remote from the breach.

Exercise 4

Meryl bought a new fridge. The fridge bore a conspicuous notice that the instruction booklet should be read in full before the fridge was used. The instruction booklet stated that the fridge should be left for three hours before being turned on, so that the refrigerant could settle. Meryl ignored the notice and the booklet and turned the fridge on immediately. There was a small explosion, damaging her kitchen. Would she be able to sue the manufacturer for negligence?

Economic loss

The cases above relate to instances of damage to person or property. The question of liability for purely economic loss is still uncertain in its scope. Economic loss usually arises in the form of profits which a business would have generated had it not been for the act complained of. Generally, if financial loss is attached in some way to physical damage it can be claimed for, but loss of pure profits is not recoverable.

Case: Spartan Steel and Alloys Ltd v Martin & Co (Contractors) Ltd 1973

The defendant's employees negligently severed an electricity cable supplying the plaintiff's factory. The plaintiff was operating a furnace at the time and the process was ruined.

Held: the plaintiff could recover for damages to the materials in the furnace and for loss of profit on that particular melting operation, but not for loss of profits on melting processes which could not take place because of the interruption to the power supply.

If the courts can identify a special relationship 'akin to contract' between plaintiff and defendant, a claim for loss of profits may succeed.

Case: Junior Books v Veitchi Co Ltd 1983

The defendants were sub-contractors engaged to lay a floor in the plaintiff's factory. Their contract was with the main contractor, not with the plaintiff. The floor was defective and had to be replaced (pure economic loss, as the only damage was to the product itself).

Held: the defendants owed the plaintiffs a duty of care. They were not producing goods for an unknown consumer; they were working for a particular person whose identity was known and who was relying on their skill and judgement as flooring contractors.

The special nature of the *Junior Books* case has been stressed in subsequent decisions, which have reverted to the award of damages for economic loss only where that loss is attached to physical loss. Thus in *Muirhead v Industrial Tank Specialities Ltd 1986* the plaintiffs were unable to recover loss of profits on lobster breeding when lobsters died due to the inadequacy of water pumps in their filtration plant.

4   Product liability

The Consumer Protection Act 1987

Part I of the Consumer Protection Act 1987 (CPA) has the advantage for the consumer that he does not have to prove negligence, nor that there was any privity of contract between him and the person he is suing. In other words the Act imposes strict civil liability, and this liability cannot be excluded by any disclaimer.

Strict product liability

Claims for losses caused by defects in a product may be brought against:

(a)   the manufacturer of the end product;

(b)   the manufacturer of a defective component (although he has a defence if he can show that he followed the instructions or specifications of the manufacturer of the end product);

(c)   an importer into the European Community

(d)   an 'own-brander'; and

(e)   a supplier, who is usually a retailer.

Because of the potential liability of the parties above, it is usual for a supplier only to be liable if he will not disclose the identity of the importer or manufacturer.

The burden of proof is on the consumer to prove that:

(a)   the product contained a defect;

(b)   he suffered damage;

(c)   the damage resulted from the defect; and

(d)   the defendant was either the producer or some other person listed above.

Defective product

A product will be found to be unsafe where it is not as safe as it is reasonable to expect. This standard of relative safety requires a court to take into account all circumstances surrounding the product, such as the way it is advertised, the time at which it was supplied, its anticipated normal use, the provision of instructions for use and even its likely misuse, in establishing the standard required. Also the benefit to society and the cost of making the product safer can be considered.

BPP Publishing

The products covered by this legislation include all goods, such as raw materials, components and packaging, plus electricity, except non-processed agricultural products and buildings.

The scope of the Act

Consumers and other users (such as the donee of an electric iron received as a gift), but not business users, can claim compensation for death, personal injury or damage to other property (but not for damage to the product itself nor for economic loss). There is unlimited liability but:

(a) a claim must be brought within three years of the fault becoming apparent;

(b) no claim may be brought more than ten years after the original supply; and

(c) where the claim is for damage to property, it must not be business property which is damaged and the amount of the damage must be more than £275.

Exercise 5

A gas cooker is made by A Ltd. A Ltd uses gas valves made by B Ltd to A Ltd's specification. A Ltd sells the cooker to C (Retailers) Ltd, which sells it to D, a private individual. The cooker explodes because the gas valve, although correctly made to A Ltd's specification, had been fitted wrongly. Only A Ltd has been negligent. Against which companies may D claim under Part I of the Consumer Protection Act 1987?

Defences

The defendant has six possible defences.

(a) 'Development risk' (the 'state of the art' defence): the state of knowledge at the time of manufacture and supply was such that no manufacturer could have been expected to detect the fault. The inclusion of this defence in the Act means that many victims of drugs which had damaging side effects may be left without a remedy. The defence was kept so as not to discourage medical research.

(b) The defect did not exist in the product when originally supplied.

(c) The product complied with mandatory statutory or EC standards.

(d) The supply was otherwise than in the course of a business.

(e) More than ten years have elapsed since the product was first supplied.

(f) The defect was wholly attributable to the design of a subsequent product into which the product in question was incorporated.

Although liability under the Act to a person who has suffered damage cannot be excluded or limited by any contract term or by a notice, parties other than the person damaged who are in the chain of distribution are free to adjust the liabilities between themselves, subject to any common law or statutory controls, such as the Unfair Contract Terms 1977.

Criminal liability

It is an offence to supply consumer goods which fail to comply with a general safety requirement: Part II of the Act. This requirement is further defined in the Act partly with reference to published safety regulations, which cover such diverse matters as furniture, prams, fireworks and nightdresses. Goods are defective if their safety does not come up to the standard normally expected by users. Instructions, presentation, distribution and the product's normal uses are all taken into account.

BPP Publishing

The general safety requirement and the safety regulations are again enforced by trading standards officers, who have a system of notices which are served on offenders.

Chapter roundup

(a) The Director General of Fair Trading works to eliminate harmful practices, seeks assurances from persistent offenders and promotes codes of practice. Some codes of practice have the force of law, but many do not.

(b) Practically all statements of fact about goods can be trade descriptions. Applying false trade descriptions to goods which are supplied or offered for supply is an offence.

(c) It is an offence to make false statements about services, accommodation or facilities deliberately or recklessly.

(d) It is an offence to make misleading statements as to price.

(e) Defences under trade descriptions legislation are mostly based on mistake or the actions of other people. They are only available if the defendant took all reasonable precautions and exercised all due diligence.

(f) A consumer suffering loss or injury may seek damages for breach of conditions implied by the Sale of Goods Act 1979, or he may sue for the tort of negligence. Alternatively he may claim against both the manufacturer and the supplier under Part I of the Consumer Protection Act 1987.

(g) It is a crime to supply consumer goods which fail to comply with a general safety requirement.

Quick quiz

1 What is the function of the Consumer Protection Advisory Committee?

2 How must a disclaimer be displayed so as to provide a valid defence under the TDA?

3 What limitations are there on the offence of making false statements relating to services, accommodation and facilities?

4 What are the general defences available in a case under TDA?

5 What must a plaintiff prove in a claim under Part I of CPA?

6 What defences are available to an action under Part I of CPA?

Solutions to exercises

1 Refusing to supply certain goods unless other goods are also bought.

Refusing to supply certain customers because they also deal with other suppliers.

Using sales staff not qualified to advise customers about special risks.

No doubt you can think of other examples.

2 (a), (c) and (d).

3 Yes: a misleading statement as to price has been made.

4 No: Meryl failed to take reasonable precautions.

5 A Ltd, and possibly C (Retailers) Ltd.

13 COMPETITION LAW

Your objectives

After completing this chapter you should:

(a) understand the main object of UK competition law;

(b) know which monopolies and mergers may be investigated, and how action may be taken;

(c) know what constitutes an anti-competitive practice, and how such practices may be investigated;

(d) know how action may be taken against restrictive trade practices;

(e) know which agreements must be registered under the Restrictive Trade Practices Act 1976;

(f) know which restrictive trade practices may be allowed to continue;

(g) be aware of the restrictions on resale price maintenance;

(h) know the restrictions imposed by Articles 85 and 86 of the Treaty of Rome.

---

1   UK competition law

The bodies which have control over UK competition policy are the Director General of Fair Trading (DGFT), the Monopolies and Mergers Commission (MMC) and the Secretary of State for Trade and Industry. Duties are imposed on them in the main by the Fair Trading Act 1973 (FTA) and the Competition Act 1980.

The role of the *Director General of Fair Trading* in competition law is as follows.

(a) He can report on *monopolies and mergers* to the Secretary of State for Trade and Industry, who may refer cases to the MMC.

(b) He may undertake initial investigations into any alleged *anti-competitive practices*.

(c) He has responsibility for registration of arrangements designed to fix prices or other *restrictive trade practices*.

(d) He can attempt to get *undertakings* from persons under investigation as to their future conduct and he then monitors that conduct.

The *MMC* acts only on directions from the Secretary of State, by whom it may either be required to investigate facts or to investigate affairs more fully if the public interest is at stake.

The *Secretary of State* at the DTI can both refer cases to the MMC and make orders which have to be followed. He also has limited power to prevent or halt the DGFT's investigations.

The public interest

For the most part the object of UK competition law is to protect the public interest. For instance the MMC in its investigations has to address the following factors under s 84 FTA.

(a) The maintenance and promotion of effective competition between UK suppliers

---

BPP Publishing

(b) The promotion of customers' interests with regard to quality, price and choice of goods and services

(c) The maintenance and promotion of a balanced distribution of industry and employment in the UK

(d) The promotion of competition in exports

(e) The use of competition to achieve the opening of markets to new entrants, the development of new products and techniques and the promotion of cost reduction

---

Exercise 1

In an industry in which there are many independent suppliers, how could the interests of small customers be adversely affected by the existence of one large customer buying 70% of the total quantity produced?

---

2 Monopolies and mergers

It is generally supposed that monopolies and large mergers of business organisations tend to operate against the public interest. A major part of UK competition law therefore concerns the regulation of monopolies and mergers.

Monopolies

A monopoly situation exists under ss 6-7 FTA if 25% or more of the goods or services of a particular kind supplied in the UK are supplied either *by* a single person or *to* a single person. For this purpose members of an interconnected group of companies are regarded as a single person. The definition also covers cases where two or more otherwise unconnected persons or companies voluntarily or involuntarily act in such a way as to prevent or restrict the operation of a free market in the goods or services in question.

There are three elements to be defined when a monopoly reference is made to the MMC.

(a) The market: 25% of the market for books is very much larger than 25% of the market for detective novels, so a careful definition of the market is required.

(b) The geographical area: if a firm confines itself to one part of the UK but has more than 25% of the market in that area then a monopoly effectively exists.

(c) Forms of supply: the same goods and services can be supplied in a number of different ways. For instance, a firm may have 25% of the market for home deliveries of milk but only 2% for milk sold over the counter.

Mergers

The FTA is also concerned with *mergers* of such magnitude that they may pose a threat to free competition. In s 64 of the Act a definition is given of the circumstances which may lead to a merger being referred to the MMC. Broadly, a qualifying merger is one which:

(a) leads to two or more enterprises ceasing to be distinct, that is they come under common ownership or control;

(b) leads to an enterprise ceasing to be carried on at all under arrangements designed to prevent competition between enterprises; or

(c) leads to assets being taken over with a value equal to or greater than a defined amount (currently £30m), and leads to a more than 25% dominance.

BPP Publishing

There are special provisions in ss 57-62 of the Act concerning newspaper mergers. Broadly speaking any newspaper merger or takeover may be referred.

The Monopolies and Mergers Commission

Only the Secretary of State for Trade and Industry may refer a merger to the MMC; the DGFT only has an advisory role.

The MMC is an independent advisory body with no executive powers. When a monopoly or merger is referred to it for consideration it must advise the government whether it believes that the public interest will be harmed.

An adverse report by the MMC is not binding on the government. But the government will usually obtain suitable undertakings from the persons concerned and will ensure that they are complied with. The Secretary of State for Trade and Industry makes the final decision; he has extensive powers to place conditions on the takeover or merger, and may even prohibit it.

3   Anti-competitive practices

The Competition Act 1980 (CA) regulates the control of anti-competitive practices (ACPs) as opposed to monopolies, mergers, restrictive trade practices and resale price maintenance. The DGFT is primarily responsible for investigations into ACPs.

An ACP is defined by s 2 of the CA as a course of conduct which restricts, distorts or prevents competition in the production or acquisition of goods or in the supply of goods and services in the UK. There must be a *course of conduct*; a single act or a series of acts which were unconnected are not ACPs.

Unless it is also a monopolist, a firm with a turnover below £5,000,000 is exempted from ACP legislation; the object is to prevent large firms from abusing their power, not to prevent new firms breaking into a market.

Types of anti-competitive practice

Most acts aimed at *resale price maintenance* are illegal under other legislation, covered later in this chapter. Generally *restrictive trade practices* are also regulated elsewhere, but there may also be an ACP here if one firm engages in a series of registrable restrictive trade practices, since this would be a 'course of conduct'. Neither *monopolies* nor *mergers* are in themselves ACPs, either because there is no 'course of conduct' or because they do not set out to restrict, distort or prevent competition.

ACPs include discriminatory pricing, forcing customers to buy entire product ranges rather than individual items and refusals to supply.

Exercise 2

X Ltd obtains a patent on a new product. This gives the company a monopoly for 20 years. While this might be anti-competitive, why is it in the public interest to grant such monopolies?

ACP investigations

It is in the DGFT's sole discretion as to whether or not to investigate an ACP, and broadly speaking at any stage he may decide that the purpose is better served by obtaining and monitoring undertakings from firms that such practices shall be left off. Once he has investigated, he publishes a report and may refer the case to the MMC which in turn submits a report to Parliament. The Secretary of State may then make an order to restrict the ACP or to remedy its effect.

Other provisions of the Competition Act 1980

The Act also provides for a form of investigation into the activities of nationalised industries and certain other bodies: ss 10 and 11. The Secretary of State may require the MMC to investigate, for example, whether such a body is abusing a monopoly position. Following an adverse report, the Secretary of State may make an order remedying the adverse effects of conduct found by the MMC to operate against the public interest.

Monopoly pricing is also covered by the CA (s 13) which allows the Secretary of State to refer any specified price to the DGFT. The price must be of major public concern: that is, of general economic importance and likely to have a significant effect on consumers.

4 Restrictive trade practices

The Restrictive Trade Practices Act 1976 (RTPA) requires that arrangements designed to fix prices or to regulate supplies of goods must be registered with the DGFT who has a duty to take proceedings before the Restrictive Practices Court. Unless it is then shown that the arrangements are in the public interest they are declared void. There can be heavy fines for infringement of these rules. The DGFT also has the duty to enforce orders made by the Court; breach of such orders is punishable as contempt of court.

The RTPA applies to agreements made between two or more persons carrying on business within the UK either in the production or supply of goods or in the supply of services. All agreements must be registered with the DGFT if they contain restrictions in respect of:

(a) prices to be charged, quoted or paid for goods or services;

(b) prices to be recommended or suggested as the prices to be charged or quoted;

(c) the terms or conditions subject to which goods or services are to be supplied or obtained;

(d) the quantities or descriptions of goods, or the scale or extent of services, to be supplied or obtained;

(e) the processes of manufacture of goods, or the form or manner in which services are to be supplied or obtained; or

(f) the person or classes of person to whom goods or services are to be supplied or from whom they are to be obtained.

The Act also extends to *information agreements*, defined as agreements between two or more persons carrying on business within the UK under which the parties exchange information with each other on the matters described above. The information so exchanged may relate to past activities, not just to future intentions.

The agreements covered by the Act do not necessarily have to be legally enforceable contracts. If two parties enter into a 'gentleman's agreement' that is sufficient to bring the matter within the scope of the Act.

There are certain agreements which are exempt from registration. Apart from a number of ordinary commercial agreements which are specifically 'excepted' in the Act, these exempt agreements include any which the Secretary of State regards as furthering a project or scheme of importance to the national economy. Examples of excepted agreements are terms relating exclusively to goods supplied (s 9), to conditions of work and to financing arrangements.

Exempt agreements cover such areas as patents, distribution rights and agriculture and forestry matters.

The Register of restrictive arrangements maintained by the DGFT is open to public inspection at the OFT.

If a registrable agreement is not registered it is void. A third party who suffers loss by the operation of a void restrictive agreement, for example a customer who has paid higher prices for goods than would have been charged if the suppliers had been competing, may sue for damages. The Director General may apply to the court for an injunction to restrain arrangements operated in contravention of these rules.

Exercise 3

Some manufacturers of domestic fuseboards agree that they will only supply one electrician in each town. Is this a registrable trade practice?

The Restrictive Practices Court

The Restrictive Practices Court is presided over by a High Court judge. Its members include both judges and laymen. Laymen are chosen for their knowledge or experience in industry, commerce or public affairs (s 3(1) Restrictive Practices Court Act 1976).

The DGFT applies to the Court for a declaration as to whether a restriction contained in a registered agreement is contrary to the public interest. If the Court decides that it is, the agreement is declared void in respect of that restriction (s 2(1) RTPA). The DGFT may then request an order from the Court prohibiting the parties from continuing in the agreement or making a new agreement to similar effect.

RTP gateways

The parties to the agreement must try to satisfy the Court that the restriction is not contrary to the public interest. To do so they must show that one or more of the following 'gateways' applies (s 10).

(a)   The restriction is reasonably necessary to protect the public against injury.

(b)   The removal of the restriction would deny to the public specific and substantial benefits or advantages.

(c)   The restriction is reasonably necessary to counteract measures taken by a third party to restrict competition.

(d)   The restriction is reasonably necessary to enable the parties to negotiate fair terms with a third party who controls a preponderant part of the market in the goods or services concerned.

(e)   The removal of the restriction would be likely to have a serious and persistent adverse effect on the general or local level of unemployment.

(f)   The removal of the restriction would be likely to cause a substantial reduction in export business.

(g)   The restriction is reasonably required for purposes connected with the maintenance of any other restriction accepted by the parties.

(h)   The restriction does not directly or indirectly discourage competition to any material degree, and is unlikely to do so.

5   Resale price maintenance

The Resale Prices Act 1976 (RPA) consolidated the law relating to resale price maintenance. The Act declares void collective agreements between suppliers or dealers and manufacturers for the enforcement of price maintenance arrangements. They are prohibited from imposing conditions for the maintenance of minimum prices at which goods are to be resold, and are also prohibited from enforcing such prices by withholding supplies from dealers who do not comply with them. However, it is still open to an *individual* supplier to recommend a minimum price for his goods, and there are exceptions to the rules on withholding supplies, as where buyers have premises or after sales services which are unsatisfactory.

Classes of goods may be exempted from the Act if to do so will be in the public interest. The only classes actually exempted are books and ethical and proprietary drugs.

An exception is made in the case of dealers who sell a supplier's goods as *loss leaders*, that is they sell the goods not for the purpose of making a profit but for the purpose of attracting customers to their premises. In this case it is not unlawful for the supplier to withhold goods from the dealer.

Suppliers or dealers who breach the provisions of the Act will not face criminal proceedings. Compliance with the Act is enforceable by civil proceedings on behalf of the Crown for an injunction or other appropriate relief. The obligation to comply with the Act is a duty owed to any person who may be affected by its contravention; breach of that statutory duty is actionable accordingly (s 24 RPA).

Exercise 4

The Net Book Agreement imposes retail price maintenance on books sold subject to its terms. Why might the agreement be argued to be in the public interest, and why might it be argued to be against the public interest?

---

6   European community competition law

Anti-competitive practices which affect only the trader within one member state of the European Community (the EC) are subject only to national legislation. However, where such practices may affect trade *between* member states, the EC rules on competition come into force. These prohibit 'all agreements between undertakings, decisions by associations of undertakings and concerted practices which may affect trade between member states and which have as their object or effect the prevention, restriction or distortion of competition within the EC'.

Quotas

Member states of the EC are prevented from restricting competition by the fact that any form of quota is strictly controlled. A quota is a restriction which limits the import, export or through-transit of goods by reference to quantity or value. The control has been extended to measures which hinder imports but are not applied to domestic products, such as requiring that the producers of an imported article must establish a business representative in the importing state.

There is generally no preclusion of prohibitions or restrictions where they can be justified on the grounds of public morality, public policy or public security. Public policy does not include the general protection of consumers. Specifically included as justifications are the protection of the health and life of humans, animals or plants, the protection of national treasures and the protection of industrial and commercial property. But any prohibition should not constitute a means of arbitrary discrimination or a disguised restriction on trade. If the restriction is arbitrary or greater than is necessary the measure cannot be justified. Thus carrying out more checks on imports from one country than from another may be unlawful, as may be inspecting imported vegetables for the presence of some harmful insect when no steps are taken to prevent or eradicate the insect in domestic produce.

Restrictions on undertakings: Articles 85 and 86

Articles 85 and 86 of the Treaty of Rome are designed to prevent the economies of specific states from enjoying particular advantages arising from the practices of business or the policies of national governments. Both Articles refer to 'undertakings' to cover any body or person engaged in commercial activities. Proceedings for infringement are brought by the Commission subject to control by the Court of Justice, but in any proceedings before them national courts may declare that an infringement has taken place. This will normally have the effect, if the infringement is embodied in a provision in a contract, that the provision will be void.

Article 85: restrictive agreements, decisions and concerted practices

Article 85 prohibits all agreements between undertakings, decisions of associations of undertakings and concerted practices which affect trade between member states and prevent, restrict or distort competition. Any such agreement or decision is void. Any agreement may, however, be justified (subject to certain conditions) and the prohibition be declared to be inapplicable if the agreement contributes to improving production or distribution or promotes technical or economic progress, while allowing consumers a fair share of the resulting benefit. But the power to make such declarations is vested in the Commission, not the national courts.

Individual agreements, which do not pose any serious threat of distorting competition (such as agreements restricting the rights of a transferee or user of intellectual property rights) may be exempted on application by the parties to the Commission and there is a general exemption for certain agreements, such as agreements for exclusive distributorships or exclusive purchasing, agreements relating to research and development up to the stage of industrial exploitation and motor vehicle distribution and servicing agreements. The Commission has issued a notice stating which agreements of a *cooperative* kind are regarded as not distorting competition, for example joint activities such as sharing market research reports, sharing financial consultancy and advice, and sharing production facilities and advertising.

Agreement is not limited to legally binding contracts: any consensual arrangement is covered so long as it is between undertakings which are *separate economic entities*: thus arrangements between a principal and his agent or between a parent company and its subsidiary are outside the Article.

Decision is not limited to decisions which are legally binding on the members of the association: any decision, including a decision to recommend a particular practice by its members, is within the article.

Concerted practice embraces activities involving contact between the parties (falling far short of legally binding agreements), but the contact may derive from the practice itself, such as where a number of companies in a trade each adhere to a traditional periodical price notification system, which enables each company to learn of the prices of competitors swiftly and concurrently. But generally merely adjusting to the practices of competitors, such as raising or lowering prices in response to competitors' price movements, is not a concerted practice.

The activities must have as their object or effect the prevention, restriction or distortion of competition. In essence, this requires evidence that the position in a member state, were it not for the agreement, would be one of more open competition. If, in fact, the businesses would not be able to compete more freely, say because of national government restrictions, then the agreement cannot be regarded as preventing competition.

Where an agreement is restrictive of competition (as it usually is) it may be justified; if it is not justified it must be declared void by the national courts and no effect may be given to it. If there are grounds for exempting the agreement under Article 85 the Commission (but not the courts) may do so. A national court may, however, refer the matter to the Commission, and businesses may make applications for individual exemptions.

Exercise 5

Give some examples of agreements which would affect trade between member states and which would therefore be likely to be void under Article 85.

Article 86: abuse of dominant position

Any abuse by one or more undertakings of a dominant position within the EC or in a substantial part of it is prohibited so far as it affects trade between member states; the list of particular abuses is similar to that set out in Article 85. Where a group of interrelated companies is involved, their conduct jointly may infringe Article 86.

An undertaking will enjoy a *dominant position* where it has power 'which enables it to hinder the maintenance of effective competition in the relevant market by allowing it to behave to an appreciable extent independently of its competitors and customers and ultimately of consumers'. Whether a dominant position is enjoyed depends upon the definition of the market in which the undertaking operates and the undertaking's overall power in respect of that market.

The 'market' is wider than the mere provision of specific goods or services; thus a supplier of bananas may influence the market for fruit generally, but not enjoy a dominant position in respect of fruit generally. On the other hand, if the market is defined as being limited to bananas, he may enjoy a dominant position. The market as a territorial entity is not limited to a particular member state: it may be smaller or larger. In certain activities the operation of the market may be on a very small scale. The position must, however, be in a substantial part of the market. If the business enjoys a monopoly or near monopoly it may be presumed to occupy a dominant position. The greater the number of competitors the smaller the percentage share which may satisfy the dominance requirement; the fewer the number of competitors the greater the requisite share. But a dominant position itself is not reprehensible: only an abuse of it is an infringement.

Chapter roundup

(a) The Director General of Fair Trading reports on monopolies and mergers, investigates anti-competitive practices, registers restrictive trade practices and seeks undertakings from persons as to their future conduct. The Monopolies and Mergers Commission and the Secretary of State for Trade and Industry may become involved in particular cases.

(b) The main objective of UK competition law is to protect the public interest.

(c) A monopoly generally exists when one person has a market share of 25% or more, either as seller or as buyer. The Secretary of State may refer such monopolies, and any mergers meeting certain criteria, to the Monopolies and Mergers Commission.

(d) Anti-competitive practices are regulated under the Competition Act 1980. The Director General of Fair Trading may investigate and report on such practices, and the Secretary of State may make orders in relation to them.

BPP Publishing

(e) Restrictive trade practices must in general be registered. They may be challenged before the Restrictive Practices Court, which will only allow such a practice to continue if one or more of eight gateways applies.

(f) Resale price maintenance is in general forbidden, but there are exceptions for books and for drugs.

(g) Under European Community law, quotas are strictly controlled. Under Article 85 of the Treaty of Rome, restrictive agreements, decisions of associations of undertakings and concerted practices are void if they affect trade between member states, they cannot be justified and they are not exempt. Under Article 86, abuses of dominant positions are forbidden.

Quick quiz

1   What is the role of the Secretary of State for Trade and Industry in UK competition law?

2   Define a monopoly.

3   What kinds of merger are affected by FTA?

4   How does the Competition Act 1980 define an anti-competitive practice?

5   List five types of agreement required to be registered under the Restrictive Trade Practices Act 1976.

6   What is an information agreement?

7   List five of the gateways available to businesses under the RTPA.

8   How may the provisions of the Resale Prices Act 1976 be enforced?

9   How may restrictions on goods within the EC be justified?

10 What is a concerted practice for the purposes of Article 85?

11 What is a dominant position under Article 86? Will such a position automatically be regarded as an infringement?

Solutions to exercises

1   The large customer could enforce a precise product specification to suit his purposes, and could demand substantial discounts, leading the suppliers to raise the price to other customers.

2   Without the possibility of obtaining patents, many companies would not invest in research and development.

3   Yes: it restricts the persons to whom goods are to be supplied.

4   The agreement sustains small and specialist bookshops, but it may keep the prices of some titles artificially high.

5   Agreements to supply at different prices in different states.

Agreements not to sell to certain states.

You may be able to think of other examples.

14 TORT

1   Tort and other wrongs

There is no entirely satisfactory definition of tort. The principle is that the law gives various rights to persons, such as the right of a person in possession of land to occupy it without interference or invasion by trespassers. When such a right is infringed the wrongdoer is liable in tort.

There is therefore a duty imposed by law to respect the legal rights of others. When a tort is committed the remedy is an action at common law for unliquidated damages, which represent such compensation as the court may see fit to award. The principles of tort are based on rights, the related duty to respect them and compensation for infringement.

Tort is distinguished from other legal wrongs.

(a)   A *crime* is an offence prohibited by law. The state prosecutes the offender and punishment is by fine or imprisonment. A tort is a civil wrong and the person wronged sues in a civil court for compensation (or an injunction against repetition).

(b)   *Breach of contract* and *breach of trust* are civil wrongs. It must be shown that the defendant was subject to the obligations of a contract or a trust and did not perform or observe those obligations. In tort no previous transaction or relationship need exist: the parties may be complete strangers.

2   Wrong and damage distinguished

When a plaintiff sues in tort claiming damages as compensation for loss he must normally prove his loss. But the necessary basis of his claim is that he has suffered a wrong. If there is no wrong *(injuria)* for which the law gives a remedy, no amount of damage *(damnum)* caused by the defendant can make him liable. *Damnum sine injuria* (loss not caused by wrong) is not actionable.

BPP Publishing

Case: Electrochrome v Welsh Plastics 1968
The defendant's lorry, driven carelessly, crashed into a fire hydrant. As a result the water supply to the plaintiff's factory nearby was cut off. The factory had to close until the supply was restored. The plaintiff claimed damages for his loss.

Held: the fire hydrant was not the plaintiff's property and so, in spite of his loss, no legal wrong had been done to him for which he could hold the defendant liable.

In some torts it is necessary to establish both wrong and loss resulting from it; this is the rule in the tort of negligence. But in other cases it suffices to prove that a legal wrong has been done and damages (possibly nominal in amount) may be recovered without proof of any loss *(injuria sine damno)*. Substantial damages may be awarded where the loss is serious, but difficult to quantify in money terms, as in cases of damage to reputation by defamation.

Mental elements

In tort, unlike crime, it is not usually necessary to prove anything about the defendant's state of mind nor is it a defence that he was innocent of any intention to do wrong. If his act was voluntary (not forced upon him) and it is a wrong, it need not be shown that he acted maliciously. But there are a few exceptions such as the tort of malicious prosecution where there must be evidence of malice. Similarly if the defendant deliberately causes loss but does so without infringing a right of the plaintiff, the latter has no remedy.

Case: Mayor of Bradford v Pickles 1895
P wished the Bradford Corporation to buy his land, adjoining the corporation's water reservoir, at a very high price. He sank a shaft on his land to divert the flow of subterranean water through it (as he was legally entitled to do). As a result less water flowed into the reservoir and it was discoloured. The corporation sued for an injunction, a court order to P to desist.

Held: the action must fail. P was exercising his rights as a landowner and was not infringing any rights of the corporation. It was immaterial that the corporation had suffered loss and that P's express motive was to inflict loss.

Cause and effect

When the plaintiff claims damages for the loss caused by the defendant's wrongful act or omission, two main issues of cause and effect may have to be considered.

(a)   Was the loss caused by a wrongful act or omission of the defendant himself? It may be a case of inevitable accident or there may be contributory negligence on the part of the plaintiff.

(b)   If the sequence of cause and effect was unquestionably begun by the defendant, how far down the ensuing chain of consequences should the court go in identifying the loss for which the plaintiff is entitled to recover damages? In tort (as in contract) there are rules on remoteness of damage.

Exercise 1

Tony plants trees in his garden. The roots remain on his land, but the trees soak up water from Peter's garden next door, thereby causing Peter's plants to wither. Is there *injuria*? is there *damnum*?

3 Remoteness of damage

When a person commits a tort with the intention of causing loss or harm which in fact results from the wrongful act, that loss or harm can never be too remote a consequence. Damages will be awarded for it.

If the sequence of cause and effect includes a new act (called a *novus actus interveniens*) of a third party or of the plaintiff, it may terminate the defendant's liability at that point: further consequences are too remote and he is not required to pay compensation for them. But where the intervening act is that of a third party who could be expected to behave as he did in the situation arising from the defendant's original wrongful act, the intervening act does not break the chain.

> *Case: Scott v Shepherd 1773*
> A threw a lighted firework cracker into a crowded market. It landed on the stall of B who threw it away. It then landed on the stall of C who threw it away and it then hit D in the face and blinded him in one eye. D sued A.
>
> *Held:* there was no break in the chain of causation from A's intentional wrongful act and he was liable to D.

Reasonable foresight

If the intervening act is that of the plaintiff himself and he acts unreasonably, for example, by taking an avoidable and foreseeable risk of injury to himself, that breaks the chain (or if it does not it may reduce his claim for loss because of his contributory negligence).

When there is a sequence of physical cause and effect without human intervention, the ultimate loss is too remote (so that damages cannot be recovered for it) unless it could have been reasonably foreseen that some loss of that kind might occur as a consequence of the wrong.

> *Case: The Wagon Mound 1961*
> A ship (the Wagon Mound) was taking on furnace oil in Sydney harbour. By negligence oil was spilled onto the water and it drifted to a wharf 200 yards away where welding equipment was in use in the repair of another ship. The owner of the wharf at first stopped work because of the fire risk but later resumed working because he was advised that sparks from a welding torch were unlikely to set fire to furnace oil. Safety precautions were taken. A spark fell onto a piece of cotton waste floating in the oil and this served as a wick, thereby starting a fire which caused damage to the wharf. The owners of the wharf sued the charterers of the Wagon Mound, basing their claim on an earlier decision that damage caused by a direct and uninterrupted sequence of physical events is never too remote even though it could not reasonably be foreseen.
>
> *Held:* the claim must fail. The earlier decision was overruled and the reasonable foresight test was laid down. Pollution was the foreseeable risk: fire was not. This was a decision of the Privy Council on appeal from Australia and as such only a persuasive precedent for English courts. But as it was a decision of the most senior English judges it is always applied in cases where the claim is for negligence.

> *Case: Hughes v Lord Advocate 1963*
> Workmen left lighted paraffin lamps as a warning sign of an open manhole in the street. Two small boys took one of the lamps as a light and went down the manhole. As they clambered out the lamp fell into the hole and caused an explosion in which the boys were injured. Evidence was given that a fire might have been foreseen but an explosion was improbable.

BPP Publishing

Held: the defendants were liable for negligence in leaving the lamps where they did. A risk of fire was foreseeable and the explosion must be regarded as 'an unexpected manifestation of the apprehended physical dangers'. It was not (as it was in the Wagon Mound case) damage of an entirely different kind.

Case: Doughty v Turner Manufacturing Co 1964
An asbestos cement lid accidentally fell into a cauldron of sodium cyanide at a temperature of 800 degrees Centigrade. The intense heat caused a chemical change in the asbestos lid as a result of which there was an explosion. The plaintiff was injured by the eruption of molten liquid. The chemical reaction leading to the explosion was previously unknown to science.

Held: a splash of sodium cyanide was foreseeable but a violent explosion was not. The result was unforeseeable and therefore too remote.

In cases of physical injury which is more serious than would normally be expected because the plaintiff proves to be abnormally vulnerable, the defendant is liable for the full amount of injury done. This is the thin skull principle: if A taps B on the head and cracks B's skull because it is abnormally thin, A is liable for the fracture.

Case: Smith v Leech Braine & Co 1962
A workman was near a tank of molten zinc in which metal articles were dipped to galvanise them. One article was allowed to slip and the workman was burnt on the lip by a drop of molten zinc. The burn activated latent cancer from which he died three years later. His widow sued for damages.

Held: damages for a fatal accident would be awarded. Some physical injury (the burn on the lip) was a foreseeable consequence. The defendants must accept liability for the much more serious physical injury (cancer) caused by their negligence.

If the plaintiff suffers avoidable loss because his lack of resources prevents him from taking costly measures to reduce his loss, he may still recover damages for it: *Martindale v Duncan 1973.*

Exercise 2

A factory owner noticed that a machine was not running smoothly. She had heard of similar cases in which the increased vibration had led to small parts flying off and causing minor injuries, so she warned the workers to check that all such parts were secure and instructed them to carry on using the machine. The motor disintegrated and part of it broke through the casing and badly injured a worker, who then sued the factory owner. Why would the factory owner be unlikely to be able to rely on either *The Wagon Mound 1961* or *Doughty v Turner Manufacturing Co 1964* in her defence?

---

4 Vicarious liability

The person who commits a tort (the *tortfeasor*) is always liable for his wrong. Others may be jointly and severally liable with him under the principle of vicarious liability. If, for example, a partner commits a tort either with the authority of the other partners or in the ordinary course of the firm's business, the other partners are liable with him.

The most important application of the principle of vicarious liability is to the relationship of employer and employee. It is often not worthwhile to sue the employee for damages since he is

BPP Publishing

Law

Notes

unable to pay them. The employer however has greater resources and may also have insurance cover.

To make the employer liable for a tort of the employee it is necessary that:

(a) there is the relationship between them of employer and employee; and

(b) the employee's tort is committed in the course of his employment.

Employment relationship

It is usually clear enough whether an employment relationship exists because of the formalities it involves (such as PAYE). Sometimes, however, it can be unclear whether a person is an employee.

Case: Cassidy v Ministry of Health 1951
The full-time assistant medical officer at a hospital carried out a surgical operation in a negligent fashion. The patient sued the Ministry of Health as employer. The Ministry resisted the claim arguing that it had no control over the doctor in his medical work.

Held: in such circumstances the proper test was whether the employer appointed the employee, selected him for his task and so integrated him into the organisation. If the patient had chosen the doctor the Ministry would not have been liable as employer. But here the Ministry (the hospital management) made the choice and so it was liable.

The course of employment

The employer is only liable for the employee's torts committed in the course of employment. Broadly the test here is whether the employee was doing the work for which he was employed. If so the employer is liable even in the following circumstances.

(a) The employee disobeys orders as to how he shall do his work.

Case: Limpus v London General Omnibus Co 1862
The driver of an omnibus intentionally drove across in front of another omnibus and caused it to overturn. The bus company resisted liability on the ground that it had forbidden its drivers to obstruct other buses.

Held: the driver was nonetheless acting in the course of his employment.

Case: Beard v London General Omnibus Co 1900
The same employer forbade bus conductors to drive buses. A bus conductor caused an accident while reversing a bus.

Held: the employer's instructions served to demarcate the limits of the conductor's duties. He was not, when driving, doing the job for which he was employed and so the employers were not liable.

(b) While engaged on his duties, the employee does something for his own convenience.

Case: Century Insurance v Northern Ireland Road Transport Board 1942
A driver of a petrol tanker lorry was discharging petrol at a garage. While waiting he lit a cigarette and threw away the lighted match. There was an explosion.

Held: the employer was liable since the driver was, at the time of his negligent act, in the course of his employment.

If the employer allows the employee to use the employer's vehicle for the employee's own affairs, the employer is not liable for any accident which may occur. There is the same result when a driver disobeys orders by giving a lift to a passenger who is injured.

210

BPP Publishing

Case: Twine v Bean's Express 1946

In this case there was a notice in the driver's part of the van that the firm's drivers were forbidden to give lifts. The passenger was killed in an accident.

Held: the passenger was a trespasser and in offering a lift the driver was not acting in the course of his employment.

Case: Rose v Plenty 1976

The driver of a milk float disobeyed orders by taking a thirteen year old boy round with him to help the driver in his deliveries. The boy was injured by the driver's negligence.

Held: the driver was acting in the course of his employment. The boy was not a mere passenger but was assisting in delivering milk.

In the numerous cases about the use of vehicles the courts have tended to widen the scope of the employer's liability by holding that if he provides a vehicle for the employee's use, the latter may be the employer's agent if he gives a fellow employee a lift (though it is not within the scope of his employment to do this: *Vandyke v Fender 1970*). So also if a vehicle is lent for the joint purposes of employer and employee as when the employer wishes to have his car delivered to a destination to which the employee (who drives it) wishes to go: *Ormrod v Crossville Motor Services 1953*.

If the employee, acting in the course of his employment, *defrauds* a third party for his own advantage the employer is still vicariously liable.

Case: Lloyd v Grace Smith & Co 1912

L was interviewed by a managing clerk employed by a firm of solicitors and agreed on his advice to sell property with a view to reinvesting the money. She signed two documents by which (unknown to L) the property was transferred to the clerk who misappropriated the proceeds.

Held: the employers were liable. It was no defence that acting in the course of his employment the employee benefited himself and not them.

Where the employer is held to be vicariously liable, he may seek an indemnity for the costs from his employee: *Lister v Romford Ice and Cold Storage Co 1957*.

Exercise 3

A research chemist employed by a drug company works in a laboratory in which, for safety reasons, all experiments involving the application of heat are forbidden. The chemist tries a reaction in which heat is spontaneously generated, and an explosion results, injuring other employees. Discuss whether the chemist acted in the course of his employment.

Independent contractors

A person who has work done not by his employee but by an independent contractor, such as a freelance plumber used by a builder, is vicariously liable for torts of the contractor in the following circumstances.

(a) The operation creates a hazard for users of the highway, as in repair of a structure adjoining or overhanging a pavement or road.

(b) The operation is exceptionally risky.

Case: Honeywill & Stein v Larkin Bros 1934
Decorators who had redecorated the interior of a cinema brought in a photographer to take pictures of their work. The photographer's magnesium flare set fire to the cinema.

Held: in commissioning an inherently risky operation through a contractor the decorators were liable for his negligence in causing the fire.

(c)   The duty is personal. For example, an employer has a common law duty to his employees to take reasonable care in providing safe plant and a safe working system. If he employs a contractor he remains liable for any negligence of the latter in his work.

(d)   There is negligence in selecting a contractor who is not competent to do the work entrusted to him.

(e)   The operation is one for which there is strict liability (see below).

5   Strict liability

In many torts the defendant is liable because he acted intentionally or at least negligently. He may escape liability if he shows that he acted with reasonable care. That is essentially the position in the tort of negligence itself. But there are also torts which result from breach of an absolute duty: the defendant is liable even though he took reasonable care.

The outstanding example of a tort of strict liability is the rule in *Rylands v Fletcher*.

'Where a person who, for his own purposes, brings and keeps on land in his occupation anything likely to do mischief if it escapes, he must keep it in at his peril, and if he fails to do so he is liable for all damage naturally accruing from the escape.'

Case: Rylands v Fletcher 1868
F employed competent contractors to construct a reservoir to store water for his mill. In their work the contractors uncovered old mine workings which appeared to be blocked with earth. They did no more to seal them off and it was accepted at the trial that there was no want of reasonable care on their part. When the reservoir was filled, the water burst through the workings and flooded the mine of R on adjoining land.

Held: F was liable, and the principle quoted above was laid down.

Many industrial processes entail the artificial ('non-natural') accumulation of water, gas or other materials which may cause damage if they escape. In such cases the occupier of the land is liable even if the escape occurs without negligence or want of care on his part. It has, however, been held in a more modern case *(British Celanese v Hunt 1969)* that not every escape of industrial materials gives rise to this strict liability. Industrial activities, as distinct from the accumulation of materials, can be a natural use of the land and so be outside the rule. In an industrial area where a business creates employment opportunities for the benefit of the community, storage of chemicals does not amount to non-natural use.

Case: Cambridge Water Co v Eastern Counties Leather plc 1991.
A firm involved in the tanning industry stored organochlorines on its premises. A nearby public water supply borehole became polluted. The plaintiff made a claim based on the rule in *Rylands v Fletcher.*

Held: storage in an industrial area was a natural use of the land; this was simply a hazard which was part of the everyday life of local inhabitants.

BPP Publishing

Exercise 4

A is the owner of a piece of land, and he knows that natural gas tends to accumulate in caverns under the land. Building works by A cause one of the caverns holding this gas to fracture, and the resulting escape of gas causes a fire on B's adjoining land. Why could B not sue A under the rule in *Rylands v Fletcher*?

---

6 Defences to an action in tort

In an action in tort the defendant may be able to rely on a defence applicable to the specific tort, such as justification in an action for defamation or that he took reasonable care in an action for negligence. But those particular defences are not available in every tort action. There are, however, general defences which may be pleaded in any action in tort. Of these general defences the most important is consent.

Consent

Volenti non fit injuria (no wrong is done to a person who consents to it) is the maxim which describes consent as a defence in tort (sometimes abbreviated merely to *volenti*). It must however be true consent, which is more than mere knowledge of a risk, and also a consent which is *freely given*.

In some cases the plaintiff expressly consents to what would otherwise be a wrong. For example a hospital patient awaiting a surgical operation is asked to give his written consent to the operation. But more often the consent is merely the voluntary acceptance of a risk of injury.

> *Case: ICI v Shatwell 1965*
> Two experienced shotfirers were working in a quarry. Statutory rules imposed on them (not their employer) a duty to ensure that all persons nearby had taken cover before making a dangerous test. As their electric cable was too short they decided to make the test without taking cover before doing so. There was a premature explosion and both were injured. They sued the employer.
>
> *Held:* they had consented to the risk. The employer was not liable since it had not been negligent nor had it committed or permitted a breach of statutory duty over safety procedures. The injured men were trained for their work and properly left to carry out safety procedures of which they were well aware.

Consent in taking a normal risk may be implied. A competitor in a boxing contest or a rugby match gives an implied consent to the risks incidental to the sports played fairly in accordance with its rules, even if the actual injury is exceptional.

In the same way a spectator at a motor race, or an employee engaged on inherently dangerous work, such as a test pilot of experimental aircraft or a steeplejack, is deemed to accept the inherent risks.

But an employee, by accepting a job or continuing in it, does not consent to abnormal or unnecessary risks created by his employer merely because the employee is aware of them.

> *Case: Smith v Baker & Sons 1891*
> S was put to work by B (his employer) in a position where heavy stones were swung over his head on a crane. Both S and B were aware of the risk. S was injured by a falling stone.

Held: S could recover damages. In working in circumstances of known risk he was not deemed to consent to the risk of the employer's negligence. This principle has been developed in later cases to impose on the employer a common law duty to provide a safe working system.

In other circumstances it has to be decided on the facts how far knowledge implies consent.

Case: Morris v Murray 1990

The plaintiff and defendant spent all afternoon drinking together with another man. despite the fact that the weather was poor, the two decided to go flying in a plane owned by the defendant, who piloted it. He took off downwind and uphill; in such conditions a different runway into the wind should have been used. The plane crashed, killing the defendant and severely injuring the plaintiff, who sued the defendant's estate. His administrators claimed *volenti non fit injuria* and/or contributory negligence on the part of the plaintiff.

Held: right from the beginning the drunken escapade was fraught with danger and, although drunk, the plaintiff knew what he was doing. It was very foreseeable that such an escapade would end tragically and so, by embarking on the flight, the plaintiff had implicitly waived his rights in the event of injury consequent on the deceased's failure to fly with reasonable care.

A person who accepts a risk in order to effect a rescue does not lose his rights against the defendant if he is injured since his consent to the risk was constrained and not freely given. But the principle only applies when the risk is taken in order to safeguard others from the probability of injury for which the defendant is responsible.

Case: Haynes v Harwood & Son 1935

The defendant's driver left his horse-drawn van unattended in a street. The horses bolted and a policeman (the plaintiff) ran out of the nearby police station to stop the horses since there was risk of injury to persons, including children, in the crowded street. He suffered injury in taking this action. The defendant pleaded volenti.

Held: the policeman (for the reasons given above) had not forfeited his claim by exposing himself to the risk.

Case: Cutler v United Dairies 1933

The horse attached to an unattended horse-drawn van bolted into an empty field. The driver called for help and a spectator who responded was injured.

Held: the spectator had consented to the risk. He was not impelled by the need to save others from danger. His claim was barred by his consent.

Exercise 5

A petrol tanker is supplying petrol to a filling station next to a busy road. A small fire starts on the forecourt, and a bystander picks up a fire extinguisher and goes to put it out. Because some petrol has been spilled, there is an explosion and the bystander is injured. If the bystander were to sue the petrol company, could the company plead *volenti non fit injuria*?

If a person creates a hazard through his own negligence and a rescuer is injured, there need not be an exceptional risk over and above the inherent risks of rescue for the negligent person to be liable for damages.

BPP Publishing

Case: Ogwo v Taylor 1987

The defendant negligently set fire to his roof. Despite being well-protected, a fireman was badly scalded by steam produced by the water from his hose hitting the flames.

Held: the defendant's action created a real risk of injury to others, of which scalding was only one example. He was therefore liable for damages.

A person who creates a risk of personal injury to others cannot contract out of his liability for personal injury or death, for instance by giving notice (in circumstances of 'business liability'): s 2 Unfair Contract Terms Act 1977.

Unavoidable accident

Accident is a defence only if it could not have been foreseen nor avoided by any reasonable care of the defendant.

Case: Stanley v Powell 1891

A member of a shooting party fired at a pheasant. A pellet glanced off a tree and injured a beater (the plaintiff).

Held: the defendant was not liable for the reasons given above.

Act of God

Act of God, which is an unforeseeable catastrophe, is a special type of unavoidable accident. This defence is rarely available.

Statutory authority

If a statute requires that something be done, there is no liability in doing it unless it is done negligently. If a statute merely permits an action it must be done in the manner least likely to cause harm and there is liability in tort, for nuisance, if it is done in some other way.

Act of State

If a person causes damage or loss in the course of his duties for the State, he may claim Act of State. But it is not a defence in any case where the plaintiff is a British subject or the subject of a friendly foreign power.

Case: Buron v Denman 1848

D was captain of a British warship who had a general duty to suppress the slave trade. He set fire to a Spanish ship carrying slaves and released them. The Crown later ratified his act.

Held: neither D nor the Crown were liable.

Necessity, mistake and self defence

An act which causes damage may be intentional. If this is so, the defence of *necessity* may be raised, provided that the act was reasonable (such as shooting a dog to prevent it worrying sheep), and either the act was done to prevent a greater evil or it was done to defend the realm.

An intentional act done out of *mistake* may occasionally be defensible if it was reasonable. Such a case may be where a person makes a citizen's arrest in the reasonable and sincere belief that the plaintiff committed a crime.

BPP Publishing

Similarly, *self defence* is a valid defence if the defendant acted to preserve himself, his family or his property, so long as the act was reasonable and in keeping with the nature of the threat. But if a blow is struck in response only to verbal attack, there is no defence.

Lastly, no claim for damages will succeed if both plaintiff and defendant were engaged in illegal activity at the time of the injury, and it arose naturally out of that activity. Hence a burglar could not sue his getaway driver for damages when the latter crashed the car: *Ashton v Turner 1980*.

Exercise 6

A lorry is carrying mirrors, stood upright and with the whole cargo being covered by a tarpaulin. The tarpaulin breaks free, exposing one of the mirrors. The sun is reflected off this mirror into the eyes of the driver of another vehicle, which then crashes injuring a pedestrian. If the lorry owner is sued by the pedestrian, which defence should he put forward?

---

7   Contributory negligence

If the damage suffered as a result of negligence was partly caused by contributory negligence of the plaintiff his claim is proportionately reduced: Law Reform (Contributory Negligence) Act 1945.

The defendant need not prove that the plaintiff owed him a duty of care. It is sufficient if part of the damage was due to the plaintiff's failure to take reasonable precautions to avoid a risk which he could foresee. If a motorcyclist, injured in a crash caused by the negligence of another driver, suffers avoidable hurt by failure to wear a crash helmet (which is compulsory) that is contributory negligence *(O'Connell v Jackson 1971)*, which will reduce damages by 15% if injury would have been less and 25% if it would not have happened at all had the helmet been worn: *Froom v Butcher 1976*. So too is failure of a front seat passenger in a car to use a seat belt. The test of contributory negligence is what caused the damage, not what caused the accident.

There is however a standard of reasonableness. Mere failure to take a possible precaution or even thoughtlessness or inattention are not contributory negligence, unless there is a failure to do what a prudent person should do to avoid or reduce a foreseeable risk. If the plaintiff is a workman working at a monotonous task or in factory noise which may dull his concentration, due allowance is made in determining whether he is guilty of contributory negligence. A child of any age may be guilty of contributory negligence but in deciding whether he has been negligent the standard of reasonable behaviour is adjusted to take account of his inexperience.

Case: Yachuk v Oliver Blais 1949
A boy of nine bought petrol from a garage stating falsely that his mother's car had run out of petrol down the road. It was supplied in an open margarine tub. The boy (and his friend of seven who accompanied him) wished in fact to play Red Indians. They set fire to the petrol and the elder was badly burnt. The garage pleaded contributory negligence by the boys.

Held: the garage was negligent in selling the petrol in this way. There was no evidence that the boys realised the danger of what they did and so it was not a case of contributory negligence.

BPP Publishing

The contributory negligence of an adult who accompanies a child is not a defence to an action by the child.

8   Remedies in tort

Damages

The amount of damages is based on the principle of compensating the plaintiff for his financial loss and not of punishing the defendant for his wrong. But there are several categories of damages related to the circumstances.

(a)   *Ordinary damages* are assessed by the court as compensation for losses which cannot be positively proved or ascertained, and depend on the court's view of the nature of the plaintiff's injury.

(b)   *Special damages* are those which can be positively proved, such as damage to clothing or cars.

(c)   *Exemplary damages* or *aggravated damages* are intended to punish the defendant for his act, and to deter him and others from a similar course of action in the future. These damages are only rarely awarded. In *Rookes v Barnard 1964* the House of Lords ruled that exemplary damages could only be awarded for torts where the defendant calculated to make more money from the tort than he would have to pay in damages (as is sometimes the situation in newspaper libel cases), where a government official acts oppressively, arbitrarily or unconstitutionally or where statute permits.

(d)   *Nominal damages* are given where the plaintiff has suffered injury, but has suffered no real damage (as in trespass to land without damage to that land).

(e)   *Contemptuous damages* are awarded where the court, although finding for the plaintiff, has no sympathy for his action.

(f)   *Parasitic damages* are awarded for infringement of a right not otherwise protected, such as a husband's loss of consortium due to his wife's injury.

Injunction

Injunction is an equitable remedy given by the court which requires an individual to refrain from doing a certain act, or orders him to do a certain act. There are two types of injunction.

(a)   An *interlocutory injunction* is awarded before the hearing of an action so as to preserve the status quo. The plaintiff enters into an undertaking to pay the defendant for any loss arising out of the granting of the injunction.

(b)   A *perpetual injunction* is granted after the full hearing and continues until revoked by the court.

Failure to comply with an injunction is a contempt of court, which then empowers the court to fine the person in default or imprison him until his contempt is purged, when he apologises and promises not to breach the injunction again.

Exercise 7

A factory has its own electrical generator. The building containing the generator is left unlocked so as to allow rapid access in the event of fire, but there is a notice on the door which reads (in full): 'High voltage. Trained electricians only'. A child of ten is negligently allowed by his parents to play near the building. The child enters the building, suffers an electric shock and is injured. To what extent could the building's owner plead contributory negligence to reduce damages payable to the child?

217

Chapter roundup

(a) A tort is a civil wrong arising from a general duty rather than from a contractual relationship.

(b) If a plaintiff has suffered damage but no legal wrong has been done, he will not succeed in his action. If a legal wrong has been done but no damage has been suffered, damages may be awarded in some cases, but they may be only nominal.

(c) In most torts, the plaintiff need not show that the defendant acted maliciously, only that he acted voluntarily.

(d) Damages will only be awarded for loss which is not too remote from the actions of the defendant. Chains of causation may be broken by the actions of others, or may become too tenuous when the consequences go beyond what could reasonably have been foreseen. However, the thin skull principle may allow damages to be awarded for unexpected damage.

(e) An employer is liable for torts committed by his employees in the course of their employment. An employee may be acting in the course of his employment even if he disobeys his employer's orders. Vicarious liability can also arise for the torts of independent contractors.

(f) The rule in *Rylands v Fletcher* defines a tort of strict liability, in which reasonable care is no defence. It covers the escape of anything brought onto the defendant's land and likely to do mischief if it escapes, but it does not cover things naturally on the land.

(g) Consent of the plaintiff is usually a defence to an action in tort, but someone who acts to save others does not consent to the risk involved in the rescue. Other defences include unavoidable accident, act of God, statutory authority, act of State, necessity, mistake and self defence.

(h) The main remedies for torts are damages (which are generally intended to compensate rather than to punish) and injunctions. Damages may be reduced to take account of contributory negligence by the plaintiff.

Quick quiz

1   What is a tort? How is it different from other legal wrongs?

2   Distinguish wrong from damage, and identify the factors which must be present for there to be liability in tort.

3   How may remoteness of damage affect a claim in tort?

4   What two factors must be present for an employer's vicarious liability to be established?

5   When is a person liable for the torts of his independent contractor?

6   What is the rule in *Rylands v Fletcher*?

7   What is the meaning and significance of the defence *volenti non fit injuria*?

8   When will the defence of necessity be effective?

9   What happens if the court finds that there was contributory negligence on the part of the plaintiff?

10 Describe the different types of damages which may be awarded.

Solutions to exercises

1   There is *damnum* but no *injuria*.

2   It was foreseeable that parts of the machine would break loose: large parts are of the same kind as (but more damaging than) small parts.

3   He did act in the course of his employment, conducting chemical experiments. He did not break the rule against the application of heat, and even if he had done so he might still have been held to be acting in the course of his employment.

4   A did not bring the gas onto his land.

5   No: the bystander acted to prevent injury to persons.

6   Unavoidable accident.

7   Not at all: the parents' negligence is irrelevant, and the child was too young to understand the risk.

15 NEGLIGENCE

1   Negligence

There is a distinct tort of negligence which is causing loss by a failure to take reasonable care when there is a duty to do so. To succeed in an action for negligence the plaintiff must prove the following three things.

(a) The defendant owed him a *duty of care* to avoid causing injury to persons or property.

(b) There was a *breach* of that duty by the defendant.

(c) In *consequence* the plaintiff suffered injury, damage or (in some cases) financial loss.

2   Duty of care

In the case of *Donoghue v Stevenson* the House of Lords ruled that a person might owe a duty of care to another with whom he had no contractual relationship at all.

> *Case: Donoghue v Stevenson 1932*
> A purchased from a retailer a bottle of ginger beer for consumption by A's companion B. The bottle was opaque so that its contents were not visible. B drank part of the contents of the bottle and topped up her glass with the rest. As she poured it out the remains of a decomposed snail emerged from the bottle. B became seriously ill. She sued C, the manufacturer, who argued that as there was no contract between himself and B he owed her no duty of care and so was not liable to her.
>
> *Held:* C was liable to B. Every person owes a duty of care to his 'neighbour', to 'persons so closely and directly affected by my act that I ought reasonably to have them in contemplation as being so affected'. In supplying polluted ginger beer in an opaque bottle the manufacturer must be held to contemplate that the person who drank the contents of the bottle would be affected by the consequences of the manufacturer's failure to take care to supply his product in a clean bottle.

This narrow doctrine has been much refined in later cases. For any duty of care to exist, three points must be proved (as stated in *Anns v London Borough of Merton 1977*).

BPP Publishing

(a)   There must be a sufficient relationship of proximity or neighbourhood between the parties (defendant and plaintiff).

(b)   The defendant should be able reasonably to foresee that carelessness on his part may damage the plaintiff.

(c)   The law should allow that duty to result in liability. In particular, liability for the acts of independent third parties has been restricted.

The comments made in *Anns* suggest that objective foreseeability leads automatically to a duty of care and that a defendant who satisfies the foresight test is therefore liable unless there are reasons (such as public policy) why he should not be liable. In *Murphy v Brentwood DC 1990*, a case with facts similar to *Anns*, the House of Lords seems to have overruled its own decision on the earlier case, and the test of liability has been tightened, both by this case and by the *Caparo* case (see below). The *Murphy* case suggests that a duty of care will be based upon proximity, a principle similar to that in *Donoghue v Stevenson* itself.

The decision in *Caparo Industries plc v Dickman 1990* has also cast doubt on whether a single general principle of negligence can provide a practical test which may apply to every situation. In particular, the concepts of foreseeability or 'neighbourhood' are little more than convenient labels to attach to different specific situations before the court which, on detailed examination, it recognises as giving rise to a duty of care.

In any given case, if a reasonable man could have foreseen the consequences then a duty of care may be owed; whether it has actually arisen or not depends on the facts. The duty may be restricted or ignored completely in the following circumstances.

(a)   A person is not normally liable for the acts of third parties, unless they were under his control. In an employment relationship, where there is control by the employer, the latter normally has vicarious liability for the acts of his servants done in the course of their employment.

(b)   Certain persons involved in judicial process are immune from all civil action, particularly judges, lawyers and jurors during a trial. Arbitrators are immune when they act in that capacity, as are valuers acting as arbitrators or quasi-arbitrators.

(c)   A person may be liable for omission, such as where an accountant carelessly leaves out part of his report, but a duty of care rarely arises from an obligation to take positive action which has not been taken.

Exercise 1

What do you think is the public policy reason why barristers acting as advocates in legal proceedings cannot be sued for negligence?

The cases below indicate the current uncertainty as to how far the principles of negligence extend.

(a)   It applies in *product liability* cases such as *Donoghue v Stevenson* itself where physical injury or damage results from failure to take proper precautions. But if there is a reasonable opportunity of avoiding the injury by intermediate inspection or by routine precautions, there is no duty to a plaintiff who could have avoided it by these means.

Case: Grant v Australian Knitting Mills 1936

G purchased from a retailer a pair of underpants made by AKM. Owing to AKM's negligence the pants still contained a bleaching chemical. G contracted dermatitis. AKM argued that G could have washed the pants before use and if he had done so would have removed the bleaching agent before it harmed him.

Held: the duty of care does not extend to preventing injury avoidable by reasonable and expected precautions at a later stage. But washing a new garment before use is not such a normal precaution. AKM was liable.

(b)   There is generally no duty to take care to prevent third parties from doing damage: mere foreseeability of damage is not enough.

Case: Perl v Camden LBC 1983

Thieves entered an empty house owned by the defendant and broke through from there into the adjacent property, stealing a number of valuable items.

Held: because there was no special relationship by which the house-owner could control the acts of the thieves, no duty of care to the plaintiffs arose.

(c)   But if the defendant is in control of third parties he has a duty of care in the exercise of that control.

Case: Home Office v Dorset Yacht Club 1970

DY's property was damaged by a number of boys who escaped at night from a Borstal institution. The escape was due to lack of care by the guards for whom the Home Office was responsible.

Held: the Home Office was vicariously liable for the negligence of its staff as it owed a duty of care to persons whose property it could be foreseen might be damaged if the boys escaped.

Economic loss

One of the most uncertain areas in the law on negligence is how far and in what circumstances there is liability for financial (usually called 'economic') loss, if it is not the direct consequence of physical damage caused by negligence. The most common example of economic loss is where a person who has suffered physical damage makes a claim for loss of business profits while the damage is put right.

But in the last twenty years successful claims have been made for loss of profits both in cases where the root cause was physical damage and in cases where no actual physical damage occurred at all.

Case: Ross v Caunters 1980

A solicitor gave negligent advice to a testator and drew up a will carelessly. A gift to the plaintiff (an intended beneficiary) failed as a result.

Held: the solicitor owed a duty of care to beneficiaries since it was reasonably foreseeable that they would be damaged by negligent advice. The beneficiary could therefore sue for loss since he was actually in mind when the solicitor drew up the will.

Liability to pay damages for economic loss is limited to situations where the parties are linked by some special relationship, such as solicitor and beneficiary or takeover bidder and accountant. In the *Caparo* case the situation was analysed as being one where the defendant knew:

(a)   of the nature of the transactions which the plaintiff had in mind;

(b)   that the advice or information would be communicated to the plaintiff; and

(c)   that it was likely that the plaintiff would rely on that advice or information when deciding whether to go ahead with the transaction in mind.

Exercise 2

As a security measure, A installs lights outside his house. The house of B, his neighbour, is thereby illuminated, and B expresses his gratitude to A for choosing a security measure which benefits both of them. A later removes the lights without warning B, and the night after he does so B's house is burgled. Could B sue A?

Nervous shock

There is a duty to take care not to cause nervous shock to a person who one can foresee might suffer in that way from one's negligence. But the liability is not to everyone who may in fact be affected.

(a)   There is a duty of care not to cause nervous shock by putting a person in fear for his own safety or by making him an actual witness to an act of negligence by which he suffers nervous shock, such as seeing his house on fire: *Attia v British Gas Plc 1987*.

(b)   When a person is injured by negligence, his relatives who learn of the accident immediately afterwards and suffer shock can recover (there is a duty not to alarm or distress them). Otherwise a person who does not witness the event cannot usually claim that a duty of care was owed to him even if he suffers shock as a result.

> *Case: McLoughlin v O'Brien 1982*
> A woman called to a hospital where her husband and three children were receiving emergency treatment shortly after an accident of which she was informed by a witness to it. She suffered nervous shock.

> *Held:* there was a duty to her as likely to be affected and so she could recover. This follows *Hambrook v Stokes 1925* (a mother heard the sound of an accident in the road where her children were playing), and was distinguished from *Bourhill v Young 1943* (a passenger in a tram heard but did not see an accident in the road alongside the tram: she saw the messy consequences afterwards but was not within the range of persons contemplated as likely to be affected).

(c)   A distinction can be drawn between those who witness an event by dint of attending it and those who witness it via a simultaneous television broadcast.

> *Case: Allcock and others v Chief Constable of South Yorkshire Police 1991*
> Numerous spectators at a football match were injured or killed due to being crushed in crowded stands. Various relatives, who had proved the infliction of various psychiatric illnesses and had established that it was the defendant's actions which caused such infliction, brought an action for damages for nervous shock.

> *Held:* even where the relatives held a sufficient degree of kinship to make it reasonably foreseeable that psychiatric illness, rather than grief and sorrow, would result, those who saw the disaster unfold through simultaneous (or recorded) broadcasts were not owed a duty of care.

BPP Publishing

3 Breach of duty of care

The standard of reasonable care requires that the person concerned should do what a reasonable man 'guided upon those considerations which ordinarily regulate the conduct of human affairs' would do and abstain from doing what a reasonable man would not do. The standard of 'a reasonable man' is not that of an average man: for instance, the standard of a 'reasonable' car driver is a very high standard indeed, and would not be lowered for a learner driver. The rule has been developed as follows.

(a) In considering what precautions should be taken or foresight applied, the test is one of knowledge and general practice existing at the time, not hindsight or subsequent change of practice.

> *Case: Roe v Minister of Health 1954*
> A doctor gave a patient an injection taking normal precautions at that time. The drug was contaminated and the patient became paralysed. At the time of the trial seven years later medical practice had been improved to avoid the risk of undetected contamination (through an invisible crack in a glass tube).
>
> *Held:* the proper test was normal practice based on the state of medical knowledge at the time. The doctor was not at fault in failing to anticipate later developments.

(b) A person who professes to have a particular skill, for example in a profession, is required to use the skill which he purports to have. But an error of judgement is not automatically a case of negligence: *Whitehouse v Jordan 1981.*

(c) In deciding what is reasonable care the balance must be struck between advantage and risk. The driver of a fire engine may exceed the normal prudent speed on his way to a fire but not on the way back.

(d) If A owes a duty of care to B and A knows that B is unusually vulnerable, a higher standard of care is expected. For example, B might be a child, an inexperienced employee given risky work to do or a person with a thin skull.

> *Case: Paris v Stepney Borough Council 1951*
> P was employed by K on vehicle maintenance. P had already lost the sight of one eye. He was hammering metal. It was not the normal practice to issue protective goggles to men employed on this work since the risk of eye injury was small. A chip of metal flew into P's eye and blinded him.
>
> *Held:* although industrial practice did not require the use of goggles by workers with normal sight, there was a higher standard of care owed to P because an injury to his remaining good eye would blind him. S had failed to maintain a proper standard of care in relation to P.

Exercise 3

An accountant advises a client to use a well known tax avoidance scheme. At the time when he does so, the Inland Revenue is challenging the scheme in the courts. In a test case, the High Court has found in favour of the Inland Revenue but the Court of Appeal has found in favour of the taxpayer, and an Inland Revenue appeal to the House of Lords is pending. If the Inland Revenue succeed, any taxpayer who has used the scheme will be substantially worse off than if he had not used the scheme. If the Inland Revenue were to succeed in the House of Lords and the client were to sue the accountant, would the accountant be able to rely on *Roe v Minister of Health 1954* in his defence?

BPP Publishing

4 *Res ipsa loquitur*

It rests on the plaintiff to show both that the defendant owed him a duty of reasonable care and that the defendant failed in that duty. If the plaintiff does not know how the accident happened it may be difficult to demonstrate that it resulted from failure to take proper care. In some circumstances the plaintiff may argue that the facts speak for themselves *(res ipsa loquitur)*: that want of care is the only possible explanation for what happened and negligence on the part of the defendant must be presumed.

To rely on this principle the plaintiff must first show that:

(a)　the thing which caused the injury was under the management and control of the defendant; and

(b)　the accident was such as would not occur if those in control used proper care.

> *Case: Scott v London & St Katharine Docks Co 1865*
> S was passing in front of the defendant's warehouse. Six bags of sugar fell on him.
>
> *Held:* in the absence of explanation it must be presumed that the fall of the bags of sugar was due to want of care on the part of the defendants. Principles (a) and (b) above were formulated in this case.

> *Case: Easson v LNE Railway Co 1944*
> A four year old boy fell through the open door of a train seven miles from its last stopping place.
>
> *Held:* the principle of *res ipsa loquitur* did not apply since the railway company was not sufficiently in control of the doors of the train. After it left the last station a passenger might have opened the door.

5 Consequential harm

A claim for compensation for negligence will not succeed if damage or loss is not proved. In deciding whether a claim should be allowed, the court considers whether:

(a)　the breach of duty gave rise to the harm; and whether

(b)　the harm was too remote from the breach.

A person will only be compensated if he has suffered actual loss, injury, damage or harm as a consequence of another's actions. The claim will not be proved if:

(a)　the plaintiff followed a course of action regardless of the acts of the defendant;

(b)　a third party is the actual cause of harm;

(c)　a complicated series of events takes place such that no one act was the cause of all the harm; or

(d)　an intervening act by the plaintiff or a third party breaks the chain of causation *(novus actus interveniens)*.

Having decided whether harm arose from a breach of duty, the court will finally look at whether the harm which occurred was reasonably foreseeable.

BPP Publishing

Exercise 4

Elizabeth left her horse in a paddock surrounded by a high fence and with only one gate, but the horse got out of the paddock and injured Jackie. Elizabeth claims that she had shut the gate securely, but Jackie claims that she had not disturbed the gate. It is certain that no other person was involved. If Jackie sues Elizabeth for negligence, what principle is Jackie likely to rely on and what defence is Elizabeth likely to put forward?

6   Negligent misstatement

There is a duty of care not to cause economic loss by negligent misstatement, but the duty exists only where the person who makes the statement foresees that it may be relied on. There must therefore be a *special relationship*. To establish such a special relationship the person who makes the statement:

(a)   *must do so in some professional or expert capacity which makes it likely that others will rely on what he says.* This is the position of an accountant providing information or advice in a professional capacity (or indeed of any other person professing special knowledge, skill and care), but the principle was recently extended to a friendly relationship with business overtones.

> *Case: Chaudry v Prabhakar 1989*
> A friend of the plaintiff undertook (as a favour) to find a suitable car for her to buy; the plaintiff stipulated that any such car should not have been involved in an accident. The friend (who knew more about cars than the plaintiff did) failed to enquire of the owner of a car (which had, to the friend's knowledge, a straightened or replaced bonnet) whether it had been in an accident. In fact the car had been in a serious accident and it was unroadworthy and worthless. The plaintiff sued the friend for £5,500.
>
> *Held:* the friend owed a duty to take such care as was reasonable in the circumstances and had broken that duty; there had been a voluntary assumption of responsibility against the background of a business transaction; hence the friend was liable for the plaintiff's loss;

(b)   *must foresee that it is likely to be relied on by another person.*

> *Case: Hedley Byrne v Heller & Partners 1964*
> HB were advertising agents acting for a new client E. If E failed to pay bills for advertising arranged by HB then HB would have to pay the advertising charges. HB through its bank requested information from E's bank (HP) on the financial position of E. HP returned non-committal replies which were held to be a negligent misstatement of E's financial resources. In replying HP expressly disclaimed legal responsibility.
>
> *Held:* there is a duty of care to avoid causing financial loss by negligent misstatement where there is a 'special relationship'. HP were guilty of negligence having breached the duty of care but escaped liability by reason of their disclaimer.

The House of Lords in this case adopted Lord Denning's tests of a special relationship laid down in *Candler v Crane Christmas 1951*:

'a special relationship is one where the defendant gives advice or information and the plaintiff relies on that advice. The defendant should realise that his words will be relied on either by the person he is addressing or by a third party'.

BPP Publishing

It is almost certain that advice given on a social occasion cannot give rise to a duty of care, unless the person giving it realised (or should have realised) that it was going to be relied upon.

The principle of liability for negligent misstatement has been refined in the area of professional negligence to take account of the test of *reasonable foresight* being present to create a duty of care.

Case: JEB Fasteners Ltd v Marks, Bloom & Co 1982
The defendants, a firm of accountants, prepared an audited set of accounts showing stock valued at £23,080. It had been purchased for £11,000, but was nevertheless described as being valued 'at the lower of cost and net realisable value'. Hence profit was inflated. The auditors knew there were liquidity problems and that the company was seeking outside finance. The plaintiffs were shown the accounts; they doubted the stock figure but took over the company for a nominal amount nevertheless, since by that means they could obtain the services of the company's two directors. At no time did MB tell JEB that stock was inflated. With the investment's failure, JEB sued MB claiming that:

(a)   the accounts had been prepared negligently;

(b)   they had relied on those accounts;

(c)   they would not have invested had they been aware of the company's true position; and

(d)   MB owed a duty of care to all persons whom they could reasonably foresee would rely on the accounts.

Held: MB owed a duty of care (d) and had been negligent in preparing the accounts (a). But even though JEB had relied on the accounts (b), they would not have acted differently if the true position had been known (c), since they had really wanted the directors, not the company. Hence the accountants were not the cause of the consequential harm and were not liable.

This case implied that an auditor should reasonably foresee that he has a legal duty of care to a stranger. The decision was confirmed in *Twomax Ltd and Goode v Dickson, McFarlane & Robinson 1983*, where the auditors had to pay damages to three investors who purchased shares on the strength of accounts which had been negligently audited.

Exercise 5

At a party, Alfred asks Bertha, a friend of his and a solicitor, about a dispute which he is having with his neighbour. Bertha suggests that Alfred comes to her office for a chat about it the next day. He does so, and Bertha gives him some advice without charge. He acts upon that advice, and in consequence loses his right to sue his neighbour. Is it likely that Alfred could sue Bertha?

The *Caparo* decision

The *Caparo* decision has made considerable changes to the tort of negligence as a whole, and the negligence of professionals in particular.

Case: Caparo Industries plc v Dickman and Others 1990
In March 1984 Caparo Industries purchased 100,000 Fidelity shares in the open market. On 12 June 1984, the date on which the accounts were published, they purchased a further 50,000 shares. Relying on information in the accounts, which showed a profit of

BPP Publishing

£1,300,000, further shares were acquired. On 25 October the plaintiffs announced that they owned or had received acceptances amounting to 91.8% of the issued shares and subsequently acquired the balance. Caparo claimed against the directors (the brothers Dickman) and the auditors because the accounts should have shown a loss of £460,000. The plaintiffs argued that the auditors owed a duty of care to investors and potential investors in respect of the audit. They should have been aware that in March 1984 a press release stating that profits would fall significantly had made Fidelity vulnerable to a takeover bid and that bidders might well rely upon the accounts.

Held: the auditors' duty did not extend to potential investors nor to existing shareholders increasing their stakes. It was a duty owed to the body of shareholders as whole.

In the *Caparo* case the House of Lords decided that there were two very different situations facing a person giving professional advice:

(a)   preparing advice or information in the knowledge that a particular person was contemplating a transaction and was expecting to receive the advice or information in order to decide whether or not to proceed with the transaction (a special relationship); and

(b)   preparing a statement (such as an audit report) for more or less general circulation which could foreseeably be relied upon by persons unknown to the professional for a variety of different purposes.

In *MacNaughton (James) Papers Group Ltd v Hicks Anderson & Co 1991*, it was stated that, in the absence of some general principle establishing a duty of care, it was necessary to examine each case in the light of the concepts of foreseeability, proximity and fairness.

The absence of a general principle establishing a duty of care was now acknowledged by the courts, so the court had to consider whether it was fair, just and reasonable for a legal duty of care to arise in the particular circumstances of each case. Lord Justice Neill set out the matters to be taken into account in considering this.

(a)   The purpose for which the statement was made

(b)   The purpose for which the statement was communicated

(c)   The relationship between the maker of the statement, the recipient and any relevant third party

(d)   The size of any class to which the recipient belonged

(e)   The state of knowledge of the maker

(f)   Any reliance by the recipient

In spite of the decision in the *Caparo* case, it is still possible for professional advisers to owe a duty of care to an individual. The directors and financial advisors of the target company in a contested takeover bid were held to owe a duty of care to a known takeover bidder in respect of financial statements and other documents prepared for the purpose of contesting the bid: *Morgan Crucible Co plc v Hill Samuel Bank Ltd and others 1990*.

Exercise 6

An electrical engineer writes a book for general publication on the safe use of electricity. The advice given is generally sound, but there are certain circumstances in which precautions not mentioned in the book should be taken. Is it likely that someone who suffers injury through not taking these precautions could sue the author for negligent misstatement?

Chapter roundup

(a) Negligence is causing loss by failing to take reasonable care when there is a duty to do so. A duty of care is owed to persons whom it could be reasonably be foreseen would be affected by the defendant's carelessness.

(b) The plaintiff may be expected to have taken reasonable and expected precautions, and defendants are not liable for the actions of third parties not under their control.

(c) Liability for economic loss is limited to cases in which there is a special relationship between the plaintiff and the defendant.

(d) Nervous shock is not generally actionable except by persons in fear of their own safety, witnesses actually present and relatives who learn of an accident immediately afterwards.

(e) The standard of reasonable care varies with the expertise of the defendant and with the circumstances, but later improvements in methods are not taken into account.

(f) Where there is no explanation for how an accident happened but want of care is the only possible explanation, the doctrine of *res ipsa loquitur* may be invoked.

(g) Damages are only recoverable for the consequences of the defendant's actions. The actions of third parties, or the actions of the plaintiff uninfluenced by the defendant's actions, may break the chain of causation and prevent damages from being awarded.

(h) Negligent misstatements by experts are actionable, but there is uncertainty about how widely a duty of care is owed. The most important recent case is *Caparo Industries plc v Dickman and Others 1990.*

Quick quiz

1 What is required to establish a valid claim for negligence?

2 How far has liability for want of care been restricted by developments in case law?

3 To what extent are damages recoverable for nervous shock.

4 Explain the significance of *res ipsa loquitur*.

5 How is a special relationship established in a case of negligent professional advice?

6 Describe the two ways in which professionals give advice, only one of which gives rise to a special relationship.

Solutions to exercises

1 An unsuccessful litigant would sue his barrister, effectively obtaining a retrial.

2 No: A is not responsible for the actions of third parties.

3 No: the accountant knew (or at least should have known) of the risk.

4 Jackie would allege *res ipsa loquitur*, and Elizabeth would plead *volenti non fit injuria*.

5 Yes: a visit to a solicitor's office is not a social occasion.

6 No: there is no special relationship between the author and the injured party.

16 OTHER TORTS

Your objectives

After completing this chapter you should:

(a)   know what constitutes conversion;

(b)   know what constitutes a private nuisance;

(c)   know what makes a statement defamatory;

(d)   be able to distinguish between libel and slander;

(e)   know what defences may be put forward to an action for defamation.

1   Conversion

Conversion is any action in connection with goods which denies or is inconsistent with the plaintiff's title.

Case: Oakley v Lister 1931

O, a demolition contractor, agreed under a particular contract to dispose of 8,000 tons of hardcore from a runway. He rented some land on a farm to store the material pending its disposal. He had sold half of it when the freehold of the farm was purchased by L. L claimed that he had bought all that was on the land and removed some of the hardcore. He forbade O from removing any more of it, threatening him with an action for trespass. O contracted to sell the remaining 4,000 tons to a third party, who withdrew on hearing of L's claims. O claimed conversion.

Held: O was a lawful tenant and the owner of the material. L was asserting rights inconsistent with O's ownership of the goods. He had to pay in damages for conversion.

To maintain an action for conversion the plaintiff must be the owner and either have the goods in his possession or be entitled to immediate possession. A person who has possession but not ownership cannot sue for conversion. A refusal to return goods to the owner on demand is a form of conversion. If there is no prejudice to the owner's rights of possession and enjoyment, there is no conversion.

Case: Fouldes v Willoughby 1841

F had put his horses on W's ferry boat but a dispute arose over the charges. W asked F to remove his horses and when F refused W put the horses ashore. F sued W for conversion.

Held: this was not conversion since W's action in putting the horses ashore in no way disputed F's ownership.

The normal remedy for conversion is damages. The value of the goods is usually determined as at the date of conversion. But in a case of wrongful detention the defendant may be ordered to return the goods.

BPP Publishing

2   Nuisance

Nuisance may be of two types, public and private.

Private nuisance

Private nuisance is unlawful interference with the plaintiff's use of his property or with his health and comfort or convenience. It often takes the form of emitting noise, smell or vibration. If A throws garden rubbish over the fence into B's garden that is trespass; if A burns his rubbish by a series of smoky bonfires which causes real discomfort to B that may be private nuisance.

In private nuisance cases it is often necessary to strike a balance between the convenience and interests of two parties. The following factors may enter into the decision.

(a)   If the activity causes significant damage to property it will generally be restrained as private nuisance. If it merely causes discomfort the advantages and disadvantages may be balanced to determine whether the activity complained of is so unreasonable as to amount to nuisance.

(b)   Causing intentional discomfort to a neighbour is very likely to be restrained as unreasonable.

> *Case: Christie v Davey 1893*
> C and D occupied adjoining semi-detached houses with a common party wall. D objected to the sounds of C's activities as a music teacher. He made very loud noises, for example banging metal trays to annoy C.
>
> *Held:* C's music lessons were a reasonable use of her house; D's deliberate racket made purely to annoy was unreasonable. D was restrained from this conduct.

In his defence the defendant may rely on the plaintiff's consent, or on statutory authority, reasonableness on his part, or lack of intention to annoy. The remedy is often an injunction to restrain the continuation of the nuisance. Damages may also be awarded. In some cases the plaintiff may resort to self-help by abating the nuisance. For this purpose he may even enter the defendant's land if the latter does not respond to a notice requesting him to abate the nuisance himself.

Public nuisance

Public nuisance is a crime for which the person at fault may be prosecuted. If a public nuisance causes damage to the plaintiff to a greater extent than to the public generally he may sue in tort. For example, parking coaches in a side street so as to obstruct it can be a public nuisance but owners of nearby houses may also be able to sue the coach company if the noise and fumes cause discomfort to them in their houses: *AG v Gastonia Coaches 1976*.

Exercise 1

Martin holds loud parties in his house, annoying his neighbour Justin. Is Justin likely to succeed in an action for nuisance:

(a) if parties are held twice a year;

(b) if parties are held once a week?

Trespass to land

Trespass to land is unauthorised interference with a person's possession of land. It is committed by deliberately coming onto the plaintiff's land, even if the defendant did not realise that he was trespassing. The plaintiff may sue even if no damage has been done, but only nominal damages will be awarded unless damage is proved. The plaintiff may also seek an injunction to prevent repetition of the trespass.

3   Defamation

The essence of a defamatory statement is that it *damages the reputation* of the person defamed, and:

(a)   lowers his standing in society;

(b)   causes him to be shunned or avoided; or

(c)   makes imputations which are damaging to him in his profession, business or occupation.

Mere insults or 'abuse', spoken in the heat of a quarrel, are not necessarily defamatory, though the distinction is not always easy to make. To say to a man 'You devil!' might not be defamatory, but to say of him that 'he is a born criminal' probably would be. The law against defamation serves to protect 'interests in reputation', reputation being the estimation other people have of you. Injury to one's own self-respect, pride or dignity without further publication is not defamation.

Defamation then involves the publishing of a statement which has the effect of causing 'right-minded persons' to think less of the person or to avoid him. If a person makes a statement which is defamatory, he may be liable to the person he has defamed, unless one of a number of recognised defences is available. If a High Court judge allows, it is possible to bring a criminal prosecution for a particularly offensive statement; in general, however, the remedy for defamation is a *civil action* to recover damages. Less often an injunction, which is a prohibition against the repetition of a defamatory statement, may be obtained.

Libel and slander

There are two distinct forms of defamatory statement.

(a)   A *libel* is typically made in writing, but it includes other statements made in a form which is likely to be disseminated widely or continuously, such as a film made for public exhibition (both sound and visual effects may be libellous), a programme broadcast by radio or television, a play (Theatres Act 1968 s 4) and effigies.

> *Case: Yousoupoff v MGM Pictures Ltd 1934*
> A film was produced in England depicting the rape of a lady by Rasputin, and his subsequent murder. The lady had been romantically linked with one of his murderers. The plaintiff, who was married to one of Rasputin's murderers, alleged that people thought she was the lady who had been raped.
>
> *Held:* a talking film, even where the defamation is only in pictures, is libellous. Hence the plaintiff did not have to show special damage to obtain her damages, as would have been necessary in the case of slander.

(b)   A *slander* is typically spoken, or in some other transitory form, such as a gesture.

The distinction between these forms is important, since slander cannot be a crime, whereas libel may be. In addition, many actions for slander will only produce a remedy if 'special loss' is proved by the plaintiff, whereas libel is actionable *per se*.

A person may sue without proof of damage if a slander:

(a) casts aspersions on his integrity or competence in his profession;

(b) alleges that he has committed a crime punishable by imprisonment *(Gray v Jones 1939)*;

(c) imputes unchastity to a woman (Slander of Women Act 1891); or

(d) imputes that he suffers from venereal disease.

'Special loss' must be proved in any other case of alleged slander to gain a remedy. This may be easier for a business client to prove; telling a supplier that his customer is a crook may lead to the latter losing a contract and so incurring special expense in loss of profit or in finding another supplier. But mental suffering and social ostracism leading to loss of habitual hospitality have been seen as special losses for individuals.

Each occasion on which a statement is made can be a separate case of defamation: there may be liability for a defamatory statement each time it is made, by whomever it is made. The defence of 'privilege' (as described later) is sometimes available to a person (such as a newspaper reporter) who repeats what was said by someone else; but in principle it is no defence to assert that the statement is only a repetition and not an original statement.

Exercise 2

A club runs a gaming machine for the amusement of its members without the necessary licence. The authorities discover this, and one of the members of the club is accused (falsely) of having informed the authorities. Why is this accusation not defamatory?

Defences to an action for defamation

Consent

It is a defence that the plaintiff gave his *consent*, possibly only by implication, to the publication of a defamatory statement about himself: *Cookson v Harewood 1932*. This sounds unlikely, but, for example, the subject of a defamatory statement made at a company meeting may fail to object to it, thereby consenting to its publication in the minutes of that meeting.

Justification

Justification is a defence; the defendant must show that the statement was true in all *material* particulars. Defamation cannot be committed by telling the truth.

Fair comment

For the defence of *fair comment* to succeed, it must be shown that the statement was a fair comment on a matter of public interest, which insofar as it gave facts they were accurate, and that the defendant was not actuated by malice (improper motive) in making the statement.

Privilege

It is a defence that the statement was protected by *privilege*, which may be absolute or qualified. This is the most important defence in practice. The difference between absolute and qualified privilege is that absolute privilege remains available as a defence despite any evidence of malice on the part of the person who makes the statement. It enables Members of Parliament, for example, to make statements with the deliberate intention of causing prejudice to the person about whom the statement is made.

Absolute privilege is given to enable a person to make statements *in the public interest*, without fear of personal liability. It extends to:

BPP Publishing

Notes

(a) statements made in Parliament, papers laid before Parliament and fair and accurate reports of Parliamentary proceedings;

(b) statements made by judges, juries, witnesses, counsel or parties in judicial proceedings and contemporary newspaper reports of those proceedings and other fair and accurate reports of those proceedings, such as the Law Reports;

(c) communications between high officers of state, in the course of their official duties;

(d) statements between solicitor and client, in some cases. (In others, only qualified privilege is given.)

Exercise 3

If justification is pleaded as a defence to an action for defamation but the defence fails, the court may award aggravated damages. Why should this be so?

The defence of *qualified privilege* evolved through case law. It was extended to newspapers (subject to certain conditions) by the Defamation Act 1952.

Qualified privilege is applicable to a statement made *without* malice or improper intent, being a statement made:

(a) by a person who has an interest or a (social, moral or legal) duty to make the statement;

(b) to a person who has a corresponding interest or duty to receive the statement.

Qualified privilege has been held to apply to:

(a) references to prospective employers or credit agencies: *London Association for the Protection of Trade v Greenlands 1916*;

(b) statements in protection of one's private interests: *Osborn v Thos Boulter 1930*;

(c) statements made by way of complaint to a proper authority;

(d) professional communications between solicitor and client.

If a statement to which qualified privilege might otherwise apply is made in circumstances which give it wider circulation than is necessary to protect the common interest, malice may be inferred, and the privilege will be lost.

Exercise 4

Janice is planning to bring an action for nuisance against her neighbour. She is discussing this with her solicitor in a wine bar, and she utters the words 'I think Mrs Smith next door to me is running a brothel'. Her words are overheard by someone who knows both her and Mrs Smith. If Janice were to be sued for defamation, would she be able to claim qualified privilege?

Chapter roundup

(a) Conversion is any action in connection with goods which denies or is inconsistent with the plaintiff's title. The plaintiff must be the owner and must have possession or be entitled to immediate possession.

BPP Publishing

(b) Private nuisance is unlawful interference with the plaintiff's use of his property or with his health and comfort or convenience. An injunction and/or damages may be awarded.

(c) A defamatory statement is one which damages the reputation of the plaintiff. In general, defamatory statements in permanent form or in radio or television broadcasts are libel, actionable without proof of special loss, whereas defamatory statements in transient form are slander.

(d) Defences to an action for defamation include consent, justification, fair comment and privilege (which may be absolute or qualified).

Quick quiz

1   What is conversion?

2   How is private nuisance distinguished from public nuisance?

3   What is the effect of a defamatory statement?

4   When may a person gain a remedy for slander without proof of damage?

5   What defences are there to an action for defamation?

Solutions to exercises

1   (a)   No: an occasional party is reasonable.

    (b)   Yes.

2   The member is being accused of upholding the law, which does not damage his reputation.

3   The defamatory statement will have been given added publicity in the course of the trial.

4   No: she gave unnecessary publicity to the allegation.

17 THE NATURE OF A COMPANY

Your objectives

After completing this chapter you should:

(a)   understand the separate legal personality of companies;

(b)   know when a company may be identified with its members;

(c)   be able to contrast a company with a partnership;

(d)   know how a company may be liable in tort and crime;

(e)   understand how public and private companies differ;

(f)   understand the relationship between holding and subsidiary companies.

---

1   The company as a legal entity

The word 'company' is generally used to describe a company formed by *registration* under the Companies Act 1985. This Act is the main piece of legislation on companies, and all statutory references in the remainder of this book are to this Act (as amended by later legislation) unless otherwise stated.

The essential feature of any corporate body is that it exists as a legal entity, or person, distinct from its members.

A company has a number of characteristics in consequence of being a legal entity separate from its members.

Limited liability. The company is liable without limit for its own debts. However it obtains its capital from and distributes its profits to its members. It may be - and usually is - formed on the basis of limited liability of members. In that case they cannot be required to contribute (if the company becomes insolvent) more than the amount outstanding (if any) on their shares.

Transferable shares. The interest of members as proprietors of the company is a form of property (measured in 'shares') which they can transfer to another person subject to any restriction imposed by the constitution of the company.

Perpetual succession. A change of membership or the death of a member is not a change in the company itself. It is a separate person which continues unaffected by changes among its members.

Assets, rights and liabilities. The assets and liabilities, rights and obligations incidental to the company's activities are assets of the company and not of its members.

The distinction between a company and its members as different legal persons (sometimes called 'the veil of incorporation') was authoritatively established by the House of Lords in 1897.

BPP Publishing

Case: Salomon v Salomon Ltd 1897

For 30 years S carried on business as sole trader. S decided in 1892 to form a registered company to which he transferred the business as a going concern. Soon after the company was formed it suffered losses. The company failed and went into liquidation. It then had £6,000 of assets left but owed £7,000 to its unsecured trade creditors and £10,000 to B under a debenture. If a secured debenture originally issued to S was valid, B would take the all remaining assets. The other creditors however argued that the security given by the debenture was invalid because 'the company was Mr Salomon in another form'.

Held: the company has a legal existence... and it is impossible to deny the validity of the transaction (the purchase of the business and the issue of the debenture) into which it has entered.

2 The veil of incorporation

The veil of incorporation means merely that a company is to be distinguished as a separate person from its members. Exceptions are made (called *lifting the veil of incorporation*) in some specific situations.

Lifting the veil by statute to enforce the law

If, when a company is wound up, it appears that its business has been carried on with intent to defraud creditors or others the court may decide that the persons (usually the directors) who were knowingly parties to the fraud shall be personally responsible for debts and other liabilities of the company: s 213 Insolvency Act 1986. This is a restraint on directors who might otherwise permit their company to continue trading fraudulently when they know that it can no longer pay its debts. Even in the absence of fraud, s 214 Insolvency Act 1986 (wrongful trading) may apply.

A *public* company must, under s 117, obtain a certificate from the Registrar before it may commence to trade. Failure to do so leads to personal liability for the directors for any loss or damage suffered by a third party to a transaction entered into by the company in contravention of s 117.

A company is identified by its name which distinguishes it from other companies. Every company is required to *exhibit its name in its correct form* outside every place of business, on its seal (if it has one) and on its business letters and other documents such as bills of exchange. If the rule is broken an officer of the company responsible for the default may be fined and, as regards business documents, he is personally liable to the creditor if the company fails to pay the debt: s 349.

Exercise 1

In *Macaura v Northern Assurance Co Ltd 1925*, M insured (in his own name) some timber which he had sold to a company of which he was the sole owner. When the timber was destroyed by fire, the insurance company was found to be not liable to pay for the loss. Why do you think this was?

Identification of a company and its members

The courts may ignore the distinction between a company and its members and managers if the latter use that distinction to evade their legal obligations.

Case: Gilford Motor Co Ltd v Horne 1933

H (the defendant) had been employed by the plaintiff company under a contract which forbade him after leaving its service to solicit its customers. After the termination of his employment H formed a company of which his wife and an employee were the sole directors and shareholders. But H managed the company and through it evaded the covenant by which he himself was prevented from soliciting customers of G.

Held: an injunction requiring observance of the covenant would be made both against H and the company which he had formed as a 'a mere cloak or sham'.

Groups of companies

A holding company must ordinarily produce group accounts in which the profits or losses, assets and liabilities of subsidiary companies are consolidated or treated as if they belonged to the holding company.

There is no general rule that commercial activities of a subsidiary are to be treated as acts of the holding company merely because of the relationship of holding company and subsidiary. But the companies may be so identified if either the one is in fact acting as agent or trustee of the other, or they are both involved in carrying on what amounts to a single business.

Case: DHN Food Distributors Ltd v Tower Hamlets LBC 1976

DHN carried on business as grocers from premises owned by a subsidiary of DHN. The subsidiary itself had no business activities. Both companies had the same directors. The local authority (the defendant) acquired the premises compulsorily but refused to pay compensation for disturbance of the business since the subsidiary which owned the premises did not also carry on the business.

Held: holding company and subsidiary should be regarded as an 'economic entity'. Accordingly there was a valid claim for disturbance since ownership of the premises and business activity were in the hands of a single group.

The courts will not extend the economic entity principle too far. It is always necessary to show that the companies were involved in a single business rather than (as is often the case) carrying on separate businesses. If a subsidiary becomes insolvent the holding company is never liable for its debts unless it guaranteed them. A mere 'comfort letter' indicating an intention to pay a subsidiary's debts is not binding.

3   Companies and partnerships

The owners of a small business have a choice whether to trade as a partnership or as a company but some professions, including solicitors, do not permit their members to practise as companies. The choice is often determined by the amount of tax likely to be paid under one alternative or the other. There are however a number of other factors of comparison.

The essential features of a partnership are stated in the same sequence below.

(a)   A partnership is the relation which subsists between persons carrying on a business in common with a view of profit: Partnership Act 1890 s 1. A partnership is *not a separate entity*: it is merely the partners as a group working in a particular relationship with each other.

(b)   Every partner is *liable without limit* for the debts of the partnership. It is possible to register a limited partnership in which some (but not all) partners have limited liability. But the limited partners may not take part in the management of the business: Limited Partnerships Act 1907. This exception is little used and is of no importance.

(c) Since partnership is a personal relationship *it ends on a change in the personnel* of the partnership.

(d) The *assets and liabilities belong to the partners* in a partnership. But they own the assets as 'partnership property' to be used in the firm's business.

(e) A partnership, unlike a company, cannot create a floating charge over its assets (such as stock in trade or book debts) as security for a loan.

Exercise 2

In *Daimler Co Ltd v Continental Tyre and Rubber Co 1916*, heard when the UK and Germany were at war, the defendant was a UK company largely owned by Germans. The plaintiff was held not to be required to pay a debt to the defendant, because the defendant should be treated as an enemy alien. What did the court have to do to ignore the fact that the defendant was a UK company?

---

4 A company's liability in tort and crime

A company can have civil liability in tort for wrongs done by its officers and employees acting on its behalf in its business. This is a normal application of the principle of vicarious liability.

There is more uncertainty about the liability of a company for a crime committed in the course of its business activity. In general there can never be liability for a crime unless the person responsible for the criminal act did it with the necessary knowledge, intent or other mental condition called *mens rea* (guilty mind). A company has no mind of its own.

It has been held that when a crime is committed by a senior employee of a company (not necessarily a director) he may be treated as the *directing mind and will* of the company which is then itself guilty of crime. This principle only applies to officers of senior status.

Where there is strict liability for a criminal offence a company may be convicted of it since the accused's state of mind - *mens rea* - is irrelevant to liability for such an offence: *Mousell Bros Ltd v London & North-Western Railway Co 1917*.

5 Public and private companies

A public company is a company registered as such under the Companies Acts with the Registrar of Companies. Any company not registered as public is a private company: s 1(3). A public company may be one which was originally incorporated as a public company or one which re-registered as a public company having been previously a private company.

A public company is such because the Registrar of Companies (referred to as 'the registrar' in the remainder of this text) has issued a certificate that the company has been registered or re-registered as a public company.

Differences between private and public companies

The more important differences between public and private companies imposed by law relate to the following factors.

(a) *Directors*. A public company must have at least two directors but a private company only one: s 282. The rules on loans to directors are much more stringent in their application to public companies and their subsidiaries than to private companies: s 330. A public company, except by ordinary resolution with special notice, may not appoint a director aged over 70: s 293.

(b) *Members*. A public company must have at least two members. A private company need only have one member. There is no upper limit on the number of members of either public or private companies.

(c) *Capital*. The main differences are:

    (i)   minimum amount of £50,000 for a public company, no minimum for a private company;

    (ii)   a public company may raise capital from the general body of investors by offering its shares or debentures to the public; a private company is prohibited from doing so.

(d) *Dealings in shares*. In practice only a public company can obtain a Stock Exchange or other investment exchange listing for its shares. Not all public companies however are listed. There are additional rules of company law relating to listed securities.

(e) *Accounts*

    (i)   A public company has seven months from the end of its accounting reference period in which to produce its statutory audited accounts. The period for a private company is ten months: s 244(1).

    (ii)   A private company, if qualified by its size, may have partial exemption from various accounting provisions. These remissions are not available to a public company or to its subsidiaries (even if they are private companies): ss 246, 248 and 250.

(f) *Commencement of business*. A private company can commence business as soon as it is incorporated. A public company if incorporated as such must first obtain a certificate from the registrar who must be satisfied that the company has allotted at least £50,000 of its share capital, paid up as to at least a quarter of its nominal value and the whole of any premium: s 372.

(g) *Identification* as public or private:

    (i)   the word 'limited' or 'Ltd' in the name denotes a private company; 'public limited company' or 'plc' must appear at the end of the name of a public company: s 25;

    (ii)   the *memorandum of association* of a public company must include a clause describing it as a public company. Nothing of this kind is prescribed for a private company.

Exercise 3

In what ways do the rules which differ between public and private companies give extra protection to investors in public companies? Why should such extra protection be given?

---

6 Holding and subsidiary companies

A company will be the *subsidiary company* of another company, its *holding company*, if:

(a) the latter holds the majority of the voting rights in the former;

(b) the latter is a member of the former and in addition has the right by voting control to remove or appoint a majority of its board of directors; or

(c) the latter is a member of the former and controls a majority of the voting rights, pursuant to an agreement with other members or shareholders;

or if it is a subsidiary of a company which is itself a subsidiary of that other company: s 736 (1).

A company (A) is a *wholly-owned subsidiary* of another company (B) if it has no other members except B and its wholly-owned subsidiaries, or persons acting on B's or B's subsidiaries' behalf: s 736 (2).

The importance of the holding and subsidiary company relationship is recognised in company law in a number of rules.

(a) A holding company must generally prepare *group accounts* in which the financial situation of holding and subsidiary companies is consolidated as if they were one person: s 227.

(b) A subsidiary may not ordinarily be a member of its holding company or give financial assistance for the purchase of the shares of its holding company: s 23 and s 151(1).

(c) Since directors of a holding company can control its subsidiary some rules designed to regulate the dealings of a public company with its directors also apply to its subsidiaries even if they are private companies, particularly loans to directors: s 330.

Exercise 4

A Ltd holds 60% of the shares in B Ltd, which holds 60% of the shares in C Ltd. A Ltd thus effectively holds 60% × 60% = 36% of C Ltd. Is C Ltd a subsidiary of A Ltd?

Chapter roundup

(a) A company is a legal entity separate from its members. It owns its own assets and has its own liabilities.

(b) A company may nonetheless be identified with its members in certain cases, generally to prevent the abuse of separate legal personality.

(c) A partnership is not an entity distinct from its members, and partners have unlimited liability for the firm's debts.

(d) A company can be vicariously liable for the torts of its employees. It may also be guilty of crimes committed by sufficiently senior employees.

(e) Public companies may, unlike private companies, offer their shares and securities to the general public. Correspondingly, they are subject to special restrictions.

(f) A group of companies comprises a holding company and one or more subsidiary companies. The control exercised by the holding company and its ownership of the subsidiaries is recognised in company law.

Quick quiz

1 What is meant by 'perpetual succession'?

2 What is the significance of *Salomon's* case?

3 In what circumstances does statute draw aside the veil of incorporation?

4 For what other reasons have the court identified a company with its members (excluding group companies)?

5 What is the 'economic entity' test applied to groups of companies?

6 State three differences between a partnership and a registered company.

7 Is a company liable for a tort or a crime committed by one of its employees?

8 State three differences between a public and a private company.

9 In what circumstances is one company a subsidiary of another?

10 Name three particular requirements made of groups by the Companies Acts.

Solutions to exercises

1 M did not have an insurable interest, because the timber belonged to the company and not to him.

2 The court had to lift the veil of incorporation.

3 The need for two directors may make it difficult for a single dishonest director to defraud investors.

A public company must produce accounts more quickly than a private company.

A public company must raise substantial capital before it may trade. It must therefore ensure that many investors (or a few wealthy investors) accept that it is reputable.

The extra protection is needed because capital may be raised from investors who have no prior contact with or knowledge of the company.

4 Yes: C Ltd is a subsidiary of B Ltd, which is in turn a subsidiary of A Ltd.

18 FORMATION OF A COMPANY

> **Your objectives**
>
> After completing this chapter you should:
>
> (a)   understand the role of the promoters of a new company;
>
> (b)   understand the position of pre-incorporation contracts;
>
> (c)   know how registration of a new company is secured;
>
> (d)   know what conditions a public company must satisfy before starting business;
>
> (e)   know how a company makes contracts.

1   Promoters and pre-incorporation contracts

A company cannot form itself. The person who forms a company is called a *promoter*.

Duties of promoters

The promoter is said to stand in a *fiduciary position* to the company and this imposes on him the obligation to make proper disclosure of any personal advantage which he may obtain from acting as promoter. The disclosure must be made either to an independent board of directors or to existing and prospective members of the company.

There are two types of profit which a promoter may make, one legitimate and the other wrongful.

(a)   A promoter who acquires interest in property before promoting a company and then makes a profit when he sells the property to the promoted company makes a *legitimate* profit provided he discloses it: *Re Lady Forrest (Murchison) Gold Mine Ltd 1901.*

(b)   A promoter who enters into and makes a profit personally in a contract as a promoter is acting wrongfully, in breach of fiduciary duty.

Remedy for breach of fiduciary duty

If the promoter does not make a proper disclosure of legitimate profits or if he makes wrongful profits the primary remedy of the company is to rescind the contract and recover its money. But sometimes it is too late to rescind because the property can no longer be returned or the company prefers to keep it. In such a case the company can only recover from the promoter his wrongful profit, unless some special circumstances dictate otherwise.

(a)   If, at the time, the promoter was *acting as the company's agent*, he is accountable to the company as his principal. But this is rarely the case since the promoter usually concludes the preliminary transaction before he begins to act as promoter and before the company exists to be his principal.

(b)   He can be made to account for legitimate profits arising from sale of property to the company if they arose from a collateral transaction, such as a mortgage of the property.

BPP Publishing

The remedies above are claims by the company against the promoter. He has no obligations at common law to individual shareholders, although he may discharge his duty to the company by disclosure to its existing or prospective shareholders. But if, as is usual in these cases, there is a prospectus offer, the promoter has a statutory liability to compensate any person who has acquired securities to which the prospectus relates and suffered loss in respect of them as a result of any untrue or misleading statement, or omission.

Liability for pre-incorporation contracts and expenses

A promoter usually incurs expenses in preparations, such as drafting legal documents, made before the company is formed. He has no automatic right to recover his expenses from the company. But he can generally arrange that the first directors, of whom he may be one, agree that the company shall pay the bills or refund to him his expenditure.

Generally pre-incorporation contracts are of two types.

(a)   The promoter makes arrangements which he intends that the company will carry out once it is incorporated.

(b)   The promoter makes a contract on the company's behalf either being unaware of, or disregarding, the fact that the company is not yet formed. He may hold himself out to be a director of what is in fact a non-existent company.

A company can never ratify a contract made on its behalf before it was incorporated. It did not exist when the pre-incorporation contract was made; it cannot be made a party to it. This principle applies to both rights and obligations.

Although ratification of a pre-incorporation contract is not possible, a company may enter into a new contract (novation) on similar terms after the company has been incorporated. But there must be sufficient evidence that the company has made a new contract. Mere recognition of the pre-incorporation contract by performing it or accepting benefits under it is to be distinguished from making a new contract.

> *Case: Howard v Patent Ivory Manufacturing Co 1888*
> By a pre-incorporation contract J agreed to sell property to the company. After the company had been formed the terms of the purchase were modified and J agreed to accept part of the price in debentures instead of cash as originally agreed.
>
> *Held:* the re-negotiation of the payment terms were sufficient evidence of a new offer and acceptance by which the company had after incorporation made a new contract.

Liability under pre-incorporation contracts is determined by s 36C(1):

'A contract which purports to be made by or on behalf of a company at a time when the company has not been formed has effect, subject to any agreement to the contrary, as one made with the person purporting to act for the company or as agent for it, and he is personally liable on the contract accordingly.'

The effect of s 36C(1) is limited.

> *Case: Cotronic (UK) Ltd v Dezonie 1991*
> A company, W B Ltd, was incorporated in 1973 but struck off the register and dissolved in 1981. A contract was entered into in March 1986 between Mrs O and W B Ltd which of course did not at that time exist; a new company bearing the same name was not incorporated until 1988.
>
> *Held:* the contract could not be saved under s 36C, since there had been no *intention* when the contract was made of forming the new company.

Exercise 1

In *Re Northumberland Avenue Hotel Co Ltd 1886* there was a pre-incorporation contract to grant a building lease to a company. After incorporation, the company took possession of the land and began to build on it. The company thus had the benefit of the contract earlier agreed. Why was the company not bound by the contract?

---

2 Registration procedures

A company is formed by the issue of a certificate of registration by the registrar. The certificate identifies the company by its name and serial number at the registry and states (if it be so) that it is limited and (if necessary) that it is a public company.

To obtain the certificate of incorporation it is necessary to deliver to the registrar prescribed documents (see below) bearing the name of the proposed company.

The documents to be delivered to the registrar are as follows.

(a) A *memorandum of association* This is normally signed by at least two subscribers. However, in the case of single member private companies it is possible for only the one member to subscribe to the memorandum. The signature(s) must be dated and witnessed. Each subscriber agrees to subscribe for at least one share: s 1(1).

(b) *Articles of association* signed by the same subscribers, dated and witnessed. Alternatively the memorandum of a company limited by shares may be endorsed 'registered without articles of association'. The statutory Table A articles then become the company's articles in their entirety.

(c) A statement in the prescribed form (known as *Form 10*) giving the particulars of the first director(s) and secretary and of the first address of the registered office. The persons named as directors and secretary must sign the form to record their consent to act in this capacity. When the company is incorporated they are deemed to be appointed: ss 10 and 13.

(d) A statutory declaration *(Form 12)* by a solicitor engaged in the formation of the company or by one of the persons named as director or secretary that the requirements of the Companies Act in respect of registration have been complied with: s 12(3).

A registration fee is payable.

The registrar considers whether the documents are formally in order and whether the objects specified in the memorandum appear to be lawful, since a company may only be registered if it has a lawful purpose: s 1. If he is satisfied, he gives the company a 'registered number' (s 705), issues a certificate of incorporation and publishes a notice in the London Gazette that it has been issued: ss 13 and 711.

Companies 'off the shelf'

Because the registration of a new company can be a lengthy business, it is often easiest for people wishing to operate as a company to purchase one 'off the shelf'. This is possible by contacting enterprises specialising in registering a stock of companies, ready for sale when a person comes along who needs the advantages of incorporation.

Exercise 2

'Off the shelf' companies cannot exist on the shelf, waiting to be bought, unless all the usual formalities of registration have already been complied with. What changes are the buyers of an off the shelf company likely to make immediately on purchase?

---

3   Commencement of business

A *private company* may do business and exercise its borrowing powers from the date of its incorporation. It is normal practice to hold a first meeting of the directors at which the chairman, secretary and sometimes the auditors are appointed, shares are allotted to raise capital, authority is given to open a bank account and any other initial commercial arrangements are made. A return of allotments should be made to the registrar: s 88. Within the first nine months of its existence the company should give notice to the registrar of the accounting reference date on which its annual accounts will be made up: s 224.

If no such notice is given within the prescribed period, companies are deemed to have an accounting reference date of the last day of the month in which the anniversary of incorporation falls.

A new *public company* may not do business or exercise any borrowing powers unless it has obtained a trading certificate from the registrar: s 117.

To obtain a trading certificate a public company makes application on Form 117 signed by a director or by the secretary with a statutory declaration made by the director or secretary which states:

(a)   that the nominal value of the allotted share capital is not less than £50,000;

(b)   the amount paid up on the allotted share capital, which must be at least one quarter of the nominal value and the entire premium if any: s 101;

(c)   particulars of preliminary expenses and payments or benefits to promoters.

The registrar must notify receipt of Form 117 in the Gazette and may accept the declaration without investigation and issue a trading certificate, which is conclusive evidence that the company is entitled to do business and to exercise its borrowing powers.

4   Company contracts

There is no special form of company contract - the same rules requiring use of written or sealed documents apply to companies as to individuals: s 36. The company must of course enter into contracts through agents. Its articles of association delegate wide powers to its directors and they may in turn permit employees to make commercial contracts under their general or specific authorisation.

A director, secretary or other authorised officer of a company may authenticate a document on the company's behalf: s 41. Provided the signature is made in this way and in the course of the company's business that person's signature is treated as that of the company: *UBAF Ltd v European American Banking Corporation 1984*.

The common seal

A company may have a 'common seal' for general use on documents, such as debentures, which it executes as deeds (s 36A(2)), though under s 36A(3), this is no longer mandatory. If a company does not have a seal, or does not use it, s 36A(4) provides that 'a document signed by a director and the secretary of a company or by two directors of the company, and expressed (in whatever form of words) to be executed by the company, has the same effect as if executed under the common seal of the company'. If a document executed by the company states on its face that it is intended to be a deed, then it takes effect as a deed on delivery.

A company may have a second 'official seal' for use on its share and debenture stock certificates. The official seal must be a facsimile of the common seal with the addition of the word 'Securities': s 40. This is convenient when the company's register of members is maintained, and new share certificates are issued, by professional registrars. They keep the register at their own premises and therefore wish to have a seal of their own to apply to share certificates.

The name of the company must be legibly engraved on its seal: s 350 (1). The seal does not usually have anything on it except the name.

Contracts with the subscribers and members

There is a special procedure to be followed by a public company if:

(a) *within two years of incorporation as a public company* it acquires property ('non cash assets') of specified value from subscribers to the memorandum; or

(b) *within two years of re-registration as a public company* (having previously been a private company) it acquires such property from persons who were members at the time of re-registration.

The general effect of these rules is that the property must be valued by an independent qualified valuer and the transaction must be approved by ordinary resolution passed in general meeting: s 104.

If these rules are broken then the company may recover the consideration or its equivalent; the agreement is then void: s 105. The minimum value which brings these rules into operation is one tenth of the nominal value of the company's issued share capital at the time. The rules do not apply however to acquisition of property in the ordinary course of business or under court supervision.

Exercise 3

What key principle of company law is reflected in the fact that a company can make contracts in the same ways as an individual can (albeit through agents)?

Chapter roundup

(a) A company is formed by its promoters. They have a fiduciary duty to the company.

(b) A company cannot be a party to a pre-incorporation contract, but such a contract can be replaced by a new contract which the company is a party to.

(c) Several documents must be submitted in order to obtain a registration certificate for a new company.

(d) A private company may commence business without further formality, but a public company must obtain a trading certificate.

(e) A company may make contracts in the same way as an individual, although it must do so through agents such as its directors. There are special rules for contracts between public companies and their subscribers.

BPP Publishing

Quick quiz

1   Define a promoter.

2   To whom should a promoter disclose any personal advantage which he obtains from the promotion?

3   What are the company's remedies for non-disclosure by a promoter?

4   How may a promoter recover from the company his expenses incurred in forming it?

5   If a company (a) acts on a pre-incorporation contract or (b) negotiates modifications of its terms, how in each case does that action affect the company's liability (if any) under the contract?

6   State the statutory rule on an agent's liability on pre-incorporation contracts.

7   Describe the documents which must be delivered to the registrar to form a company limited by shares.

8   How may a new enterprise avoid the complexities of registration?

Solutions to exercises

1   Taking the benefit of a contract does not amount to a novation.

2   The buyers are likely to change the company's name and its directors.

3   Separate legal personality.

19 PUBLICITY

<table>
<tr><td colspan="2">Your objectives</td></tr>
<tr><td colspan="2">After completing this chapter you should:</td></tr>
<tr><td>(a)</td><td>know the main sources of information about a company;</td></tr>
<tr><td>(b)</td><td>know what information is available from the Companies Registry;</td></tr>
<tr><td>(c)</td><td>know the required scope of accounting records;</td></tr>
<tr><td>(d)</td><td>know the contents of and rights of access to the statutory registers;</td></tr>
<tr><td>(e)</td><td>know how a company's annual report and accounts must be prepared and circulated;</td></tr>
<tr><td>(f)</td><td>understand how auditors are appointed and removed from office;</td></tr>
<tr><td>(g)</td><td>know the duties and powers of auditors.</td></tr>
</table>

1   Accountability

Public accountability

It is a basic principle of company law that the advantages of trading through a separate corporate body (especially if its members have limited liability for its debts) should be matched by requiring the company to provide information about itself which is available to the public. Anyone who is interested in a company, typically because he intends to do business with it and perhaps to give it credit, can thus find out who owns and manages it and what its financial position was at the date of its latest accounts.

The basic sources of information about a UK company are as follows.

(a) Its *file at the Companies Registry* (situated in Cardiff but with a search room in London) in which the registrar holds all documents delivered to him by the company for filing. Any members of the public may inspect the file (called 'making a search') on payment of a small fee and may obtain copies of the documents in it.

(b) The *registers and other documents* which the company is required to hold at its registered office (or in some cases at a different address of which notice is given to the registrar). Here too there are statutory rights of inspection.

(c) The *London Gazette* (published two or three times a week by HMSO) in which the company itself or the registrar is required to publish certain notices.

Constructive notice

Until 1989, the availability of information from the company's file at the registry was matched by a general principle of 'constructive' or 'deemed' notice. Because a member of the public had the opportunity of inspecting documents on the file he was treated in law as if he had done so. However, s 711A now provides as follows.

'A person shall not be taken to have notice of any matter merely because of its being disclosed in any document kept by the registrar of companies (and thus available for inspection) or made available by the company for inspection.'

Two specific exceptions to this are provided.

(a)   S 416 retains the presumption that any person who is taking a charge over the company's property has notice of any item requiring registration in the charges register, which is in fact disclosed in the register when the charge is created.

(b)   Certain land charges registered at Companies House are deemed to comprise actual notice.

However, there is a general duty to make reasonable enquiries and failure to do so means that a person may still be treated as having notice: s 711A(2).

Internal accountability

A different aspect of the requirement that information must be given exists within a company. The management of the company is in the hands of the directors and they must be accountable to the members.

(a)   The members have a statutory right to receive a copy of the annual accounts, together with the auditors' and directors' reports: s 238.

(b)   Various transactions and interests of the directors must be disclosed in the accounts or entered in a register or other documents which members may inspect.

(c)   Any loans to directors and transactions with the company in which they have a material interest must be disclosed in the accounts: s 232.

(d)   There is a register of directors' interests in shares or debentures: s 325.

(e)   In some cases, such as long-term service agreements or compensation for loss of office, disclosure to members is merely the first step and the transaction is terminable or void unless the members then approve it in general meeting: ss 319 and 312.

Exercise 1

Peter receives and reads a copy of the Companies Registry file on X Ltd. In legal proceedings relating to subsequent events, he claims that he should not be treated as having had notice of the contents of the file. Why is he misinterpreting s 711A?

---

2   The companies registry and the DTI

In its memorandum of association a company must state whether its registered office is to be situated in England (which includes Wales) or in Scotland: s 2. If in England its file is held at the Companies Registry at Cardiff and microfiche copies of the file contents are available for inspection in London. If the registered office is in Scotland the company's file is at the registry at Edinburgh.

Anyone is allowed to inspect a copy of documents held by the registrar or, if these are illegible or unavailable, the document itself: s 709(1). A person may demand the certificate of incorporation and a certified copy of any other document.

Contents of the registry file

On first incorporation the company's file includes a copy of its certificate of incorporation and the original documents presented to secure its incorporation. Every document delivered to the registrar in compliance with company law is added to the file.

If a company has been in existence for some time the file is likely to include each year's annual accounts and return, copies of special, extraordinary and some ordinary resolutions passed in general meeting, a copy of the altered memorandum or articles of association if they have been altered and notices of various events such as the appointment of a receiver or liquidator, a change of directors, secretary, auditors or address of registered office. If a company issues a prospectus, a signed copy with all annexed documents is delivered for filing. Even this list is not exhaustive.

The London Gazette

The registrar is required to give notice in the *London Gazette* of the receipt of any of the following documents (s 711 (1)):

(a) various resolutions, statements, notices and reports;

(b) a notice of change of directors;

(c) an annual return or annual accounts;

(d) a notice of change of address of the registered office;

(e) a court order for compulsory winding up or dissolution of a company or the liquidator's return of the final meeting in liquidation.

He also gives notice of the issue of a certificate of incorporation and the receipt of Form 117 for a trading certificate. He adds to the file a copy of any certificate of re-registration, for example a private re-registered as a public company, which he may issue.

Company forms

All standard documents required to be delivered to the registry must be 'in the prescribed form'. These are printed forms in standard A4 size prescribed by statutory regulation (The Companies (Forms) Regulations 1979) so that the lay-out, content and size of the forms is uniform. Companies obtain their own supplies from specialist commercial law stationers.

Exercise 2

What is the purpose of giving notice of certain documents in the *London Gazette*, when the complete file on any company is available for inspection?

---

3 Company records and registers

Contents of accounting records

A company is required by s 221 to keep accounting records sufficient to show and explain the company's transactions. At any time, it should be possible:

(a) to determine with reasonable accuracy the company's financial position; and

(b) to ascertain that any balance sheet or profit and loss account prepared is done so in accordance with the Act.

Accounting records may be kept in the form of bound books or in any other manner decided by the directors: s 722. If another method is used (such as loose-leaf binders or computer records) added precautions must be taken to prevent falsification: s 723; the company and its officers may be fined if they default in this respect.

Accounting records should be kept at the company's registered office or at some other place thought fit by the directors. Where accounting records are kept outside the UK, say by a branch of a UK company, accounts and returns must be made every six months to the UK.

Accounting records should be open to inspection by the company's officers: s 222. They have a right of inspection of all records, although the court has no statutory power to compel a company to allow its accounting records to be inspected. Note particularly that a *shareholder* is not given the right to inspect accounting records although the Articles of Association, the directors or an ordinary resolution may confer the right.

Registers

The statutory registers which a company must keep (with the relevant sections) are:

(a)   the register of members: s 352;

(b)* the register of directors and secretaries: s 288;

(c)   the register of directors' interests in shares and debentures of the company: s 325;

(d)* the register of charges: s 411;

(e)* minutes of general meetings of the company: s 382;

(f)   minutes of directors' and managers' meetings: s 382;

(g)   (if the company is a public company) the register of substantial interests in shares (3% or more of the nominal value of any class of shares): s 211.

Those items which are marked * must be kept at the registered office. The others may be kept at the registered office or at certain other places. Items (c) and (g) serve to amplify the register of members and therefore must be kept at the same place as that register.

Companies with debentures issued nearly always keep a register of debentureholders, but there is no statutory compulsion to do so. If a register of debentureholders is maintained, it should not be held outside England and Wales, and should be kept at the registered office. If it is not kept there, the registrar should be informed of its whereabouts: s 190.

The *register of members* lists the company's shareholders.

The *register of charges* contains details of charges affecting the company property or undertaking, and should provide brief descriptions of property charged, the amount of the charge and the name of the person entitled to the charge. Any person may inspect the charges register; members and creditors may inspect free of charge.

In addition to keeping a register of charges, a company must also keep copies of every instrument creating a charge at its registered office: s 411. Any member or creditor may inspect the copies and register without a fee; others may inspect the register for such a fee as may be prescribed.

Exercise 3

If shareholders in a company have no right to inspect accounting records, how can they tell whether the company is doing well or badly?

The *register of directors and secretaries* must contain the following details in respect of a director who is an individual: s 288:

(a)   present and former forenames and surnames;

(b)   residential address;

(c)   nationality;

(d)   business occupation;

(e)   particulars of other current and former directorships held in the last five years;

(f)   date of birth.

Where a director is a corporation, details must be shown of its name and registered or principal office. Similar details must also be shown regarding the company secretary. The register must include shadow directors as well as normal directors.

The register must be open to inspection by a member (free of charge), or by any other person (for a fee).

The *register of directors' interests in shares and debentures* must be maintained by the company (s 324), showing details of holdings as notified by directors under s 325 and Schedule 13 para 14. It must also enter details of rights granted to directors, irrespective of whether the directors notify the company.

Annual return

Every company must make an annual return to the registrar under ss 363 - 364A, giving the following information.

(a)   The address of the registered office of the company: s 364.

(b)   The address (if not the registered office) at which either the register of members or any register of debentureholders is kept: s 364.

(c)   The type of company it is and its principal business activities: s 364.

(d)   The total number of issued shares of the company up to the date on which the return was made up, and their aggregate nominal value: s 364A.

(e)   In respect of each class of shares, the nature of that class and the total number of issued shares to the date of the making up of the return, and their nominal value: s 364A.

(f)   The names and addresses of members of the company at the date of the return, and those who have ceased to be members since the last return. This list should be indexed or alphabetical: s 364A.

(g)   The number of shares of each class held by members at the return date, along with details of shares of each class transferred since the date to which the last return was made up and the dates on which the transfers were registered: s 364A.

(h)   If (f) and (g) have been fully covered in either of the preceding two returns, only changes in membership and share transfers need be noted: s 364A.

(i)   Where a private company has elected to dispense with the laying of accounts and reports before the company in general meeting under s 252, or to dispense with the holding of the AGM under s 366A, this fact should be stated: s 364.

(j)   Names and addresses of the directors and secretary and, in the case of each indexed director, his nationality, date of birth, previous occupation and other directorships: s 364

Exercise 4

Why might a prospective investor in a company want to know about previous directorships held by the directors?

4   Accounts and audit

Annual accounts

The directors must, in respect of each accounting reference period of the company:

(a)   prepare a balance sheet and profit and loss account (s 226);

(b)   lay before the company in general meeting accounts for the period: s 241 (with exceptions as described below); and

(c)   deliver to the registrar a copy of those accounts: s 242.

The accounts must be made up to a date which falls within the period seven days before or after the end of the accounting reference period: s 223. The accounting reference period is fixed to begin on the day after the expiry of the previous period and to end on the company's chosen accounting reference date: s 224.

The company's board of directors must approve the annual accounts and this approval must be signified by a director's signature on the balance sheet: s 233. When copies are circulated the name of the director who signs must be stated.

A company is required to lay its accounts and the directors' and auditors' reports before members in general meeting (unless it is a private company which has dispensed with this requirement under s 252 by an elective resolution): s 241. It must deliver a copy to the registrar within a maximum period reckoned from the date to which the accounts are made up: s 242. The permitted interval between the end of the accounting period and the issue of accounts is seven months for a public and ten months for a private company.

There are certain reliefs and special provisions relating to:

(a)   *the first accounts of a company following its incorporation:* broadly the first accounts may cover any period of 6-18 months: thereafter the accounts follow the normal annual cycle: s 224;

(b)   *small or medium sized companies* need not deliver to the registrar full accounts but only abbreviated versions: s 246. The size limits for small and medium sized companies are based on turnover, assets and number of employees.

The accounts must be audited and the auditor's report must be attached to the copies issued to members, delivered to the registrar or published. But a company which is 'dormant' may exclude this requirement: ss 235, 233 and 250. The accounts must also be accompanied by a directors' report giving information on a number of prescribed matters: s 234. It must contain a balanced review of the development of the business of the company (and any subsidiary undertakings) during the financial year and at the end of it, and must state the directors' recommendations on the application, retention and distribution of profits: s 234(1). The report must be formally approved by the board and signed by a director or the secretary: s 234A.

Circulation of accounts

Each member and debentureholder is entitled to be sent a copy of the annual accounts, together with the directors' and auditor's reports, at least 21 days before the meeting before which they shall be laid: s 238(1). Anyone else entitled to receive notice of a general meeting, including the company's auditor, should also be sent a copy. At any other time any member or debentureholder is entitled to a copy free of charge within seven days of requesting it: s 239(1).

A listed public company may prepare a summary financial statement (SFS) to be circulated to members instead of the full accounts, provided its constitution allows: s 251(1). The summary may be sent:

(a)   to any member who has expressly agreed to receive any such a statement; and

(b)   to any member who has failed to respond to a notice from the company enquiring whether the member wishes to receive a summary.

Adoption of accounts by members

The accounts must be laid before members in general meeting. It is usual to deal with the accounts at each year's Annual General Meeting. But it is not obligatory to do so: the accounts may be considered at an Extraordinary General Meeting.

When the accounts are laid before a general meeting it is usual to propose a resolution that they be 'adopted' or approved. This gives the members present an opportunity to ask pertinent questions and to make criticisms or suggestions. The approval of the accounts is regarded as a vote of confidence in the directors. If however the accounts are not 'adopted' they are still the accounts and their validity is not affected. But to reject the accounts is an expression of members' lack of confidence in the directors.

Exercise 5

Why should public companies be required to file their accounts more quickly than private companies, given that public companies are likely to be larger and to have more work to do in preparing accounts?

The auditor

Every company (except a dormant private company) must appoint an auditor (s 384) who must be a member of a recognised supervisory body (s 25 CA 1989) and not be a member of or connected with the management of the company: s 27 CA 1989. Corporate bodies are allowed to act as auditors.

The appointment of auditors

The first auditor of a new company is appointed by the *directors* to hold office until the conclusion of the first general meeting at which the accounts are considered: s 385. The directors or the company in general meeting may also appoint an auditor to fill a casual vacancy: s 388.

In the ordinary way the *members* appoint the auditor at each general meeting at which the accounts are considered, to hold office until the next such meeting, that is to audit and report on the accounts to be prepared for that subsequent meeting.

If the members fail to appoint an auditor at the general meeting at which the accounts are considered, the company must, within seven days of the meeting, give notice to the Secretary of State who has power to appoint an auditor: s 387.

BPP Publishing

A *dormant private company* may be exempted from the requirement to appoint an auditor and have an audit if it passes a special resolution to this effect: ss 388A and 250. A company is dormant if there has been no significant accounting transaction apart from the issue of subscriber shares.

Whoever appoints the auditor has power to fix his remuneration for the period of his appointment. It is usual when the auditor is appointed by the general meeting to leave it to the directors to fix his remuneration by agreement. Such remuneration must be disclosed in a note to the accounts: s 390A.

The termination of an auditor's appointment

An auditor may be *removed* from office before the expiry of his appointment by passing an ordinary resolution in general meeting: s 391. Special notice to the company is required: s 391A.

An auditor may *resign* his appointment by giving notice in writing to the company delivered to the registered office: s 392. Alternatively he may simply decline to offer himself for re-election.

In his notice of resignation or on ceasing to hold office for any reason (s 394) the auditor must deposit at the company's registered office either:

(a)   a statement that there are no circumstances connected with his resignation which he considers should be brought to the notice of members or creditors of the company; or

(b)   a statement disclosing what those circumstances are.

On receiving the auditor's notice of resignation the company must send a copy of it to the registrar. If the auditor's notice contains a statement of circumstances the company must also (unless the court holds it to be defamatory) send a copy to every person entitled to receive a copy of the accounts: s 392(3). S 394(3)(a) provides similar requirements where the statement of circumstances is *not* in connection with an auditor's resignation.

An auditor who includes in his statement of resignation a statement of the circumstances connected with it has the following additional rights:

(a)   to circulate (through the company) to members a statement of reasonable length of the reasons for his resignation (unless it is defamatory);

(b)   to requisition an Extraordinary General Meeting at which he will explain his reasons;

(c)   to attend and speak at any meeting at which his resignation or the appointment of his successor is to be considered: s 392A.

Changes of auditor

Whenever a resolution is to be proposed at a general meeting for the appointment of an auditor who is not the auditor who was appointed on the last occasion (however the change may arise), or if it is a resolution for the removal of an auditor before the expiry of his year of office, 28 days' special notice must be given to the company and the company must notify its members and the auditor concerned. This serves to bring to the notice of members and the auditor any changes of auditors: s 391A.

Duties and powers of auditors

The statutory duty of an auditor is to report to the members whether the accounts give a true and fair view and have been properly prepared in accordance with the Companies Act: s 235. To fulfil this duty, the auditor must carry out such investigations as are necessary to form an opinion as to whether:

(a)   proper accounting records have been kept and proper returns adequate for the audit have been received from branches;

(b)   the accounts are in agreement with the records: s 237; and

(c)   the information given in the directors' report is consistent with the accounts: s 235(3).

If the auditor is satisfied on these matters they need not be mentioned in the report.

The auditor's report must be read before any general meeting at which the accounts are considered and must be open to inspection by members. The auditor may also attend any meeting after resigning at which his successor is appointed and also the meeting at which his office would have expired.

Auditors have wide statutory powers to enable them to obtain whatever information they may require for the purpose of their audit. In particular they may inspect books and records and call on officers of the company for information or explanations: s 389A. It is a crime for an officer of a company to make a false statement to an auditor if it is misleading, false or deceptive in a material particular and is made knowingly or recklessly (with indifference as to its truth): s 389A(2).

Exercise 6

When an auditor ceases to hold office, he *must* deposit a statement under s 394. What could go wrong if he were merely permitted to deposit a statement?

Chapter roundup

(a)   Companies must disclose information about themselves to the public, so that other persons doing business with them can assess their financial position.

(b)   With only two exceptions, persons are not deemed to be aware of information merely because it is disclosed at the Companies Registry.

(c)   The file on a company at the Companies Registry includes its memorandum and articles, annual reports and accounts, the names of the directors, copies of certain resolutions and some other information. The receipt of certain documents is published in the *London Gazette*.

(d)   A company's accounting records must enable the company's financial position to be determined at any time. They may be inspected by a company's officers, but not by its members.

(e)   A company must keep several statutory registers, and some of them must be kept at the registered office. In most cases both the members and the public have a right of access.

(f)   Annual accounts, accompanied by a directors' report, must be prepared and circulated. The accounts are approved by the directors, and they may be adopted by the members in general meeting. Listed public companies may circulate summary financial statements.

(g)   The members of a company appoint an auditor, who must report on the annual report and accounts. There are rules on the termination of an auditor's appointment designed to make it difficult to get rid of an auditor before he makes an adverse report.

BPP Publishing

Quick quiz

1   What are the main sources of information about a company's affairs provided by law?

2   When is a person deemed to have notice of certain items on file at the registry?

3   Where is a company's file held and what might it contain?

4   List three documents in respect of which the registrar gives notice of receipt in the *London Gazette*.

5   What must a company's accounting records make it possible to do?

6   Name six registers which may be held by a company (including relevant section numbers of the Companies Act) and state where they must be held

7   Who may inspect copies of an instrument creating a charge?

8   What details about directors must the register of directors contain?

9   Who adopts a company's accounts?

10   What interval is allowed after the end of the period covered by accounts for laying the accounts before a general meeting and delivering a copy to the registry?

11   What reports must be attached to the accounts?

12   Who may be sent a listed public company's summary financial statement?

13   By whom may auditors be appointed (a) in normal circumstances and (b) in special circumstances?

14   What is the procedure by which an auditor may resign his appointment? By what means may he bring to the notice of members a disagreement between him and the directors?

15   On what matters does an auditor need to form an opinion when preparing his audit report?

Solutions to exercises

1   S 711A covers cases where someone did not in fact have notice. Peter did have notice.

2   Changes in a company's file need to be publicised, so that interested parties do not have to check the whole file for changes every few weeks.

3   They receive the company's annual report and accounts.

4   Directors might have been associated with either successful companies or failed companies.

5   Public companies can offer shares to the general public, so available information should be as up to date as possible.

6   He could resign without making any comment, leaving the members unaware of difficulties.

BPP Publishing

20 MEMORANDUM AND ARTICLES

Your objectives

After completing this chapter you should:

(a)   know the contents of a company's memorandum;

(b)   know the rules on the names of companies;

(c)   understand the importance of a company's registered office;

(d)   know how a typical modern objects clause is drafted;

(e)   understand the distinction between objects and powers;

(f)   understand the doctrine of *ultra vires*, and how it is severely limited by statute;

(g)   know the function of a company's articles;

(h)   know how a company's articles may be altered;

(i)   understand the extent to which the memorandum and articles create contractual relations.

---

1   Purpose and contents of the memorandum

The purpose of the memorandum and articles of association (for short 'the memorandum' and 'the articles') is to define what the company is and how its business and affairs are to be conducted. The memorandum sets out the basic elements. The articles are mainly internal rules.

For historical reasons these are two separate documents. If there is any inconsistency between them the memorandum prevails.

The original memorandum must be presented to the registrar to obtain registration of the new company. It is usually signed by at least two persons ('the subscribers') who agree to become the first members. In the case of single member private companies, however, it is now possible for only the member to subscribe to the memorandum of association. Whenever the memorandum is altered a copy of the complete altered text must be delivered to the registrar for filing: s 18.

Contents of the memorandum

The memorandum of a private company limited by shares is required by s 2 to state:

(a)   the *name* of the company;

(b)   whether the *registered office* is to be situated in England and Wales, or Scotland;

(c)   the *objects* of the company;

(d)   the *limited liability* of members;

(e)   the *authorised share capital* and how it is divided into shares.

The items on this list are referred to in this chapter as 'compulsory clauses'.

BPP Publishing

The memorandum of a public company contains the above particulars and also a sixth statement (placed second in order) that the company is a public company: s 1(3).

Every memorandum must also end with a *declaration of association* by which the subscribers state their wish to form the company. Each subscriber must, opposite his signature, state the number of shares (in practice always one share only) which he agrees to take.

2 The company name

The name of the company serves to identify it and to distinguish it from any other company. For this reason, and to control the use of company names which might mislead the public, the registrar has statutory powers of control over the choice of names.

The choice of name (whether the first name or a name adopted by change of name later) of a limited company must conform to ss 25 to 31, as follows.

(a) The name must *end* with the word(s):

    (i)   *public limited company* (abbreviated *plc*) if it is a public company; or

    (ii)   *limited* (or *Ltd*) if it is a private limited company.

(b) No company may have a name which is the same as that of any existing company appearing in the statutory index at the registry. For this purpose two names are treated as 'the same' in spite of minor or non-essential differences; for instance the word 'the' as the first word in the name is ignored. 'John Smith Limited' is treated the same as 'John Smith & Company Ltd': s 26(3).

(c) No company may have a name the use of which would in the registrar's opinion be a criminal offence or which he considers offensive: s 26(1).

(d) No company may have a name which in the registrar's opinion suggests a connection with the government or a local authority or which is subject to control (unless of course its use is officially approved): s 26(2). Words such as 'International' or 'British' are only sanctioned if the size of the company matches its pretensions. A name which suggests some professional expertise such as 'optician' will only be permitted if the appropriate representative association has been consulted and raises no objection.

Change of name

A company may change its name by passing a special resolution and obtaining the registrar's certificate of incorporation that he has registered the company under a new name: s 28. The certificate makes the change effective from when it is issued, though the company is still the same legal entity as before.

The registrar can compel a company to change its name (within such time as he may allow) if:

(a) the name is the same as or in the registrar's opinion too like the name of another company which was or should have been on the register when the name was adopted, or if misleading information or assurances were given to secure registration: s 28; or

(b) the company's name gives so misleading an indication of its activities as to be likely to cause harm to the public: s 32.

Exercise 1

A supplier is proposing to sell goods on credit to ABC Ltd, which he knows is owned by very wealthy individuals, well able to pay any debts. Why should the supplier pay attention to the (compulsory) 'Ltd' in the company's name?

Passing-off action

Any person may seek an injunction to restrain a company from using a name (even if duly registered) which suggests that the latter company is carrying on the business of the complainant or is otherwise connected with it (a *passing-off* action). But the complaint will not succeed if the complainant lays claim to the exclusive use of a word which has a general use.

Display of company names and other particulars

A company must:

(a) paint or affix outside every office or place of business its name in a conspicuous position and in easily legible letters. Failure to do so is punishable by fining the company and its officers in default: s 348;

(b) engrave on its seal (if it has one) its name in legible letters: s 350;

(c) mention its name in legible characters on all business letters and official publications and other communications, bills of exchange, orders for money or goods issued by the company, invoices, receipts and letters of credit: s 349.

On its business letters, invoices and order forms a company must state in legible letters the following particulars required by s 351.

(a) The company's place of registration, that is either England and Wales or Scotland.

(b) The address of its registered office. It is not sufficient to state the registered office address; it must be *identified* as the registered office address.

(c) Its registered number.

Business names other than the corporate name

Most companies trade under their own registered names. But a company may prefer to use some other name. If it does so it must:

(a) state its registered name and its address on all business letters, invoices, receipts, written orders for goods or services and written demands for payment of debts;

(b) display its name and address in a prominent position in any business premises to which its customers and suppliers have access;

(c) on request from any person with whom it does business give notice of its name and address.

Exercise 2

In *Aerators Ltd v Tollit 1902* the plaintiff took action to prevent the formation of another company with a name which included the word 'aerators'. Why did the plaintiff's passing-off action fail?

3   Registered office

The memorandum does not state the address of the registered office but only that it will be situate in England and Wales. This fixes the domicile of the company which, unlike other matters comprised in the memorandum, is unalterable.

The first address of the registered office is given in the documents presented to secure incorporation.

At any time thereafter the directors may alter the address of the registered office. But the new address, like the old, must be within the country specified in the memorandum. The registered office need not have any close connection with the company. Some companies arrange with their accountants or solicitors to make the latter's office premises the registered office of the company.

If the address of the registered office is changed, notice of the new address must be given to the registrar and the change takes effect after the registration: s 287(3). Documents may still be served on the company at the former address for a further 14 days.

The importance of the registered office is that:

(a)   if a legal document, such as a notice or writ to commence legal proceedings, has to be served on a company this may be done by delivering it at the registered office or by sending it by post (preferably recorded delivery) to that office: s 725. The company cannot then deny that it has received the document;

(b)   various registers and other documents are held either at the registered office or in some cases at another address.

4   Objects

The objects clause sets out the 'aims' and 'purposes' of the company. It is usually very broadly drafted, so that the company's actions cannot be challenged as outside its objects. A clause ending as follows is not uncommon.

'to carry on any other business, trade or enterprise which may be advantageously carried out, in the opinion of the directors, in connection with or ancillary to the general business of the company'.

Objects and powers

Also contained in the objects clause will be a list of permissible transactions (or express powers). These may include powers to lease and construct buildings, employ and remunerate staff, sub-contract work and so on. The most common and most important express powers are to borrow funds, to give security by creating charges over property, and to give guarantees.

The list of express powers may be long and detailed. This is to avoid the uncertainty caused by the fact that some powers to enter into transactions in the pursuit of the company's objects may only be *implied*. The danger here is that powers can only be implied to *further* the objects. Hence any action which does not promote the objects and is not an express power, may not be effective as an implied power.

Independent objects

It is common practice to include a statement in the objects clause of the memorandum stating that each 'object' or 'power' should be construed as stating a separate object. This is done to avoid the interpretation of a clause as an express power to be exercised only in support of main objects.

BPP Publishing

Object as a 'general commercial company'

It is now possible to register a company with objects which merely state that the company's object is to 'carry on business as a general commercial company': s 3A. The legislation specifically states that this means that:

(a)   the object of the company is to carry on any trade or business whatsoever; and

(b)   the company has power to do all such things as are incidental or conducive to the carrying on of any trade or business by it.

Alteration of objects

A company may by special resolution alter its objects (s 4(1)).

S 5 provides a procedure for a dissenting minority to apply to the court to modify an otherwise valid alteration of the objects clause. The conditions are that:

(a)   application to the court must be made within 21 days from the passing of the special resolution to alter the objects; and

(b)   the applicants must hold in aggregate at least 15 per cent of the issued share capital or 15 per cent of any class of shares. They must not originally have voted in favour of the alteration nor consented to it.

Once such an objection is made the alternative which was approved can only come into effect insofar as the court allows: s 4(2). The court can arrange for the parties to come to an agreement (s 5(4)) as it can, say, order the company to buy the dissenting minority's shares: s 5(5).

Exercise 3

A company is set up with the object of making and selling computers, and with the power to borrow or lend money. Why would the directors not be empowered to run a moneylending business?

Ultra vires

Since a company's capacity to contract is defined in its objects clause it has always followed that, however widely this is drawn, some acts would be beyond its capacity. The Latin term for this is *ultra vires*; in principle, the law would not allow such an act to be legally enforceable because of lack of capacity. However, this doctrine's effect is now severely restricted by legislation.

A company's contractual capacity as it affects third parties

S 35(1) Companies Act 1985 (as amended) provide as follows.

'The validity of an act done by a company shall not be called into question on the ground of lack of capacity by reason of anything in the company's memorandum.'

Note that neither the company nor a third party can plead *ultra vires* to escape their obligations, since the section operates in favour of both parties.

S 35A(1) Companies Act 1985 provides as follows.

'In favour of a person dealing with a company in good faith, the power of the board of directors to bind the company, or authorise others to do so, shall be deemed to be free of any limitation under the company's constitution.'

263

There are a number of points to note about s 35A(1).

(a)   The section applies in favour of the *person dealing with the company*.

(b)   In contrast with s 35(1), good faith is required. It is up to the company to prove lack of good faith in the third party, however, and this may turn out to be quite difficult.

(c)   The section covers not only acts beyond the capacity of the company, but acts beyond 'any limitation under the company's constitution'. This includes not only the memorandum and articles, but also resolutions of the members and other agreements made by them.

The combined effect of the above legislation (enacted in 1989) is to abolish the effect of the *ultra vires* rule in relation to acts done between a company and third parties, unless the third party acts in bad faith *and* the directors acted outside their authority. In future almost all such acts will be capable of validation, at the instance of either party.

A company's contractual capacity as it affects members

The effect of the *ultra vires* rule continues to operate *internally* between the company and its members.

S 35(2) provides that as follows.

'A member of a company may bring proceedings to restrain the doing of an action which, but for subsection (1) would be beyond the company's capacity; but no such proceedings shall lie in respect of an act to be done in fulfilment of a legal obligation arising from a previous act of the company.'

This means that a member can gain an injunction to restrain an *ultra vires* act before it is done but, after the event, there will be no right to challenge the action.

The directors have a duty (to the company) to ensure that the assets of the company are not used for *ultra vires* purposes. If they have breached this duty, the situation is dealt with by s 35(3).

'It remains the duty of the directors to observe any limitations on their powers flowing from the company's memorandum; and an action by the directors which but for subsection 35(1) would be beyond the company's capacity, may only be ratified by the company by special resolution. A resolution ratifying such action shall not affect any liability incurred by the directors or any other person; relief from any such liability must be agreed to separately by special resolution.'

Protection of the company in contracts with directors

Sections 35 and 35A could be used to validate questionable transactions between the directors and the company . S 322A deals with this situation, providing as follows.

'Where a company enters into a transaction to which the parties include:

(a)   a director of the company or its holding company; or

(b)   a person connected with such a director or a company with whom such a director is associated;

and the board of directors, in connection with the transaction, exceed any limitation on their powers under the company's constitution, the transaction is voidable at the instance of the company.'

The section also provides that, whether or not the transaction is avoided, the persons covered by the section (and any director who authorised the transaction) is liable to account to the company for profit made or loss and damage caused. The transaction will *not* be voidable if it is ratified by ordinary or special resolution (depending on circumstances), where third party rights intervene, or if restitution can no longer be made.

Exercise 4

The directors of H Ltd must, under the company's articles of association, obtain the permission of the members before selling any land belonging to the company. Jane, an outsider, knows this and knows that no such permission has been obtained. She contracts to buy some land from the company for half of its market value, acting in collusion with the directors. Before completion, the members discover what has happened and take legal action to stop the sale going ahead. Could Jane rely on s 35A(1)?

---

5   Articles of association

The articles of association deal mainly with the internal conduct of the company's affairs - the issue and transfer of shares; alterations of capital structure; calling general meetings and how they are to be conducted (including members' voting rights); appointment, powers and proceedings of directors; dividends; accounts and the issue of notices. If the company has more than one class of shares the rights of a class and the procedure for varying them is usually set out in the articles.

The memorandum differs from the articles in that it deals with the constitution of the company mainly as it affects outsiders. In case of conflict the memorandum prevails over the articles. It is possible to alter the standard clauses of the memorandum (with one exception, namely the clause specifying country of origin) but special restrictions and procedures make it less easy to do so. The articles, however, may as a general rule be altered simply by passing a special resolution. Clauses which could be included in the articles may be placed in the memorandum in order to make it more difficult to alter them.

Table A articles

A company limited by shares may have its own full-length special articles, or it may adopt all or any part of the statutory standard model articles (known as Table A) made under s 8. Private companies usually have a short form of articles which state that Table A is to apply subject only to a few exclusions or modifications deemed desirable for the company.

As regards form, the articles must be printed and divided into numbered paragraphs: s 7(3). The first articles presented to obtain registration of a new company are signed by the subscribers to the memorandum, dated and witnessed. But if new or altered articles are adopted later the copy of the text to be delivered to the registrar need not be signed.

Whenever any alteration is made to the articles a copy of the altered articles must be delivered to the registrar within 15 days, together with a signed copy of the special resolution by which the alteration is made: ss 18 and 380.

6   Alteration of the articles

A company has a statutory power to alter its articles by special resolution: s 9(1). This means that if a special resolution is properly moved and carried at a general meeting by a 75% majority of votes cast, the alteration is valid and binding on all members of the company.

Alteration of the articles is restricted by the following principles.

BPP Publishing

(a)   The alteration is void if it conflicts with the Companies Act or with the memorandum.

(b)   In various circumstances, such as to protect a minority (s 459) or in approving an alteration of the objects clause (s 5(5)), the court may order that an alteration be made or, alternatively, that an existing article shall not be altered. The leave of the court is then required if the relevant article is later to be altered to vary it from the terms approved by the court.

(c)   A member may not be compelled by alteration of the articles to subscribe for additional shares or to accept increased liability for the shares which he holds unless he has given his consent: s 16.

(d)   An alteration of the articles which varies the rights attached to a class of shares may only be made if the correct variation procedure has been followed to obtain the consent of the class (s 125). A 15 per cent minority may apply to the court to cancel the variation under s 127.

(e)   An alteration may be void if the majority who approve it are not acting *bona fide* in what they deem to be the interests of the company as a whole (see below).

(f)   A person whose contract is contained in the articles cannot obtain an injunction to prevent the articles being altered, but he may be entitled to damages for breach of contract.

Exercise 5

Robert holds 10% of the shares in C Ltd. A special resolution is voted for by all the other shareholders (Robert voting against) to alter the articles so as to make each member liable to contribute an extra £10 per share. Robert is told that as his holding is less than 15%, he must accept this. Is this true?

---

7   The memorandum and articles as contracts

A company's memorandum and articles bind, under s 14:

(a)   members to company;

(b)   company to members (but see below);

(c)   members to members; but not

(d)   company to third parties.

The members are deemed to have separately covenanted to observe the articles and memorandum. The principle that only rights and obligations of members are covered by s 14 applies when a member seeks to rely on the articles in support of a claim made as an outsider.

Case: Eley v Positive Government Security Life Assurance Co 1876
E, a solicitor, drafted the original articles and included a provision that the company must always employ him as its solicitor. E became a member of the company some months after its incorporation. He later sued the company for breach of contract in not employing him as a solicitor. The case turned partly on technical points which no longer arise since the law (The Statute of Frauds) has been changed.

Held: E could not rely on the article since it was a contract between the company and its members and he was not asserting any claim as a member.

266

S 14 gives to the memorandum and articles the effect of a contract made between (a) the company and (b) its members individually. It can also impose a contract on the members in their dealings with each other as illustrated by the case below.

Case: Rayfield v Hands 1958
The articles required that (a) every director should be a shareholder and (b) the directors must purchase the shares of any member who gave them notice of his wish to dispose of them. The directors, however, denied that a member could enforce the obligation on them to acquire his shares.

Held: there was 'a contract ... between a member and member-directors in relation to their holdings of the company's shares in its article' and the directors were bound by it.

Exercise 6

In *Beattie v ECF Beattie Ltd 1938* the articles provided that disputes between the company and its members should be submitted to arbitration. B, the managing director, was sued by the company to recover money improperly paid to him. Although B was a member, why could he not insist that the dispute be submitted to arbitration?

Chapter roundup

(a)   A company's memorandum states basic facts such as the company's name and its objects.

(b)   A company's name must not be the same as that of any existing company, and it must not be inappropriate in certain ways. The use of a name likely to be confused with one already in use may be restrained by a passing-off action. A company's name must be displayed so that outsiders know who they are doing business with.

(c)   A company must have a registered office, at which documents may be served on it.

(d)   A company's objects are set out in its memorandum. It is the modern practice to state the objects in very broad terms, so that advantage may be taken of any commercial opportunity. The powers of a company, if not stated to be independent objects, may only be exercised in furtherance of the company's objects.

(e)   A company's objects may be altered by special resolution of the members, but a dissenting minority may have a right to object.

(f)   Even if an act of a company is outside the scope of its objects and therefore *ultra vires*, its validity cannot usually be called into question. However, the company may have a remedy when the directors contract with the company in excess of their powers.

(g)   A company's articles of association set out its detailed constitution. A company may adopt a standard set of articles (Table A), or it may write its own articles. The articles may be changed by special resolution, but certain changes require the consent of the members directly affected.

(h)   A company's memorandum and articles create contractual relations affecting the members, but only in their capacity as members.

Quick quiz

1   What are the compulsory clauses of a public company's memorandum (in correct order)?

2   To what do the signatories to the memorandum commit themselves?

3   On what grounds may the registrar refuse to register a company name?

4   What is the procedure for voluntary change of name by a registered company?

5   On what grounds may the registrar order a company to change its name?

6   What particulars must appear on the letterhead of a company which carries on a trade?

7   What is a 'business name' and what requirements apply to a company if it uses such a name?

8   May a company change the address of its registered office?

9   Describe the general content of a modern objects clause.

10   Who may object to an alteration of the objects clause?

11   Can a member of the company challenge an *ultra vires* action of the company after it has been done?

12   How is a company protected in respect of transactions entered into by the company with its directors beyond the limits of the latter's authority?

13   Is a company limited by shares obliged to adopt Table A in force at the time of the company's formation as its articles?

14   How may a company alter its articles?

15   What is the result if a company alters its articles so that in their altered form the articles conflict with (a) the Acts or (b) the memorandum or (c) a separate contract with another person?

16   May an alteration of the articles deprive a member of rights accrued under the articles before alteration? May it impose new obligations on him?

17   To what extent are the articles a contract between the company and its members?

Solutions to exercises

1   The shareholders are not liable for the company's debts (beyond any amount unpaid on their shares). Their wealth is therefore not available to the company's creditors.

2   'Aerators' is a word in general use.

3   The power is restricted to use in connection with the company's object.

4   No: Jane has not acted in good faith.

5   No: a member may not be compelled to accept increased liability for his shares.

6   He was being sued as managing director, not as a member.

21 SHARE CAPITAL AND DIVIDENDS

Your objectives

After completing this chapter you should:

(a) know what different amounts of share capital may be stated;

(b) know how shares are allotted;

(c) know what consideration for shares is acceptable;

(d) understand rights issues and bonus issues;

(e) know the difference between ordinary shares and preference shares;

(f) know how class rights may be varied;

(g) know how shares are transferred and how transfers may be restricted;

(h) understand the significance of share certificates;

(i) understand the concept of maintenance of capital;

(j) know how a company is prevented from reducing its capital except in restricted circumstances;

(k) know the powers of directors in relation to dividends;

(l) know what profits may be distributed and the consequences of paying excessive dividends.

---

1 Types of capital

The term 'capital' is used in several senses.

(a) *Authorised share capital* is the total amount of share capital which the company is authorised to issue by the capital clause of its memorandum. This total must be divided into shares of fixed amount (called the *nominal* or *par* value of the shares). It can be increased as prescribed in the articles (usually an ordinary resolution suffices).

(b) *Issued share capital* (or allotted share capital) is the nominal value of the shares which have been allotted and issued to members. A company need not issue all its share capital at once. If it retains part this is *unissued* share capital.

(c) *Called up share capital* is the aggregate amount of calls for money or other consideration which members are required to pay (or have paid in applying for shares): s 737. If for example a company has issued 70 £1 (nominal) shares, has received 25p per share on application and has called on members for a second 25p, its *called up* share capital is £35 (50p per share). When the members pay the call the *paid up* share capital is then £35 also. Capital not yet called is *uncalled capital*.

(d) *Reserve liability* is any uncalled capital which the company has resolved by special resolution shall only be called up in the course of winding up: s 120. For example a company might issue all its authorised capital of, say, £1,000,000 (in £1 shares), call up 75p per share and resolve that the balance of 25p should be reserve liability. As a result

---

£25,000 (obtainable from members) is held back as a reserve against liabilities arising in winding up. Such arrangements are uncommon.

Loan capital, in contrast with the above, is the term used to describe borrowed money obtained usually by the issue of debentures. Loan capital is a liability owed to creditors. It is quite different from share capital which represents the interests of members as proprietors of the company. In general, debts must be discharged in priority to any return of capital to shareholders.

Shares may be classified, according to their respective rights, as ordinary share capital or preference share capital.

2 Allotment of shares

The allotment of shares is a form of contract. The intending shareholder applies to the company for shares. This is an offer which the company accepts by allotting shares to him.

Procedure for allotment of shares

The allotment of shares of a private company is a simple and immediate matter. Public companies listed on The Stock Exchange usually follow a two-stage procedure.

(a) They first issue a renounceable *allotment letter* (or similar document) which the original allottee may for a limited period (up to six weeks) transfer to another person by signing a form of renunciation (included in the letter) and delivering it to the transferee. The original allottee or the ultimate renouncee, sends in the allotment letter with a completed application for registration of the shares in his name. No entry is made in the register of members when the allotment letter is first issued.

(b) On receipt of *application for registration* the company enters the name of the applicant in the register of members and delivers a return of allotments to the registrar made up to show who is then on the register. The applicant becomes a member by *entry on the register* and receives a share certificate from the company.

Except where renounceable allotment letters are issued, the name of the allottee is usually entered in the register soon after, and as a direct consequence of, the allotment of shares to him. He then becomes a member: s 22.

Subscribers to the memorandum become members of the company as soon as it is incorporated and their names should be entered in the register of members without any decision to allot shares to them.

Directors' powers to allot shares

It is long established practice to delegate to the board of directors (as part of their general management functions) the decision on the terms of the contract of allotment and the power to allot shares. The directors may only exercise the power of allotment if they are properly authorised to do so, either by the articles or by ordinary resolution passed in general meeting.

S 80 requires of a public company that the authority to allot shall be given until a specified date and for a specified period of not more than five years. A private company may confer authority to allot shares for an *indefinite* period, or for a fixed period longer than five years.

BPP Publishing

Exercise 1

Z Ltd has an authorised share capital of 20,000 £2 shares. It issues 60% of these shares, but only calls upon members to pay 70% of the nominal value, in three equal annual instalments. All members pay the amounts required on time. What is the company's paid up share capital after the second instalment is paid?

Pre-emption rights: s 89

If a company proposes to allot shares described as 'equity securities' wholly for cash it has a statutory obligation (subject to certain exceptions) to offer those shares to holders of similar shares in proportion to their holdings s 89.

The offer must be made in writing in the same manner as a notice of a general meeting is sent to members. It must specify a period of not less than 21 days during which the offer may be accepted. If not accepted within that period the offer is deemed to be declined: s 90.

Equity securities subject to the rules just explained are broadly ordinary shares whenever issued for cash. But subscribers' shares, preference shares, bonus issues and shares allotted under an employees' share scheme are exempt from these restrictions which would be inappropriate to them: s 94.

Equity securities which have been offered to members in this way but are not accepted may then be allotted on the same (or less favourable) terms to non-members.

A *private* company may by its memorandum or articles permanently exclude these rules so that there is no statutory right of first refusal: s 91.

Any company may, by special resolution resolve that the statutory right of first refusal shall not apply: s 95. For public companies, the period of disapplication is limited to five years.

Consideration for shares

Every share has a nominal value and may not be allotted at a discount to that. In allotting shares every company is required to obtain in money or money's worth consideration of a value at least equal to the nominal value of the shares: s 100. To issue shares 'at par' is to obtain equal value, say, £1 for a £1 share. If shares are allotted at a discount on their nominal value the allottee must nonetheless pay the full nominal value with interest at the appropriate rate (5%).

The no-discount rule only requires that, in allotting its shares, a company shall not fix a price which is less than the nominal value of the shares. It may leave part of that price to be paid at some later time by whoever then holds the shares.

Payment for shares

The price for the shares may be paid in money or 'money's worth', including goodwill and know-how: s 99. It need not be paid in cash and the company may agree to accept a 'non-cash' consideration of sufficient value. For instance, a company may issue shares in payment of the price agreed in the purchase of a property. The allotment of shares as a bonus issue is for full consideration since reserves, which are shareholders' funds, are converted into fixed capital and used to pay for the shares: s 99(4).

Private companies

A private company may allot shares for inadequate consideration by acceptance of goods or services at an over-value. This loophole has been allowed to exist because in some cases it is very much a matter of opinion whether an asset is or is not of a stated value.

Public companies

The more stringent rules which apply to *public companies* regarding consideration and payment are as follows.

(a) Future services are not to be accepted as consideration: s 99(2).

(b) The company must, at the time of allotment, receive at least one quarter of the nominal value of the shares and the *whole* of any premium.

(c) Non-cash consideration may not be accepted as payment for shares if an undertaking contained in such consideration is to be, or may be, performed more than five years after the allotment: s 102.

(d) Any non-cash consideration accepted must be independently valued (except when shares are being issued in return for shares in a company being taken over): s 103.

(e) Within two years of receiving its certificate under s 117, a public company may not receive a transfer of non-cash assets from a subscriber to the memorandum, unless its value as consideration is less then 10% of the issued nominal share capital and it has been independently valued and agreed by an ordinary resolution: s 104.

Allotment of shares at a premium

A company may be able to obtain consideration for new shares in excess of their nominal value. The excess, called 'share premium', must be credited to a share premium account (s 130) to which certain restrictions apply.

Return of allotments

Within one month of allotting shares, a company must deliver to the registrar a return of allotments in the prescribed form showing what shares have been allotted, to whom and for what consideration: s 88.

Rights and bonus issues

A *rights issue* is an allotment (or the offer of it by renounceable allotment letter) of additional shares made to existing members. If the members do not wish to subscribe for additional shares under a rights issue they may be able to sell their rights to other persons and so obtain the value of the option.

A *bonus issue* is more correctly but less often called a capitalisation issue (also called a scrip issue). The articles of a company usually give it power to apply its reserves (including its undistributed profits) to pay up unissued shares and then to allot these shares as a bonus issue to members.

Exercise 2

How might existing members of a company be unfairly treated if pre-emption rights did not exist, even assuming that all new shares were issued for their full market value?

---

3   The nature of shares and types of share

A share is a form of property, carrying rights and obligations. It is by its nature *transferable*. A member who holds one or more shares is by that fact a shareholder.

If no differences between shares are expressed it is assumed that all shares have the same rights. It is unnecessary to classify them as *ordinary shares* since there are no others. But there is no objection to doing so.

A company may at its option attach special rights to different shares, for example as regards dividends, return of capital, voting (or less often the right to appoint a director). Any share which has different rights from others is grouped with the other shares carrying identical rights to form a *class* in distinction from shares with different rights included in another class.

The most common classes of share capital with different rights are *preference shares* and *ordinary shares*; there may also be ordinary shares with voting rights and ordinary shares (often distinguished as 'A' ordinary shares) without voting rights.

Preference shares

The essential characteristic of any preference share is that it carries a prior right to receive an annual dividend of fixed amount, say a 6% dividend. There are no other *implied* differences between preference and ordinary shares though there are often express differences between them.

As regards the priority dividend entitlement, four points should be noted.

(a)   The right is merely to receive a dividend at the specified rate before any other dividend may be paid or declared. It is not a right to compel the company to pay the dividend if it declines to do so.

(b)   The right to receive a preference dividend is deemed to be cumulative unless the contrary is stated. If, therefore, a 6% dividend is not paid in year 1, the priority entitlement is normally carried forward to year 2, increasing the priority right for that year to 12%.

(c)   If a company which has arrears of unpaid cumulative preference dividends goes into liquidation, the preference shareholders cease to be entitled to the arrears unless:

   (i)   a dividend has been declared though not yet paid when liquidation commences; or

   (ii)   the articles (or other terms of issue) expressly provide that in a liquidation arrears are to be paid in priority to return of capital to members.

(d)   Holders of preference shares have no entitlement to participate in any additional dividend over and above their specified rate.

In all other respects preference shares carry the same rights as ordinary shares unless otherwise stated. If they do rank equally they carry the same rights, no more and no less, to return of capital, distribution of surplus assets and voting. In practice, it is unusual to issue preference shares on this basis. More usually, it is expressly provided that:

(a)   the preference shares are to carry a priority right to return of capital; and

(b)   they are not to carry a right to vote or they only do so in specified circumstances such as failure to pay the preference dividend, variation of their rights or a resolution to wind up.

When preference shares carry a priority right to return of capital the result is that:

(a)   the amount paid up on the preference shares, say £1 on each £1 share, is to be repaid in liquidation or reduction of capital before anything is repaid to ordinary shareholders; but

(b)   unless otherwise stated the holders of the preference shares are not entitled to share in surplus assets when the ordinary share capital has been repaid.

Exercise 3

J Ltd has some £1 8% preference shares and some £1 ordinary shares in issue. Nothing is stated about the rights attaching to the preference shares. Abigail holds 100 preference shares and 500 ordinary shares. In years 1 and 2, no dividend is paid. In year 3, a 9% dividend is declared on the ordinary shares. How much does Abigail receive in year 3?

4 Variations of class rights

The holders of issued shares have vested rights which can only be varied by the company with the consent of all the holders or with such consent of a majority as is specified in the articles.

The usual procedure for variation of class rights requires that an *extraordinary resolution* (giving approval) shall be passed by a *three-quarters majority* cast either:

(a) at a *separate meeting* of the class, or

(b) by *written consent*: s 125(2).

Minority appeals to the court

Whenever class rights are varied under a procedure contained in the memorandum or articles a minority of holders of shares of the class may apply to the court to have the variation cancelled: s 127. The objectors together must:

(a) hold not less than 15% of the issued shares of the class in question;

(b) not themselves have consented to or voted in favour of the variation; and

(c) apply to the court within 21 days of the consent being given by the class: s 127 (2) and (3).

The court can either approve the variation as made or cancel it as 'unfairly prejudicial': s 127 (4). It cannot, however, modify the terms of the variation or approve it subject to conditions. To establish that a variation, although approved by a three-quarters majority of the class, is 'unfairly prejudicial' to the class, it must generally be shown that the majority who voted in favour was seeking some advantage to themselves as members of a different class instead of considering the interests of the class in which they were then voting.

5 The transfer of shares

To obtain transfer of the legal ownership of shares two conditions must be satisfied.

(a) A 'proper instrument of transfer' must be delivered to the company which may not enter the transfer in its register until this is done: s 183(1).

(b) If, as is general practice with private companies, the articles give to the directors power to refuse to register a transfer and the directors exercise their power in proper way, the contractual restriction imposed by the articles operates to prevent a transfer of legal ownership.

It is standard practice in unlisted companies nowadays to use the stock transfer form authorised for general use by the Stock Transfer Act 1963: s 1. This can be used to transfer fully paid shares irrespective of any provision in the articles requiring some other form and must be signed but not sealed: s 2 Stock Transfer Act 1963. Transactions on The Stock Exchange are effected using sold transfer and bought transfer forms.

BPP Publishing

Transfer procedures in unlisted companies

The unlisted company transfer procedure is that the registered holder (the 'seller') completes and signs the stock transfer form and delivers it with his share certificate to the transferee (the 'buyer') who completes the transfer and pays stamp duty before delivering it to the company (with the seller's share certificate) for registration. The buyer becomes the holder and legal owner of the shares only when his name is entered in the register of members: s 22. The company issues to him a new share certificate within two months (s 185) and cancels the old one.

Transfer procedure for Stock Exchange transactions

The sequence of action for a transfer of shares listed on the Stock Exchange is as follows.

(a)   A shareholder, acting through a stockbroker, agrees to sell shares at a specified price.

(b)   The broker sends a 'TALISMAN *Sold* transfer' to his client, who signs the transfer and returns it to the broker with his share certificate. The shareholder thereby sells his shares to SEPON (Stock Exchange Pool Nominees Ltd).

(c)   The broker sends the documents in to the Centre, which *certifies* the transfer and returns it for presentation to the company, to effect the transfer to SEPON.

(d)   The share transfer is registered by the company, with SEPON as the transferee. Each listed company maintains a running SEPON account for this purpose.

(e)   At the end of each account period SEPON issues 'TALISMAN *Bought* transfers' to the ultimate purchasers, and these transfers are presented to the company for registration in the names of the buyers. Thus SEPON sells the shares to the new investor.

Exercise 4

In *Re Holders Investment Trust Ltd 1971*, a scheme to substitute unsecured loan stock for preference shares was voted through by the holders of the vast majority of the preference shares, because they (as holders of 52% of the ordinary shares) would benefit overall. On what ground do you think the court forbade the change in preference shareholders' rights?

Restrictions on transfer of shares

Although it is no longer legally necessary to do so the articles of private companies usually provide that the directors may refuse to register a transfer of any share, whether fully or partly paid. The articles of a public company may impose this restriction but the company cannot have a Stock Exchange listing for its shares if the transfer of fully paid shares is restricted.

If the directors have a power under the articles to refuse a transfer they should exercise that power properly. Otherwise the transfer must be registered and the court may order rectification of the register for that purpose.

(a)   To exercise their power the directors must consider the transfer and take an active decision to refuse to register it.

(b)   The directors in reaching their decision must act *bona fide* in what they consider to be the interest of the company. But the court is reluctant to intervene.

(c)   The articles should either authorise the directors to refuse in their absolute discretion to register a transfer, or specify grounds of refusal.

(d) The power of refusal must be exercised within a reasonable time from the receipt of the transfer. A company is required to give notice of any refusal within two months: s 183(5).

The articles may also restrict the right of transfer of shares by giving to members a right of first refusal of the shares which other members may wish to transfer. Any such rights are strictly construed. A member who wishes to accept such shares must observe the terms of the articles; a member wishing to sell shares will not be permitted to evade his obligation to make the offer.

5 Share certificates

Within two months of allotting shares or receiving a transfer a company must have ready for delivery a certificate of the shares allotted or transferred (unless the transfer is rejected). This is a formal written declaration that the person named is entered in the register as the holder of the shares specified: s 185. A company listed on The Stock Exchange has the shorter time limit of 14 days.

A share certificate is not a document of title but is *prima facie* evidence of ownership: s 186. The company therefore requires the holder to surrender his certificate for cancellation when he transfers all or any of his shares.

Estoppel and share certificates

If a company issues a share certificate which is incorrect it is estopped from denying that it is correct but only against a person who has relied upon it and thereby suffered loss.

> *Case: Re Bahia & San Francisco Railway Co 1868*
> T was the registered holder of 5 shares. S and G forged a transfer of the shares to themselves and presented it for registration with T's share certificate which they held as her brokers.
>
> The transfer was registered and a new share certificate was issued to S and G as shareholders. S and G sold the shares to B and another person who were duly registered as holders. T had the shares re-registered in her name since the forged transfer was a nullity. B and the other purchaser claimed the value of the shares from the company as damages.
>
> *Held:* the claim was valid.

Apart from ownership the company may be similarly estopped from denying the correctness of the certificate in other respects; for example, if the certificate states that the shares are fully paid the company cannot deny that this is so.

Share warrants

If authorised by its articles, a company limited by shares may issue share warrants which are negotiable instruments transferable by delivery: s 188. A warrant entitles its bearer to shares specified therein and allows him to transfer those shares by delivery of the warrant. On the issue of a share warrant the company removes the name of the registered holder from its register of members. He (or the person to whom the warrant may be transferred) is then only a member to the extent that the articles may provide. The company does not know who has the warrant. The bearer may subsequently surrender it for cancellation and the company must then enter the bearer's name in the register as a member: s 355.

Exercise 5

In *Re Hackney Pavilion Ltd 1924*, a company's two directors were unable to agree on whether to register a share transfer, and neither had a casting vote. Why was the company then forced to register the transfer?

7 Maintenance of capital

The capital which a limited company obtains from its members as consideration for their shares (and its right to call for payment of the balance (if any) still owing on its shares) is sometimes called 'the creditors' buffer'. No one can prevent an unsuccessful company from losing all or part of its capital by trading at a loss. But insofar as subscribed capital remains in the hands of the company it must be held for the payment of the company's debts and may not be returned to members (except under procedures which safeguard the interest of creditors). That is the price which members of a limited company are required to pay for the protection of limited liability. They cannot be compelled to pay more than the amount due on their shares but they cannot recover what they or their predecessors have subscribed for the shares unless the company's debts have been paid.

Share premium account

As explained previously a company which obtains for its shares a consideration in excess of their nominal value must transfer the excess to a share premium account: s 130.

The permitted uses of share premium are:

(a)   to make an issue of fully paid bonus shares;

(b)   to make an authorised reduction of capital. Such reductions are strictly controlled;

(c)   to pay capital expenses, such as the preliminary expenses of forming the company;

(d)   to pay a discount on the issue of shares or debentures;

(e)   to pay a premium (if any) paid on the redemption of debentures: s 130(2).

Private companies (but not public companies) may also use a share premium account in purchasing or redeeming their own shares out of capital. This procedure is strictly controlled.

Redemption or purchase by a company of its own shares

There is a general prohibition against any voluntary acquisition by a company of its own shares, though there is no objection to accepting a gift: s 143.

The prohibition is subject to exceptions. A company may:

(a)   purchase its own shares in compliance with an order of the court;

(b)   issue redeemable shares and then redeem them (out of distributable profits or the proceeds of a new issue);

(c)   purchase its own shares under certain specified procedures; and

(d)   forfeit or accept the surrender of its shares.

Purchase of own shares

Companies are allowed to purchase shares provided certain safeguards were followed. A limited company may now *purchase its own shares* (whether issued as redeemable or irredeemable):

(a) out of profits or the proceeds of an issue of new shares; or

(b) if it is a *private company*, out of capital.

For redemption or purchase of shares out of capital there is a long and involved procedure which includes the following steps.

(a) A statutory declaration must be made by the directors (supported by a report of the auditors) to the effect that after the payment is made the company will be able to pay its debts and to carry on its business for at least a year to come: s 173; these must also be delivered to the registrar: s 195.

(b) Shareholders must approve the payment by passing a *special resolution*. In this decision any vendor of shares may not use the votes attached to the shares which he is to sell to the company: s 173.

(c) A member who did not vote for the resolution and a creditor (for any amount) may within five weeks apply to the court to cancel the resolution, which may not be implemented until the five weeks have elapsed: s 176.

(d) A notice must be placed in the *Gazette* and in an appropriate national newspaper, or every creditor must be informed: s 175.

If the company goes into insolvent liquidation within a year of making a payment out of capital the persons who received the payment and the directors who authorised it may have to make it good to the company.

Exercise 6

Why are elaborate precautions not needed when a company buys its own shares out of profits or the proceeds of an issue of new shares?

Financial assistance for purchase of own shares

Giving financial assistance to a third party to enable him to buy the company's shares can take many forms. Hence it is difficult to prohibit altogether or to regulate. The relevant rules (ss 151 - 158) comprise a general prohibition, a procedure by which a private company may give such assistance and a complex set of definitions and exceptions intended to determine which transactions are or are not prohibited.

Subject to exceptions it is not lawful for a company to give any financial assistance for the purpose of the acquisition of shares either of the company or of its holding company or to discharge liabilities incurred in making the acquisition. The prohibition applies to assistance given either directly or indirectly, before or after, or at the time of the acquisition. 'Financial assistance' is elaborately defined to mean a loan, a guarantee or indemnity or security, purchase of such rights from a third party and 'any other financial assistance given by a company which reduces to a material extent, its net assets': s 152.

Two main tests have to be applied to any suspect transaction.

(a) What was its *purpose*? It is not objectionable if its principal purpose was not to give financial assistance for the purchase of the shares nor if it was an incidental part of some larger purpose of the company: s 153(1)(a).

(b) What was the state of mind of the directors in approving the transaction? Did they act in *good faith* in what they deemed to be the interests of the company and not of a third party: s 153 (1)(b).

BPP Publishing

A private company may give financial assistance for the acquisition of its own shares or the shares of its holding company, subject to the following conditions of ss 155 - 158.

(a) The financial assistance given must not reduce the net assets of the company or, if it does, the financial assistance is to be provided out of distributable profits.

(b) There must be a statutory declaration of solvency by the directors of the company (with a report by the auditors) of the same type as is prescribed when a private company purchases its own shares by a payment out of capital.

(c) A special resolution must be passed to approve the transaction. Normally this is a resolution of the company which gives the assistance. But if that company is a wholly owned subsidiary which assists the acquisition of shares of its holding company the members of the latter company must pass the resolution.

(d) A right to apply to the court is given to members holding at least 10% of the issued shares (or of a class of shares). To permit them to exercise this right there is a four week delay in the implementation of the resolution.

Three other specific exceptions are made. A company is not prohibited from entering into any of the following transactions: s 153(4).

(a) Making a loan if lending is part of its ordinary business, and the loan is made in the ordinary course of its business. This exception is restricted to money-lending companies. But it would permit a bank to make a loan to a customer on standard terms even though he then used the money to invest in shares of the bank.

(b) Providing money in good faith and in the best interests of the company for the purpose of an employees' share scheme or for other share transactions by *bona fide* employees or connected persons.

(c) Making loans to persons (other than directors) employed in good faith by the company with a view to those persons acquiring fully paid shares in the company or its holding company to be held by them as beneficial owners.

Loss of capital in a public company

If the net assets of a public company are half or less of the amount of its called up share capital there must be an extraordinary general meeting: s 142. The duty to call the meeting arises as soon as any of the directors comes to know of the problem. When the directors' duty arises they must issue a notice to convene a meeting within 28 days of becoming aware of the need to do so. The meeting must be convened for a date within 56 days of their coming to know the relevant facts. The purpose of this procedure is to enable shareholders to consider 'whether any, and if so what, measures should be taken to deal with the situation'.

Exercise 7

Alison borrows money to buy shares in a manufacturing company, which is a public company and is not her employer. The loan is for five years, but the lender may demand early repayment. The lender does so, because he is concerned that Alison may soon become unable to pay her debts. The lender suggests that Alison asks the company to guarantee the loan, in return for which he will not demand early repayment. He says that the use made of the loan is immaterial, because the purchase of shares has already been made. Would the company be allowed to give the guarantee?

8 Dividends

Payment of dividends

Dividends may only be paid by a company out of profits available for the purpose: s 263. The power to declare a dividend is given by the articles which usually follow the model of Table A.

(a) The company in general meeting may declare dividends but no dividend may exceed the amount recommended by the directors: Table A Article 102.

(b) The directors may declare such interim dividends as they consider justified: Article 103.

(c) Dividends are normally declared payable on the paid up amount of share capital. For example a £1 share which is fully paid will carry entitlement to twice as much dividend as a £1 share 50p paid: Article 104.

(d) A dividend may be paid otherwise than in cash: Article 105. Without such a provision, payment must be in cash.

(e) Dividends may be paid by cheque or warrant sent through the post to the shareholder at his registered address: Article 106. If shares are held jointly payment of dividend is made to the first-named joint holder on the register.

A shareholder (including a preference shareholder) is not entitled to a dividend unless it is declared in accordance with the procedure prescribed by the articles and the declared date for payment has arrived.

Distributable profits

The profits which may be distributed as dividend are 'accumulated realised profits, so far as not previously utilised by distribution or capitalisation, less accumulated realised losses, so far as not previously written off in a reduction or reorganisation of capital duly made': s 263(3).

The word 'accumulated' requires that any losses of previous years must be included in reckoning the current distributable surplus.

Dividends of public companies - the full net worth test

The above rules on distributable profits apply to all companies, private or public. A public company is subject to an additional rule which may diminish but cannot increase its distributable profit as determined under the above rules.

A public company may only make a distribution if its net assets are, at the time, not less than the aggregate of its called-up share capital and undistributable reserves. The dividend which it may pay is limited to such amount as will leave its net assets at not less than that aggregate amount: s 264(1).

Undistributable reserves are defined in s 264(3) as:

(a) share premium account;

(b) capital redemption reserve;

(c) any *surplus* of accumulated unrealised profits over accumulated unrealised losses (known as a revaluation reserve);

(d) any reserve which the company is prohibited from distributing by statute or by its memorandum or articles.

BPP Publishing

Relevant accounts

The question whether a company has profits from which to pay a dividend is determined by reference to its 'relevant accounts' which are generally the latest audited annual accounts: s 270. Relevant accounts must be properly prepared in accordance with the requirements of the Companies Acts. If the auditor has qualified his report on the accounts he must also state in writing whether, in his opinion, the subject matter of his qualification (if it relates to statutory accounting requirements) is material in determining whether the dividend may be paid: s 271.

Infringement of dividend rules

Any member of a company may apply to the court for an injunction to restrain the company from paying an unlawful dividend. A resolution passed in general meeting to approve it is invalid and does not relieve the directors of their liability.

The company is entitled to recover an unlawful distribution from its members if at the time of receipt they knew or had reasonable grounds for knowing that it was unlawful: s 277. If only part of the dividend is unlawful, if it exceeds the distributable profits by a margin, it is only the excess which is recoverable. If a member knowingly receives an improperly paid dividend a derivative action cannot be brought by him against the directors.

The directors are liable to make good to the company the amount unlawfully distributed as dividend if they caused an unlawful dividend:

(a)   if they recommend or declare a dividend which they know is paid out of capital.

(b)   if without preparing any accounts they declare or recommend a dividend which proves to be paid out of capital;

(c)   if they make some mistake of law or interpretation of the memorandum or articles which leads them to recommend or declare an unlawful dividend. But in such cases the directors may well be entitled to relief under s 727 (acts performed 'honestly and reasonably').

The directors may however honestly rely (in declaring or recommending a dividend) on proper accounts which disclose an apparent distributable profit out of which the dividend can properly be paid. They are not liable if it later appears that the assumptions or estimates used in preparing the accounts, although reasonable at the time, were in fact unsound.

Exercise 8

In year 1, H Ltd suffers a realised loss of £1,000. In year 2, it has a realised profit of £9,000 and pays dividends totalling £4,700. In year 3, it suffers a realised loss of £500. What total dividend could be paid at the start of year 4?

Chapter roundup

(a)   Any company has an authorised share capital, an issued share capital, a called up share capital and a paid up share capital. All of these amounts may differ.

(b)   Shares may be allotted to investors immediately on application, or alternatively renouncable allotment letters may be issued. The directors normally have power to allot shares, but in a public company they may not be given authority to allot for more than five years at a time. Existing members have pre-emption rights in relation to ordinary shares issued wholly for cash unless these rights have been disapplied.

(c)   The consideration for shares need not be cash, but some forms of consideration are excluded or subject to special restrictions in the case of public companies.

(d)   Shares may be allotted at a premium. A return of allotments must be made. Shares may be issued in rights issues and bonus issues.

(e)   Shares may have different rights attaching to them. The most common distinction is between ordinary shares and preference shares. Preference shareholders have certain standard rights in comparison to ordinary shareholders unless the contrary is stated.

(f)   Class rights may be varied, but a minority may have a right of objection to the court.

(g)   There are standard procedures for the transfer of shares. The directors of a company may be given the power to refuse to register a transfer, but they must exercise such a power properly.

(h)   A share certificate is prima facie evidence of ownership of shares, and a company may be estopped from denying its correctness.

(i)   The paid up capital of a limited company is the investment of the members to which the creditors may have recourse if need be. Its reduction is therefore carefully controlled. Shares may be issued as redeemable and then redeemed, and shares may be purchased, but only in such a way as to maintain the company's capital. A private company may purchase its own shares out of capital subject to certain safeguards designed to ensure the company's continued solvency. The giving of financial assistance by a company for the purchase of its own shares is severely restricted. If a public company suffers a severe loss of capital the members must consider the situation.

(j)   The directors of a company determine what dividends, if any, are to be declared. The members have no right to insist on the payment of a dividend.

(k)   Dividends may only be paid out of accumulated realised profits less accumulated realised losses. Public companies are subject to a further restriction, the full net worth test. The permissible level of dividend payments is determined by reference to the 'relevant accounts'. Excessive dividends may in certain cases be recovered from the members or from the directors.

Quick quiz

1   Distinguish between authorised, issued and called up share capital.

2   Describe the procedure by which a person who holds a renounceable allotment letter may (a) transfer his rights and (b) obtain registration of his shares in his name.

3   What are the statutory rules under which directors may be authorised to allot shares?

4   In respect of which share issues must a company give to its members a right of first refusal? When may this be disapplied by (a) a private and (b) a public company?

5   What statutory rules apply to the issue of shares of a public company in relation to the consideration given for the shares?

6   What is a return of allotments?

7   What is (a) a rights issue and (b) a bonus issue?

8   Describe the rights of preference shareholders in respect of their dividends.

9   What other distinctive class rights are normally defined for preference shares?

10 What is the usual procedure for obtaining the consent of holders of a class of shares to variation of their class rights?

11 What statutory right of objection exists in favour of the minority of a class who have been outvoted at a class meeting held to approve a variation of class rights?

12 To what principles should directors conform if they wish to make a valid refusal of a share transfer?

13 What is the legal significance of a share certificate?

14 In what ways may funds standing to the credit of the share premium account be used?

15 What are the exceptions to the general rule that a company may not acquire its own shares?

16 What resources may (a) a public company and (b) a private company use to purchase its own shares?

17 Give examples of transactions expressly excepted from the prohibition on giving 'financial assistance' for the purchase of the company's shares.

18 By what procedure may a private company lawfully give financial assistance for the purchase of its own shares or the shares of its holding company?

19 What are the duties of the directors of a public company whose assets fall to half or less of its called up share capital?

20 What is the Table A procedure for declaration of (a) an interim and (b) a final dividend?

21 What profits may lawfully be distributed as dividends?

22 What rule may prevent a public company from distributing as dividend profits which a private company might lawfully distribute?

23 What are 'relevant accounts' and what is their significance?

24 What is the position of the directors if, *after payment of a dividend*, it is discovered that they have recommended or declared a dividend which is not covered by sufficient distributable profits?

BPP Publishing

Solutions to exercises

1   $20,000 \times £2 \times 60\% \times 70\% \times 2/3 = £11,200$.

2   A new member could obtain control of the company if enough shares were issued to him.

3   $100 \times 8\% \times 3 + 500 \times £1 \times 9\% = £69$.

4   The holders of the vast majority of the preference shares sought an advantage as members of a different class (the ordinary shareholders).

5   The directors did not take an active decision to refuse to register the transfer.

6   There is no reduction of non-distributable capital.

7   No: assistance after the acquisition of shares is forbidden.

8   $£(- 1,000 + 9,000 - 4,700 - 500) = £2,800$.

22 LOAN CAPITAL AND CHARGES

Your objectives

After completing this chapter you should:

(a) know what powers a company has to borrow money;

(b) know what a debenture is, and understand the role of a debenture trust deed;

(c) be able to distinguish between fixed and floating charges;

(d) know the rules on the priority of charges and on the registration of charges;

(e) know the ways in which debentureholders may enforce a company's obligations to them.

1   Borrowing

A company whose objects are to carry on a trade or business has an implied power to borrow for purposes incidental to the trade or business. The objects clause, however, nearly always contains an express power to borrow. It is usual not to impose any maximum amount on the company's capacity to borrow (though it is possible to do so). In delegating the company's power to borrow to the directors it is usual, and essential in the case of a company whose shares are listed on The Stock Exchange, to impose a maximum limit on the borrowing arranged by directors.

If there is a power to borrow there is also a power to create charges over the company's assets as security for the loan: *Re Patent File Co 1870*.

A public company initially incorporated as such cannot borrow money until it has obtained a certificate under s 117. Only a public company may offer its debentures to the public and any such offer is a prospectus; if it seeks a listing on The Stock Exchange then the rules on listing particulars must be followed.

2   Debentures

Any document which states the terms on which a company has borrowed money is a debenture (a written acknowledgement of a debt): s 744. It may create a charge over the company's assets as security for the loan. But a document relating to an unsecured loan is also a debenture in company law (though often called an unsecured loan note in the business world to distinguish it from a secured debenture).

Debenture trust deeds

There maybe a *debenture trust deed*. It is usually a long and elaborate legal document whose main elements are as follows.

(a)   A trustee for prospective debentureholders is appointed.

BPP Publishing

(b) The nominal amount of the debenture stock is defined, which is the maximum amount which may be raised then or later. The date or period of payment is specified, as is the rate of interest and interest payment dates.

(c) If the debenture stock is secured the deed creates a charge or charges over the assets of the company (and often of its subsidiaries which are parties to the deed for that purpose).

(d) The trustee is authorised to enforce the security in case of default and, in particular, to appoint a receiver with suitable powers of management.

(e) The company enters into various covenants, for instance to keep its assets fully insured or to limit its total borrowings; breach is a default by the company.

(f) There are provisions for a register of debentureholders, transfer of stock, issue of stock certificates, and meetings of debentureholders at which extraordinary resolutions passed by a three-quarters majority are decisions binding on all debentureholders.

Comparison of shares and debentures

There are important differences between shares and debentures.

(a) A shareholder is a proprietor or owner but a debentureholder is a *creditor* of the company. A shareholder as a member may vote at general meetings; a debentureholder has no such right as a member, though exceptionally he may have votes if the Articles and the deed allow.

(b) In liquidation debentures, like other debts, must be repaid in full before anything is distributed to shareholders.

(c) Interest at the agreed rate must be paid on debentures even if it is necessary to pay out capital in doing so. A shareholder only receives dividends if they can be paid out of distributable profits and the company decides to declare a dividend.

(d) A company has no statutory restriction on redeeming or purchasing its debentures (unless prohibited by the terms of the debenture). It may usually re-issue debentures which have been redeemed. There are elaborate rules to regulate the redemption or purchase by a company of its own shares.

Exercise 1

A company offers 10% preference shares and 7% debentures to investors. Ignoring tax considerations and the repayment of capital, why might an investor prefer the debentures?

---

3 Charges

A charge over a company's assets gives to the creditor (called the 'chargee') a prior claim (over other creditors) to payment of his debt out of those assets. Charges are of two kinds.

(a) *Fixed or specific charges* attach to the relevant asset as soon as the charge is created. A fixed charge is best suited to fixed assets which the company is likely to retain for a long period.

(b) *Floating charges* do not attach to the relevant assets until the charges crystallise.

A floating charge attaches to all the company's assets of the relevant description at the time of crystallisation, so it may be given over current assets. A floating charge over 'the undertaking

BPP Publishing

and assets' of a company (the most common type) applies to fixed assets as well as to current assets.

Crystallisation of a floating charge means that it is converted into a fixed charge on the assets owned by the company at the time of crystallisation. Events causing crystallisation are:

(a) the liquidation of the company;

(b) cessation of the company's business;

(c) active intervention by the chargee, generally by way of appointing a receiver over the assets of the company subject to the security or exercising a power of sale;

(d) if the charge contract so provides, when notice is given by the chargee that the charge is converted into a fixed charge;

(e) automatically on the occurrence of some specified event, without notice from the chargee, if the charge contract so provides;

(f) the crystallisation of another floating charge if it causes the company to cease business.

Priority of charges

If different charges over the same property are given to different creditors it is necessary to determine their priority. Leaving aside the question of registration, the main points in connection with the priority of any charges are as follows.

(a) Legal charges (legal mortgages of land or of shares) rank according to the order of creation.

(b) An equitable charge (any charge other than a legal mortgage of land or of shares) created before a legal charge will only take priority over the latter if, when the latter was created, the legal chargee had notice of the equitable charge.

(c) A legal charge created before an equitable one has priority.

(d) Two equitable charges take priority according to the time of creation.

It is always possible to vary these rules by agreement of both creditors.

If a floating charge is created and a fixed charge over the same property is created later, the fixed charge will rank first since it attached to the property at the time of *creation* but the floating charge attaches at the time of *crystallisation*.

4 Registration of charges

If a company creates a fixed or floating charge over its assets the charge should usually be registered within 21 days of its creation: s 398(1). It is primarily the duty of the company to register the charge but particulars may also be delivered by another person interested in the charge: s 398(1). The registrar files the particulars in the 'companies charges register' which he maintains (s 397) and notes the date of delivery. He then sends copies of the particulars and of the note of the date of registration delivered to the company and chargee: s 398(5).

The effect of non-delivery

Non-delivery within 21 days results in the charge being void against an administrator, liquidator or person acquiring an interest in the charged property.

(a) The charge will be void even if insolvency proceedings or the acquisition of an interest in the property occur *within* the 21 days prescribed for delivery, *if* the particulars are not in fact delivered during this period: s 399(1).

(b) Creditors who subsequently take security over property and duly register their charge within 21 days will take precedence over a previous unregistered charge. This will be the case even if the later chargee had *actual notice* of the previous unregistered charge (unless the later charge was expressed as being subject to the earlier charge).

Non-delivery of a charge means that the sum secured by it is payable forthwith on demand, even if the sum so secured is also the subject of other security: s 407(1).

Late delivery of particulars

If the charge was not registered within 21 days, it is possible to perfect the charge by late delivery under s 400(1), so that it will not be void against an administrator, liquidator or acquirer of an interest if insolvency proceedings on the acquisition of an interest happens *after* registration. If it occurs on the same day then there is a rebuttable presumption that the relevant event happened first.

Exercise 2

On 1 January, a company mortgages its factory to A as security for a £50,000 loan. On 1 February, the same factory is mortgaged to B as security for a £40,000 loan. On 1 March, C takes a floating charge over all the company's assets as security for a £60,000 loan, and on 1 April D takes a floating charge over all the company's assets as security for a £20,000 loan. All charges are registered within 21 days of creation, except that C's charge is not registered.

On 1 August, the company goes into liquidation. The factory is worth £120,000 and the company's other assets are worth £12,000. The company has no other liabilities. How much do each of A, B, C and D receive?

5 Debentureholders' remedies

Any debentureholder is a creditor of the company with the normal remedies of an unsecured creditor. He could:

(a) sue the company for debt and seize its property if his judgement for debt is unsatisfied;

(b) present a petition to the court for the compulsory liquidation of the company;

(c) present a petition to the court for an administration order.

A *secured* debentureholder (or the trustee of a debenture trust deed on behalf of secured debentureholders) may enforce the security. He may:

(a) take possession of the asset subject to the charge if he has a legal charge (if he has an equitable charge he may only take possession if the contract allows);

(b) sell it (provided the debenture is executed as a deed);

(c) apply to the court for its transfer to his ownership by foreclosure order (rarely used and only available to a legal chargee);

(d) appoint a receiver of it.

6 Receivers

The debenture (or debenture trust deed) usually gives power to the debentureholders (or their trustee) to appoint a receiver in specified circumstances of default by the company. The debenture also provides that the receiver, when appointed:

(a) shall have suitable powers of management and disposal of the assets under his charge; and

(b) shall be an agent of the company and not of the debentureholders by whom he is appointed. The purpose of this stipulation is to safeguard the debentureholders against liability for any wrongful act of the receiver.

A receiver may be appointed under a fixed or a floating charge. He takes control of the assets subject to the charge as a means of enforcing the security for the benefit of the secured creditor by or for whom the receiver is appointed.

Administrative receivers

A receiver who is appointed under a floating charge extending over the whole or substantially the whole of the company's property is called an *administrative receiver*. He is in charge of the company's business and therefore he has to manage it, and he must be a qualified insolvency practitioner.

An administrative receiver is automatically given a long list of statutory powers, unless the debenture provides to the contrary. These include powers:

(a) to borrow money and give security;

(b) to carry on the business of the company;

(c) to sell the company's property;

(d) to transfer the business of the company (or part of it) to a subsidiary.

Unless appointed by the court, the receiver is an agent of the company unless or until it goes into liquidation. As agent:

(a) he is personally liable on contracts made in the course of his duties as receiver;

(b) he is entitled to an indemnity for that liability out of the company's assets; and

(c) he can bind the company by his acts.

The function of a receiver is to manage or to realise the assets which are the security with a view to paying out of those assets what is due to the debentureholders whom he represents (plus the expenses including his own remuneration). If he is able to discharge these debts he vacates his office of receiver and the directors resume full control.

Exercise 3

A lender to a company takes a fixed legal charge over the company's only premises and a floating charge over the company's assets and undertaking. The company defaults at a time when its premises are worth much less than the debt but the company's inventory is very valuable. How should the lender proceed?

Chapter roundup

(a) Companies generally have powers to borrow and to create charges over assets;

(b) A debenture is a written acknowledgement of a debt. An issue of debentures may be accompanied by a debenture trust deed, appointing a trustee to look after the interests of the debentureholders and imposing constraints on the issuing company.

(c) A debentureholder is a creditor of the company, and the company must pay interest and repay capital on the due dates. A shareholder has no automatic right to the payment of dividends, and share capital is normally only repaid on a liquidation.

BPP Publishing

(d)   A company may create fixed or floating charges over its assets as security for money borrowed. A fixed charge is given over specific assets, whereas a floating charge attaches to whatever assets of a given class the company has at the time of crystallisation.

(e)   Charges must be registered within 21 days of their creation. There are rules on the priority of charges, and late registration may cause a charge to lose its priority.

(f)   Debentureholders have the usual remedies of any creditor if amounts owing to them are not paid on time. Secured debentureholders may take and sell the assets they have a charge over, or they may appoint a receiver.

Quick quiz

1   State three matters on which a debenture trust deed normally makes provision.

2   Compare the legal position of a debentureholder and a shareholder.

3   What are the characteristics of a floating charge?

4   In what circumstances does a floating charge crystallise and what is the effect of its doing so?

5   In what circumstances will a fixed charge created later than a floating charge take priority over the floating charge?

6   What is the effect of non-delivery of particulars of a charge?

7   What remedies are available to (a) a secured and (b) an unsecured debentureholder?

Solutions to exercises

1   Interest must be paid on time even if the company makes a loss. Dividends need not be paid, even if the company makes a profit.

2   A receives £50,000 and B receives £40,000. D receives £20,000 and C receives the remaining assets, £22,000.

3   The lender should appoint a receiver under the floating charge, to sell as much of the inventory as is needed to pay the debt.

BPP Publishing

23 DIRECTORS

Your objectives

After completing this chapter you should:

(a) understand the role of directors;

(b) know how directors may be appointed;

(c) know the rules on the disclosure of directors' shareholdings

(d) know the other required disclosures concerning directors;

(e) know how a director's term of office may come to an end;

(f) know when a person may be disqualified from being a director;

(g) understand the fiduciary position of directors;

(h) know the extent of directors' duty of care;

(i) know the restrictions on directors' interests in company contracts and on loans to directors;

(j) know the extent of directors' powers and the rules on board meetings;

(k) understand the position of a managing director;

(l) know how members can control directors;

(m) understand the position of outsiders when directors exceed their actual authority;

(n) understand the role of the company secretary.

1   Who and what is a director?

There is no comprehensive definition of a company director. But any person who occupies the position of director is treated as such: s 741. The test is one of function. The directors' function is to take part in making decisions by attending meetings of the board of directors. Anyone who does that is a director whatever he may be called. A person who is given the title of director, such as 'sales director' or 'director of research', to give him status in the company structure is not a director in company law unless by virtue of his appointment he is a member of the board of directors. Undischarged bankrupts and disqualified persons may not be directors.

Shadow directors

A person (other than a professional advisor merely acting in that capacity, for example, an accountant or solicitor) not appointed as a director is a director for legal purposes if the board of directors is accustomed to act in accordance with his directions or instructions. He is called a *shadow director*.

Alternate directors

A director may if the articles permit him to do so (Table A Articles 65 - 69) appoint an *alternate director* to attend and vote for him at board meetings which he himself is unable to attend. An alternate director is a director to whom the relevant rules of company law apply.

BPP Publishing

A director may also be an employee of his company. Since the company is also his employer there is a potential conflict of interest which in principle a director is required to avoid. To make it possible for an individual to be both a director and employee the articles (Table A Article 84) usually make express provision for it but prohibit the director from voting at a board meeting on the terms of his own employment. If the articles permit, a director may also have some connection, say as a consultant or professional adviser, with the company and earn remuneration paid by the company in that capacity. Directors' service agreements are open to inspection by members and any service agreement which the company is not free to terminate within five years is only valid in that respect if approved in general meeting.

Other conditions on directors

If the articles provide for it (Table A Article 84) the board may appoint one or more directors to be managing directors. A managing director does have a special position and has wider apparent powers than any director who is not appointed a managing director.

One company may be a director of another. In that case the director company sends an individual to attend board meetings as its representative.

Every company must have at least one director and for a public company the minimum is two: s 282. There is no statutory maximum but the articles usually impose a limit.

The same person may be a director (if there is more than one) and also company secretary. A sole director may not also be secretary. Another company may be either director or secretary. To prevent avoidance of the rules, it is provided that if Company A, which has a sole individual director (X), is sole director or secretary of Company B then X may not be secretary or sole director respectively of Company B: s 283(4).

2 Appointment of directors

The documents delivered to the registrar to form a company include a form giving particulars of the first directors and signed by them to signify their consent: s 13(5). On the formation of the company those persons become the first directors.

Once a company has been formed any appointment of directors in addition to or in replacement of previous directors is made as the articles provide. Most companies follow Table A in providing for co-option of new members by existing directors and election of directors in general meeting. But the articles may exclude retirement by rotation or permit some person, such as the holding company or a major shareholder, to appoint one, several or all directors. It is a matter of choosing whichever procedure is convenient.

Rotation of directors

Table A Articles 73-80 on retirement and re-election of directors ('rotation') provides that:

(a) every year one third shall retire; at the first annual general meeting (AGM) of the company they all retire (Article 73);

(b) retiring directors are eligible for re-election (Article 80);

(c) the directors themselves may fill a casual vacancy by co-option - such an appointee must stand for re-election at the next AGM after his appointment and does not count in determining the one-third to retire by rotation; the company in general meeting may also elect new directors (Article 79);

(d) a managing director or any other director holding executive office is not subject to retirement by rotation and is excluded in reckoning the one third in (a) above (Article 84).

Register of directors and secretaries

A company must keep at its registered office, where any person may inspect it, a register of its directors and secretaries showing:

(a) the name of each director/secretary;
(b) his address;
(c) his nationality;
(d) his date of birth;
(e) particulars of his business occupation and other directorships.

Items (c), (d) and (e) above apply only to directors, not to the company secretary.

Exercise 1

A company adopts Table A as its articles. It has ten directors. During one year, four of them die and the remaining directors co-opt two replacement directors. How many directors will retire at the next AGM?

---

3 Directors as shareholders

There is no general rule that a director must be a shareholder nor any rule which prohibits him from being one. The articles may however require that each director shall be the registered holder of a specified number of shares (called 'qualification shares').

If a director does hold shares or debentures, he is required to give notice to the company and the company must enter the information in a register of directors' interests which is kept with the register of members (normally at the registered office). This register too is open to inspection by the public. The register must be kept at the company's registered office or, if the register of members is kept at a place other than the registered office, at the place where the register of members is kept. In the latter case, notice of the location must be given to the registrar: Sch 13 para 25.

The register must be available for inspection by members and other persons to the same extent and subject to the same conditions as in the case of the register of members. The register must be produced at the commencement of every AGM of the company and be available for inspection during the meeting by any person attending. The rules as to the supplying of copies of the register, and the powers of the court to compel inspection and to direct the supplying of copies, are the same as in the case of the register of members. The directors' report issued with the annual accounts must state each director's interests in shares and debentures at the beginning and end of the year (unless disclosed in the accounts).

4 Disclosures concerning directors

Loans to directors

A company may not (subject to exceptions) enter into a loan or similar transaction with a director of the company or of its holding company nor (in the case of a public company or its subsidiary) with a person connected with such a director. If any such loan (whether prohibited or permitted) existed during the year prescribed particulars must be included (subject to limited exceptions) in the annual accounts for the year: s 232.

Directors' interests in contracts

There are similar requirements for disclosure in the annual accounts of transactions in which a director had directly or indirectly (for example through another company) a material interest: Sch 6 para 1. The other directors may decide whether a director's interest is 'material' (and requires disclosure).

Inspection of directors' service contracts

A company must make available for inspection by members a copy or particulars (if there is no written service agreement) of contracts of employment between the company or a subsidiary and directors of the company: s 318.

There are two exceptions to the general rule (s 319).

(a)   If the service contract requires the director to work wholly or mainly outside UK only brief particulars (the director's name and the duration of the contract) need to be given.

(b)   If the contract will expire or if the company can terminate it without compensation within a year, no copy or particulars need be kept available for members' inspection.

The copy or particulars must be available either at the registered office, or at the principal place of business in England.

Prescribed particulars of directors' emoluments must be given in the accounts and also particulars of any compensation for loss of office and directors' pensions: Sch 5.

6   The termination of directorships

A director may always vacate his office by resignation (Table A Article 81 provides for resignation by notice in writing given to the company) or by not offering himself for re-election when his previous term of office ends under the rotation rules. Obviously office is also vacated on the death of a director or on the dissolution of the company. In addition there are statutory provisions for removal from office and for disqualification.

The articles may provide for the removal of a director from office. But if the director also has a service agreement he may still be entitled to compensation for its breach by his dismissal.

In addition to any provisions of the articles for removal of directors, a director may be removed from office by ordinary resolution of the members (passed by a simple majority) of which special notice to the company has been given by the person proposing it: s 303. On receipt of the special notice the company must send a copy to the director who may require that a memorandum of reasonable length shall (unless it is defamatory) be issued to members; he also has a right to address the meeting at which the resolution is considered: s 304.

This statutory power of removal overrides the articles and any service agreement (but the director may claim damages for breach of the agreement). The power is, however, limited in its effect in two ways.

(a)   A member who gives special notice to remove a director cannot insist on the inclusion of his resolution in the notice of a meeting unless he qualifies by representing members who either have one twentieth of the voting rights or are at least 100 members on whose shares an average of at least £100 has been paid up: s 376.

(b)   A director may be irremovable if he has weighted voting rights and can prevent the resolution from being passed.

BPP Publishing

Retirement of directors

A director of a public company is deemed to retire at the end of the AGM following his 70th birthday: s 293(3). This rule is disapplied if the articles permit him to continue or if his continued appointment is approved by the general meeting. It is the duty of directors to disclose their ages to the company for the purposes of this rule: s 294.

Exercise 2

In *Bushell v Faith 1969*, the company had three members who were also the directors and each held 100 shares. On a resolution to remove a director, that director was to have three votes per share while other members were to have one vote per share. Could a director prevent a resolution to remove him from being put forward? Could he prevent it from being passed?

---

7   Disqualification of directors

Table A Article 81 provides that a director must vacate office:

(a)   if he is disqualified by the Act or any rule of law (for example if he ceases to be the registered holder of qualification shares);

(b)   if he becomes bankrupt or enters into an arrangement with his creditors;

(c)   if he becomes of unsound mind;

(d)   if he resigns by notice in writing;

(e)   if he is absent for a period of six consecutive months from board meetings held during that period without obtaining leave of absence and the other directors resolve that he shall on that account vacate office.

Statutory disqualification of directors

The Company Directors Disqualification Act 1986 (CDDA) provides that a court may disqualify any person from being (without leave of the court) a director (including a shadow director), liquidator, administrator, receiver or manager of a company's property or in any way directly or indirectly being concerned or taking part in the promotion, formation or management of a company: s 1. The terms of the disqualification order are thus very wide. They have been held to include acting as a consultant to a company.

The court may make an order on any of the following grounds.

(a)   A person is convicted of an indictable offence in connection with the promotion, formation, management or liquidation of a company or with the receivership or management of a company's property: s 2 CDDA.

(b)   It appears that a person has been persistently in default in relation to provisions of company legislation requiring any return, account or other document to be filed with, delivered or sent or notice of any matter to be given to the registrar of companies: s 3 CDDA.

(c)   It appears in the course of the winding up of a company that a person has been guilty of fraudulent trading (the person does not actually have to have been convicted of fraudulent trading) or has otherwise been guilty, while an officer or liquidator of the company or receiver or manager of its property, of any fraud in relation to the company or of any breach of his duty as such officer etc: s 4 CDDA.

(d) The Secretary of State acting on a report made by the inspectors or from information or documents obtained under the Companies Act, applies to the court for an order believing it to be expedient in the public interest.

(e) A director has participated in wrongful trading: s 10 CDDA.

The court must make an order where it is satisfied:

(a) that a person has been a director of a company which has at any time become insolvent (whether while he was a director or subsequently); and

(b) that his conduct as a director of that company makes him unfit to be concerned in the management of a company: s 6 CDDA.

Exercise 3

Susan was a director of a company which, a month after her resignation, became insolvent. She was also responsible for wrongful trading while a director of another company. Does it follow that she will be disqualified from being a director (assuming that a court considers the matter)?

---

8   Fiduciary duties of directors

Directors are said to hold a fiduciary position (a position in which they must serve faithfully) since they make contracts as agents of the company and have control of its property.

The directors owe a fiduciary duty to the company to exercise their powers *bona fide* in what they honestly consider to be the interests of the company: *Re Smith & Fawcett Ltd 1942*. The effect of this rule is seen in cases on gifts made to persons not employed by the company.

Case: Re W & M Roith Ltd 1967
The controlling shareholder and director wished to make provision for his widow, but did not want to leave her shares. His service agreement therefore provided her with a pension for life on his death.

Held: the object of this was to benefit the widow, not the company, and hence could be rescinded.

In exercising the powers given to them by the articles the directors have a fiduciary duty not only to act *bona fide* but also only to use their powers for a proper purpose.

The directors owe a fiduciary duty to avoid a conflict of duty and personal interest. It is unnecessary to show that the company has been prejudiced in any way by the conflict of interest.

A director may not obtain any personal advantage from his position of director without the consent of the company for whatever gain or profit he has obtained.

Case: Industrial Development Consultants Ltd v Cooley 1972
C was managing director of the company which provided consultancy services to gas boards. A gas board declined to award a contract to the company but C realised that he personally might be able to obtain it. He told the board of his company that he was ill and persuaded them to release him from his service agreement. On ceasing to be a director of the company C obtained the contract. The company sued him to recover the profits of the contract.

Held: C was accountable for his profit.

Exercise 4

In *Regal (Hastings) Ltd v Gulliver 1942*, the company had an investment opportunity, but insufficient capital. It formed a subsidiary and subscribed some of the necessary capital, while the directors and others subscribed the rest. The result was that the directors made a substantial profit, and the company had lost nothing because it could not have made the investment without their help. However, the directors still had to account to the company for their profit. Which of the above rules on directors' duties was applied?

---

9 Directors' duty of care

Directors have a common law duty of care to show reasonable competence. A director is expected to show the degree of skill which may reasonably be expected from a person of his knowledge and experience: the standard set is personal to the director.

In the absence of ground for suspicion and subject to normal business practice, he is entitled to leave the routine conduct of the business in the hands of its management and may trust them, accepting the information and explanation which they provide, if they appear to be honest and competent.

Company's action against negligent directors

The company may recover damages from its directors for loss caused by their negligence. But something more than imprudence or want of care must be shown. It must be shown to be a case of gross negligence.

10 Directors' dealings with their company

There are several statutory rules forbidding or restricting transactions affecting or involving directors.

Directors' interests in company contracts

A director shall always 'declare the nature of his interest', direct or indirect, in a contract or proposed contract with the company (s 317). The disclosure must be made to the first meeting of the directors at which the contract is considered or (if later) the first meeting held after the director becomes interested in the contract.

The shareholders' approval is required for any contract or arrangement by which the company buys from or sells to a director of the company or of its holding company or a person connected with any such director property which exceeds £100,000 in value or (if less) exceeds 10 per cent of the company's net assets (subject to a minimum of £2,000 value): s 320.

A company must disclose in the annual report and accounts any contract or arrangement with the company (or a subsidiary) in which a director, directly or through a connected person, has an interest which is material. The other directors may decide that a director's interest in a contract is not material for disclosure. But contracts of a value not exceeding £1,000 or (if greater) not exceeding one per cent of the company's assets (subject to a maximum of £5,000) are exempt from this disclosure requirement: s 232 and Sch 6.

BPP Publishing

If a director's service contract extends for longer than five years and under its terms the company either cannot terminate by notice or can only terminate it in specified circumstances (s 319(6)), the company can in fact terminate it at any time with reasonable notice. However, such a contract will only be valid if it is first approved by an ordinary resolution: it cannot later be ratified.

Loans to directors (ss 330-338)

Every company is prohibited by s 330 from:

(a) making a loan to a director of the company or of its holding company;

(b) guaranteeing or giving security for a loan to any such director;

(c) taking an assignment of a loan which, if made originally by the company, would have been contrary to (a) and (b);

(d) providing a benefit to another person as part of an arrangement by which that person enters into a transaction forbidden to the company itself by rules (a), (b) or (c).

There are the following general exceptions to these rules.

(a) A company may make a loan or give a guarantee or security in respect of a loan to a director which is also its holding company: s 336.

(b) A company may fund a director to enable him to perform his duties provided that the money is approved in general meeting before or afterwards; if it is made available before approval is obtained, it must be approved at or before the next AGM and must be repaid within six months of that AGM if not so approved: s 337.

(c) A money-lending company may advance money to a director, provided it is done in the normal course of business and the terms are not more favourable than the company would normally allow: s 338.

(d) A company may make a loan of up to £5,000: s 334.

(e) Group members may lend to each other: s 333.

(f) A holding company may make loans to directors of its subsidiaries, provided they are not directors of, nor connected to directors of, the holding company.

Relevant companies

There are more stringent rules for 'relevant companies' which include any public company and any private company which is a member of a group which includes a public company. The same basic rules apply to relevant as to other companies. In addition:

(a) the exceptions described in (b) and (c) above are limited to a maximum of £10,000 and £100,000 respectively, although a bank is only restricted to the £100,000 limit if the loan is to buy a residence: s 338;

(b) there are restrictions on indirect means of enabling a director to obtain goods or services on credit;

(c) a company transaction with a third party who is connected with one of its directors is subject to the same rules as apply to its transactions with a director himself.

Exercise 5

A company is to buy from a director a piece of land worth £3,500. The company's net assets are worth £80,000. The other directors consider that the director's interest is material. Must the shareholders approve the contract? Must the contract be disclosed in the annual report and accounts?

298

11 Directors' powers

The powers of the directors are defined by the articles. It is usual (Table A Article 70) to authorise the directors 'to manage the business of the company' and 'to exercise all the powers of the company'. They may then take any decision which is within the capacity (as defined by the objects clause) of the company unless either the Act or the articles themselves require that the decision shall be taken by the members in general meeting.

Board meetings

The articles confer powers on the directors collectively and not upon individual directors (unless appointed as managing directors). The directors should therefore exercise their powers by holding board meetings at which collective decisions are taken.

The articles usually leave the directors free to decide when and how board meetings shall be held. No period of notice is prescribed by law nor need a notice of a board meeting disclose the business to be transacted. Any member of the board may call, or require the secretary to call, a meeting. Reasonable notice should be given to all members sufficient to enable them to attend unless the articles (Table A Article 88) provide that directors who are abroad are not entitled to receive notice.

Minutes must be kept of the proceedings of board meetings and when signed by the chairman are evidence of those proceedings. The directors (and also the auditors for the purpose of their audit) have a right to inspect the minute book. No one else has nor need the minute book be kept at any particular place: s 382.

The directors are usually authorised by the articles (Table A Article 72) to delegate any of their powers to a *committee* of the board or to a *single director* either for a specific transaction or as managing director.

Managing and other working directors

If the articles provide for it (as they usually do) the board may appoint one or more directors to be managing directors. In his dealings with outsiders the managing director has apparent authority as agent of the company to make business contracts. No other director, even if he works full time, has that *apparent* authority as a director, though if he is employed as a manager he may have apparent authority at a slightly lower level. The managing director's *actual* authority is whatever the board gives him, and the board may change the limits of that authority, if necessary breaching his service agreement to do so.

12 Members' control of directors

The members of a company appoint the directors and may remove them from office under s 303. They can also, by altering the articles, re-allocate powers between the board and the general meeting. The members therefore have some control over the directors. But the directors are not agents of the members who can be instructed by the members in general meeting as to how they should exercise their powers.

> *Case: John Shaw & Sons (Salford) Ltd v Shaw 1935*
> In exercise of their general management powers given by the articles the directors began legal proceedings in the name of the company. The defendants who were shareholders (and directors) convened an EGM to pass a resolution that the action against them should be discontinued. The board challenged this decision.
>
> *Held:* the general body of shareholders 'cannot themselves usurp the powers which by the articles are vested in the directors'. The resolution passed by the EGM was therefore invalid.

Exercise 6

In *Holdsworth & Co v Caddies 1955*, a managing director had a service agreement under which his duties related to several companies in a group. The board confined his duties to one subsidiary. Were they entitled to do so?

---

13 Liability of the company for unauthorised acts of directors

The powers given to 'directors' by the articles are only vested in persons who *are* directors. If they have not been properly appointed or if they have ceased to be directors they do not have the directors' powers under the articles. But a person who deals with a company through persons who appear to be and who act as directors can usually enforce the contract. It is provided that the acts of a director or manager are valid notwithstanding any defect that may afterwards be discovered in his appointment or qualification: s 285 and Article 92. But to bring this statutory rule into operation there must be an appointment which is later found to be defective. It does not extend to a case where no appointment at all is made or the 'director' has ceased to be a director.

The 'indoor management' rule

The articles may reserve to the company in general meeting power to authorise certain transactions or impose on the directors some rule of procedure such as fixing a quorum of two or more for board meetings. The rule in *Turquand's* case is that the outsider who deals with the directors (or apparent directors):

(a)   is deemed to be aware of the requirements or restrictions imposed by the articles; but

(b)   is entitled to assume (unless he knows or should suspect the contrary) that these internal rules have been observed.

> *Case: Royal British Bank v Turquand 1856*
> Under the articles the directors could only borrow for the company such amounts as might be authorised by ordinary resolution passed in general meeting. A resolution was passed but it was defective since it did not specify the amount which the directors might borrow. The directors issued to the bank a debenture for £2,000 believing that they had authority to do so. The bank did not know of the defective terms of the resolution and had no legal right to inspect it since no copy of an ordinary resolution (of this type) is filed at the registry. The company went into liquidation and the liquidator (Turquand) argued that the company had no obligation to repay the loan since the loan contract (debentures) had been made without the authority required by the articles (of which the bank must be deemed to be aware - the doctrine of constructive notice of a company's basic public documents).
>
> *Held:* the bank must be deemed to be aware that the directors needed authority to borrow but it was also entitled to assume that authority had been properly given since the bank had no means of discovering whether a valid resolution had been passed.

Turquand's case and the Companies Act 1989

The status of the rule in *Turquand's* case is questionable in the light of the amendments made to the Companies Act 1985 by the Companies Act 1989. The new ss 711A, 35(1), 35A and 35B all impact on this position. S 711A abolishes the doctrine of constructive notice as it applies to documents held by the registrar, or made available to the company for inspection. This strikes out a basic premise of *Turquand's* case. However, s 711A(2) specifically provides

300

that the abolition does *not* affect the question whether a person is affected by notice of any matter by reason of a failure to make such enquiries as ought reasonably to be made: that is, a person is deemed to have constructive notice if he did not bother to make reasonable enquiries.

The combined effect of the new provisions certainly overlap with the rule in *Turquand's* case. An *ultra vires* act is now almost always validated. In relation to *intra vires* actions beyond the delegated powers of directors, it is clear that s 35A covers very similar situations to *Turquand's* case, and that it applies in some situations where *Turquand's* case does not.

Exercise 7

How might the outcome in *Turquand's* case have differed if the bank had been a member of the debtor company?

Agency by holding out

Holding out is a basic rule of the law of agency: if the principal (the company) holds out a person as its authorised agent it is estopped (against a person who has relied on the representation) from denying that he is its authorised agent and so is bound by a contract entered into by him on the company's behalf.

This situation usually results from the board of directors permitting a director to behave as if he were a managing director duly appointed when in fact he is not. As explained above a managing director does, by virtue of his position, have apparent authority to make commercial contracts for the company. If the board allows a director to enter into contracts, being aware of his dealings and taking no steps to disown him, the company will usually be bound.

> *Case: Freeman & Lockyer v Buckhurst Park Properties (Mangal) Ltd 1964*
> A company carried on a business as property developers. The articles contained a power to appoint a managing director but this was never done. One of the directors of the company, to the knowledge but without the express authority of the remainder of the board, acted as if he were managing director in finding a purchaser for an estate and again in engaging a firm of architects to make a planning application. The company later refused to pay the architect's fees on the grounds that the director had no actual or apparent authority.
>
> *Held:* the company was liable since by its acquiescence it had represented that the director was a managing director with the usual authority of that office.

14 The company secretary

Every company must have a secretary and a sole director must not also be the secretary. The directors of a public company must take all reasonable steps to ensure that the secretary is suitably qualified for his post by his knowledge and experience. Under s 286, a public company secretary may be anyone who:

(a)   was the secretary or his assistant on 22 December 1980;

(b)   has been a public company secretary for at least three out of the five years previous to appointment;

(c)   is a member of the Institute of Chartered Secretaries and Administrators or of one of several accountancy bodies;

(d) is a barrister, advocate or solicitor in the UK; or

(e) is a person who, by virtue of holding or having held any other position or being a member of any other body, appears to the directors to be capable.

The Act does not define the general duties of a company secretary since these will vary according to the size of the company and of its headquarters. The standard minimum duties of the secretary are:

(a) to make the arrangements incidental to meetings of the board of directors. The secretary usually convenes the meetings (Table A Article 88), issues the agenda (if any), collects or prepares the papers for submission to each meeting, attends the meeting, drafts the minutes and communicates decisions taken to the staff of the company or to outsiders, for instance a refusal of the directors to approve the transfer of shares;

(b) to maintain the register of members (unless this work is contracted out to professional registrars), to enter in transfers of shares and to prepare share certificates for issue to members. The secretary also keeps the other statutory registers and prepares the notices, returns and other documents which must be delivered to the registrar.

The secretary as agent

It is a general principle of agency law that if a person is employed in a capacity in which he does certain things for his principal he has *apparent* authority to bind his principal by such actions on his behalf, unless the principal has denied him that authority and the other party has notice of the restriction. In 1971 the Court of Appeal applied this principle and recognised that it is a normal function of a company secretary to enter into contracts connected with the administration of the company.

Case: Panorama Developments (Guildford) Ltd v Fidelis Furnishing Fabrics Ltd 1971
B, the secretary of a company, ordered cars from a car hire firm, representing that they were required to meet the company's customers at London Airport. Instead he used the cars for his own purposes. The bill was not paid, so the car hire firm claimed payment from B's company.

Held: B's company was liable, for he had apparent authority to make contracts such as the present one, which were concerned with the administrative side of its business. The decision recognises the general nature of a company secretary's duties. The court also said that, if the issue had arisen, it might not have treated the secretary as having apparent authority to make *commercial* contracts such as buying or selling trade goods, since that is not a normal duty of the company secretary.

Exercise 8

Would a company secretary ordering office stationery be likely to be treated as acting within his apparent authority in a plumbing company? Why might the position differ if the company traded as a stationer?

Chapter roundup

(a) A director is a person who takes part in making decisions by attending board meetings, whether or not he is called a director. Directors may also be employees of their company, with contracts of employment. A private (but not a public) company may have only one director, but a sole director may not also be the company secretary.

(b) Directors are generally elected by the members. Table A provides for the rotation of directors.

(c) Directors need not be members unless the articles require them to be, but they may be members. Any shareholdings must be disclosed in a register of directors' interests.

(d) Loans to directors, directors' interests in contracts and the terms of directors' service contracts must all be disclosed.

(e) A director may resign. He may also be removed from office, either in accordance with the articles or by an ordinary resolution of the members.

(f) A director may be required by the articles to vacate office in certain circumstances. Any person may be disqualified from being a director under the Company Directors Disqualification Act 1986.

(g) A director holds a fiduciary position, and must act in the best interests of his company. If he makes a personal profit from his position he may be required to account for it to the company.

(h) A director has a duty of care, and is expected to show the degree of skill which may reasonably be expected from a person of his knowledge and experience.

(i) A director must declare any interest he has in a contract with the company, and such interests may have to be disclosed in the annual report and accounts. There are severe restrictions on loans by companies to their directors.

(j) Directors have the power to manage their company. This power is exercised in board meetings. A managing director has apparent authority to make contracts for the company on his own.

(k) The members of a company cannot tell the directors how to exercise their powers, but they can remove the directors.

(l) The acts of an irregularly appointed director are valid. Under the indoor management rule, an outsider is entitled to assume that internal formalities required by a company's articles have been observed. However, this rule is now less important than it was because of legislation contained in the Companies Act 1989.

(m) If a director is allowed to represent that he is a managing director, he may come to have the apparent authority of a managing director.

(n) Every company must have a company secretary, and the secretary of a public company must be appropriately qualified. The secretary is effectively the company's chief administrative officer. He has apparent authority to make administrative contracts, but not commercial contracts.

BPP Publishing

Quick quiz

1 What is meant by the expressions (a) 'shadow director' and (b) 'alternate director'

2 What are the rules about the number of directors?

3 What particulars must be entered in (a) the register of directors and secretary and (b) the register of directors' interests, and where must each be kept?

4 What information is available to members concerning the terms of employment of directors?

5 What are the practical limitations on the members' statutory powers to remove a director from office?

6 Give the grounds, included in the Table A model articles, for disqualification of a director from continuing to hold office in the company.

7 Upon what grounds *may* a director be disqualified by a court order from holding office? When *must* the court disqualify him?

8 What are the main elements of a director's fiduciary duty?

9 What standard of competence is expected of directors?

10 What are the disclosure requirements of a director in relation to a contract of the company in which he has an interest?

11 What are the main exceptions to the general rule against a company making a loan to one of its directors?

12 What is the standard (Table A) formula by which the powers of the directors are defined?

13 What are the rules on notice to call a board meeting?

14 In what respect is it material to a person dealing with a company that he reasonably believes that the company representative is a managing director?

15 Are members in general meeting allowed to exercise powers which under the articles are delegated to the directors?

16 State the rule in *Turquand's* case.

17 In what circumstances is a secretary prohibited from also being a director of the company?

18 Who may be appointed secretary of a public company?

19 State the standard minimum duties of a company secretary.

Solutions to exercises

1 (10 - 4)/3 + 2 = 4.

2 A resolution to remove a director could be put forward against his wishes, but he could prevent it from being passed (by 300 votes to 200).

3 Susan might be disqualified, but she need not be (unless her conduct while a director of the insolvent company makes her unfit to be concerned in the management of a company).

4 The rule that directors must not obtain any personal advantage or profit from their position.

5 The shareholders need not approve the contract, but it must be disclosed in the annual report and accounts.

6 Yes, despite the consequent breach of his service agreement.

7 The bank would have known that the required resolution had not been passed, so it would probably have lost its right to repayment of the loan.

8   The company secretary would be acting within his apparent authority in a plumbing company. If the company traded as a stationer, the contract might be a commercial contract outside the company secretary's apparent authority.

24 MEETINGS

Your objectives

After completing this chapter you should:

(a) understand the difference between annual and extraordinary general meetings;

(b) know how a meeting may be validly convened;

(c) know when special notice of a resolution is required, and how it is given;

(d) know how a resolution may be requisitioned;

(e) know what must be stated in the notice convening a meeting;

(f) be aware of the rules on proxies;

(g) be able to distinguish between ordinary, extraordinary and special resolutions;

(h) know the rules governing elective and written resolutions;

(i) know how votes are conducted, and appreciate the effect of the assent principle.

1   Types of meeting

Although the management of a company is in the hands of the directors, the decisions which affect the existence of the company, its structure and scope, are reserved to the members in general meeting.

There are two kinds of general meeting of members of a company, annual general meetings (AGMs) and extraordinary general meetings (EGMs).

Annual general meetings

The rules are as follows.

(a) Every company must hold an AGM in each (calendar) year: s 366.

(b) S 366A allows a private company to dispense with the holding of an AGM by the passing of an elective resolution. An election has effect for the year in which it is made and subsequent years. In any such year affected by the resolution any member, by notice to the company not later than three months before the end of the year, may require the holding of an AGM in that year.

(c) Not more than 15 months may elapse between meetings. But provided that the first AGM is held within 18 months of incorporation, the company need not hold it in the year of incorporation or in the following year: s 366.

(d) If a default is made, the Department of Trade and Industry on application of any member may call the AGM and give whatever directions are necessary, even to modify the articles or fix a quorum of one. In this case the company may resolve that this meeting also constitutes the AGM of the year in which it is held: s 367.

(e) A notice convening an AGM must be in writing and in accordance with the articles. At least 21 days notice should be given; shorter notice is valid only if all members entitled to attend agree: s 369.

BPP Publishing

(f)   The notice must specify the meeting as an AGM: s 369.

It is usual, but not obligatory, to transact at an AGM the 'ordinary business' of the company if so described in the articles.

Extraordinary general meetings

The *directors* have power to convene an EGM whenever they see fit: Table A Article 37.

The directors may be required to convene an EGM by *requisition of the members*. The rules (s 368) are as follows.

(a)   The requisitionists must hold at least 10% of the paid up share capital carrying voting rights.

(b)   They must deposit at the registered office a signed requisition stating the objects of the meeting, that is the resolutions which they intend to propose.

(c)   If the directors fail within 21 days of the deposit of the requisition to convene the meeting, any reasonable expenses of the requisitionists in convening the meeting are then payable by the company and recoverable from the directors.

(d)   The date for which an EGM on requisition of the members is called must be within 28 days of the issuing of the notice.

Exercise 1

Give some examples of events which might lead to an EGM, bearing in mind that the ordinary management of a company is entrusted to the directors and not the members.

---

2   Convening a meeting

A meeting cannot make valid and binding decisions until it has been properly convened.

(a)   The meeting must be called by the board of directors or other competent person or authority. If however there is some irregularity in the board meeting which convenes a general meeting and the members in general meeting nonetheless pass the resolutions proposed this may be taken as a waiver of irregularity.

(b)   The notice must be issued to members in advance of the meeting so as to give them 14 days notice of the meeting (21 days if a special resolution is to be proposed). The members may agree to waive this requirement.

(c)   The notice must be sent to every member (or other person) entitled to receive it, but it need not be sent to a member whose only shares do not give him a right to attend and vote (as is often the position of preference shareholders), nor need it usually be sent to a joint holder of voting shares who is not the first named holder on the register. If, however, the business to be done must by law be disclosed to all members (for example proposals to pay compensation to directors for loss of office requiring approval under s 312) then notice of it must be sent even to members who are not entitled to vote on it).

(d)   The notice must include any information reasonably necessary to enable shareholders to know in advance what is to be done.

Special notice of a resolution

Special notice must be given *to the company* of the intention to propose a resolution:

(a) to remove an auditor or to change the auditor: s 391A;

(b) to reappoint a director aged more than 70 where the age limit applies: s 293;

(c) to remove a director from office or to appoint a replacement after removal: s 303.

When special notice is given under s 379 the sequence is as follows.

(a) The member gives special notice of his intention to the company at least 28 days before the date of the meeting at which he intends to move his resolution. If, however, the company calls the meeting for a date less than 28 days after receiving the special notice that notice is deemed to have been properly given.

(b) On receiving special notice the company may be obliged under s 376 to include the resolution in the AGM notice which it issues. But in other circumstances the company (the directors) may refuse to include it in their notice. If the company gives notice to members of the resolution it does so by a 21 day notice to them.

(c) If special notice is received of intention to propose a resolution for the removal from office of a director (under s 303(2)) or to change the auditor (under s 391A) the company must forthwith send a copy to the director or auditor so that he may exercise his statutory right to defend himself by issuing a memorandum and/or addressing the meeting in person.

Requisitioning a resolution

It usually rests with the directors to decide what resolutions shall be included in the notice of a meeting. But (apart from the requisition of an EGM) members can take the initiative if they represent at least 5% of the voting rights or are at least 100 members holding shares on which there has been paid up an average per member of at least £100: s 376. These members may, under s 377:

(a) by requisition delivered at least six weeks in advance of an AGM require the company to give notice to members of a resolution which they wish to move;

(b) by requisition delivered at least one week in advance of an AGM or EGM require the company to circulate to members a statement not exceeding 1,000 words in length (unless the court declares it to be defamatory).

In either case, the requisitionists must bear the incidental costs unless the company otherwise resolves. The company need not comply if the court is satisfied that the procedure is being used to obtain needless publicity for defamatory material.

Content of notices

The notice of a general meeting must give the date, time and place of the meeting, and an AGM or a special or extraordinary resolution must be described as such. Information must be given of the business of the meeting sufficient to enable members (in deciding whether to attend or to appoint proxies) to understand what will be done at the meeting.

In issuing the notice of an AGM it is standard practice merely to list the items of routine business to be transacted, such as the declaration of dividends, the election of directors and the appointment of auditors and fixing of their remuneration.

Non-routine business may be transacted equally validly at an AGM or at an EGM. In either case its nature makes it necessary to set out in the notice convening the meeting the full text of the relevant resolution.

Exercise 2

David, a shareholder in Q Ltd, wishes to include a resolution in the notice of an AGM about to be sent to members. The directors do not wish to include his resolution. He holds 4% of the votes, but his paid up share capital is £15,000. Can he force the inclusion of his resolution?

3 Proxies

Any member of a company which has a share capital, if he is entitled to attend and vote at a general or class meeting of the company, has a statutory right (s 372) to appoint an agent, called a proxy, to attend and vote for him. The rules are as follows.

(a) A meeting of a *private* company may only appoint one proxy who may, however, speak at the meeting.

(b) A member of a *public* company (who may be a nominee of two or more beneficial owners of the shares whose voting intentions conflict) may appoint more than one proxy but his proxy has no statutory right to speak at the meeting (this is to prevent the use of professional advocates at large meetings).

(c) The proxy need not himself be a member of the company.

(d) Whether it is a private or a public company the proxy may vote on a poll but not on a show of hands.

The articles may vary condition (a) for private companies. Both public and private company articles may vary condition (d): proxies voting on a show of hands.

4 Types of resolution

A meeting reaches a decision by passing a resolution. There are five kinds of resolution.

(a) An *ordinary resolution* is carried by a simple majority of votes cast (over 50%).

(b) An *extraordinary resolution* is carried by a 75% majority of votes cast.

(c) A *special resolution* is carried by a 75% majority of votes cast.

21 days' notice is required for a meeting at which a special resolution is to be put forward, but only 14 days' notice is required if only ordinary and extraordinary resolutions are to be put forward.

(d) An *elective resolution* may be passed by a *private* company:

    (i) to confer authority to issue shares indefinitely or for a fixed period which may exceed five years: s 80A;

    (ii) to dispense with the laying of accounts before a general meeting, unless a member or the auditors require it: s 252;

    (iii) to dispense with holding an AGM unless a member requires it: s 366A;

    (iv) to reduce the 95% majority needed to consent to short notice under ss 369(4) or 378(3), to a figure of not less than 90%;

    (v) to dispense with the annual appointment of auditors (so that the incumbent auditors are automatically reappointed): s 386.

To pass such a resolution, *all* the members entitled to attend and vote must agree: s 379A. 21 days notice is required and the resolution must be registered within 15 days.

An elective resolution may be revoked by ordinary resolution (s 379A(3)) but this must also be registered: s 380(4).

(e)   A *written resolution* is available to private companies. Anything that a private company could do by a resolution of a general meeting or a class meeting may be done, by a written resolution. All members entitled to attend and vote must sign the resolution (s 381A(1)). Note the following restrictions.

   (i)   A written resolution cannot be used to remove a director or auditor from office, since such persons have a right to speak *at a meeting*.

   (ii)   A written resolution must be sent in advance to the auditors, who have seven days to serve notice that the resolution should be considered at a meeting; the resolution cannot take effect unless they do not reply, they declare that no such meeting is needed, or the meeting is held.

A signed copy of every special and extraordinary resolution (and equivalent decisions by unanimous consent of members) must be delivered to the registrar for filing. Some ordinary resolutions, particularly those relating to share capital, have to be delivered for filing but many do not.

Exercise 3

Distinguish special resolutions from resolutions requiring special notice.

Voting and polls

The rights of members to vote and the number of votes to which they are entitled in respect of their shares are fixed by the articles. One vote per share is normal but some shares, for instance preference shares, may carry no voting rights in normal circumstances. To shorten the proceedings at meetings the procedure is as follows.

(a)   *Voting on a show of hands.* On putting a resolution to the vote the chairman calls for a show of hands. One vote may be given by each member present in person: proxies do not vote. The chairman declares the result. Unless a poll is then demanded, the chairman's declaration (duly recorded in the minutes) is conclusive.

(b)   *Voting on a poll.* If a real test of voting strength is required a poll may be demanded. The result of the previous show of hands is then disregarded. On a poll every member and also proxies representing absent members may cast the full number of votes to which they are entitled. A poll need not be held forthwith but may be postponed so that arrangements to hold it can be made.

A poll may be demanded as provided by the articles, but in any case:

(a)   by not less than five members;

(b)   by member(s) representing not less than one tenth of the total voting rights;

(c)   by member(s) holding shares which represent not less than one tenth of the paid-up capital.

5   The assent principle

The purpose of holding general meetings with all the formality which they entail is to give each member the opportunity of voting (in person or by proxy) on the resolutions before the meeting. If the meeting is not properly convened and conducted its purported decisions are not binding on any member who disagrees with and challenges them. His right to do so exists whether he was absent from the meeting or attended it but was in the minority. But this is a protection given to a dissenting member. If every member in fact agrees it would be pointless and wrong to allow any non-member to dispute the validity of the unanimous decision purely on the grounds that unanimity was achieved in some informal way. Accordingly a unanimous decision of the members is often treated as a substitute for a formal decision in general meeting properly convened and held, and is equally binding.

Chapter roundup

(a) Major decisions affecting a company are taken by the members in general meeting. Every company must hold AGMs, except for private companies which have decided not to by elective resolution. EGMs may be called by the directors or requisitioned by a sufficiently large number of the members.

(b) A meeting must be properly convened. Certain resolutions can only be included in the agenda if special notice has been given to the company. The directors can exclude a resolution unless a sufficiently large number of the members force its inclusion.

(c) Any member entitled to attend and vote may send a proxy to the meeting instead.

(d) Resolutions may be ordinary, extraordinary or special. A private company may also pass an elective resolution or a written resolution.

(e) Voting is normally by a show of hands, although a poll may be demanded.

(f) Under the assent principle, a unanimous but informal decision of the members may be treated as a substitute for a formal decision in general meeting.

Quick quiz

1   What are (a) the intervals and (b) the period of notice fixed by law for an AGM?

2   How may an EGM be convened?

3   List the routine items of business of an AGM for which it is unnecessary to include a detailed description in the notice.

4   State the rules on proxies.

5   Describe the types of resolution which may be passed at a general meeting and the requirements applicable to each.

6   For what purposes may a private company use an elective resolution?

7   Describe the procedure for taking a vote at a company general meeting

8   Who may demand a poll?

9   What is the assent principle?

Solutions to exercises

1   The directors might all die or otherwise become incapable of acting.

It might become impossible for the company to carry on its business, because of (say) a fire or a change in the law.

You can probably think of other examples.

2   No.

3   A special resolution is passed by a 75% majority, and needs 21 days' notice *to the members*.

Special notice of a resolution (which may be an ordinary resolution) is given *to the company* at least 28 days before the relevant meeting.

25 SHAREHOLDERS

Your objectives

After completing this chapter you should:

(a) understand how persons become and cease to be members of companies;

(b) know the contents of a register of members;

(c) know how the position of a beneficiary of a trust which owns shares may be protected;

(d) know what interests in shares must be notified;

(e) know how the principle of majority rule is restricted in order to protect minorities;

(f) be aware of the powers of the DTI to investigate companies.

1   Becoming a member

A member of a company is a person who has agreed to be a member and whose name has been entered in the register of members: s 22(2). Entry in the register is essential. Mere delivery to the company of a transfer does not make the transferor a member.

Subscribers to the memorandum are deemed to have agreed to become members of the company. The subscribers are liable to pay an amount equal to the nominal value of their shares unless the company waives its rights against them by allotting all the authorised share capital to other persons.

2   Ceasing to be a member

A member ceases to be a member if:

(a) he transfers all his shares to another person and the transfer is registered;

(b) he dies;

(c) he becomes bankrupt and his shares are registered in the name of his trustee;

(d) he is a minor who repudiates his shares;

(e) he is the trustee of a bankrupt member and disclaims his shares;

(f) the company forfeits or accepts the surrender of shares or sells them under a lien;

(g) the company is dissolved and ceases to exist.

3   The register of members

Every company must, under s 352, keep a register of members and enter in it:

(a) the name and address of each member and the class (if more than one) to which he belongs unless this is indicated in the particulars of his shareholding;

BPP Publishing

(b) if the company has a share capital, the number of shares held by each member. In addition:

    (i) if the shares have distinguishing numbers, the member's shares must be identified in the register by those numbers; and

    (ii) if the company has more than one class of shares the member's shares must be distinguished by their class, such as preference or ordinary shares;

(c) the date on which each member became and eventually the date on which he ceased to be a member. The company must preserve entries relating to former members for 20 years from the date of ceasing to be a member: s 352(6).

Any member of the company can inspect the register of members of a company without charge; a member of the public has the right of inspection but must pay a fee.

Location of register

To make the right of inspection effective, the company is required to hold its register of members either at its registered office or at any other place at which the work of making up the register is done. But if the register of members is kept elsewhere than at the registered office:

(a) notice of the place at which the register is held must be sent to the registrar (and notice of any change of that address). It must also be shown in the annual return; and

(b) the alternative address at which the register is kept must be within the same country as the registered office.

Exercise 1

Judy sells all her shares in a company to Simon. The contract for the sale is made on Monday, Simon pays Judy on Wednesday and the transfer is registered on Friday. Which of the two is a member on Thursday?

---

4 Shares held on trust

An English company is forbidden to make any note on its register of a trust relating to its shares. The company deals with the registered holder as the legal owner of his shares and is not concerned with the fact that he may hold the shares as nominee or trustee: s 360.

Stop notices

If a beneficiary gives notice to an English company that he has an interest in shares registered in the name of another person, the company will return the notice stating that it is not permitted to accept it. The beneficiary may however protect his interests by serving a *stop notice*. Thereafter the company may not register a transfer of the shares to which the stop notice relates without giving written notice to the person who has served the stop notice on the company. After giving notice the company must wait for 14 days before registering the transfer, and during that time the beneficiary can, if he wishes, apply to the court for an injunction to prohibit the transfer.

5 Substantial shareholdings

Any person who acquires a notifiable interest in voting shares of a public company must give notice (with prescribed particulars) to the company of his interest: s 198. Thereafter so long as his interest is above the minimum he must give similar notice of all changes: s 202. The company on receiving the information must enter it in a register of interests in shares which is open to public inspection: s 211.

A person has a notifiable interest when he is interested in at least 3% of the shares: ss 198-201. Disclosure must be made to the company within two days: s 202. A person has an interest even if shares are held in someone else's name: thus substantial investors cannot conceal themselves by using nominees to hold their shares.

On its side the company may (and on the requisition of 10 per cent or more (in share value) of its members, must) call on anyone (not necessarily a member) to declare whether he has a notifiable interest: s 212 and s 214.

Exercise 2

On 1 June Lisa buys 500 shares in a company with 50,000 shares in issue. On 4 June she buys a further 400 shares, on 12 June she buys a further 700 shares and on 20 June she buys a further 2,000 shares. By what date must she disclose her interest to the company?

---

6 Minority protection

The rule in *Foss v Harbottle*

Ultimate control of a company rests with its members voting in general meeting since (among other things) the directors are required to lay annual accounts before a general meeting and may be removed from office by a simple majority of votes. But if the directors hold a majority of the voting shares or represent a majority shareholder the minority has no remedy unless the rules of minority protection apply.

> *Case: Foss v Harbottle 1853*
> A shareholder (Foss) sued the directors of the company alleging that the directors had defrauded the company by selling land to it at an inflated price. The company was by this time in a state of disorganisation and efforts to call the directors to account at a general meeting had failed.
>
> *Held:* the action must be dismissed since:
>
> (a)   the company as a person separate from its members is the only proper plaintiff in an action to protect its rights or property; and
>
> (b)   the company in general meeting must decide whether to bring such legal proceedings.

Common law rules

Case law recognises a number of limitations to the principle of majority control (the rule in *Foss v Harbottle*) and in those cases permits a minority to bring legal proceedings. The decisions are not entirely consistent but the principles are generally summarised as follows.

(a)   No majority vote can be effective to sanction an act of the company which is illegal.

BPP Publishing

(b) If the law or the company's articles require that a special procedure shall be observed, say alteration of the articles by special resolution, the majority must observe that procedure and their decision is invalid if they do not do so.

(c) If the company under majority control deprives a member of his individual rights of membership, he may sue the company to enforce his rights.

> *Case: Pender v Lushington 1877*
> The articles gave members one vote for each 10 shares held by them but subject to a maximum of 100 votes for each member. A company which was a large shareholder transferred shares to the plaintiff to increase its voting power. At the meeting the chairman rejected the plaintiff's votes. The plaintiff sued and the company relied on the argument that only the company itself could object to an irregularity of voting procedure.
>
> *Held:* the plaintiff's votes were a 'right of property' which he was entitled to protect by proceedings against the company.

(d) If those who control the company use their control to defraud it (or possibly to act oppressively to a minority) the minority may bring legal proceedings against the fraudulent (or oppressive) majority. Otherwise a wrong would be without remedy since the majority would prevent the company from taking action.

Exercise 3

Edwards v Halliwell 1950 was a trade union case, but the relevant law was the same as for companies. Rules (equivalent to articles) stated that members' subscriptions could only be increased by a two thirds majority of votes cast in a members' ballot. A meeting decided to increase the subscriptions, but no ballot was held. Which common law rule was applied to declare the increase invalid?

Statutory rules

Any member may now apply to the court for relief under s 459 on the grounds that the company's affairs are being or have been conducted in a manner which is unfairly prejudicial to the interests of the members generally or of some part of the members. Application may also be made in respect of a particular act or omission which has been or will be prejudicial. It is not necessary to show that there has been bad faith or even an intention to discriminate against the minority. But the complaint must be based on prejudice to the member as a member and not, for example, as an employee or as an unpaid creditor. Whatever the basis of the petition the court will take account of the surrounding circumstances and conduct of the parties.

> *Case: Re Noble & Sons (Clothing) Ltd 1983*
> B had provided the capital but left the management in the hands of N, the other director, on the understanding that N would consult B on major company matters. N did not do so and B confined himself to enquiries to N on social occasions; he accepted N's vague assurances that all was well. The petition followed from a breakdown of the relationship.
>
> *Held:* B's exclusion from discussion of company management questions was largely the result of his own lack of interest. His petition was dismissed.

When a petition is successful the court may make whatever order it deems fit - though the petitioner is required in presenting his petition to state what relief he seeks. It may include, under s 461:

(a) an order regulating the future conduct of the company's affairs: for example that a controlling shareholder shall conform to the decisions taken at board meetings *(Re H R Harmer Ltd 1958);*

(b) an authorisation to any person to bring legal proceedings on behalf of the company. The company is then responsible for the legal costs;

(c) an order requiring the company to refrain from doing or continuing an act complained of;

(d) provision for the purchase of shares of the minority by either the controlling shareholder or the company;

(e) inclusion in the memorandum or articles of provisions which may only be altered or removed thereafter by leave of the court.

Investigations by the Department of Trade and Industry

The Department of Trade and Industry (the DTI) has statutory power to appoint an inspector to investigate the affairs or ownership of a company (ss 431-432, 442-443).

The DTI must appoint inspectors if a court so orders. In addition, it may appoint inspectors to investigate the affairs of a company:

(a) if the company itself applies: s 431;

(b) if application is made by members who are not less than 200 in number or who hold at least one tenth of the issued shares (or, if the company has no share capital, by at least one fifth of the members). The applicants may be required to produce evidence to show good reasons for their application and to give security (not exceeding £5,000) for the costs of the investigation: s 431;

(c) if the DTI considers that the affairs of the company have been conducted in a fraudulent or unlawful manner (or that it was formed for a fraudulent or unlawful purpose) or in a manner unfairly prejudicial to some part of its members or that members have not been given all the information with respect to its affairs which they might reasonably expect: s 432.

Exercise 4

The controlling shareholders of a company resolve to replace the directors with new directors who will work to increase efficiency by reducing the number of employees. John, a minority shareholder and senior employee, is made redundant by the new directors. Why could he not apply for relief under s 459?

Chapter roundup

(a) A person becomes a member of a company by being entered in the register of members. He ceases to be a member when he dies, when the company ceases to exist or when all of his shares are registered in the name of another person.

(b) The shareholdings of all members are recorded in the register of members. No notice of a trust may be included in the register, but the position of a beneficiary may be protected by serving a stop notice on the company.

(c) Any person interested in at least 3% of a company's shares must notify the company.

(d) In general, majority rule prevails, but this principle is restricted to protect minorities. There are several common law restrictions, and under statute law any member may apply for relief if the company's affairs are conducted in a way which is unfairly prejudicial to some or all of the members.

(e)   The Department of Trade and Industry may appoint inspectors to investigate a company.

Quick quiz

1   In what ways may a person (a) become and (b) cease to be a member of a company?

2   What particulars must be entered in a register of members and where must the register be kept?

3   Who may inspect a register of members?

4   In what circumstances (if any) is a company affected by notice from a third party of his interest in shares registered in a name not his own?

5   Describe briefly the methods by which a person who has an interest in shares registered in another person's name may be required to disclose his interest. To which shares do the rules relate and to whom is the disclosure to be made?

6   What is the rule in *Foss v Harbottle*?

7   State the main exceptions to the principle of majority control.

8   On what grounds may a shareholder obtain a statutory remedy against a controlling majority?

9   When may the DTI appoint inspectors to investigate a company's affairs?

Solutions to exercises

1   Judy (she is on the register on Thursday).

2   50,000 × 3% = 1,500 shares, so Lisa must disclose her interest by 14 June (two days after 12 June).

3   If a special procedure must be observed, decisions ignoring that procedure are invalid.

4   He would be applying as an employee and not as a member.

BPP Publishing

26 LIQUIDATIONS AND OTHER INSOLVENCY PROCEDURES

Your objectives

After completing this chapter you should:

(a) know how a company may come to be dissolved;

(b) understand the effects of a decision to liquidate a company;

(c) know the grounds for compulsory liquidation;

(d) be able to distinguish between a members' and a creditors' voluntary liquidation;

(e) know how each type of liquidation proceeds;

(f) understand the role of a liquidation committee;

(g) understand the position of contributories;

(h) know the powers and duties of liquidators;

(i) understand the effects of an administration order and the position of an administrator;

(j) understand when and how a voluntary arrangement may be made.

Statutory references in this chapter are to the Insolvency Act 1986 unless otherwise stated. 'CA' denotes the Companies Act 1985

1   Methods of dissolution

Dissolution occurs when a company's name is removed from the register. At this point it ceases to exist. There are a number of ways in which this may be done.

(a) By the registrar, under s 652 CA, if it appears to him that the company is defunct.

(b) By order of the court under s 427(3)(d) CA following a scheme of arrangement under s 425: no winding up is necessary as the company is transferring its business.

(c) By Act of Parliament (very rarely used).

(d) By cancellation of registration on application for judicial review by the Attorney-General. This may be invoked if the registrar has erroneously registered a company with illegal objects: *R v Registrar of Companies (ex p Attorney General) 1980*.

(e) On application by the official receiver for early dissolution: s 202.

(f) On completion of a compulsory liquidation.

(g) On completion of a voluntary liquidation.

BPP Publishing

2 Liquidations

Most dissolutions follow liquidation or 'winding up' (the terms are used synonymously). The assets are realised, debts are paid out of the proceeds, and any surplus amounts are returned to members.

Liquidation begins with a formal decision to liquidate. If the members in general meeting resolve to wind up the company that is a *voluntary* liquidation. This may be either a members' or a creditors' voluntary liquidation, depending on whether the directors believe that the company will or will not be able to pay its debts in full.

A company may also be obliged to wind up by a *compulsory* liquidation, ordered by the court on a petition usually presented by a creditor or a member.

Whether liquidation is voluntary or compulsory it is in the hands of the liquidator (or joint liquidators), who take over control of the company from its directors. Liquidators' actions are valid even if the appointment or qualifications are defective; no further share dealings or changes in membership will be permitted (unless the court sanctions a rectification or other change); and all invoices, orders, letters and other company documents must state prominently that the company is in liquidation.

Exercise 1

What is the point of requiring that all documents state that a company is in liquidation, given that the members and creditors are likely to be aware of that fact?

---

3 Compulsory liquidation

A petition is presented to the Chancery Division of the High Court (or, if the company has an issued and paid up share capital not exceeding £120,000 in the county court of the district in which the registered office is situated): s 117. The petition will specify the ground for compulsory winding up and be presented (usually) either by a creditor or by a member (called a 'contributory' in the context of liquidation). The standard grounds for compulsory liquidation are listed in s 122.

(a) The company has by special resolution resolved that it should be wound up by the court.

(b) The company, incorporated as a public company, has failed within a year to obtain a trading certificate.

(c) The number of members of a public company has been reduced to below two. This used to apply to private companies, but single member private companies are now allowed.

(d) The company has not commenced its business within a year of incorporation or has suspended its business for a year.

(e) The company is unable to pay its debts: s 122(1)(f). This is the most common ground.

(f) The court considers that it is just and equitable to wind up the company: s 122(1)(g). This ground may be used by a dissatisfied member.

Company unable to pay its debts

A creditor who petitions on the grounds of the company's insolvency may rely on any of three situations to show that the company is unable to pay its debts: s 123.

BPP Publishing

(a)   A creditor (or creditors) to whom the company owes more than £750 serves on the company at its registered office a written demand for payment and the company neglects, within the ensuing 21 clear days, either to pay the debt or to offer reasonable security for it.

(b)   A creditor obtains judgement against the company for debt, and attempts to enforce the judgement but is unable to obtain payment, because no assets of the company have been found and seized.

(c)   A creditor satisfies the court that, taking into account the contingent and prospective liabilities of the company, it is unable to pay its debts. The creditor may be able to show this:

   (i)   by proof that the company is not able to pay its debts as they fall due: the *commercial insolvency test;* or

   (ii)   by proof that the company's assets are less than its liabilities: the *balance sheet test.*

At the hearing other creditors of the company may oppose the petition. If so, the court is likely to decide in favour of those to whom the larger amount is owing. But the court may also consider the reasons for the differences between the creditors:

The just and equitable ground

Orders have been made for liquidation on the just and equitable ground in the following situations.

(a)   The substratum of the company has gone: the main object of the company can no longer be achieved.

(b)   The company was formed for an illegal or fraudulent purpose or there is a complete deadlock in the management of its affairs.

(c)   The understandings between members or directors which were the basis of the association have been unfairly breached by lawful action.

(d)   The directors deliberately withheld information so that the shareholders have no confidence in the company's management.

Exercise 2

In *Re a Company (No 003729 of 1982) 1984*, the petitioner for compulsory liquidation had demanded a sum due under a contract from the company. The company had disputed the amount due, and had only paid part of the sum demanded. The petitioner therefore claimed that the company had neglected to pay a debt. Why do you think the petitioner failed?

Proceedings for compulsory liquidation

When a petition is presented to the court a copy is delivered to the company in case it objects. It is advertised so that other creditors may intervene if they wish.

If the petition is presented by a member (a contributory) he must show (in addition to suitable grounds for compulsory liquidation) that the company is *solvent* or alternatively refuses to supply information of its financial position, and that he has been a registered shareholder for at least six of the 18 months up to the date of his petition.

320

Once the court has been petitioned, a provisional liquidator may be appointed by the court: s 135. The Official Receiver is usually appointed, and his powers are conferred by the court. These usually extend to taking control of the company's property and applying for a special manager to be appointed (ss 144 and 177).

Effects of an order for compulsory liquidation

The effects of the order, which may be made some time after a provisional liquidator is appointed, are as follows.

(a) The Official Receiver (an official of the DTI whose duties relate mainly to bankruptcy of individuals) becomes liquidator: s 136.

(b) The liquidation is deemed to have commenced at the time (possibly several months earlier) when the petition was first presented. If compulsory liquidation follows voluntary liquidation already in progress liquidation runs from the commencement of the voluntary liquidation: s 129.

(c) Any disposition of the company's property and any transfer of its shares subsequent to the commencement of liquidation is void unless the court orders otherwise: s 127. The court will decide whether to validate a disposition made under s 127.

(d) Any legal proceedings in progress against the company are halted (and none may thereafter begin) unless the court gives leave. Any seizure of the company's assets after commencement of liquidation is void: ss 130 and 128.

(e) The employees of the company are automatically dismissed. The provisional liquidator assumes the powers of management previously held by the directors.

(f) Any floating charge crystallises.

The assets of the company may remain the company's legal property but under the liquidator's control unless the court vests the assets in the liquidator. The business of the company may continue but it is the liquidator's duty to continue it with a view only to realisation, for instance by sale as a going concern.

Within 21 days of the making of the order for winding up (or of the appointment of a provisional liquidator) a *statement of affairs* must be delivered to the liquidator verified by one or more directors and by the secretary. The statement shows the assets and liabilities of the company and includes a list of creditors with particulars of any security which creditors may hold and how long it has been held: s 131.

Meetings of contributories and creditors

The Official Receiver has 12 weeks to decide whether or not to convene separate meetings of creditors and contributories. The purpose of these meetings would be to provide the creditors and contributories with the opportunity to appoint their own nominee as permanent liquidator to replace the official receiver, and a liquidation committee as their representative to work with the liquidator. (In cases of conflict, the creditors' nominee takes precedence over the members' nominee.) If the Official Receiver believes there is little interest and that the creditors will be unlikely to appoint a liquidator he can dispense with a meeting, informing the court, the creditors and the contributories of the decision. He must then call a meeting if at least 25 per cent in value of the creditors require him to do so: s 136.

If the creditors do hold a meeting and appoint their own nominee he automatically becomes liquidator subject to a right of objection to the court: s 139. Any person appointed to act as liquidator must be a qualified insolvency practitioner.

At any time after a winding up order is made, the Official Receiver may ask the Secretary of State to appoint a liquidator. Similarly, he may request an appointment if the creditors and members fail to appoint a liquidator: s 137.

Completion of compulsory liquidation

When the liquidator completes his task he reports to the DTI, which examines his accounts. He may apply to the court for an order for dissolution of the company. The order is sent to the registrar who gives notice of it in the *London Gazette* and dissolves the company: s 205.

Exercise 3

Following an order for compulsory liquidation of a company with debts of £120,000, meetings of the creditors and contributories are held. The creditors nominate Paul as liquidator, whereas the contributories nominate Sharon. Paul claims that he can realise the company's assets within a month for £100,000, whereas Sharon claims that she can run the business and sell it as a going concern for £140,000 within six months. If nobody reconsiders his or her position, who will be appointed liquidator?

---

4 Voluntary liquidation

There are two types of voluntary liquidation, a members' voluntary liquidation where the company is solvent and a creditors' voluntary liquidation where the company is insolvent and the members resolve to liquidate in consultation with creditors.

Members' voluntary liquidation

The type of resolution to be passed varies with the circumstances of the case: s 84. A company may by *extraordinary* resolution resolve to wind up because it cannot, by reason of its liabilities, continue its business. This enables an insolvent company to go into liquidation on a 14 day notice. A company may, by *special* resolution (giving no reasons), resolve to wind up.

The winding up commences on the passing of the resolution. A liquidator is usually appointed by the same resolution (or a second resolution passed at the same time).

Declaration of solvency

A voluntary winding up is a members' voluntary winding up *only* if the directors make and deliver to the registrar a declaration of solvency: s 89. This is a statutory declaration that the directors have made full enquiry into the affairs of the company and are of the opinion that it will be able to pay its debts, together with interest (at the rate applicable under s 189(4)) on those debts, in full, within a specified period not exceeding 12 months. If the liquidator later concludes that the company will be unable to pay its debts he must call a meeting of creditors and lay before them a statement of assets and liabilities: s 95.

The liquidator calls special and annual general meetings of contributories to whom he reports. Within three months after each anniversary of the commencement of the winding up the liquidator must call a meeting and lay before it an account of his transactions during the year: s 93. When the liquidation is complete the liquidator calls a meeting to lay before it his final accounts: s 94.

After holding the final meeting the liquidator sends a copy of his accounts to the registrar who dissolves the company three months later by removing its name from the register: s 201.

Creditors' voluntary liquidation

If no declaration of solvency is made and delivered to the registrar the liquidation proceeds as a creditors' voluntary liquidation even if in the end the company pays its debts in full: s 96.

322

To commence a creditors' voluntary liquidation the directors convene a general meeting of members to pass an extraordinary resolution. They must also convene a meeting of creditors (s 98), giving at least seven days notice of this meeting. The notice must be advertised in the *London Gazette* and two local newspapers. The notice must either:

(a) give the name and address of a qualified insolvency practitioner to whom the creditors can apply before the meeting for information about the company; *or*

(b) state a place in the locality of the company's principal place of business where, on the two business days before the meeting, a list of creditors can be inspected.

The meeting of members is held first and its business is to resolve to wind up, to appoint a liquidator and to nominate up to five representatives to be members of the liquidation committee.

The creditors' meeting should preferably be convened on the same day at a later time than the members' meeting, or on the next day, but in any event within 14 days of it. One of the directors presides at the creditors' meeting and lays before it a full statement of the company's affairs and a list of creditors with the amounts owing to them. The meeting may (if the creditors so wish) nominate a liquidator and up to five representatives to be members of the liquidation committee. If the creditors nominate a different person to be liquidator, their choice prevails over the nomination by the members.

The effect of voluntary winding up

Unlike a compulsory winding up, there is no automatic stay of legal proceedings against the company and the employees are not automatically dismissed.

Exercise 4

Why do the creditors of a company ordinarily have no role in a members' voluntary liquidation?

---

5 Liquidation committee

A liquidation committee may be appointed in a compulsory liquidation and in a creditors' voluntary liquidation. It usually comprises an equal number of representatives of members and of creditors (in a creditors' voluntary liquidation limited to a maximum of five from each side). The committee meets once a month unless otherwise agreed and may be summoned at any time by the liquidator or by a member of the committee: Sch 8.

The general function of the committee is to work with the liquidator, to supervise his accounts, to approve the exercise of certain of his statutory powers and to fix his remuneration. Like the liquidator himself members of the committee are in a fiduciary position and may not secure unauthorised personal advantages, for example by purchase of the company's assets.

6 Contributories

Shareholders and past shareholders are called *contributories*. A contributory may have to contribute funds to meet a company's debts if the shares which he holds or previously held are partly paid or if it is found that the rules on consideration have been breached in the allotment of the shares as fully paid.

If it is necessary to make calls on contributories the liquidator draws up an 'A' List of contributories who were members at the commencement of the winding up and a 'B' List of contributories who were members within the year preceding the commencement of winding up. A B List contributory has liability limited by the following principles.

(a)   He is only liable to pay what is due on the shares which he previously held and only so much of the amount due on those shares as the present holder (an A List contributory) is unable to pay.

(b)   He can only be required to contribute (within the limits stated in (a) above) in order to pay those debts of the company incurred before he ceased to be a member which are still owing.

No contributory who ceased to be a member more than a year before the commencement of liquidation can be liable.

7   Powers of liquidators

In order to perform his function satisfactorily, the liquidator is given certain powers, contained in Sch 4. His basic function is to obtain and realise the company's assets to pay off its debts.

All liquidators may, with the relevant sanctions:

(a)   pay any class of creditors in full;

(b)   make compromises or arrangements with creditors;

(c)   compromise any debt or questions relating to assets;

(d)   take security;

(e)   bring or defend legal proceedings (without sanction in a voluntary liquidation): s 167;

(f)   carry on the business in a way beneficial to the winding-up (without sanction in a voluntary liquidation).

His subsidiary powers, given to enable him to perform the above, include selling assets, giving receipts (often under seal), receiving dividends, drawing bills of exchange, raising money, appointing agents and doing any other necessary things.

8   Duties of liquidators

Given the wide-ranging powers invested in a liquidator, he has certain duties.

(a)   He must exercise his discretion personally. Although he may delegate clerical tasks and those which he cannot perform personally (for which he can appoint agents), a liquidator cannot delegate his duty to use his judgement, even to the court. However, if it is in the interest of the company's creditors and contributories, and in any case if the nature of the business requires it, a liquidator may ask the court to appoint a manager with special skills.

(b)   He stands in a fiduciary relationship to the company, its creditors and contributories.

(c)   He must cooperate with the official receiver.

(d)   He must notify the liquidation committee of (i) dispositions to a connected person, and (ii) all matters of concern.

A liquidator must keep *records of proceedings*. He must keep a record of all receipts and payments and, if the company continues trading, a trading account should be kept. An

BPP Publishing

account must be submitted to the Secretary of State every 12 months, the first one being accompanied by a summary statement of affairs and an explanation of why assets referred to therein have not been disposed of. A final account must be submitted within 14 days of leaving office. On request, creditors and contributories are entitled to free copies of accounts, and the Secretary of State may order them to be audited.

A liquidator must *act quickly* in carrying out his duties, and not delay for lack of obvious funds.

Liquidators must *keep minutes* of the proceedings and resolutions of creditors', contributories' and liquidation committee meetings.

After six months of voluntary liquidation, the liquidator must pay the balance of funds not required for day-to-day running of the liquidation into a special account at the Bank of England (the Insolvency Services Account). Money received in a compulsory liquidation must be paid into this account immediately, unless the liquidator has express authority from the DTI to operate a local bank account.

The registrar is entitled to receive reports on a voluntary liquidation at the end of twelve months and every six months thereafter.

Exercise 5

J Ltd is in liquidation with debts of £70,000. The company has one asset, a building. Tony would pay £100,000 for the building, but he refuses to deal with a company in liquidation. The building is therefore sold to a company owned by the liquidator for £90,000, and then re-sold to Tony for £100,000. All the creditors of J Ltd are paid in full. What duty, if any, has the liquidator breached?

9 Alternatives to liquidation

Winding up a company is a fairly drastic step involving the cessation of trading, the disposal of assets and the final dissolution of the company. There are alternatives to liquidation when a company is insolvent to some degree.

(a) *Administration:* under this procedure a moratorium is imposed by the court on creditors' actions against the company while an insolvency practitioner attempts to solve the problem.

(b) *Voluntary arrangement with creditors:* by means of this the company itself, under the supervision of an insolvency practitioner, arranges with creditors for a way of sorting out the problems surrounding it.

10 Administration orders

If a company is not yet in liquidation but is already, or is likely to become, unable to pay its debts the company itself, its directors, or any of its creditors, including unsecured creditors, may present a petition to the court to make an administration order in respect of the company: s 9(1). The broad effect of such an order is to put an insolvency practitioner in control of the company with a defined programme, and meanwhile to insulate it from pressure by creditors. The administration order provides an alternative for the unsecured creditor to suing for the debt in the courts or petitioning for winding up. For the secured creditor it is an alternative to both these solutions and to putting in a receiver.

BPP Publishing

Effectively the secured creditors have a right of veto over the making of an administration order. This is because anyone petitioning for an administration order must give notice of the fact to anyone who is entitled to put in a receiver or to anyone who has actually put one in. The secured creditor on receiving the notice can then appoint a receiver. If he does, an administration order cannot be made. If a receiver is already in place and the secured creditor does not consent to that receiver stepping down, then again an administration order cannot be made. On the other hand once an administration order is made it is no longer possible for a creditor to appoint a receiver.

Once a winding up resolution has been passed or the court has ordered the company to be wound up, an administration order can no longer be made. On the other hand once an administration order has been made it will no longer be possible to petition the court for a winding up order.

The petition for administration

The first step is to present a petition to the court for an administration order: s 9. In order to make an order the court must be satisfied that:

(a)   the company is or is likely to become unable to pay its debts; and

(b)   the making of an administration order is likely to achieve one or more of:

   (i)   the survival of the company and its undertaking as a going concern;

   (ii)   the approval of a voluntary arrangement;

   (iii)   the sanctioning of a scheme of arrangement under s 425 CA;

   (iv)   a more advantageous realisation of the company's assets than would be effected in a liquidation.

The effect of the administration *petition* is to impose a standstill on any move:

(a)   for voluntary liquidation;

(b)   for seizure of the company's goods in execution of a judgement for debt;

(c)   to re-possess goods obtained on hire purchase, rental or retention of title arrangements;

(d)   for the institution of any legal proceedings against the company.

It does not, however, prevent the presentation of a petition for compulsory liquidation, though no *order* may be made while the petition for an administration order is pending, nor does it prevent a receiver from being appointed.

Exercise 6

A petition for an administration order is made on 1 August, and the order is made on 15 August.

(a)   Could a receiver have been appointed on 8 August?

(b)   Could a petition for compulsory liquidation have been presented on 8 August?

The administration order

If the administration order is made, the above temporary measures become permanent; in addition no petition may be presented for compulsory liquidation nor may any administrative receiver be appointed: s 11. Other effects of an administration order are as follows.

(a) In addition to the powers given to a receiver an administrator may challenge past transactions of the company with a view to having them reversed by court order.

(b) An administrator may, with the sanction of the court or with the charge-holder's agreement, sell property of the company subject to a fixed charge: s 11. He may also sell property subject to a floating charge and in this case the charge is then transferred to the proceeds of sale: s 15.

(c) A supplier of goods on hire purchase or retention of title terms may not, unless the administrator consents or the court gives leave, re-possess those goods: s 11(3). The powers of sale described in (b) extend to goods in this category: s 15(2).

(d) The administrator acts as the company's agent (s 14), but he does not have statutory liability on contracts. A person dealing with an administrator in good faith is entitled to assume that he is acting within his powers: s 14(6).

(e) As regards contracts, the administrator can be prevented by injunction from refusing to carry on with a contract made by the company.

The administrator

The court appoints an insolvency practitioner to be the administrator of the company; in that capacity he has all the statutory powers of an administrative receiver. In addition he may remove any director from office, appoint directors and call meetings of creditors and of members: s 14. With the approval of the court he may also dispose of, free of encumbrance, property of the company until then subject to a charge and also property in its possession under a hire purchase, rental or retention of title agreement. But if he does so, a sum equal to the market value of the property (the net proceeds topped up if necessary) must be applied in repayment of the previously secured debt, or in meeting the claims of the persons whose goods have been sold: s 15.

The order must be publicised.

(a) All company correspondence and documentation must bear the administrator's name and state that an order has been made: s 12.

(b) The administrator must give notice to the company (immediately), the registrar (within 14 days) and the creditors (within 28 days): s 21.

An administrator is entitled to receive a statement of affairs. Within three months (or such longer time as the court may allow) he must produce and circulate a statement of his proposals for implementing the purpose of the administration order. Copies go to the creditors; members receive copies or a notice is published to inform them where they may apply for a copy. The administrator next calls a meeting of creditors, on 14 days' notice, to consider and, if thought fit, approve his proposals. He then reports to the court on the result of the meeting. If the proposals have been approved, the administration order will continue in force so that they may be implemented. If the proposals have not been approved the court is likely to discharge the order: s 24(5).

In approving the administrator's proposals, the creditors' meeting may resolve to appoint a creditors' committee to work with the administrator: s 26. They may modify his proposals, but only if he agrees to each change: s 24.

Exercise 7

An administrator of a company with three factories proposes to close and sell one factory and to buy new equipment for the two remaining factories. The creditors are generally in favour of the proposed sale, but will not under any circumstances agree to spending money on new equipment. The administrator will not agree to the sale unless new equipment is to be bought. What is the likely outcome?

---

11 Voluntary arrangements

The insolvency of a company may of itself increase its debts and/or reduce its resources. An insolvent company may cease to trade, it may default on its commercial contracts because its suppliers will no longer do business with it, or it may dismiss its employees who are thereby entitled to redundancy payments. Hence it can be in the interest of creditors to accept a compromise with a company rather than insist on its adopting formal insolvency procedure. They are particularly likely to agree to do so if there is a prospect of selling the company's business as a going concern or of pulling it back into solvency by reorganisation or improved management.

A *voluntary arrangement* is either a composition (part payment) in satisfaction of a company's debts or a scheme of arrangement of its affairs: s 1(1). A scheme of arrangement might, for example, be an agreed postponement or rescheduling of payment of debts pending reorganisation or sale of the business.

The initiative in proposing a voluntary arrangement may be taken either:

(a)   by the directors, if the company is not already in liquidation nor subject to an administration order; or

(b)   by a liquidator or administrator in office at the time.

In either case the initiative proceeds under the guidance of an insolvency practitioner (called 'the nominee' at this stage) but in case (a) the company is not formally insolvent. The nominee holds separate meetings of members and of creditors and lays before them his proposals for a voluntary arrangement.

If both meetings approve it, the voluntary arrangement becomes binding on the company and on all creditors concerned: s 5. But there are safeguards which significantly limit the possibility of effecting a binding arrangement.

(a)   Any secured or preferential creditor whose rights are affected by the arrangement is not bound by the scheme unless he has expressly consented to it: s 4.

(b)   Any creditor or member of the company may raise objections to the scheme before the court by showing either (i) that it is unfairly prejudicial (it discriminates against him) or (ii) that there has been a material irregularity in relation to one or other of the meetings: s 6. If the court upholds such an objection, it may revoke or suspend the arrangement or order that revised proposals shall be submitted to further meetings for approval.

If the company is in liquidation or is subject to an administration order when the arrangement is approved, the court may make a suitable order to terminate or suspend those proceedings. An insolvency practitioner, now called a supervisor, implements the arrangement. He may be, but need not be, the same practitioner who was nominee at the initial stage.

BPP Publishing

Exercise 8

A company has debts of £100,000 (all unsecured) and assets which could be sold to raise £30,000. There are at present 20,000 ordinary shares in issue. If the company can overcome its temporary difficulties, it is likely to prosper. Two possible voluntary arrangements have been suggested.

(a) The debts could be exchanged for £80,000 unsecured debentures carrying no interest, repayable in five years time.

(b) The debts could be exchanged for 20,000 ordinary shares. No dividends would be paid on any shares for five years.

If, in five years time, the company is likely to have assets of £180,000 and no liabilities (except the unsecured debentures if issued), which arrangement are the creditors likely to prefer? Why might they prefer the other arrangement?

Chapter roundup

(a) When a company is dissolved, it is removed from the register and ceases to exist. This can happen in several ways, but the most common way is liquidation. In a liquidation, a company's assets are disposed of, its debts are paid so far as possible and any surplus is paid to the members.

(b) A compulsory liquidation may be petitioned for on any of several grounds, but the most common ground is that the company is unable to pay its debts. A provisional liquidator (usually the Official Receiver) is appointed on the presentation of a petition, and if the court is satisfied an order for winding up is then granted. A statement of affairs is prepared and meetings of contributories and creditors may be held in order to appoint a replacement liquidator. The liquidator reports to the DTI on the completion of his work.

(c) If a company is solvent, it may go into members' voluntary liquidation. The liquidator holds meetings of contributories, and prepares final accounts once he has finished his work.

(d) A creditors' voluntary liquidation is also instigated by the members, but a meeting of the creditors must also be held. The creditors may nominate a liquidator and their choice prevails over the members' choice. A liquidation committee may be appointed to work with the liquidator.

(e) In any liquidation, contributories may be called upon to provide funds to meet the company's debts if they hold partly paid shares or if they disposed of such shares within the year preceding the commencement of the winding up.

(f) A liquidator may pay and compromise debts, and may conduct legal proceedings. He stands in a fiduciary relationship to the company, and he must exercise his discretion personally and keep records.

(g) If a company is in temporary difficulty, it, its directors or any of its creditors may apply for an administration order. Once an administration order has been made, a receiver cannot be appointed and the court cannot be petitioned for a winding up order. The administrator then has time to devise a scheme to save the company from insolvency.

(h) It may benefit creditors and members to enter into a voluntary arrangement under which debts are paid in part or exchanged for shares or securities, rather than putting the company into liquidation.

Quick quiz

1   Describe how a company may be dissolved.

2   Give three grounds on which an order may be made by the court for compulsory liquidation of a company.

3   What grounds may be asserted in a creditor's petition to establish that the company is unable to pay its debts?

4   What is the result likely to be if other creditors oppose a creditor's petition for compulsory liquidation?

5   Give two examples of circumstances which can provide 'just and equitable' grounds for compulsory winding up.

6   What are the effects of an order for compulsory liquidation on those who have dealings with the company?

7   What meetings are called by the Official Receiver and for what purposes?

8   What type of resolution is passed to put a company into voluntary liquidation?

9   What is a liquidation committee? When is it appointed? What does it do?

10   In what circumstances and within what limits may a previous holder of shares be liable to contribute towards the payment of the company's debts although he has transferred his shares to some other person before the company goes into liquidation?

11   What are the main powers of liquidators?

12   How far may a liquidator delegate his duties?

13   What accounting records must a liquidator keep? To whom must he submit records?

14   How do liquidations, receiverships and administrations interact?

15   What is the effect of an administration order once made?

16   How may a secured creditor ensure that he is not affected by a company's voluntary arrangement?

Solutions to exercises

1   Persons with no previous dealings with the company need to be warned before they make contracts with the company.

2   The company had not neglected to pay: it was deliberately disputing the amount due.

3   Paul: the creditors' choice prevails.

4   It is expected that all creditors will be paid in full, so there is no need for them to interfere.

5   He has breached his fiduciary duty to the company.

6   (a)   Yes

     (b)   Yes

7   The court will discharge the administration order.

8   The creditors are likely to prefer (b), giving them wealth of £180,000 × 20,000/40,000 = £90,000 in five years time. They might prefer (a) if they doubted the accuracy of the forecast of assets.

REVIEW FORM

Name:

College:

We would be grateful to receive any comments you may have on this book. You may like to use the headings below as guidelines. Tear out this page and send it to our Freepost address: **BPP Publishing Ltd, FREEPOST, London W12 8BR**.

Topic coverage

Objectives, exercises, chapter roundups and quizzes

Student-friendliness

Errors (please specify and refer to a page number)

Other

BPP publishing